[redacted]

Notes on Love in a Tamil Family

A

Book

The Philip E. Lilienthal imprint
honors special books
in commemoration of a man whose work
at the University of California Press from 1954 to 1979
was marked by dedication to young authors
and to high standards in the field of Asian Studies.
Friends, family, authors, and foundations have together
endowed the Lilienthal Fund, which enables the Press
to publish under this imprint selected books
in a way that reflects the taste and judgment
of a great and beloved editor.

Notes on Love in a Tamil Family

MARGARET TRAWICK

University of California Press
BERKELEY LOS ANGELES LONDON

The Publisher wishes to acknowledge the generous support of the Associates of the University of California Press.

University of California Press
Berkeley and Los Angeles, California

University of California Press, Ltd.
Oxford, England

Library of Congress Cataloging-in-Publication Data

Trawick, Margaret.
Notes of love in a Tamil family / Margaret Trawick.
p. cm.
"A Philip E. Lilienthal book."
Bibliography: p.
Includes index.
ISBN 0-9520063-6-7 (alk. paper)
1. Tamil (Indic people)—Families. 2. Love. 3. Tamil (Indic people)—Social life and customs. 4. Trawick, Margaret. I. Title.
DS432.T3T73 1990
306.8′08994811—dc20 89-4954
CIP

Printed in the United States of America

1 2 3 4 5 6 7 8 9

The paper used in this publication meets the minimum requirements of American National Standard for Information Sciences – Permanence of Paper for Printed Library Materials, ANSI Z39. 48-1984. ∞

Contents

Figures

Plates

Acknowledgments

Several organizations underwrote the years of freedom I spent in India and America learning what I needed to learn in order to write this book and then writing it. The Social Science Research Council funded my first extended period of fieldwork from January 1975 through July 1976. It was during this time that I met the principal protagonist of this book, S. R. Themozhiyar, and began taking lessons from him. The National Endowment for the Humanities (NEH) provided financial support during the summer of 1979, when Themozhiyar came to America and continued his lessons to me. The American Institute of Indian Studies (AIIS) provided support for my stay in Tamil Nadu in 1980. The Rockefeller Foundation and again AIIS supported my work in Tamil Nadu in 1984. I completed the manuscript in 1987–1988, as a resident scholar at the School of American Research in Santa Fe, New Mexico. Funds for my scholarship there were provided by NEH. I am grateful to all of these organizations for their generosity and their encouragement.

For nearly two decades of constant inspiration and teaching full of erudition, challenge, and surprise, I am grateful to my two mentors at the University of Chicago, McKim Marriott and Paul Friedrich. May my mind be ever young and ever growing, as are the minds of both these great scholars.

For reading and commenting on portions of this manuscript in various stages of production, I am grateful to Jonathan Haas, Jane Kepp, Pauline Kolenda, Owen Lynch, George Marcus, McKim Marriott, Gananath Obeyesekere, A. K. Ramanujan, and David Spain. For reading the entire manuscript when it was almost finished and providing numerous insights and suggestions, together with lavish praise (so nourishing to my beleaguered ego), I am especially grateful to Errol Valentine Daniel. I owe special thanks also to Kim Vanatta and Mary Rzepski, whose friendship and counsel have bettered both my life and my work.

I am indebted to Daniel and Abraham Egnor for making me see the world through different eyes. Certainly neither this book nor anything like it would have been written had Dan and Abe not been born to me. May this work which has brought so much strangeness into their young lives benefit them somehow in the future.

I am grateful to Keith Egnor for enduring so much hardship for my sake. May he find a path more true to his own nature, and may it lead him to joy.

I am indebted to Ken Butler for bringing me in out of the rain and giving me the home of my dreams together with unconditional affection, all quite unearned. Without Ken I would not have been able to keep on living and keep on writing.

For their patient instruction, good humor, encouragement, and understanding, I am grateful to hundreds of people in Tamil Nadu, of whom I can here name only a few. K. Paramasivam, P. Shanbagavalli, P. Kanakkasabhapathi, B. R. Lakshmi, M. Laxmana Iyer, L. Chandra, and P. Raghava Reddiar all assisted me in very substantial ways.

Most of all I am indebted to my guru S. R. Themozhiyar and to his guru, his wife's sister, R. Sulochana (Anni). They, together with all the members of their household, gave me food, shelter, advice, companionship, protection, knowledge, cheer. But these are ordinary gifts, that ordinary people might give. I am indebted to this family more for gifts of a higher order, magical gifts of the ancient kind, which change the recipient into another being. Through such gifts, they killed and recreated me. Now they are always with me, no matter where I go.

Note on Transliteration

VOWELS

Tamil vowels are of three kinds, short, long, and diphthong. Short vowels are relatively unstressed, lax, and of short duration. Long vowels are relatively stressed, pronounced, and of longer duration.

Short vowels:

a	as in English c*u*p
i	as in English p*i*t
e	as in English p*e*t or (word initial) *ye*t
u	as in English p*u*t
o	as in English b*oo*k or f*ou*ght

Long vowels:

ā	as in English T*o*m
ī	as in English f*ee*d
ē	as in English r*ai*d or (word initial) *yay*
ū	as in English f*oo*l
ō	as in English h*o*pe

Diphthongs:

ai	as in English b*i*te (only shorter, more lax)
ow	as in English t*ow*n

CONSONANTS

Consonants like vowels are of two kinds: short, or single, and long, or double. Short or single consonants are relatively unstressed, lax, and of brief duration. Long or double consonants are relatively stressed, pronounced, and of longer duration.

Consonants are also divided into "hard" (stops and fricatives), "soft" (nasals), and "middle" (liquids, flaps, and glides). Single hard consonants in certain word-initial positions or after other hard consonants are pronounced as though they were double.

Finally, there are six points of articulation for Tamil consonants: labial, dental, palatal, alveolar, retroflex, and velar. There is one hard consonant and one soft consonant at each point of articulation.

Hard consonants:

Single:

velar	k	as in English *g*old or *h*ello
palatal	c	as in English *s*igh
retroflex	ḍ	something like English la*dd*er
dental	t	something like English *th*is
labial	p	as in English ru*bb*er
alveolar	ṟ	as in (British) English hu*rr*ah

Double:

velar	kk	as in English *k*ing or lu*ck*y
palatal	cc	as in English *ch*air or i*tchy*
retroflex	ḍḍ	something like English pu*t-d*own
dental	tt	something like English *t*op
labial	pp	as in English *p*eo*p*le
alveolar	ṟṟ	something like (American) English *tr*ee

Soft consonants:

velar	ṅ before k	as in English thi*n*k
palatal	ñ	as in English ora*n*ge or Spanish ma*ñ*ana
retroflex	ṇ	something like English thu*n*der
dental	n before t or word-initial	as in English pa*n*ther
labial	m	as in English *m*other
alveolar	n	as in English hu*n*ter

Middle consonants:

palatal	y	as in English *y*es
labial	v	as in English ho*v*er or bo*w*er
alveolar flap	r	as in (British) English Ha*r*old
alveolar liquid	l	something like English si*ll*y

retroflex flap	ṛ	something like (American) English hu*rr*ah
retroflex liquid	ḷ	something like English mi*l*d

When a Tamil word first appears in a section or chapter of this book, it is italicized. After that, it is left unitalicized. Proper names (people, places, deities, and texts) are not italicized and are generally spelled without diacritical marks (e.g., Anni and Ayya instead of Aṇṇi and Ayyā. Where a common English spelling exists for a proper name, this spelling is used instead of a more technically accurate transcription (e.g., Ganesan instead of Kaṇēcan, Mohana instead of Mōkanā).

Prologue

A Note on Theory

We anthropologists have inner cosmologies of our own, of course. Most of us would freely admit it. We hold tight to our visions and our dreams, even if it means keeping our eyes closed much of the time.[1]

One of our most compelling dreams, one that we hold tightest to, is the dream of wholeness, the vision of a world whose meaning is contained within itself, of a life that is complete, of a place where all things touch. That wholeness is for us (modern people) only a dream, that we lack it and that it is something we long for has been repeatedly revealed to us by the weavers of some of our greatest current cosmologies—Durkheim, Freud, Marx, Sapir—dreamers of wholeness themselves, who convinced us (anthropologists) to believe in that dream, showed us that it was lost, and inspired us to travel to the most distant corners of the earth in hopes of its recovery.[2]

Like many other people in the world, we are inclined to give our vision of wholeness the shape of a living body. In this form it is called "the organic metaphor." Many of us have called this "metaphor" too mystical, or too optimistic, yet we have perpetuated it covertly in structural linguistics and structural anthropology. When we read Jakobson's description of the growth of language in the child, there comes before our minds an image of the primordial cell dividing into members of a whole which complement each other lovingly and completely: mama and papa, and in between, the child, mediating, differentiating, and completing the golden triangle.[3] The art of Levi-Strauss unfolds a grander vision of text after text—in no matter what diverse environments, languages, and material media—linking together analogically, lending meaning to each other, sharing an underlying code (again, like the cells of a body), and allowing for the manifestation of every form of life and its opposite, in a world where all the texts know and complete each other.[4]

But in Levi-Strauss's work there is from the beginning, and increasingly as his explorations widen, a realization that completeness is not in any one self, or set of selves, or in any one culture, or set of cultures, but always over the horizon of one's knowledge, however vast. And finally, there is a recognition that the self-existent, underlying code for which one searches (now, following Victor Turner, we may call it *logos*) is nowhere, and (in Boon's words) "only the voyage is real."[5]

Presently that branch of anthropology concerned with "thought-systems," "language," and "symbols" has been broken into (inevitably) by other disciplines, and feeling its own integrity lost, is entering a new phase.[6] In this phase, a radically decentered view of the human condition emerges, in which the image of an underlying, unifying code is seen to be a tyrannous illusion, communication is less to be valued than polyphony or even discord, the self is intrinsically and as a consequence of its very inception not whole, and meaning, as either the intended goal or the intending source of action, whatever gives wholeness to being, cannot be found to "exist" at all. Some people call this phase "post-modern." All they mean by the use of this term is that intellectuals in the current age no longer are able to believe that they have arrived at the beginning of Utopia; we can no longer consider perfection to be within our grasp. Imperfection is what we live with. It is life. Thus for anthropologists, the boundless, ragged, and plural collection of things called "context" has become more real than the neat, discrete, and well-ordered thing called "text"; and "performance" with all its flaws and slips has become more real and more interesting than the never-realized perfection of potential we call "competence."[7]

In this book what I wish to do is take an ethnographic situation and describe it in such a way as to try to mediate between the old wholistic and the new decentered visions of the human condition. This must sound grandiose. What I mean is that my book stands more or less self-consciously between these two poles. On the one hand, I wish to recognize that the *desire* for wholeness is an important presence in some if not all cultures, that it is something that could be said to have been shared by myself and my companions in the ethnographic situation to be described, and that it was indeed what brought us together into this situation in the first place. That we had this desire in common might be attributed to the fact that we both come from "logocentric," Indo-European-dominated civilizations, or it might not, I don't know.[8] That we are not unique in this respect among ethnographer–informant teams appears to me probable.

On the other hand, I would like to take as presupposed the necessary and intrinsic nonwholeness both of the self and of culture, and the from-the-beginning plurality of both of these (maybe fictional) entities.

In modern ethnography, plurality and the absence of wholeness are facts to which we return again and again, both on the level of culture and on the level of the self—in, for instance, studies of pluralistic societies; studies of spirit-possession; on-the-ground studies of language; and studies seeking to determine other people's ideas of what a "person" or a "self" is.[9] But for the most part, wholeness is still taken as normative, plurality and fragmentation as unusual and to-be-explained.

One advantage of taking plurality as basically the way things are is that it makes us realize that the ethnographic situation (confrontation between "field worker" and "native") is not really all that strange, and it may make us feel more comfortable about focusing on that situation for what it is and playing it as it lays. Since we are no longer searching for an underlying code, we may allow our writing to be less abstract, not so far removed from our experience. We may not feel so inclined to pretend in our monographs that we don't exist.[10] We may be able to act upon the faith that "culture" is created only in the confrontation between cultures,[11] as "self" is created only in the confrontation between selves. When we see ourselves as co-constructors of culture at culture's boundaries, there may evolve a more symmetrical relationship between ourselves on one side of the boundary and our informants on the other. We may be able to come to terms with the fact that "meaning" cannot be pinned down, is always sought but never apprehended, is never this and never that, never here nor there but always in between, always inherently elusive and always inherently ambiguous. We may come to accept this ambiguity as that which is created by us and our informants and that which binds us to them. We may accept it as the closest we will ever come to the fulfillment of our desire.

CHAPTER ONE

What Led Me to Them

ABOUT THE AUTHOR

More than a quarter of my life has passed since I began writing this book. Its heart has stayed constant during this time, but its features have changed and changed again as I have moved and taken it with me from one world to another to another. It is beginning to look to me now as I look to myself, like a beaten-up suitcase with a lot of stickers on it.

The story I tell in this starting chapter describes the events that led up to my living with a South Indian Tamil family some years ago and to my writing about them now. One or two pages are about my pre-India days and about what I think led me to go to India in the first place. The rest of this chapter is about some of the things I learned in India from Indians—in particular, from one person—about how what I learned from experience meshed or failed to mesh with what I learned from books, and about how a Tamil poem, partially and for a brief time, became my life. A few stanzas of this poem are presented later in this chapter. These stanzas are complex and much of what they refer to is foreign to people of this country, so I offer an explication of them which is partly my own and partly that of the man who taught them to me. You, reader, may find these poem-fragments dense and strange, but don't for that reason ignore them, for in fact they are alive, and they are stronger than they seem, clad as they are in my homespun translations. Behind the translations and explications are the Tamil songs that are the reason for this book. This book is built to hold them, and through it they may be heard to echo by those who listen closely. They are the voices of people who lived hundreds of years ago, but they are also the voices of people who live now. The things I want you to know but haven't the power to say, these other voices will tell you.

The remaining chapters of this book are about exactly what the title says, love in a Tamil family, the family of the man who taught me the poem. These chapters describe different aspects of Tamil family life that touch upon love—kinship organization, childrearing, sexual relations, habits of speaking, rules of behavior. The central topic of this book—in Tamil, *anpu,* in English, "love"—is a feeling, and my approach to the study of this feeling has been through feeling. I have tried throughout the course of my research and writing to remain honest, clear-headed, and open-minded, and to follow the dictates of reason and empirical observation in my descriptions and analyses of the events I have sought to comprehend. But I have not attempted to be "objective" in the common sense of this term. I have never pretended to be be disinterested or uninvolved in the lives of my informants, and I have never set my own feelings aside. Only by heeding them have I been able to learn the lessons that I try, in this volume, to pass on.

I was born in 1948. My father, a psychiatrist, spent the war as a naval doctor in China and Okinawa, and he brought home paintings and tapestries of landscapes, birds, horses, courtly lovers, heavens, earths, and hells. I lived many hours of my childhood in those pictures. My mother's best friend from her childhood in Los Angeles was Hisako Nishihara. After the bombing of Pearl Harbor, Hisako's relatives were put in detention camps, though they were American citizens. Both mother and Hisako loved the beauty of life forms. They were honors students in bacteriology at UCLA. When I was about twelve I came across mother's college notebooks, which she had saved, filled with pencil drawings of microbes, each drawing precise and exquisite. Hisako became a laboratory assistant. Mother became a medical secretary. Both of them married their doctor-bosses at the end of the war and spent the remainder of their lives as housewives.

I was raised in Kentucky, my father's native home. Mother never felt completely happy there. One of her adulthood friends was Alene Dorsey, a black woman from the tobacco- and pig-growing area outside of Louisville; Alene's natal home had been a shack lined with newspaper. She wanted something better for her family now, but the segregation laws in effect in Kentucky at that time blocked her every effort. She was eighteen when she went to work for my mother, put our household in order, and started helping to raise me. I think I was three or four. I remember once listening to the song "My Old Kentucky Home" (" . . . 'tis summer, the darkies are gay. . .") and asking Alene, "Are you a darkie?" and Alene bursting into tears.

Mother spoke often of the stupidity of racism and xenophobia. She praised the beauty of Japanese culture. When I went to college, I consid-

Plate 1. A sivalingam.

ered majoring in Japanese, but didn't. Perhaps it was too cool and northern for me. I loved biology, philosophy, religion, poetry, math, language. I didn't much like people. I ended up majoring in anthropology, as a strange kind of compromise between these various loves and as a concession to the species to which I grudgingly owed allegiance. I thought that if I could learn to see human beings as a part of nature, I might learn to love them better. I read the classics in anthropology as they were assigned. Emile Durkheim's organic metaphor (society is an organism) and Claude Levi-Strauss's structuralism (mythic thought is wild thought, wild thought is as patterned and well-ordered as a wild plant) delighted me. When it came time to choose an area for field research, I chose India.

Like the Asian brides I had heard of, I devoted my life to India before I had even met it. I went to graduate school in anthropology, determined to become a specialist in India.

"You know," said an older woman anthropologist to me and my human husband, Keith, "this will mean long periods of time away from home."

"We know," we answered eagerly, excitedly.

Unlike an Asian bride, I calculated that if my marriage with India got too rough, I could always divorce myself from it. But I was wrong.

The college I went to was Harvard, but Keith was not a Harvard man. I never liked Harvard men. I liked tough, working-class ones like Keith. My mother's father was Irish, a worker in the steel mills of Pittsburgh from the age of twelve. Mother idolized him. I was a populist to the core and a lover of the underdog. Like a female coyote, if two males had ever battled for me (none ever did) I would have gone with the loser.

I chose to do my field work in South India probably because, through my mother, I am Irish. In many ways, South India is to North India as Ireland is to England. South India has been dominated politically and culturally by North India for many centuries. Tamils in particular, the most populous of South Indian ethnic groups (defined by the language they speak) take pride in their identity and more than once in this century have attempted to establish a separate Tamil nation. Also like the Irish, Tamils believe in strong sentiment: rage, grief, compassion, affection, desire, laughter, and ecstasy are openly and frequently displayed in the streets and courtyards of Tamil Nadu. And like the Irish, Tamils value the gift of gab: fabulous conversationalists, storytellers, singers, and poets abound among them.

TRADITIONAL INDIA

Now the first thing that this book is about is the way that India both exceeds and shatters Western expectations, the way it both exceeded and shattered mine. Of course there are the stereotypes: India is "more spiritual" than the West, its people "impoverished," "nonmaterialistic," "fatalistic," and "other-worldly," its society structured according to a "rigid caste hierarchy," its women "repressed" and "submissive," its villagers "tradition-bound" and "past-oriented," their behavior ordered by "rituals" and constrained by "rules" of "purity" and "pollution." These words are not just products of popular Western fantasy. Scholars and specialists in South Asian culture use them often.[1] But one thing I learned in India was that these words are *just* words, *our* words, to refer to certain scattered events occurring in South Asia. The propositions they imply are partial truths, half truths, and anyone going to India who expects all of Indian life to conform to them will find herself merely deluded and confused. It would almost be better, I think, if we could abandon such words, all those words that imply explanation and understanding of such a large place as India, at least those words whose referents are only scholarly abstractions, certainly those words over which academic people fight. Alas, if you wish to address the academic specialists, you must use them.

I have tried, anyway, in my own narrative not to lean on such words too much. This has not been difficult, because they explain very little of what I experienced in India. The women I knew there, for instance, were more aggressive than me, more openly sexual than me, more free in their criticisms of their men than me. Here in America I often get in trouble for arguing, losing my temper, speaking my mind. But in Tamil Nadu, one of my woman friends, Anni, asked me pointedly, "Is it your habit to bow and defer to *everyone*?" My personality in Tamil Nadu was no more sweet and obliging than it is in America; if anything, I was more short-tempered there. As for Anni, she was milder than many Tamil women I knew—indeed, she was known for her patient and loving nature. But when she accused me, through her question, of excessive deference, she was not being sarcastic. Compared to her, I was a little mouse. The notion of the repressed and submissive Indian woman simply did not apply to the people among whom I lived—and yet in some ways it did. Anni would not have been Anni without her fidelity to her men and her ability to endure hardship for their sake, to do without while they did with. She was proud of these qualities of hers and wore them fiercely. They entitled her to speak freely and to walk with her head held high.

Hierarchy ("the rule of the sacred") in India also was not what I expected. Ritual status unsupported by worldly power counted for very little in the places where I lived. The highest caste in Anni's village, for instance, the caste with the greatest "ritual status" or "purity," the Brahmans, were a poor minority and were ordered about by the landowners rather rudely. "Ritual purity" was, more than anything else, a matter of material exchanges, a matter of food and a matter of sex. It was essentially what we would call a physical state, not what we would call a spiritual one. What we would call "spiritual purity," what Tamils call a "pure heart," *tūymaiyāna manacu,* was often, if anything, opposed to ritual purity. South Indian devotional religion, *bhakti*, has as one of its basic precepts the renunciation of ritual purity for the attainment of divine grace. It is based on the simple idea that love is the way to freedom—love that knows no boundaries, love that is common to all. People reviled for their lack of ritual purity, people of "untouchable castes," *tīṇḍā inaṅkaḷ,* could claim by dint of this very lack to be most pure at heart. The suffering borne by those in states of social defilement itself made possible the heart's more genuine purity. The clean and prosperous, it was said, felt no need of gods. The entrance of deities into the bodies of certain people during states of possession was proof of those people's inner purity. A god would not enter an unclean place. But most of the possessed, all of those possessed regularly by gods or goddesses, were members of lower, "less clean" castes. In order to be filled with the grace of God, they said, you had to have a kind of hunger, a kind of emptiness inside. Those on top never knew such emptiness. And yet the shamans and shamanesses, having a deity's power in them, gained by that fact a degree of worldly influence that many a village Brahman might have envied.

Ritual purity, then, was not a dominant principle, certainly not *the* reigning principle, on the so-called spiritual level. But neither was it dominant on the so-called material level. Regarding food, ritual purity was a matter of the "higher" feeding (in the closest and most intimate sense) the "lower." But what did it matter whether food at a feast was cooked and served by Brahman hands when they had no power over its distribution? The questions that mattered most to people concerning food were, Who owns the land on which it is grown? How much do the workers who grow it get paid? Who can buy it and who can sell it and for how much? Who cares enough for me to see that I am fed? Who trusts me enough to let me feed them? Who will go hungry for my sake? Who will share meals with me? Who is truly one with me, who my friend? Such questions were asked with respect not only to food, but to many other kinds of bodily and material exchanges, from the loaning of money to the offering of smiles and caresses. And they were asked not only within a family, but between families, between castes, between species of animals, men, and gods.

Emotion, power, and the interest in form that we call ritual were all tied up together, all shaded into each other. Worldly power was not just a matter of who owned the land and the money. It was also a matter of who had the unpredictable, dangerous love of the laborers, the landowners, the voters, the politicians, and the deities. Religion was not just a "belief-system" that started where empirical knowledge left off. It was not an imaginative superstructure spun off of a hard material infrastructure. It was not a restricted, sacred domain cordoned off from the everyday, the profane. It was *matam,* "madness," a connection with chaotic, invisible powers, present in all places, in all times. It was personality, it was the physiology of plants and animals, it was economics, it was sex. It was *not* "not real." Kinship organization, in the same way, was much more than just "social structure," a stable architectural framework through which generations passed. It was also a form of poetics, a set of biochemical equations, a web of deep-seated longings. It could hardly be called a "structure" at all, for protean variability in form was intrinsic to it, and it was composed of those things that structural anthropologists are always trying to get away from—unique and unpredictable human personalities. And yet beyond all these, there seemed to be in the kinship ideal of South India something stable and eternal, for which all were reaching.

India has often been called a "traditional" society. What some people mean by this is that Indians live in a world resembling our own past. Of course, this isn't true. It is also not true, as is often claimed, that Indians look to the past for all the best things, so that they resist change as a matter of principle. On each of my visits to Tamil Nadu, I found to my dismay (for I was probably seeking some kind of Eden myself) that things were changing fast. New kinds of rice were being grown, new kinds of song were being sung, new kinds of marriage contracted. People realized that things were not necessarily getting better—some of the changes were definitely for the worse. Certain changes were widely regarded as evil, but were accepted and perpetuated even by the people who purportedly disapproved of them—the spread of the dowry system was a case in point. Other changes were generally regarded as desirable—for instance the acceptance of widow-remarriage—but were much more slowly being put into practice. (Dowry marriage is a practice associated with North India and with Brahmans; widow-remarriage with people of lower castes.) Some relatively superficial changes were blatantly visible—many more vehicles on the road. Other much deeper changes were more hidden—many more children in school. Sometimes a change that might be expected to kill tradition revitalized it: the abundance and popularity of movies in South India in this century did not so much drown out folk themes as give them a new and powerful medium. Religious cults such as those of the "disease goddesses" grew stronger even as the old systems of patronage and the old diseases were replaced with more modern ones. Sometimes a change intended to be revitalizing turned out killing: old men said the new high-yield rice burned the belly and did not appease hunger. Moreover it was a risky crop to grow; it required just the right amount and kind of rain at just the right times, expensive fertilizers and insecticides, and a large and reliable labor pool that had to be well paid. Relying on such rice, you either lived in style or you starved, farmers told me. Yet it was a status crop, and everyone who could afford to grow it did.

To escape such changes, anthropologists often go to "remote" villages, or at least old towns, where things are quieter. But change is everywhere—that the whole world is always changing is part of received, "traditional" Indian wisdom.

EARLY EDUCATION

Our first extended visit to India came in 1975. Keith was thirty-one, I was twenty-six, our son Daniel was four months in the arms. We lived in Madras, the fourth largest city in India, capital of Tamil Nadu. Keith had left his job as a high school teacher to come with me. I was doing my dissertation research on "concepts of the body in South India." While I was there, the object of my quest metamorphosed into "Tamil theories of life processes." Perhaps this was my way of seeking nature within culture, order and beauty within the chaos and ugliness that is humankind. Educated in the principles of cultural anthropology, I wanted something whole and human, which yet was not deliberately manufactured by human beings nor identical with them, something that grew spontaneously among them and could not be explained by history or individual agency, something lawful but unpredictable, unified but collective, conscious but unconscious, detailed, alive, concrete, abstract, ideal, transcendent. Most of all what I searched for should be something true, beautiful, and Indian that had never before been captured in either Indian or Western books, but could be captured in mine. To find this thing was not an easy task.

I went searching for "good informants." Mostly I found two kinds: (1) scholars who quoted to me from books; (2) ordinary folks who couldn't understand what I was doing or what I wanted of them and were afraid to try and answer my abstract philosophical questions. The months rolled by. We visited villages, thinking of a move, but we were strangers everywhere and no place seemed satisfactory. Every kind of person was in Madras city. I thought if I just kept trying, I would find a way to fit things together. I continued to visit people who for some reason or other might have something interesting to say about life processes, and I tried to get to know the people around me, to befriend them, at least not to alienate them, to live according to their rules, whatever those might be.

Meanwhile Keith was going crazy with the craziness of a Third World city—the heat, the sickness, the not knowing how to live, how to cook, how to speak, how to sleep, most of all the people who mocked his great lumbering T-shirted figure, walking to the corner store to buy a dozen eggs, carrying a naked, sunburnt baby in the crook of one muscular arm. I tried to follow, and make him follow, the precept that "the native is always right." No matter how strange or mean people seemed, I tried to accept them and make him accept them. We began to quarrel seriously.

I was going crazy myself in a different way, frequently sick, frequently angry, always searching, following every lead, for what I wasn't quite sure, and I wondered why I had come to this place, dragging my family along, in pursuit of what I was beginning to think was a chimera: cultural form.

Then, slowly, my luck began to change. I met a brilliant shamaness; I met a slightly dotty but wise old doctor; I met some women who worked in the doctor's paddy fields; I met the Tamil scholar Themozhiyar. Everything I have learned about Tamil Nadu since then stems from these encounters.

The doctor and Themozhiyar were the ones who interested me most, at first. The doctor lived in a village at the southern end of Tamil Nadu, Themozhiyar had spent his whole life in or near Madras, hundreds of miles from the doctor's home. The doctor was old—past eighty. Themozhiyar was young—not quite forty. The doctor was a Brahman and identified strongly with the Brahman community; he wore the topknot of old-fashioned Saiva Brahmans (worshippers of Siva); he was fluent not only in Tamil but in English, Sanskrit, and Malayalam. Sanskrit is the language of the great Brahminical texts. In the region where this doctor lived, Tamil shades into Malayali. Through the languages that he knew, the doctor was in close contact both with the laborers of his district and with the savants of the subcontinent. Themozhiyar, in contrast, knew only Tamil and some Telugu, the language of his ancestors. He had never learned any English; he said he was frightened of it and of math; he was also frightened, he said, of people with many degrees. Unlike the doctor, he did not try to get to know the untouchable laborers of his village; he feared being changed by them. Thus his knowledge was more circumscribed, and perhaps for this reason more unified, than that of the doctor. Themozhiyar was of a "high non-Brahman caste" and the feelings he expressed about Brahmanism were mixed. He had been involved in the Tamil self-respect movement, which was anti-Brahminical. If Themozhiyar and the doctor, whose name was Mahadeva Iyer, had met, they would probably have disliked each other, their backgrounds and their philosophies were so different. So in certain ways, my two prize informants balanced each other nicely.

But the two men had many things in common as well: both were serious Saivas, both were vegetarians, both were landowners, both were extremely literate, both were teachers, and both were talkers: they would both ramble on and on about all kinds of topics and the things they said were amazing. I couldn't find these things in books. Mahadeva Iyer talked about medicine, about sickness and its treatment, about cooking, about his pet bull, about his family, about the mountains that grew behind his village, about the North Pole, the British administrators, the forest demons, the magicians and yogis he had known, about the Vedas, the English and Sanskrit alphabets, about house construction, embryogenesis, the marriages of people and of trees, about cosmic and social forces, about life in general. He knew the old Sanskrit medical texts well and often explicated parts of them for me. His explications generally went far beyond anything the texts themselves said.

Themozhiyar talked about Tamil literature—he had read widely, and knew many verses by heart, and he believed them, lived them, in much the same way that Mahadeva Iyer believed in and lived the Sanskrit medical texts, but with less skepticism and compromise. Themozhiyar was a kind of fundamentalist when it came to the literature of Tamil Saivism. He had a religious attitude toward the older, secular literature as well. He believed (because the old poems said), that the souls of the dead were visible floating in the empty sky, that a swan could separate milk from water, that crabs would die if you disturbed them during lovemaking, that bats defecated through their mouths, that if you spat on a chicken before you brushed your teeth in the morning, the chicken would be poisoned. It was all rather touching and incredible to see this practical, educated, city-wise man profess these silly ideas, and sillier ones still, and chastise me as though I were a foolish child for doubting them. But the silly merged with the profound. Themozhiyar spoke often of events in his own life, as a way of illustrating for me passages of literature that I was trying to learn about. He also drew upon what he called *potu aṟivu*, "common knowledge." Like Mahadeva Iyer's explanations of medical texts, Themozhiyar's explanations of Tamil texts were in no way determined by the texts themselves, and yet they were continuous with them; they were something new growing out of the texts, like seedlings out of the forest floor, whose sources could only be guessed.

The things that Themozhiyar said that I thought of as silly were of course only silly to me, with my American-educated, female point of view, which had its own blind spots. As I listened to Themozhiyar, and as I listened to Mahadeva Iyer, a pattern emerged in the picture of the world that each man was drawing for me. The trees, the mountains, the medicines, the households, and the poems that they spoke of all had certain distinctive things in common. They all were linked through an extensive network of metaphors. They all fit a common framework, and it was one that I had never seen before I came to Tamil Nadu. The large hard mountains encompassed the fertile paddy land as men guarded their women. The eyes blossomed, the breasts wept, and the fields breathed forth their powerful spirits rhythmically. All living hardness softened, all softness melted, and all fluid substance was sublimated into power, into spirit, into new life. Hard consonants contained and were animated by the soft breathy spirit of vowels. The bones of the saint melted with love for God, releasing his soul to join the invisible, passionate cosmic dancer. The tough barky tree poured its life forth in the form of a tender fruit, consummated in ripening, in sweetening, in being consumed as the body of a ripe woman is softened and loosened and consumed as she pours her life into others, as a man's member weakens and diminishes as it pours forth its spirit, its feeling, and fluid seed into a new generation. These were the forces turning the world in which Mahadeva Iyer and Themozhiyar lived. All the things they said were arranged around these forces. It had just been a matter of time, of collecting a large enough number of seemingly unconnected bits of information, before I began to see the interlocking patterns into which they all fell.

After eighteen months in Tamil Nadu, I returned home and wrote my dissertation about these patterns, describing in detail an array of the different pieces of information that fit them. A great number of the pieces had been given me by Themozhiyar. A slightly smaller number had come from Mahadeva Iyer. The remainder came from scattered sources, the most important of these sources being Mahadeva Iyer's agricultural laborers, with whom I had spent much time.

I wasn't sure whether my dissertation would be accepted, because it failed to adhere to many of the conventions of anthropological research and writing. However, it was interesting and original, it contained a fair amount of useful information, and it was very coherent: all the pieces fit together closely. The dissertation passed, and I was told that I should publish it.

I never did publish it—it is on file at Chicago if anyone wants to see it—and my reasons for not publishing it were these: first, I felt concerned that my sources were not broad enough. I knew that many people doing anthropology had relied as heavily as I on one or two principal informants. It was not necessarily wrong to do this, as long as you were honest about it, I felt. A single articulate human being can open many doors, and there were precedents for such a narrow focus in a number of anthropological classics. What troubled me more was the knowledge that both Mahadeva Iyer and Themozhiyar were men—high-caste, highly educated, landowning men at that. I did not want to believe that Tamil culture—that *any* culture—was made only, or even mostly, by such men. I knew there was something more. In the back of my mind, during all this time, there remained Alene Dorsey, my black other mother, smart but denied education, strong but denied political power, loving, segregated. I do not congratulate myself on this degree of remembrance of Alene. But at least it was enough to give me pause, to make me think twice about what these high-caste men, in their beautiful words, were telling me.

Besides Alene, there was another influence: in Tamil Nadu itself there had been the shamaness. An untouchable woman with no schooling, no land, no money, many children to support, her husband irregularly employed and earning little, she was astonishingly eloquent and resourceful. Like my two male informants, she too wove a world with words for me, but I could not put her into my dissertation because what she told me did not fit at all with what they said. Nor was it their world turned upside down: that would have been too easy. It was a completely different set of visions—tougher, angrier visions, more bitter, more questioning ones. I learned from her, as well as from Anni and others, how illusory was the ideal of the soft and yielding, submissive Indian woman.

In subsequent visits to Tamil Nadu—in part, perhaps as penance for the high-caste masculine bias of my dissertation—I sought out untouchable women, recorded their words, took them seriously, and was greatly rewarded for doing so, for there are artists and philosophers among them from whom we have much to learn. My few publications to date are mainly about these women.

But there are other, less noble, reasons why I backed away from publishing by dissertation.

As the first stint of my field work in Tamil Nadu picked up and became more exciting and I knew at last the direction in which I was going, things got worse for Keith. I was spending increasing amounts of time away from the house, leaving him alone with the baby. He bought wood and hand tools and constructed a playpen, his body covered with sawdust and sweat as he labored in the hundred-degree heat of the afternoon. He could have hired a carpenter to do the job for him, but that was not the point. He befriended other Americans living in Madras, but he was the only one who had no reason of his own to be in India. He spent several afternoons a week at the American consulate, reading the New York Times. He began to speak about returning to Chicago.

Often I would go out in the evenings, when social life begins to stir in Tamil Nadu. The scorching sun drives people into the shade in the afternoon, but as soon as it is gone, the streets fill with men and women, and businesses reopen. The shamaness held regular healing sessions in the evenings, and Themozhiyar conducted his temple lectures in the evenings.

In the village of Tiruvānmiyūr, at the sourthern end of Madras, there is an old temple called the Sri Maruntiswaran Koil, "The Temple of the Lord of Medicine." It was here that I first met Themozhiyar. I had visited the temple because I was interested in "indigenous medicine," as a set of activities dealing with life processes. I came there one day to see what I might find. It was a peaceful place, unlike the temples closer into town which are filled with frenetic activity. Not much seemed to be going on here at all. Goats grazed around the temple courtyard. People had started to build a large stone archway at the entrance to the temple, but it was never finished. The ocean was nearby, and its breezes kept the air constantly cool. By the temple tank (most temples have these man-made ponds next to them) there grew a tree with burlap bags hanging from it. It smelled bad. Someone told me the bags contained placentas.

No one was there at the temple that day, so I wandered around undisturbed. The most striking thing inside it was a large gilded and brightly painted statue of a being called the Kamadhenu, "The Cow of Desire." It had the body of a cow, lifting its feet prancingly like a show horse, and it had the erect and fanned out tail of a peacock. Instead of a cow's head, it had the head of a woman, with a cherubic face that smiled sweetly with inviting red lips. A small tiger voluptuously licked the cow's udder.

Also inside the temple was a special sivalingam. The Sivalingam is the Lord Siva's erect penis. It is to Siva as the cross is to Jesus—his holy sign, and also a sharp reminder of the essence of his character. Though veils of prudery sometimes partly mask it, Saivism is a religion of the erotic; it is an ancient religion that has had time to grow, and its roots go deep down; its poetry and its iconography plumb the soul.

The sivalingam in this temple was different from most, in that it was not hand-carved. Instead, it was some kind of natural rock formation, something like a stalagmite, shaped like a partly melted candle. It was kept in, or around it had been built, a small dark alcove, illuminated only by the daylight that filtered in.

Later someone gave me a tiny pamphlet, of the kind that are published semianonymously by the tens of thousands in India, explaining the history of the Sri Maruntiswaran Koil. The story was that once the Kamadhenu lived in the forest, and nearby in the same forest was a sivalingam, which she loved. Every day she would visit it and bathe it in her milk. But one day an evil hunter, a king, came through the forest and pursued the Kamadhenu, trying to kill her. She fled, but when she reached the sivalingam, she turned to face her pursuer. Placing her hoof upon the sivalingam for support, she sprang upon the hunter and killed him. Then she turned again and found that the sivalingam had been crushed by her hoof. Still, having been enveloped so often in her warm sweet milk, it loved her, and forgave her for destroying it. That is why even today we may see this sivalingam, crushed and partly melted, standing in the darkness.

One other thing caught my attention on the first afternoon that I visited this temple. This was a banner strung between two pillars, announcing that someone named Pulavar Themozhiyar would lecture at the temple every Tuesday evening on the topic of a text called Tirumantiram. Tirumantiram, "The Sacred Spell," was one of the books of the Saiva canon that I had wanted to read. It was supposed to describe the means to immortalization of the body and along the way it was supposed to describe from its own point of view all the life processes—conception, birth, growth, death, and the movements of the soul—together with social customs associated with these processes at the time that the book was written, a thousand years ago. I returned to the temple the following Tuesday evening to hear the lecture.

Keith came with me, carrying Daniel, so perhaps as a young family we made an auspicious sight. We found that the temple was almost empty, but in one of the outer rooms, open to the night, there was a middle-aged man, seated cross-legged on the floor, speaking in formal tones to a group of older men seated around him. The speaker had a mahogany-colored face and body but his teeth were gleaming white and his tongue was pink as a rose petal. His mouth was the first thing one noticed about him; the second thing was his voice. Next his hands, then his eyes, then his feet.

Some of the old men gestured to us to come and sit down among them. I did so. Keith took Daniel and carried him around in the courtyard of the temple to keep him quiet. The speaker was saying that the body is layered, like a lotus flower. The outer layers are large and tough, the inner layers are soft and small, the fragrance comes from within the inner layers. He made the shape of a lotus with one of his hands. His gestures were fluid. His palms were pink like his tongue. As he spoke, he looked from one to another of the members of his audience. Periodically, his eyes paused at mine. His left eye was slightly askew, so that when he looked at me, he seemed to be meeting my gaze and avoiding it simultaneously. After he finished speaking he stood up and some of the old men prostrated themselves before him, touching his feet. They told me to bow to him too, so I did. His calves were bowed, his toes were rough and barky and darker than the earth. When I stood up, I saw that he was shorter than me by about three inches. He left the temple, conversing companionably with some of the men. I wanted to talk with him but he would not speak with me or look at me after the lecture. It was about ten o'clock when Keith and Dan and I got home. I tried to explain to Keith what had been said in the lecture, but as I wasn't sure myself what it was all about, I did not do a very good job.

In the following weeks, I returned to the temple by myself, to hear subsequent lectures. Still, Themozhiyar would not talk with me. Then one evening one of the old men—his name was Ganesan—asked me about myself and started up a conversation in that way. He was kind and friendly, and we ended up chatting for a long time. After a while he asked me was it true, as all his friends believed, that Westerners had no rules at all governing their behavior, that the women could do anything, go with anyone they wanted any time. I told him no, not at all. He said, that's the way it seems in the movies. I said, you must know that the movies aren't true. He said he knew they mixed truth with lies, but all that he and his friends knew of America was what they saw in the movies. He asked me why I came to the lectures. I told him I was interested in learning as much as I could about Tirumantiram. He said, "You know, you're not like our children; they're not the least interested in these old books."

Ganesan approved of my wanting to learn about Tamil literature, but he said that I would not be able to cover very much ground at the rate we were going. At the temple, Themozhiyar expounded upon one verse of Tirumantiram each week and there were three thousand verses in all. Why didn't I ask him to come to my home and give me private lessons? I told Ganesan I didn't think he would come—he seemed rather shy. Ganesan said, "Of course he will come!" Especially if I paid him. I asked Ganesan, "Will you arrange it?" A few days later, Themozhiyar appeared at my house, accompanied by Ganesan and two other male friends. He delivered a formal lecture to all of us, and then left. The next week he came again, alone, and lectured to me again. Daniel, in the next room, started crying in the middle of the lecture, and I excused myself to go and nurse him. Themozhiyar smiled, stretched his legs out in front of him, laid his head back on his hands and relaxed.

After that he came every week, and the lectures quickly broke down into question-and-answer sessions, and then into conversations, on every topic that he or I could think of. In the great anthropological tradition of kinship studies, following in the footsteps of the famous Bronislaw Malinowski (author of *The Sexual Life of Savages*), I felt it was an important part of my research to learn something about native theories of where babies come from. Gently, innocently, via the mediation of Tirumantiram, I broached this topic with Themozhiyar. At his request, I had made a list of all the sections of Tirumantiram that I was especially interested in reading. One item on this list was a chapter entitled *Karu Uṯpatti* ("Embryogenesis"). I had already looked at this chapter and found it rather benignly obscure. But Themozhiyar's lessons about it to me were something else again. They were subtle, disturbing erotic quasi-poems of his own creation.

Spring in Tamil Nadu is not what it is here. By March, the fire wind, as they call it, is blowing strongly. In January or February, I forget which, Keith had gotten a letter from the school in Chicago where he taught, asking him to come home and teach there again. He had written back immediately, "Yes, I'm coming." I found myself telling him angrily, "Go. Just go." Keith, I'm sorry. On March 1, 1976, Keith got on the plane. Daniel and I stayed on in Tamil Nadu for six more months. Themozhiyar continued his visits. The time came when he said to me, "What we're doing is a selfish thing, very selfish." I argued with him, and won my case, but knew that he was right. At the end of August, on Daniel's second birthday, we flew home.

INITIATION

Themozhiyar's letters to me were sometimes difficult to decipher. For instance, he would write long paragraphs expounding on the importance of what is called in Tamil *poruḷ*, a word that we translate as "meaning, substance, thing, important thing, wealth, money." He said there was drought, the harvest was bad, he wanted to perform charitable acts for poor children but was unable to do so. I deduced from such letters that he wanted me to send him money. I was saddened by this, because from my point of view, friendship was not consistent with begging for gifts. It took me a long time to understand and accept that from his point of view such begging meant something quite different. Once in response to a *poruḷ*-letter I wrote back apologizing that, being a student with a very small income, I did not have enough cash to send him a gift-check that month. He answered, saying, "You are to be pitied. I thought that you were a fertile tree. I know now that you are a bald tree."

Often he wrote and spoke in such metaphors. He had told me that this was the civilized (*nākarikamāna*) way of speaking. For instance, he said,

Plate 2. The Kamadhenu.

if a wife speaks angrily to her husband, the husband should express his discontent by saying, "There is too much salt in the stew." Of his own wife Padmini he said, "She is like a jackfruit—tough on the outside, sweet on the inside." When he was unhappy with Padmini and I asked him, "What about the jackfruit?" he said, "The jackfruit emits a sweet sticky fluid that attracts many flies, and traps them." He said I was like the plaintain. "What are the characteristics of the plantain?" I asked. "It is a plant that has many uses," he said.

In 1978, I received a letter from him that seemed to be brimming with joy. "Something wonderful is about to emerge," he wrote, "like a lotus from the mud, like a pearl from a shell." A few months later, his son Jnana Oli was born.

Themozhiyar saw himself as my guru and me as his student. He wanted me to believe in his god and to follow his path toward that god. He referred to me as a *muṟaiyillāta poruḷ*, a "lawless thing," whose life had no order and followed no rule. Out of pity, he said, he would lift me up. The ceremony of worship and meditation that he conducted he referred to as *vaṛipāḍu*, "taking the path." When I was still in Madras, he had performed initiation (*gurudiksha*) on me, by surprise and against my mild protests, by giving me a secret mantra of twenty syllables. I accepted the role of disciple, as being the most appropriate one under the circumstances, though as I got to know Themozhiyar better I found it increasingly difficult to bow to him, even as a nominal gesture. I argued with him frequently, as did his other students, but I was probably more vehement and stubborn than they. I wanted to learn from him, but I also wanted to be in control of the situation in which the two of us found ourselves. I told him that he should consider me a child, that in my ignorance of Tamil culture I *was* a child, and needed to be taught everything from the foundation up. Themozhiyar agreed to that. I acted as humbly and innocently as was possible for me. But I did not enjoy being treated as an inferior.

There was one long poem that Themozhiyar wanted me to read. The name of the poem was Tirukkōvaiyār. It was written by the most famous of Tamil Saiva saints, Māṇikkavācakar. Themozhiyar had been lecturing about this poem, verse-by-verse, week-by-week, to a group of his students in Saidapet. He told me that in this poem, the Lord Siva takes the form of a woman, and the questing soul, *uyir,* is the man who loves her. He said that it was a very difficult poem, that few people read it and most did not understand it because of its complex grammar. I was interested in the part about God being a woman. In Indian devotional literature, it is common for the worshipper to enter into an erotic relationship with Siva or Vishnu, but in most cases, the worshipper becomes (in his male imagination) female, the frustrated but faithful mistress of her divine lord, who has a multitude of girlfriends and who generally misses his dates with all of them. The subordination of human to divine is, in this literature, analogized with the subordination of wife to husband. The contrast between the necessary fidelity of the one and the fickle freedom of the other is notable. Tirukkōvaiyār sounded different to me, and better. If in this poem the oversexed and unruly Lord Siva played the role of a Tamil woman, he would have, for a change, to toe the line.

For three years, Themozhiyar and I corresponded. To me, our relationship was a meeting of two worlds normally very distant from each other. I thought that if we could simply learn to understand each other, and beyond that, if we could learn to work together, to be colleagues and coequals, to create something together, then we would have achieved a change in anthropology, a change in the way that civilizations deal with each other. My visions were very broad and, now I realize, absurdly grandiose. But they were not unworthy visions. Other people in my field were also attempting to change "informants" into "colleagues" and simultaneously to change the idea of culture from something fixed to something dynamic, to realize that culture, whatever it is, is constantly being created and recreated among people who are different from each other, even as different from each other as Themozhiyar and I. My mentors in America encouraged me to continue learning from Themozhiyar and working with him on joint projects. The idea of building a bridge between two great human civilizations obsessed me. For years my life revolved around this dream.

This dream and one other, totally opposite one: to get away from human beings as much as possible, to live with my small family back in the woods, to need little money, to be undisturbing of the world, and undisturbed. After all this time of being an anthropologist, I still believed more in Nature than in Culture. Life in India had fanned the flame of my belief from both sides. While I was there I was never able to be alone with just the trees and the birds; people and their intensity were everywhere; moreover, they crowded around me, following me and keeping close tabs on me wherever I went. I longed more than ever for the cool wild woods of my home, for solitude. At the same time I saw that in India, Nature had not been so much conquered and paved over as it is here. This force that Tamils call *iyaṯkai*, "that which is as it is," made cracks in everything human-constructed and sent its tendrils through. People had no choice but to live with it, so they did. The materials of their lives were mostly just what was at hand. A coconut shell and a stick made a ladle, mud and grass made a house. Every object of possible use was recycled many times. To people in Tamil Nadu who lived this way, making do was a stark necessity. To me, it was an admirable skill. In my final months in Madras, I learned to eat less and less until I was never hungry at all, wore the same old clothes until they were rags, and felt quite blissfully happy. I must have been quite a sight when I got back home. You can live on nothing in India, because so many people have to. In America, no one will let you. But for a while I tried.

In 1979, I received a small summer grant to work on translating Tirukkōvaiyār. I was intending to go to India to do it, but early in the spring, Keith and I decided to buy a piece of abandoned farmland out in the country near where we worked and build our own house on it. So I used the grant to bring Themozhiyar here.

Themozhiyar had little sense of the world beyond Tamil Nadu. When I picked him up at Kennedy airport and drove him the three hundred miles via Route 17 back to central New York State, he watched the vast stretches of forestland rolling by and finally asked suspiciously, "Where are all the people? Where are all the cattle?" In the late afternoon, in a heavy cold rain, we arrived at our home—a battered old twenty-foot trailer in the middle of a field of weeds. Keith, Dan, and I had just moved in ten days before. We were planning to build our house near the trailer. Themozhiyar looked around at the weeds in despair. "There's not even a path," he said.

For him it must have been a paradoxical situation indeed. We owned a car—a possession that only the wealthiest of Tamil people could boast of—and yet we had no house. We owned twenty fertile acres, a considerable holding by Tamil standards, and yet we had left it all in wild trees and goldenrod. He asked me if cattle would eat goldenrod. I said I didn't know. He asked me what maples were good for. Firewood or lumber, I said, but we planned to leave the healthy trees standing. "You must cut it all down," he commanded. "Plant mango trees." Mangoes won't grow in this part of the country, I told him. "Plant apple trees, then. What a terrible waste this is." I told him it would be a big job to cut down twenty acres of secondary growth and hardwood, plow it, and plant it. Keith and I had neither the skill nor the time nor the energy nor the tools to do this. "Get laborers to do it," he said. "Where are your laborers?" I told him we had none. In this country we could not afford to pay even one person to work for us.

He kept saying over and over again, "This country is not like Tamil Nadu. The trees are different, not a single tree is the same. The sky is different. The people are different." We lived in the midst of such opulence, *oru vaḷamāna nāḍu,* "a rich country" he called it often, looking out on the wanton deep green of the summer woods. And we had such nice white skin. He said he knew if he stayed here long enough, his skin would get paler too. And yet our customs were so barbaric. Even the milk, he said, tasted like blood.

I thought he might like to try a vegetarian pizza. But when I brought home the box and opened it, his eyes widened with horror. "It looks like a corpse," he said, "With the pus and the blood oozing out." I said, "You know it's not that. The white is cheese, made out of milk. You drink milk. And the red is tomatoes. Your wife at home cooks with tomatoes all the time." He said, "Yes, but she doesn't mix it all up and display it and make it beautiful [*aṛakupaḍuttamāḍḍāṅka*] like you do." Beauty and death are an ancient association in Tamil Nadu.

Both Keith and I kept trying to educate Themozhiyar. We wanted to show him the good things about ourselves and our country. But he refused to be educated. He had not come for that. He had come to educate *us*. He had come as my guru. Tamil knowledge was the best of all knowledge, he said, and he, Themozhiyar, already knew everything there was to know. I protested, "Ayya, there are many things you don't know. For instance, you don't know English." "I have all the necessary knowledge [*tēvaiyāna aṟivu*]," he said. "All the rest nobody needs."

Themozhiyar's ignorance of English had consequences not only for him but for us, on many levels. For one thing, it meant that he was unable to communicate directly with anyone but me during his stay in America. If he wanted to speak, he had always to do it through me. I learned the powers of an interpreter, then, and was glad I had never had one in India. The temptation to edit the things people said to each other was sometimes very great. I wanted to protect Themozhiyar from the contempt of my friends. Once, for instance, he wanted to tell a professorial friend of mine that he admired Adolph Hitler. But what did he know of Adolph Hitler? That name meant something completely different to him than it did to us. Did he know about the holocaust? No. And how many times had I embarrassed my Tamil associates by saying ignorant things to relative strangers when I was in the field? How many times would they have covered up for me if they had been able?

The worst thing was that Themozhiyar couldn't talk with Keith. During the three months that he was living with us in the trailer, the two of them could only communicate with each other through gestures and facial expressions. When I talked with one, the other felt left out and angry. How could he know what was being said? We might be talking about him in front of his face, we might be mocking him, and he wouldn't know it. A silent bond of suffering grew between them and both of them grew more critical of me as the summer progressed. Why had I created this situation? Keith was building our house single-handedly. Often he needed help. Themozhiyar and I did assist him whenever we could but it wasn't enough. I should have been up there helping all the time. The summer was growing short. Themozhiyar was there to explicate the poem to me. He had a job to do, for which he was being paid, for which he had been brought halfway around the world. He seemed to feel a heavy weight of responsibility. At the rate of five stanzas a day for ninety days we could get through the poem. Each stanza took between one and two hours. The house also had to be livable by fall. The trailer was on loan and had to be returned. The conflict was impossible, and there was no way that Themozhiyar and Keith could work things out directly between themselves.

Finally, Themozhiyar's not knowing either my language or my culture even to the extent that I knew his meant that true collaboration between us of the kind I dreamed of would always be impossible. He did all the teaching. I did all the learning. I had great power over him because he didn't know my world and didn't want to know it. I think now that the possibility of such power was just what attracted me to him in the first place. To me he was the perfect informant. His knowledge of his own "traditional" culture was tremendous, and he did wonderful things with this knowledge: he could make his own thoughts out of it, and he could convey these thoughts in words to me, in such a way that hidden connections could be seen and flashes of recognition would occur. He made his culture alive, he was one of the cells on the meristem, he was one of the builders. At the same time, he was "pure," he was remarkably free of "Western influence." He could not anticipate my responses to what he said, because he was unfamiliar with the medium in which my mind had grown, and so he could not defend himself against me. If he intended to show himself to me at all (at least this much was his choice), he would have to show himself to me as he would to one of his own people. To me as a wilderness-seeking anthropologist, he was virgin territory.

I know the implications of all this now. I do not like them. But I don't believe that they render what I learned from Themozhiyar or about him false. I also don't believe that there was any better way that I might have proceeded. Should I not have tried to learn about a person from another culture? Should I have objectified him more? Treated him as a piece of data? Should I have kept him at a distance because he was male and I was female? Would I have learned as much if I had done so? Would I have cared as much about what happened to him and his family afterwards?

Every day Themozhiyar and I sat down in the grass underneath a young walnut tree that had grown from the richly manured ruins of an old barn, I with my pen and paper and tape recorder, Themozhiyar with his voice, and there he sang the poem to me verse by verse, explained it to me and lectured about it to me, daily for three months, often for eight hours a day, until he was hoarse and tired. Alongside his chanting and his lectures he provided a simple Tamil definition of each word in the poem and a careful explanation of the meaning, or meanings, of each verse as he read it. If the absence of English in our conversations crippled us in one way, it freed us (and especially me) in another, by forcing me to think in Tamil, rather than trying to translate everything into English before I understood it.

The poem Tirukkōvaiyār is about love between two strangers, a man and a woman, from two different lands. It is also about the abstract universal unbounded creative divine force Themozhiyar called *civam* (whence the name of Lord Siva, *civaperumān,* derives) and its love for the bounded soul of a human being. In order to love this finite soul, be loved by it and free it, civam enters into a finite form, the form of the guru. Thus the poem is also about the love between guru and disciple, how each travels a long way and changes very much in order to meet the other, how each, out of love, causes pain to the other, how each, out of love, endures this pain. As Themozhiyar taught the poem to me, it also became a poem about the two of us.

THE PROCESS OF EMBODIMENT

I have said that one theme of this book is the way that India both exceeds and shatters our Western expectations. A second theme of this book is the fluid relationship between ideal and experience in India, within and among Indian minds. By "ideal" I mean high-level mental creations: myths, philosophies, sciences, songs, poems, and the like—those rarified aspects of culture for which India is famous. By "experience" I mean what happens to ordinary Indian people in their day-to-day lives, on the ground, in the mud. Ideal and experience are my own categories—*our* own categories—but perhaps as long as we realize that they stand for realities that are in fact inseparable, we will not go too far astray. In India they are related to each other as food and spirit, feeling and flesh: they are constantly being transformed one into the other.

Similar relations have been discussed by Indologists before, under the rubric of Great and Little Tradition, Text and Context.[2] The Great Tradition was the world of Sanskrit written texts, by means of which the literati throughout South Asia communicated with each other, by means of which they created the rules, the high ideals, that they thought all people should follow. The Little Tradition was the mass of village praxis and local lore, all the unwritten (or largely unwritten) "manners, customs, and ceremonies" by means of which ordinary people ordered their lives, the multiplicity of contexts in which the rules of the texts might or might not be more or less enacted.

Central to the anthropological studies that produced the labels Great and Little was the understanding that in India, ideas and ideals are not Platonic. They are neither changeless nor inviolable, sacred though they may be. Rules stand in a cyclic relation to praxis, as the high does to the low, as the Great does to the Little, as the ideal does to the real. Each is constantly turning into the other and changing it.

Thus in India great ideas have no self-existence. Great texts are like spirits out of bodies—they need flesh, matter, circumstantiality, to give them shape, to make them real. And so they take a thousand forms, and every form is real. Also they have no self-existence in that they are not unique. Great stories, great images, great ideas turn up again and again in many different places. Great texts are anthologies, compilations, collections. The greatest of the Indian epics, the Mahabharata, is like a forest all of whose species grow elsewhere, and there are even whole other forests like it. Likewise Tirukkōvaiyār, "The Holy Flower-Chain," the poem/story/myth that Themozhiyar taught to me, is a collection of images and phrases many if not all of which are found elsewhere in Tamil literature. It is a daisy chain, and the fields are full of daisies.

It is true in a very concrete sense to say that great texts are like spirits out of bodies, for in India, people live these texts. Myths, for instance, which tell the stories of gods, folktales which tell the stories of heroes and heroines, poems and songs which tell the stories of anonymous lovers, and finally, nowadays, movies which tell the stories of modern human beings—people in India take these as more than entertainment, they take them to heart, so that a person's life may become an enactment of a story and vice versa. Heroes and gods are persons who live;[3] their spirits exist and come down into living bodies, not at random. There is a complex relationship, and a partial identity, between the personality of a possessing spirit and the personality of the possessed. During trance, there may be a complete merger between the person's experienced life, and the storied life of the spirit, but even outside of such set apart mental states, some degree of identification remains between a living person and a beloved hero, deity, or story.

This being so, when you are trying to understand a story told in India it becomes important to consider the life of the person telling the story, and when you are trying to understand a person it becomes important to listen to the stories that that person tells. It is also important to recognize the ways in which one may lead to alterations in the interpretation or enactment of the other. The story may change to fit the life; the life may change to fit the story.

Performance of a text both embodies it and pluralizes it. Performance pluralizes a text both by fragmenting it into different forms and merging it with different contexts, and by putting the different voices the text contains into actual different people. For myths, poems, stories, and so forth, if they involve one personality, usually involve more than one. If they are enacted, they are dramatized and have multiple actors. When a drama is on a stage, it is usually fairly clear who are the actors and who is the audience, and in what direction the bulk of the messages are traveling. When a drama is carried out as part of real life, then these boundaries become blurred.

In an anthropological situation, the ethnographer, willing or not, must form part of the context of performance, part of the audience, and sometimes, part of the act. Especially in intensive, face-to-face studies of small groups of people, this must be true. A firsthand anthropological study then becomes, deliberately or not, a study of intercultural communication, and a study of cultural change. For every performance of a story, every living of it, changes the script, and when personalities of different cultures get involved in such a drama, it becomes especially interesting to see what things change, and what things remain the same.

Tirukkōvaiyār is a story about relationships between personalities that can be played out between real people. In playing it out with me, perhaps Themozhiyar was performing his own ethnographic experiment, trying to find out for himself how truly universal are the sentiments expressed in this work which he held sacred. But he was also just doing his normal job as a teacher. In all of his lectures to all of his classes, Themozhiyar took it as his task to demonstrate the oneness of the sacred literature (which was a kind of esoteric lore) with what he called *vārkkai,* "life," represented by nonesoteric folklore, what he called *potu aṟivu,* "common knowledge." His students therefore bestowed upon him the title *vāṛviyal pulavar* which means something like, "professor of the nature of life." Life, he said, was an expansion or opening up (*virivu*) of the text; the text was a condensation or gathering up (*tokuppu*) of life. Hence it was his specific goal to bring his and his listeners' experience into congruence with the text that he taught, and vice versa. Inasmuch as all experience is concrete and unique, his exegesis of the text was unique. But the tradition he followed, of fleshing out an ideal by giving it his own life form, was one shared by people throughout Tamil Nadu.

THE SAME OLD STORY

The earliest Tamil poetry, written about two thousand years ago, is of two kinds: poetry of the interior (*akam*), and poetry of the exterior (*puṟam*). Akam poetry is love poetry. Puṟam poetry is about the warlike exploits of kings. Tirukkōvaiyār, written about a thousand years ago, merges these two genres, describing simultaneously the love between a man and a woman, and the terrifying mythic exploits of the Lord Siva—how he skinned an elephant, how he broke the teeth of the sun, how his town is heavily fortified and frequented by tigers. The link between these two worlds is made by means of metaphor and metonymy: the heroine is said to be like, or to be from, the fortified town of Siva, called Tillai (after a flower that grows there) or Puliyūr (tiger town) or Cittampalam (the small space, the meeting ground, the space of consciousness inside the heart). This city is the holy city, but it is also hard to reach, armed and dangerous—like the heroine herself, whose eyes and breasts and lower body parts are frequently called "weapons." The link between beauty, especially sexual beauty, and death is a very important component of this poem.

Some specialists in early Tamil literature say that the early Tamils considered women to harbor a very dangerous, sacred power that had to be kept circumscribed in order to be useful and nondestructive to men. Poems like Tirukkōvaiyār keep seeming to say that a woman's sexuality can kill. This of course is only one-quarter of the full circle: only a man's point of view and only the dark side of that. The bright side is that a sexy woman has the power not only to feel but to give heavenly bliss, and having this power, she commands respect.

Akam poetry all follows a certain pattern. The two strangers, boy and girl, meet in a wild but beautiful place, the forested mountainside. There they engage in clandestine union and for a brief time all is ecstasy—mingled with some fear. Hardship comes when the heroine (*talaivi*), who is always very young, just barely blossomed, leaves behind her family to elope with the hero (*talaivan*). The heroine's girlfriend (*tōṛi*), who shares all her feelings and secrets, laments her going, as does the heroine's mother and the tōṛi's mother, the heroine's foster mother (*cevili tāy*). After eloping with her, the hero leaves the heroine alone to go off and perform his worldly exploits, while she waits anxiously. He is a long time in returning, and she fears that he may not return at all. At some point along the line, they wed (the formal wedding is never described in this poetry), and she bears a child. The hero then begins to visit other women. In some poems, the other woman (*parattaiyil*) speaks, and then it becomes quite clear that to the ancient Tamil poets, this woman-out-of-bounds is neither a sorceress nor a villainess, but simply a human female with human feelings. She is sad and embittered because she feels used by the hero; she knows that his first loyalities are to his family, and that he is not hers to keep. Meanwhile the wife, the heroine, almost sympathetic to the other woman, toughly endures her husband's infidelity, making a few sharp comments along the way.

In the early akam poetry, each poem describes one scene in this family drama, as seen through the eyes of one of its participants: the hero, the heroine, the heroine's mother, her girlfriend, her foster mother, the hero's companion, the other woman. Tirukkōvaiyār strings four hundred of such vignettes together, to form a whole saga, fitting the pattern described above.

In both Tirukkōvaiyār and its earlier prototypes, the sexual sentiments and images are quite graphic and unrestrained, and yet they are subtle, because they are never expressed directly but always through metaphor. Sometimes the metaphors are obvious, even to the Western reader; other times they are not. The honey-filled, curly hair of the heroine is often mentioned, but the notion of pubic hair is never directly stated, only strongly implied. The young heroine admires the color and vigor of her lover's genital equipment, but in her admiring poem, she doesn't point to his body; instead she points to a certain flower that springs up on the mountainside where he comes from, the *kuṟiñci* that has "such black stalks." The lonely abandoned wife defiantly tells her disloyal husband that she doesn't need his presence to satisfy her: she can be quite happy thinking about him and masturbating—but she doesn't say it in just this way. Rather she compares herself to her little boy playing with and pulling on his toy chariot, happy in his fantasy that it is the real thing. In this way, many aspects of human sexual sentiment are hidden in Tamil poetry, waiting still for readers to uncover them. The fact that these sentiments are expressed in a "civilized" way, so that we can never know for sure, when we read a given poem, that this or that exactly is what is meant, only increases the erotic intensity of this ancient art form.

WHAT THEY SAID

Out by the weed field near our trailer, Themozhiyar commenced his explication of Tirukkōvaiyār to me. We worked outside whenever the sun was shining. The twelve-year-old girl who lived next door babysat for Dan, who now was four, while we did the poem, and Keith labored on the house a hundred feet away. During that summer, we read through verse 307. Themozhiyar chose to stop there, on an odd number. To stop on a round number (say, 300) would have been inauspicious, he said. Below are a few of the verses that we read, together with some (polished and tidied up) excerpts from the notes that I took while he lectured.

2. Ayyam (Doubt)

pōtō vicumpō punalo paṇika ḷatupatiyō
yātō aṟikuva tētu mariti yamanviḍutta
tūtō anaṅkan tuṇaiyō iṇaiyili tollaittillai
mātō maḍamayi lōvena niṉṟavar vāṟpatiyē

[In a flower? In the sky? In the water?
In a snake's hole? Where?
Harder than anything to know
is the dwelling-place of this soul-grabbing
death's messenger, this helper of the killing,
beautiful, sickness of desire,

this lady of the matchless, ancient city of the Lord,
this innocent bird of bright plumage, or whatever
in the world it is that stands before me now.]

The poem begins with a man's terror of a woman whom he suddenly sees when he is out hunting. She is beautiful and she seems like part of the wild forest to him. He does not know how to categorize her. He does not know what she is or where she comes from. She seems to be grabbing his soul, she has great power, so she must come from the heavenly city, or perhaps she is dragging him off to his death.

But her power over him is only the power of his own desire for her. When he is able to see that she is "just a woman" he is able to relax . . . somewhat.

3. Teḷital (Clarification)

pāyum viḍaiyaran tillaiyan nāḷpaḍaik kaṇṇimaikkum
tōyum nilattaḍi tūmalar vāḍum tuyarameyti
āyum mananē aṇaṅkallaḷ ammā mulaicumantu
tēyum maruṅkuṟ perumpaṇait tōḷic ciṟunutalē

[Like the fortress of Siva, the springing bull-king,
her eyes are armed! But they blink, and her feet
are dampened in the soil,
and those flowers she wears will die.
Oh my poor, pained, searching mind! She's no god!
Just a small-browed, broad-shouldered little girl,
whose waist bends under the burden
of those big motherly breasts.]

Able to recognize that this creature is, after all, human, and that her anomalous appearance is just that of a child recently turned woman, and seeing that she has troubles of her own, in the form of that very body that so awes him, the man loses his terror.

5. Uḍkōḷ (Taking Inside)

aṇiyum amiṟtumen nāviyum āyavan ṟillaiccintā
maṇiyumpa rārāṟi yāmaṟai yōnaḍi vāṟttalarin
piṇiyum ataṟku maruntum piṟaṟap piṟaṟaminnum
paṇiyum puraimaruṅ kuṟperun tōli paḍaikkaṅkaḷē

[Perfect beauty, sweet, sweet god-food,
my breath and soul is he
who is the heart-crystal, he
who is hidden, whom the gods
do not know,
by whose origin
the unblessed sicken. Like that sickness, and

like its healing are the weapon-bright eyes
of this broad-shouldered girl, whose small belly is a
snake
or a lightning bolt, flashing, and again
flashing.]

"As a snake spreads its hood in anger," comments Themozhiyar, "the heroine spreads the place at the lower end of her snake-like waist in desire." [I recall that Madhavi, the beautiful twelve-year-old courtesan in the Tamil epic *Cilappatikāram*, is said to have a pubis like a cobra's hood.] "When she does this," he continues, "a brief strong feeling like lightning comes again and again."

"God does three kinds of work," he dictates to me. "first, he is an ornament [*aṇi*—"perfect beauty"]. An ornament gives light and beauty to those who wear it, but it stands apart.

"Second, he is *amiṛtam* ["god food," the nectar of immortality, the essence of life, a sweet distillate of all the bodily fluids]. Amiṛtam issues from the soul like a spring and causes a feeling of flourishing to blossom. The crown of the head is the place from which amiṛtam flows. He gives us this feeling by being close to us. That is why it is called amiṛtam [*amiṛ*, "be immersed, plunge, sink, drown"; more conventional scholars would say that Tamil amiṛtam is from Sanskrit *amṛta*, "deathless"].

"Third, he is the breath [*āvi*, "spirit"], the feeling within feeling. Causing feeling to mount he is one with us and fulfills us.

"This lord who is three shines as light in the place called Tillai and gives us all. The gods are unable to know him. Hiding, he shines. Those who do not worship his feet are immersed in great sorrow. In the same way, it is said of the girl who has wide shoulders and a narrow, snake-like waist, that one look of her eyes gives great pain and another look heals that pain."

6. Teyvattai Makiṛtal (Rejoicing at What God Has Done)

vaḷaipayil kīṛkaḍa niṉṟiḍa mēlkaḍal vānnukattin
tuḷaivaṟi nērkaṟi kōttenat tillaittol lōnkayilaik
kiḷaivayin nīkkiyik keṇḍaiyaṅ kaṇṇiyaik koṇḍutanta
viḷaivaiyal lālviya vēṉnaya vēṉteyva mikkaṉavē

[As though a stake planted upright in the eastern sea
where coiled conches live
found a wide yoke floating from the western sea
and pierced it like a needle,
something broke this girl, with her fish-like eyes
from her kind on the mountain of the ancient one
and brought her here to me.

But for that act of fate, I wonder at nothing,
hope for nothing, have no other god.]

For Tamils, the "eastern sea" would be the Bay of Bengal, which borders Tamil Nadu itself, and the "western sea" would be the Arabian Ocean which borders the mountainous Malabar coast. The two seas meet in the Indian Ocean to the south. In Tamil, *mēl* means both "high" (in all senses) and "west," while *kīḻ* means both "low" and "east," because the western part of southern India is mountainous while the eastern and central parts are relatively low and flat. In earlier times, *mēlnāḍu*, "western country, high country," referred to Kerala and Karnataka. Nowadays it refers to Europe and America.

In this poem, the heroine comes from a "high" place because she is the guru, the form of god come down to rescue the soul (or alternatively, because she is a wild mountain girl while he is a civilized, lowlands king). Hence Themozhiyar comments, assuming the voice of the *talaivan*, the hero, who speaks this verse: "The stake planted in the ocean is my pride. I am lost in the ocean of rebirth because of it. The guru in the form of the heroine [*talaivi*] comes and accepts me [*ēṟṟukkoṇḍatu*] like a yoke upon a stake. This is the fruit of my good deeds in the past."

Themozhiyar continues on the subject of eyes: "The heroine has 'fish-like eyes,' or eyes like those of a fish. A fish does not sleep. It does not sit on the eggs that it lays. By means of its sight [*pārvai*], by gazing at the eggs, it causes them to break and the baby fish to hatch out. The guru, *civam,* by means of its sight, gives every kind of good to the soul. It causes the soul to blossom. This is the strength [*vallamai*] of the guru's sight."

15. Iḍamaṇittukkūṟi Vaṯpuṟuttal (Comforting by Describing the Places)

varuṅkuṉṟa moṉṟurit tōṉṟillai yampala vanmalayattu
iruṅkuṉṟa vāṇa riḷaṅkoḍi yēyiḍa reytalemmūrp
paruṅkuṉṟa māḷikai nuṇkaḷa pattoḷi pāyanummūrk
karuṅkuṉṟam veṇṇiṟak kañcuka mēykkuṅ kanaṅkuṟaiyē

[Listen, tender vine living on the dark mountain
of the one who skinned the mountainous
elephant—don't be sad,
for the light will shine off the limestone palace
of our home mountain, and flow onto the blackness
of your home mountain, and make it white.]

A mythic theme is evoked here which is present also in one of the songs sung by the untouchable agricultural laborers in Themozhiyar's village. In this song, a dialogue between two lovers, each says to the other, "You come from a black rock mountain; your mother's house is made of black rock." The song ends with the confession, "You and I are a matched pair; we are both from the house of black people." Another aspect of the same theme appears in a famous story about a dispute between Siva and his wife Parvati.[4] Siva mocks Parvati by telling her, "Your body against my body is like a black snake coiled around a white tree." Parvati, offended at this slur against her color, goes off to do austerities and acquire a golden skin for herself.

South Indians take skin color very seriously. In marriage arrangements, it tends to override all other considerations of beauty. A bride is supposed to be paler in color than her husband. If a young woman is very dark, even if she is very attractive, talented, smart, and good-natured, she may have trouble finding a marriage partner. The problem has been aggravated (or perhaps created) by the hierarchical social relation obtaining between South Indians, who are mostly quite brown, and North Indians, who are somewhat paler. Pale color is just one of the marks of superiority that northerners hold against southerners. The color sensitivity of South Indians has been further aggravated by the presence in India of British and other Europeans, who are both more powerful and whiter than "the natives," and who often bring their racist attitudes to India and spread them around there. Finally, people who labor every day outdoors in the sun of course become darker in color than people who don't, and since physical labor indicates absence of wealth and low social status in India, a sunburned skin is a marker of that low status.

On the mythic level, the black-white contrast is a symbol of the male-female contrast, the purity of Siva and the fertility of Sakti. Siva is white (Siva's name means "red," but red means pale and fair to Tamils when they are speaking of skin.) The precious male sexual fluid that Siva has in abundance and frequently spills on the earth is white. The lightning, the fire, and the beam from the eyes with which he is often associated are white. The ashes with which he covers himself are white. Siva's consort, the goddess Sakti, in many of her forms is black. Many of the "village goddesses" (carnivorous, spurned by Brahmans, powerful but ambiguous as to status) who are wedded to Siva are black. The earth with which they are associated is black. While Siva harbors fire, they control the rain. Against Siva's red, they like to wear green.

This verse of Tirukkōvaiyār is about the male's whiteness flowing onto the female's darkness. Each one's "home mountain" could be each one's body, because people's bodies are thought to be made from and matched to the substances of their homes, and because the pubis is like a mountain. The whiteness flowing could be the sexual fluid that passes between them.

Themozhiyar's explication of this verse to me said, "Here the heroine is sorrowing because the hero has to leave her. The hero tries to comfort her by pointing out how close their homes are to each other: 'You see that house like a mountain painted white—it is so close to your town that your town, the black mountain of Kailasa [Siva's home], is white from the reflection. Therefore, don't be sad; we live close to each other.' He is saying that his home is so glorious and hers so humble that hers will be blessed merely by the reflection of his. But by calling her home black and his home white, he only makes things worse. The heroine's sorrow will increase.

"The heroine [*talaivai*] is an emanation of god [*civakuru*]. Is it possible, then, for her to mourn? Does God feel sorrow?

"When you raise something yourself, and you must part with it, of course you feel sorrow. A mother feels sorrow on parting with her child, even though her love is smaller than God's—she gives milk to lessen her own pain. To be cared for in her age, she gives what is asked. God gives without asking—we did not ask for eyes or nose or world or soul or flowers or trees—he just gave them. When we fail, will he not weep? Without question, he will weep."

19. Pāṅkanai ninaital (Remembering his Friend)

pūṅkanai yārpunaṟ ṟenpuli yūrpurin tampalattuḷ
āṅkenai yāṇḍukoṇḍāḍum pirānaḍit tāmaraikkē
pāṅkanai yānanna paṇpanaik kaṇḍip paricuraittāl
īṅkenai yārtaḍup pārmaḍap pāvaiyai yeytataṟkē

[In the heart's meeting place,
in the wise town of tigers,
with its bright crying flower-crowded water,
there the one close to me took me
dancing with his lotus-like feet.
Having found such a friend,
if I tell him what's been given,
who can keep me from getting
this simple little doll?]

Here the hero recalls his male companion, whom he likens to Siva, because the friend is as close to him as Siva, who enslaved him (*āṇḍukoṇḍān*) in an ecstatic love in a heavenly place. The hero feels that his companion, who is his partner in this great, prior love, will surely be able to help him carry off the lesser affair he is trying to have with a woman.

22. Kaṟariyuraittal (Speaking Abusively)

uḷamām vakainammai yuyyavan tāṇḍuceṉ ṟumparuyyak
kaḷamām viḍamamir tākkiya tillaittol lōnkayilai
vaḷamām potumparin vañcittu niṉṟorvañ cimmaruṅkul
iḷamān viṟitteṉ ṟōviṉṟem maṇṇal iraṅkiyatē

[The ancient one of Tillai
turned poison to ambrosia in his throat,
freeing the gods. He frees us as befits our hearts,
by coming and enslaving us, then leaving us.
On his mountain in a fertile garden pit
there lurks a vine-waisted girl
staring out with deery eyes.
Why does our great king
condescend to love her?]

There is considerable male–female antagonism in this poem. Not only do the hero and the heroine cause each other endless grief, but the hero's male friend (*pāṅkan*) and the heroine's female friend (*tōṟi*) each do everything they can to keep the two lovers apart. These same friends also are supposed to act as helpers and go-betweens for the lovers. Here the hero's male companion is angry with the hero for falling in love with a woman and tells him that her female charms are just a dirty low trap. He is trying to keep the hero on his side.

The reference to Siva "enslaving us then leaving us" perhaps picks up on the motif of the previous stanza, in which the love between the two men is likened to the blissful encounter between god and devotee. Is the companion accusing the hero of loving him and leaving him as Siva does to the soul?

The reference to Siva turning "poison to ambrosia in his throat" has to do with a Sanskrit myth in which the primal ocean was churned by the gods and one of the products of its churning was a poison, which Siva swallowed in order to save the gods from its destruction. Another product of the churned ocean was *amirtam*, the sweet liquid nectar of the gods, which bestows immortality upon them. This poem has Siva turning the poison into amirtam in his throat. The allusion to this particular act of Siva's seems unconnected to the rest of the poem unless we realize that in Tamil thought, amirtam is considered to be a transformation of semen, which also holds a man's life essence. Tamil Siddha yogis are believed to bring their semen up into their heads and to carry out this transformation of semen to amirtam at a place behind their throats. They feed only on this amirtam created by their own bodies and dripping into their throats, in a kind of eternal narcissistic cycle. As long as they keep themselves to themselves in this way, they will remain deathless. In this verse of Tirukkōvaiyār about homosexual love, mention of amirtam (read semen) in the throat is apt.

125. Tōṟivantukūḍal (The Girlfriend Unites with Her)

ponnanai yāṉṟillaip poṅkara vampun caḍaimiḍainta
minnanai yānaruḷ mēvaḷar pōnmel viralvarunta
mennanai yāimaṟi yēpari yēlveri yārmalarkaḷ
innana yānkoṇarn tēnmaṇan tāṛkuṛaṟ kēyvanः

[Like losers of the grace
of the lightning man who wears
in his soft hair frothing snakes,
the golden one of Tillai,
don't let your gentle fingers long
for a soft bud, deer-like one, don't pick it,
when I have brought these scented flowers,
suited to your fragrant hair.]

Here the girlfriend of the heroine beseeches the heroine to stay with her and not to go yearning after the hero. The "frothing snakes" in the "soft hair" of the "lightning man" all of course evoke male sexuality, which the girlfriend is warning the heroine to avoid. In Tamil idiom, the flower is a symbol of the vagina; the bud is a symbol of the penis. In previous verses, the hero has repeatedly attempted to offer a gift to the heroine—first a leaf, then a leaf bud, then a flower bud—but each gift is refused by the mediating girlfriend. In this stanza the girlfriend is telling the heroine that the flowers she brings are more appropriate to the heroine's own female nature than is the kind of gift the hero has to offer, or in other words, it is better for a woman to love another woman than it is for her to love a man.

Themozhiyar comments briefly:

"There is a custom in Tamil Nadu for a family to wait until late at night to eat, lest a guest should come. If the family eats early and goes to bed, the guest may come and go away hungry, or sleep on the doorstep hungry. Here the heroine Civam, having fed one guest, is waiting for another to come. She is about to pick a flower bud when her girlfriend Tiruvaruḷ ["Holy Grace"] comes and tells her, 'I have brought blossomed flowers, what do you need that bud for?' The blossomed flowers are ripened souls; the closed bud is an unripened soul."

126. Āḍiḍam pukutal (Entering the Dancing Place)

a<u>r</u>ukāl ni<u>r</u>aimalar aimpāl ni<u>r</u>aiyaṇin tēnaṇiyār
turukān malarttottut tōkaitol lāyamel lappukuka
ci<u>r</u>ukāl maruṅkul varuntā vakaimika encirattin
u<u>r</u>ukāl pi<u>r</u>arkkari yōnpuli yūranna oṇṇutalē

[I have placed many blossoms in your five-parted hair
full of bees. O peacock-girl, now
you're a thick bunch of flowers! So come back gently
into your old home.
Here your body's small middle place
will not be so hurt.
For you are like the tiger town, o bright-browed one,
of the being who is hard for others to gain, whose feet
lie upon my head.]

Again the girlfriend entreats the heroine to stay with her, to dance and play like she used to with her childhood friends, to remember the pleasures they used to give each other, to not assume the burdens and pain of adult man–woman love.

100. Kulamu<u>r</u>aikū<u>r</u>i Ma<u>r</u>uttal (Refusing Because of the Customs of the Families)

tenkam paṛankamu ki<u>n</u>kulai cāḍik katalice<u>rr</u>uk
koṅkam paṛanat toḷirkuḷir nāḍḍinai nīyumaikūr
paṅkam palavan paraṅku<u>nr</u>i<u>r</u> ku<u>nr</u>anna māpataippac
ciṅkan tiritaru cīrūrc ci<u>r</u>umiyen tēmoṛiyē

[Fierce one you belong to a cool bright land where
the coconut falls on the betel nut
and crushes the bananas
and the honey fills the field.
But our sweet-talking little girl lives
in a dark wild town where
the lion hunts the terrified elephant
on the mountain of our half-woman lord.]

Here the girlfriend of the heroine speaks to the hero, trying to convince him to give up his love for her, because their backgrounds are different and they are not suited to each other.

Themozhiyar, assuming the voice of the girlfriend, paraphrased her speech:

"You who are the soul [*ānmā*] live within a world whose boundaries are the pleasures of the senses. The heroine lives in a place beyond the pleasures of the senses. The place where she lives is a high place. The place where you live is a low place. To think that you can leave a low place and go to a high place is not in any way appropriate.

"The trees are all *māyā* [illusion, deception, magic]. The coconuts, betel, and bananas are all pleasures. The soil on which the honey and fragrance of those pleasures flow is the heart, the rejoicing in it is the light, the coolness is the bliss. You come from that land.

"Our Civam whom we call the sweet-talker [*tēmoṛi*] lives in the small town called *cittamparam* [the meeting ground, the small space, the space within the heart where Siva dances his cosmic dance]. In that town wanders the lion of God who causes the beasts of the senses to tremble. The town is on the high mountain where the Lord of the Meeting Ground [*ampalavan*] lives, who has the mother [*ammai*] as one half of himself."

"Many things are upside down in this poem," Themozhiyar concluded. "Here on the surface it is being said that his situation is better than hers—he lives in a land flowing with honey, she lives in a land where elephants and tigers wander. But beneath the surface we see that he lives in a land of illusion, she lives in a land frightening to him, a difficult land free of illusion, high in the mountains."

As Themozhiyar lectured me thus, a number of thoughts ran through my mind. I thought about how his name, *tēmoṛi*, "sweet-talker," enters this poem (The English spelling of his name that he himself used, "Themozhiyar," came from the mode of transcription used by British missionaries and linguists in the nineteenth century.). Themozhiyar had gotten this nickname as a child and it had stuck, but it is normally an epithet for girls, as the poem shows. I thought about him playing the role of the guru, Civam, who is a girl, the heroine in this poem, and about how he had told me that really he was a female at heart, who had been born as a male just in order to be able to go out in the world and teach. I thought about the contrasts between my dwelling-place and his. He had written home to his children that he was living on the edge of a huge terrifying wild forest. All of his land back home was civilized and cultivated. It was dry, too, and not many trees at all grew there. And it was flat. He thought of the hilly region where we lived as "mountainous." I thought about how embarrassingly rich we were compared to him. We could have anything at all we wanted to eat, any time—all the milk, all the honey, all the almonds (he loved almonds), all the butter, all the fruit, all the rice—anything. He was very impressed by this, and yet he was very angry when he learned we had no little mud deity to guard the boundaries of our garden, no planting rituals, no astrology, nothing like that at all. "You people live for nothing but pleasure!" he exclaimed once in a fury.

But pleasure wasn't evil in his eyes. He was always telling me that Civam was feeling, feeling was all. Finally we came to the last verse we would read together that summer. It was about love, about how no one person, not even God, can find joy alone. Perhaps it was also about how no one heart can know completely what the truth is, for truth like love is boundless and can never be embraced by one person alone.

307. Kalaviyinpaṅkūṟal (Speaking the Sweetness of Mingling)

ānanta veḷḷat taṛuntumo rāruyir īrurukkoṇ
dānanta veḷḷat tiḍaittiḷait tālokkum ampalañcēr
ānanta veḷḷat taṟaikaṛa lōnaruḷ peṟṟavarin
ānanta veḷḷamvaṟ ṟātumuṟ ṟātiv vaṇinalamē

[As though one full soul, drowning in a sea of bliss,
became two, and there in the endless sea danced,
like those with the grace
of the lord of the meeting place,
that will never dry up and will never reach its end,
our sea of bliss is this shining love.]

AMBIGUITY

"The gods hate what is obvious," says a very old Indian proverb. "The gods love what is obscure." In India the sacred is obscure because it is beyond the capacity of any one mind to know it fully. It is intrinsically and paradoxically out of reach, both beyond and within. (Tamils say their word for "God," *kaḍavuḷ*, is from *kaḍa*, "cross over," and *uḷ*, "be inside.") By definition and by its very nature, the sacred is both far away and hidden. The gods are buried deep in the darkness of their temples, and even there, what can be seen by dim flamelight is only the form, a temporary, finite reality. The spirit itself is hidden within this form, and it can never be seen directly, it is always invisible. By definition what can be seen is form, are forms, bodies (*rupa, uruvam*). What unifies the many forms, what lies within them, is, by definition, unable to be seen.

In its essential nature, the Indian sacred is formless and one, but in the bounded world of the senses it is always formed and many. The forms it takes are not ordinary forms, being changeable, contradictory, not as they appear.

South Asian deities, therefore, are not consistent. Each has a dual nature; each is split. In Sri Lankan Buddhism the king of the demons

Mara is the mirror image and cross-cousin of Buddha the king of the gods. As cross-cousins, Buddha and Mara are affines. They are welded together as male and female. They need each other. When Mara is conquered he is not expelled from the kingdom of the Buddha (as the devil is expelled from the Christian God's heaven), rather he is enfolded within it.[5]

The Hindu gods, Siva and Vishnu, the light one and the dark one, like Buddha and Mara are rivals and affines: in South Indian myth, Siva is the husband of Vishnu's sister. Siva even begets a child upon Vishnu him/herself. Not long ago the worshippers of Vishnu and Siva fought each other. Each was evil to the other. The more they fought, the more they became alike.[6]

Vishnu in his form as Krishna dwells together with his mistress Radha in the one body of the Bengali saint Caitanya. In the body of the saint, the male and female halves of divinity are merged, yet somehow they remain two, not one, so that they may continue to enjoy the pleasure of their differences.

Siva, whose sign is the phallus, is said to be half female. In his form as Ardhanariswaran, his body is split down the middle, woman on the left, man on the right. He is the king of ascetics—men who give up all physical pleasures and keep their sexual power within themselves. He is also king of philanderers; he makes love to his yogini wife as well as to many others not out of any sense of duty or altruism but for the sake of pleasure only; the heat of his desire is a terror to all around. The ashes on his body represent both self-mortification and self-gratification. Like the sun he is eternally burning himself out.[7]

Within himself, the Sri Lankan Buddha is also dual, both vital and burnt to ashes, like Siva. The remains of his cremated mortal body, his hair, teeth, and bones, are kept within monuments called *stupa*. In form, a stupa is shaped like a sivalingam. The Buddha's remains are called *dātu*, which means "semen" or "seed." The Buddha was a renouncer of desire, but his seed bestows fertility on the land all around.[8]

The great goddess of Hinduism, too, is split. As Gowri she is golden; as Kali she is black. As Mari and Sitala, she is rain and she is the cool one, but her body is burning and her thirst unquenchable and she makes the bodies of others burn with pox diseases.[9] In many of her stories she undergoes a sudden change, from murderous to benevolent, from horrible to beautiful, or the other way round. In her person are combined the purest and the most defiled of states. Mari has the head of a Brahman and the body of an untouchable. She is married both to a base "low-status" demon and to Siva.[10] Draupadi has five potent husbands and yet she is a virgin.[11] The divine female has a crude and rampant sexual appetite, and with it a powerful thirst for blood, and yet she is perfectly self-controlled, chaste, and anorexic.

Though male deities in South Asia are not considered (by Western scholars) to exemplify the qualities of man as male, female deities are thought to stand in some direct way for woman as female. (This view should be reexamined, but for now I will let it be.) It is said that women themselves are sacred, in a way that men are not, and therefore women themselves are split and ambiguous, as goddesses are. Unbound, they are the source of all destruction; bound, they are the source of all blessings.[12] Their milk is the purest of foods, their menstrual blood (from which their milk is thought to be made) is the vilest of poisons.[13] As sisters they are altruistic friends and sacred protectors, as wives they are dangerous potential destroyers.[14] As virgins and daughters they are bearers of deadly weapons and they are gifts fit only for divine receivers.[15] As wives of a god (*devadāsis*) they are whores.[16] As mothers, they are the goddess herself, desired and forbidden, life-giving and killing.[17]

To some Tamil men, woman stands for the whole experience of life itself. "Life," *vāṛkkai*, is only married life, life with a woman (or, if you are a woman, with a man). The wife is *samsāra*, "the one who goes around with you," the world of the senses. Sexual pleasure is *inpam*, "sweetness," something you taste. Marriage is *maṇam*, a word that means both "union" and "fragrance." Sexual fluid is *intiriyam*, "sensation." To make love to a woman is to "experience" her (*anupavikka*).

The experience of life itself, the multiplicity of finite sensations given by the body, is the most general form assumed by the hidden, infinite sacred. The experience of life itself, *māyā*, is ambiguous for this reason. Dreams, theater, fiction, myth, and other kinds of experience that Westerners think of as "not real" are not completely bounded off from ordinary life in India. If something bad must happen in a play or a ritual, special precautions must be taken to keep the event out of ordinary life; the actor who plays a murderer or a villain, for instance, must pray that his role and his acts be confined to the stage.[18] Ritual theatre, as for instance, the demon exorcism ceremonial in Sri Lanka, involves people pretending to be creatures they are not, and yet what happens in the ceremony is real, it is not pretend.[19] Play-acting fades into spirit possession, in which mythic personalities become active in everyday life. The personalities of possessing spirits fade into the personalities of the possessed. When a shaman or shamaness is sitting on the porch speaking to you, the voice of a spirit may suddenly break in; it is not always clear who is acting, who is speaking, in the body of someone in regular contact with a god. Philosophers discuss and storytellers write about how easily dreaming can be mistaken for waking, how impossible it is to know for sure, when you move from one world to another, whether you are waking up or falling asleep.[20] In present-day villages, gods and ancestors speak to living people in dreams. Through such channels, all the different levels of being flow into each other.

Is it any wonder, then, that South Asians are reported by Western observers to enjoy generating multiple interpretations of everyday events,[21] to apply different standards of behavior to different contexts,[22] to avoid giving absolute answers to simple questions,[23] to accept contradictions in their world without trying to resolve them,[24] to treat reality as a vast jigsaw puzzle with most of the pieces lost?[25]

If one wishes to give a form to the infinite sacred, whether this form is of myths, or of mud, or of one's own living person, one must create something ambiguous. Words are a very good medium from which to construct such a form. All kinds of complex ambiguities can be built out of words. I think it is just for this reason that Tamils pour so much of themselves into words, so much of their religious expression into poetry.

One striking feature of Tamil poetry is the high degree of ambiguity contained within it. Poems are set up in such a way that they are subject to a variety of discrepant interpretations. Of course many kinds of verbal art in many languages are characterized by ambiguity of this sort. Sanskrit is famous for it. Many scholars have noted the layer upon layer of diverse interpretation piled upon Sanskrit texts, especially those texts presenting themselves as condensations of some much wider body of knowledge subsequently lost. I do not know whether it has ever been suggested that the authors of these highly condensed sutras and samhitas *intended* for their work to be interpreted in many ways. Certainly in other Sanskrit genres, especially in satirical works and in the kinds of courtly poetry whose aim was to display the poet's virtuosity at verbal game-playing, the intentionality of the ambiguity is clear.[26]

In Tamil poetry intentional ambiguity takes the form of a set of well-established (but for the most part, unnamed) conventions. Many (though not all) of these conventions are shared with Sanskrit.[27] For instance, often what might be called phantom words or phrases appear—formulaic phrases that would cause the reader or listener automatically to think of some particular referent, but which in the context of the poem, must mean something else: *tīvinai*, "evil karma" may have to be read as "the work of fire"; *maṉṟatte nampi*, "believing in the meeting place (of Siva)" may have to be read as "our younger brother (left) the plaza." In verse 3 of Tirukkōvaiyār, there appears the phrase *ammā mulai*. *Ammā* means "mother," *mulai* means "breast." But if we interpret *ammāmulai* in the context of verse 3 to mean "mother's breast"—the first interpretation that would come to anyone's mind—we run into some trouble, because the referent of the phrase in this context is the breast of the heroine, who is not a mother, and certainly not the mother of the speaker, the hero. We could get around the problem, as I have done in my translation, by interpreting the phrase to mean "motherly breasts." Themozhiyar went even further by interpreting *ammāmulai* in this context as *am-mā mulai*, "those big breasts," thus evading completely the mother–son desire overtones that this phrase, in a poem about sexual love, evokes.

The highly condensed and elliptical quality of much Tamil poetry, including Tirukkōvaiyār, inclines it to ambiguity. We think we are hearing one thing and find we are hearing another. Surprising counterpoints in the language become revealed, displaying the tensions upon which people who think in that language subsist. Relations that ordinarily remain convert and uncognized, become overt and known. The hidden formless in this way takes a form and "comes out."

A THEORY

Indian society is very old, wide, and diverse. It is truly hard to know whether there is anything that holds it all together. There are some institutions that are quite widespread on the subcontinent: the worship of certain deities, with certain stories told about them; the organization of each local populace into castes; the ranking of castes from high to low. It has been said that a certain concept of the sacred unites Hindu India, a notion of the sacred as all, as whole.[28] I have tried to suggest here that ambiguity is intrinsic to Hindu concepts of the sacred, and that like the sacred, ambiguity is not confined to a small piece of the Hindu world, but pervades it all, from speech to sexuality, from dreaming to blood. If it is at all legitimate to think of "Indian culture" as an organic whole, a system that can be modeled and described as such, then ambiguity must be a key component of that whole, a key feature of the communicative system by which that whole is maintained. If the creation of hierarchy is one way of pulling plural ways of life and plural ways of seeing into a unit while still keeping them plural, then surely the use of ambiguous communicative forms is another, less oppressive, and more free-spirited way of doing the same thing.

But perhaps this vision, also, is too grandiose. If so, then we may drop to a lower level, but still remain somewhat abstract, and focus not on intentional ambiguity itself as something that happens often in India and takes peculiarly Indian forms. Intentional ambiguity in Indian life is a third major theme of this book.[29]

Intentional ambiguity, of the Indian variety, is more than just anomaly or unclassifiable otherness, more than something ouside the structure that has somehow to be dealt with, more than just an ad hoc way of getting from one category to another, and more than the kind of once-a-year chaos that is needed to keep some orders well-defined. Intentional ambiguity is not interstitial ambiguity, marginal, liminal ambiguity characteristic of what is dismaying or strange to people, but ambiguity at the heart of things, openly embraced where it is found, emphasized where it is hard to perceive, and created where it could not otherwise exist.

Intentional ambiguity may occur in many communicative media, on many levels of analysis. In a word or a simple part of an utterance it may take the form of polysemy sharpened by context, rather than resolved by it, or of two or more mutually exclusive interpretations for the word, both or all of which are plausible (or even indicated by the speaker to be intended) within the context of a given utterance, each of which would cast the whole utterance in a different direction, cause it to yield different consequences. Intentional ambiguity in a complex utterance may take the form of opposition between two "figures" perceivable in the utterance, or between two or more possible, mutually exclusive, interpretations of the utterance, both or all of them fitting, in some way, the act or scene in which they are embedded, but each of them constraining in a different way the possibilities for interpretation of the act or scene in which they are embedded. Where alternative figures present themselves within a single form, there may be no indication in the figures themselves or in their surroundings as to which figure is to be allowed or disallowed. Intentional ambiguity in an act may involve the simultaneous keying, or cluing in, of mutually exclusive interpretive frames for the act, or the discrepancy between possible intentions of the act. In a text, intentional ambiguity may involve the merger of previously distinct voices, or sudden disharmony among voices that previously were thought to be one. In an image it may appear as an alternation of gestalts, or as mutual accommodation among contrasting images occupying a single "mental space" (as in an Escher drawing). In a person, intentional ambiguity may be displayed as warring personalities within the person, or as discrepant presentations of self. This list, of course, by no means exhausts the possibilities.

THE FAMILY

In 1980, I returned to India to finish reading Tirukkōvaiyār with Themozhiyar and at the same time to try and do a general study of forms of

Plate 3. S. R. Themozhiyar.

ambiguity in Tamil. I was inspired to do this partly by what I had seen of Tamil poetry, including Tirukkōvaiyār, with all its hidden metaphors, its plays on words, its layers of meaning, its mergers of different worlds, its many interpretations. Partly I was inspired by modern Western literature on Indian culture, in which the ambiguity of the sacred in India, and the centrality of the sacred to all of life there, are two strong and recurrent themes. Partly I was inspired by what I had learned from Themozhiyar and my other Tamil friends, for whom double entendre, irony, and various other forms of indirection seemed to be a preferred way of communicating. My plan was to consider both written and spoken materials, with an eye to ambiguities, and see if any regularities emerged. For "spoken materials" I hoped to tape-record natural conversations, or failing this, to keep my ears open all the time and write down when I could as much as I remembered.

Keith decided not to come with me on this trip. He wanted to stay home and continue work on the house and the garden. He was angry with me for going. I didn't blame him. But I wished he would come. Daniel, approaching his sixth birthday, did come. Arriving in India with Dan, I felt alone, helpless, and worried. I did not even know how to manage an Indian kitchen yet. I did not know what I was going to do with Dan while I worked.

Plate 4. Left: Offerings to the sun; below: Sivamani

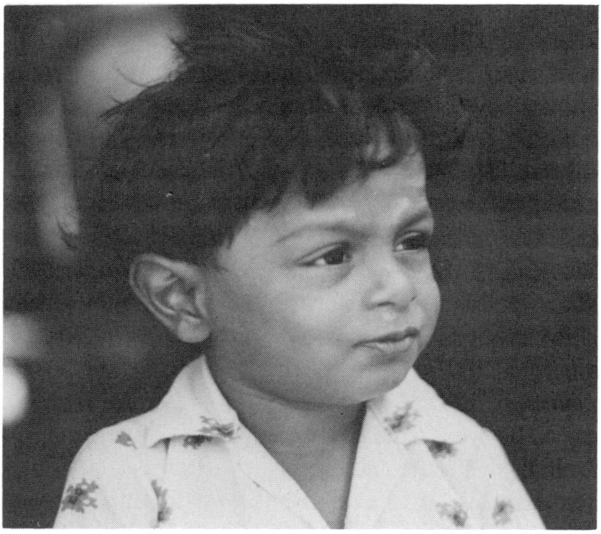

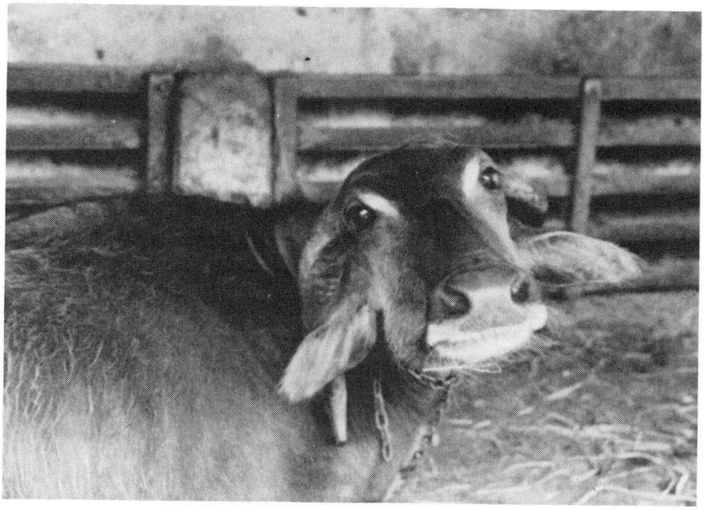

Plate 4. Above: A friendly buffalo; right: the kitchen

But when I disembarked at the Madras airport, there stood Themozhiyar and all his family, with big smiles on their faces. They took Dan in hand, they carried our luggage on their heads, they led us to a bus stop, and we all loaded on a bus that went to their village. Before I knew what was happening, Dan and I were living there.

For a while, Dan and I stayed in a separate little house across a wide lakebed from the village. Themozhiyar had built the little house with money I had given him. He called it his *maḍam*, his monastic retreat. He had named it Aruḷjnānapperuveḷi, "The Great Space of Divine Wisdom." The family called it Peruveḷi, "the great space," for short. Sometimes they called it "the temple." Themozhiyar was also building a rice mill and a concrete threshing ground. He believed that these would provide a steady income for his family. A well had been dug and a gasoline-powered pump had been installed nearby. The pump was used to water a vegetable garden, a quarter-acre paddy field, and a stand of small banana trees that had all been recently planted. Much of this had been done with the money I had given him, that he had saved. My contribution had totalled about $2500.

Themozhiyar lived with his wife, his wife's sister, her husband, all their children, and various other relatives. The house where they all lived, together with about twenty acres of paddy land adjacent to the village, belonged to the wife's sister's husband. Themozhiyar owned just the four acres he had bought recently, with the buildings he had put on it.

While Themozhiyar and I worked in the retreat during the days, reading Tirukkōvaiyār, Daniel stayed in the family house, playing with the four children his age. When these children went to the village school, the women of the house kept Dan entertained, looking after him as they looked after their babies and toddlers. At night, Dan slept with me in the retreat. Themozhiyar's wife and her sister brought us our meals when we were there. Otherwise, we ate with them in the main house. The women quickly ascertained our favorite foods—yogurt, butter, and fruit—expensive foods, and provided these and a variety of delicious meals for us in enormous abundance. Their generosity was embarrassing. Daniel grew. I put on ten pounds. All of our needs and more were met. When I went to Madras and returned home late at night, someone would be waiting for me at the bus stop, flashlight in hand. Countless batteries and cassettes were obtained for my tape recorder. A taxi was procured once at 2 A.M. for an emergency medical run to the city fifty miles away. A tricycle was bought for Dan to ride on; the concrete tank by the well was filled regularly for him to swim in. When people came to stare at me, they were driven away.

Plate 5. Annan instructs Jnana Oli to fold his hands in greeting.

More impressive to me still was the way this high-caste family responded when I became interested in their field laborers, who were untouchable to them, and invited them into Themozhiyar's religious retreat, where I was staying, so that I could record their songs. They did not raise any objections, though I knew that of their own accord they would never have let untouchables near their sacred Peruveḷi. Moreover, they gave us privacy, leaving me alone with the singers because they said "they will sing more freely that way." Which was true, for many of the songs were sung against them. They helped me find more singers, and they helped me transcribe the songs, and they did a fair and accurate job.

At first, I spent most of my time in the retreat, but as the days wore on, I found myself more and more with the family in the main house. They were interesting people; they were relaxed in my presence; I was lonely.

The focus of my attention gradually shifted from the poem to the household. There it was easy for me to observe ordinary conversation on an everyday basis. As I lived with them, and became personally involved with them, unconsciously (as it seems to me now) the focus of my attention shifted. I came to see that Themozhiyar's textual exegeses were hooked into the everyday affairs of his family—his life in the family gave the ancient poetry the meaning it had for him. When I saw him in the context of his family, he seemed much more like an ordinary human being to me, and the sacred poetic realm into which he had occasionally lifted me came down out of the stratosphere. This sacred realm was not profaned, though, and I was not disillusioned. For I learned that in the everyday life of the members of this household, and especially for Themozhiyar and his sister-in-law who formed its emotional center, the principle of love, *anpu*, was not just a high ideal, it was the way they lived. Many of their acts were explained by them, or could be understood by me, only in terms of this principle. Anpu was sacred to them: it was their highest value; it pervaded every part of their lives; it gave these lives their meaning. And as I was trying to understand the uses of ambiguity in the poem and in the household, it struck me more and more that the most ambiguous thing of all was this anpu.

The members of this household were not Themozhiyar's natal family. He had joined them when he married one of their members. Since he had run away in his childhood, he had no other home. The head of the family was a man whom Themozhiyar called Annan (*aṇṇan*, "older brother"). His wife was addressed by everyone as Anni (*aṇṇi*, "older brother's wife"). Anni's father's sister, who was also Annan's mother, remained in the household but was old and crippled and no longer had any real power there. Anni's younger sister, Padmini, was Themozhiyar's wife. Mohana also spent much time in this household. She was the cross-cousin of Anni and Padmini and was married to one of their brothers. Anni had an eighteen-year-old daughter, an eight-year-old daughter, and a six-year-old son. Padmini had an eight-year-old daughter, a six-year-old daughter, and a two-year-old son. Mohana had a two-year-old son.

Although they were landlords, this family was poor, having barely enough money to keep their children nourished. I bought them a cow and helped them complete the rice mill, and perhaps it was for the sake of money that they tolerated me as they did, though they themselves would deny this vehemently. As impoverished landlords, they were not at all uncommon. The cost of rice was fixed, laborers demanded higher wages, crops often failed, they faced litigation on all sides. Many middle-class families were better off than this one; many more were worse off. There were tensions within this family, as there are in virtually any large family. Disputes sometimes occurred over serious economic questions, but I never observed any quarrels over allocation of resources within the household, and I am inclined to think, as Anni did, that friction among people living together was an inevitable part of life.

How representative of Tamil families in general was Themozhiyar's family? This question haunted me. I could see that in the view of Tamils themselves, there was nothing especially surprising about this family's behavior, certainly nothing pathological. They were actively involved in a wide social network and they had many friends from the city and from villages who came into the house and participated in household affairs. None of the kinds of behavior I describe in this book were kept hidden from view. All of them, including the quarrels, were accepted as natural by people who dropped in. Still, I myself wondered, and many colleagues back home asked, whether Themozhiyar and his family were not more idiosyncratic than most, since many of the things they did contradicted what earlier ethnographic reports from South India had led me, for one, to expect.

For this reason, in 1984 I went back to Tamil Nadu to "observe" other families and live with them, as I had lived with Themozhiyar's family. I hoped in this way to get a better sense of what was truly unusual about Themozhiyar's family, as well as of what was common. I stayed this time in a village near Madurai, several hundred miles from where Themozhiyar's family lived. But in this village I was not able to establish with anyone the degree of intimacy I had achieved with Themozhiyar's family. So I contented myself with interviewing a relatively large number of people in the village and in the city for relatively brief periods (about an hour per person) on the topic of family relations. The interviews were open-ended. The content of these interviews supplements at some points in this volume what I learned from Themozhiyar's family. A hundred of the 150 interviewees were from the one village. The rest were from the cities of Madras and Madurai. The preponderance of interviewees were Paraiyars, Kallars, and Gounders. The remainder were Acaris, Chettiars, Vellalars, Nayakars, Brahmans, and Muslims. Although there was considerable variation among these different interviewees, for the most part they confirmed what I saw in Themozhiyar's household. Every basic expression of anpu that I saw in his family I also observed among many other families. Paradoxical behavior was often explained in terms of the feeling of anpu. The assertions I make in the following pages about Tamil love would be considered by most Tamils to be banalities—too obvious to be worth writing a book about. Only Americans seem to need convincing.

METHODOLOGY

My open-ended but prearranged interviews with relative strangers were, as I have just indicated, carried out in the absence of chances to do better enthnography. The better ethnography was the kind I carried out in Themozhiyar's household. I never formally interviewed anyone there.

I suspected when I commenced fieldwork, and I became more convinced as I went along, that structured interviews when used as a means of understanding culture are unreliable tools at best. There is nothing to prevent respondents from lying, from saying the opposite of what they believe, and they *will* lie at exactly the most crucial moments: important truths are too valuable to be handed out to just anybody. There may be "paralinguistic" messages—tone of voice, facial expression—openly telling us, "This is a lie." But how are we, as outsiders, to pick them up? How inscribe them on our tape recorders or questionnaires? Beside the "problem" of lying, there are, to obstruct the interview's achievement of its aim, the well-known "problems" of the leading question, of informants trying to tell you what you want to hear, of the context-sensitivity of people's behavior, verbal or otherwise. To many people, the informational content of what they say is not nearly as important as the personal relationship they establish in saying it. And this relationship is established largely through indirection, hidden messages, subtle responses to context. Finally there is the problem that the interview question, coming as it does from out of the blue and far away, runs the danger, even on a purely semantic-informational level, of missing its target completely. For instance, if one wants to know whether Tamil speakers believe, as Americans are said to, in the idea of "blood kinship," one might ask one's respondents, "Do different groups differ as to the content of their blood?" To this question, one will receive a negative answer. "All blood is one," people will say. One might conclude that for Tamils, blood is not implicated in ideas of kinship. Yet throughout the Tamil-speaking world, the term *ratta pācam*, "blood bond," is used to describe and explain the feeling of attachment that exists between close kin (for example, Question: "Why are you so concerned about how badly your brother was injured?" Answer: "*Ratta pācam*.") Unless an ethnographer were incredibly lucky, he or she would not think to phrase a question in terms of ratta pācam, unless he or she had already heard that term used elsewhere. Finally one has to admit that one is not in control, especially not in exclusive control, of the research project, or of the kind of knowledge one receives during the project's course. Learning a culture, like learning a language, is largely an unconscious process, which means precisely that one cannot control it. Plain waiting, listening, and hoping seem to be the most useful things one can do, most of the time.

So I waited, listened, and hoped. In Themozhiyar's household, I did not use my tape recorder. I tried a few times, but the family would not stand for it. I attempted to record in writing as accurately as I could what I heard and saw, but usually I had to wait until I was alone to write down what I had observed. Any anthropologist undertaking participant-observation experiences this difficulty. Because I was not able to use my tape recorder for natural conversations, the quotations from Themozhiyar's family that I included in my notes, and subsequently have used in this book, are not precise, having been filtered through my memory, usually after a lapse of several hours or days. Some Tamil phrases jumped out at me when I heard them. These are included, in Tamil, in the text.

Most of the things that I saw happen or heard said, happened or were said spontaneously, and not in response to any maneuvering or "elicitation" on my part. I did ask many questions, but they were usually about specific events that I did not understand.

For the most part, I have not attempted to hide the specificity of my experience under blanket generalizations. I have, however, taken the liberty of referring to the work of other writers on India and of bringing in my own observations made outside the context of Themozhiyar's family, when they seemed relevant. The chapter on kinship goes most far afield in this respect, attempting to relate the very local and personal experiences of individuals to much broader, general patterns. Much of the information I have drawn upon that comes from outside of Themozhiyar's family also did not result from systematic interviews, but was caught, as it were, on the wing. When in the following chapters I organize my notes in such a way as to show the reader patterns I have perceived, there will be a patchwork effect, for in many places I have simply put together numbers of separate observations which I consider in retrospect to belong to the same category, to express the same or related ideas or values. What these patterns reflect is something fabricated jointly by Themozhiyar's family and me, what I feel I learned as a consequence of certain experiences that they, often deliberately, put me through. This book is a residue of those experiences. Inasmuch as I have tried to make sense of what I learned, there are some loose ends bridged by my common sense, and there are some leaps of faith. At these junctures, the reader will have to decide for himself whether to trust these bridges, and/or whether to jump with me.

As my emotional involvement with Themozhiyar's family intensified, my life with them (and theirs with me) got rockier rather than easier. I often quarreled with them. I couldn't help it: they themselves were fighters. Sometimes it seemed to me that they were needlessly hurting themselves and each other, and I found it impossible then to keep my mouth shut. The women, though they took good care of me, saw me more as a rival then an ally. I was—I could not help being—an intrusion in their lives. The hardest part for all of us was that we grew attached to each other's children. When I left, so blinded had I become by my own emotions that I asked the women if I could take their children back to America with me. I offered them all the benefits of American affluence. There would be frequent back and forth visits. The children's own mothers would always remain the children's own mothers.

The refusal of my offer was gentle but very firm. The women asked if they could keep my Dan with them.

Shortly before Daniel and I returned to America, Themozhiyar and I completed our study of Tirukkōvaiyār. Again, we did not end on a round number, but stopped at the second-to-last verse of the poem. Themozhiyar steadfastly refused to read the last verse to me.

In this second-to-last verse the heroine, now a mother, speaks her mind. True to poetic formula, the hero has betrayed the heroine by making her a mother and then deserting her to court another woman. The other woman stops by the heroine's house one day. The heroine tells the hero what happened.

399. Parattaiyaikkaṇḍamaikūṟipulattal (Lamenting after Having Met the Other Woman)

ayuṟa vāynam akankaḍaik kaṇḍuvaṇ ḍēruruḍḍum
vaiyuṟu vāḍkaṇ maṛavait taṛuvamaṟ ṟunmakanē
meyyuṟa vāmitun nillē varukena veḷkic ceṉṟāḷ
kaiyuṟu mānmaṟi yōnpuli yuṟanna kārikaiyē

[A lady came,
meek as the deer our lord holds in his hand,
fearsome as the tigers that frequent his town.
Wondering, she saw our wide doorstep, then
she embraced our child rolling his strong chariot, our
child with his spear-bright eyes.
But she hid her face and fled when I told her
"This is your son, truly as of your own body.
Enter, for this is your home."]

CHAPTER TWO

Generations

THE PAST

" . . . her feet are dampened in the soil . . . "

Tirukkōvaiyār, 3.

Kanakkamma was born around 1920 in the rocky dryland village of Malaiyanur in eastern Tamil Nadu. With her were born two older sisters, one younger brother, and a younger sister. At the age of ten she married, left her home village, and moved into the house where I met her half a century later. There were forty people in the household when she married, she told me, "all eating from the same pot," and her husband's family had been in the same house for forty generations. They were Reddiars, whose ancestral home was in the north, in Andhra Pradesh. (Andhra Pradesh is the southernmost of the three "pradeshes." Its name is Sanskrit and means Land of the South, but it is north to Tamil Nadu, which is a Tamil name meaning Tamil Land. Previously Tamil Nadu was called Madras State, after the British administrative center, the city of Madras, which was located within that state. Now Tamil Nadu, at least in name, is its own point of reference, to the pride of some but the dismay of others.)

Kanakkamma remembered kindly the past authority of both British and Brahmans. The place where she lived now, Tamil Nadu, was not, to her mind, her real home; the language she spoke was not her real language. However, even Kanakkamma did not know how long ago her people and her husband's people had left Andhra and come further south. Reddiars had long been one of the wealthier castes in eastern Tamil Nadu. They counted among their members many large landholders, and they were the "dominant" caste in many villages in the Chingleput area, where Kanakkamma lived. Members of other castes depended upon the patronage of Reddiars for their survival.

Figure 1. Cast of Characters

Anni—"Older Brother's Wife." Tough, kind, aggressive, thoughtful, articulate, self-deprecating, sharp-tongued. About forty years old, runs the household. Innovative, faithful, proud. Takes orders from no one. Sometimes gets her way through martyrdom. Tall, well-built, graceful, casual. Deep-set eyes, leathery skin, heavy mouth, battered hands. Most devoted friend of her sister's husband, Ayya.

Annan—"Older Brother." Anni's husband. About fifty. Owner and manager of the family property, has a law degree. Tall, thin, slightly stooped, unsure of himself, easily persuaded, not a talker, enjoys caring for the small children. Strong sense of responsibility, inclined to formality, believes in principles, reads religious texts. Smiling, eager to please. Sometimes loses his temper.

Padmini—"Lotus-born." Anni's younger sister, about thirty years old. Married to Ayya. Tall as Anni, extremely thin, loud voiced, given to frequent, violent outbursts of anger. Passionate, fun-loving, sensual, rebellious, needing to prove herself. Proud, hard-working, never admits to suffering, physically very weak. Inseparable from her cousin, Mohana.

Ayya (Themozhiyar)—"Lord." Husband of Padmini. About forty. Much shorter than Padmini, stout and barrel-chested, bow-legged, balding, dark-skinned, tender black eyes, radiant smile. Charismatic Saiva guru, brilliant speaker, insightful explicator of religious texts, synthesizer. Has been writing poems since childhood, all kept. Streetwise, responsible, level-headed. Vain, silly, stubborn, pompous. Believes he is a saint. Leader of a group of Madras businessmen who have been friends since boyhood. Hard worker, good interviewer, good tailor, sews all the women's clothing. Frequently weeps, enters trance daily. Slowly building a financial base for his family.

Mohana—"Enchantress." Orphaned cross-cousin of Anni and Padmini, married to one of their brothers. About thirty years old. Tall, very slender, dark-skinned. Fun-loving, rebellious, devoted to Padmini. Not confident, mistreated by her in-laws, dependent for her survival on the continued friendship of her female cousins. Artistic, has learned to sew from Ayya.

Tambu—"Little Brother." Brother of Anni and Padmini, husband of Mohana. Tall, dark, lean, seems like a friendly guy. Rarely visits the house. Ostracized from the family for drinking, smoking, not getting a job, not taking care of Mohana.

Figure 1. Cast of Characters (continued)

Attai—"Father's Sister." Father's sister and mother-in-law of Anni. Mother of Annan. Adopted and raised Padmini and Mohana. In her seventies now, heavy, crippled, losing eyesight and hearing. Kind and patient, neglected, resigned. Most enjoys conversation and reading. Taught herself to read when she was a child.

Paddi—"Grandmother." Mother's mother to Anni and Padmini. In her eighties. Toothless but still spry.

Porutcelvi—"Woman of Substance." Younger sister of Ayya, school teacher, lives in Madras with her only daughter. Husband in the merchant marine, rarely home. Articulate, literate, independent. Intensely dislikes Padmini, adores Ayya.

Anuradha—Eighteen-year-old daughter of Anni. Pretty, quiet, helpful, always smiling, college-educated. First child of her generation born in this household.

Mangaiyarkkaraci—"Queen of Ladies." Saucy eight-year-old daughter of Anni. Smart. Often gets in fights.

Arivaraci—"Queen of Knowledge." Eight-year-old daughter of Padmini. Quiet, good, self-deprecating, easily frightened, frequently ill.

Umapathi—"Lord of Uma" (a name of Siva). Six-year-old son of Anni. Oldest male child in the family. Very proud, rough and tough, competitive, likes to mock and tease. Tries never to cry, but does not always succeed. Often criticized by the adults. Staunch friend of Daniel.

Arulmori—"Language of Grace." Six-year-old daughter of Padmini. Cheerful, pretty, confident, self-sufficient. A fluent reciter of poetry.

Jnana Oli—"Light of Wisdom." Two-year-old son of Ayya and Padmini. Angelic face, pellucid speech, everybody's darling, knows he's a charmer, absolutely self-assured.

Sivamani—"Jewel of Siva." Two-year-old son of Mohana. Cute and dimpled, the family fall-guy, not neglected but not quite taken seriously. Swollen belly.

Vishvanathan—"Lord of All." Twenty-year-old distant cousin of Anni and Padmini. Lives with this family as a quasi-servant, running errands, doing easy tasks. Scornful of education as well as of physical labor. Talks like a bumpkin, bodily not very strong. Loves motorized vehicles. Admires village big men. Aspires to wealth like theirs and independence from his family.

Figure 1. Cast of Characters (continued)

Ram Tilakam—Twelve-year-old distant cousin living with this family as a servant. Quiet and smiling, very tiny, given cruelly heavy work to do, but treated affectionately by the children, who call her Tilakakka ("Sister Tilakam"). Goes with the family on outings, gets decent clothing, bathes with the women of the family and is groomed by them.

Modday—"Baldy." Servant of the family in her mid-twenties. Belongs to the Nayakar caste. Gets the heaviest work, dressed in rags, poor food. Somehow she is remarkably strong. Tries to take care of her daughter Ponni, but is rarely given the time.

Ponni—"Goldy." Two-year-old daughter of Modday. Neglected and severely malnourished.

Peggymma—"Peggy-Mother." Ayya's student from America, living with his family. Quiet, not aggressive, often withdrawn, moody and emotional, unsure of herself, finicky about drinking water. Concerned about her family, families in general. Trying to learn Tamil. Trying to take notes inconspicuously.

Daniel—Peggymma's six-year-old son. Cerebral, empiricist, water-loving. Frequently sick, but always looking healthier than any of the other children in the household. Best friends with Umapathi. Pampered by all, given the best, sometimes mercilessly teased.

The family into which Kanakkamma married was a leader in its village, owning much land and many cattle. The "mother tongue" (*tāy moṛi*) of Reddiars is Telugu, the language of Andhra, of the north, the language of their sacred texts. According to Kanakkamma, Telugu was a "higher" language than Tamil. It was higher because it had much Sanskrit mixed in it. Learned Brahmans spoke it. Lower castes in the village, seeking to raise their status, spoke Telugu in imitation of their patrons. Kanakkamma's *tāy māman,* her own mother's brother—her father-in-law—owned a whole library full of Telugu books and was highly educated in Telugu, she said. "Where are those books now?" she once lamented to herself, then she turned to me and asked me (since I was studying Tamil), "Why don't you learn our Telugu?" But it would not have done me much good if I had learned it, as even Kanakkamma herself had long since forgotten how to speak it.

In Kanakkamma's youth, her family and her husband's family had been strict Vaishnavas, worshippers of Vishnu. They sang Telugu hymns to Vishnu and they wore the *nāmam*, the sign of Vishnu, painted on their

Plate 6. Paddi and Attai prepare banana flowers for cooking.

foreheads. Now they had become Saivas, worshippers of Siva, the god of the South, and the hymns that they sang to their god were in Tamil. I noticed that all of the people in the household over the age of fifteen had Vaishnava names, but none of the children did.

The *kula tēvam*, the family deity, of the household was an old grandmother who had lived in the house during the days of Muslim rule. Her story was told to me by Kanakkamma's daughter–in–law, Sulochana. On the festival of Ayudha Puja, Hindus worshipped their tools and weapons, and there was a rule that the weapons should not be removed from the place of worship until the day was over and the ceremonies completed. On that day, one married couple from the family had gone to worship at a Vishnu temple on a nearby mountain. On the same day, the family received word that Muslims were on their way to attack the village. The men went out without their weapons to meet the Muslims, and all of them were killed. The one grandmother was left alone in the house with all the children. She took a rope with a series of loops on it such as is used to tie a string of cattle, put the loops around the children's necks, and decapitated them all, then killed herself, so that the family would not have to face the shame of being plundered and raped by the Muslims. The couple returned from the mountain just as the Muslims arrived at the house. The Muslims saw the scene of carnage in the courtyard and felt pity and admiration for the courage of the grandmother. They said that hencefor-

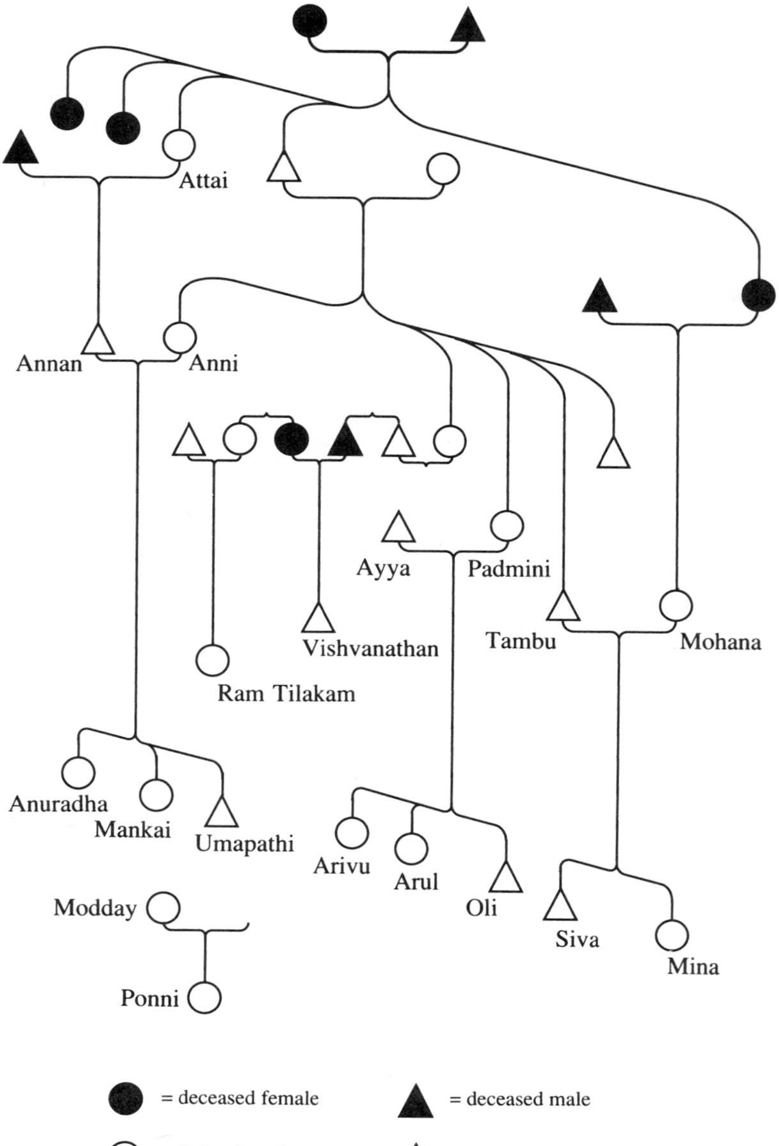

Figure 2. The family tree.

ward there would be no tax on that house. Such was the spirit of Reddiars, in days long past.

The family worshipped this grandmother, whom they called Periyamakālakshmiyammā, together with another kula tēvam called Vīrarākavapperumāl, whose temple was at Tiruvaḷḷur near Madras. This was the deity that the couple in the story had gone to worship. Kanakkamma's only son, the head of the household now, had been named after this deity, but no one in the family knew Vīrarākavapperumāl's story—or so they said when I asked. They worshipped the two, the male and the female deity, as partners. They would offer the female of the couple, the spirit of the defiant old grandmother, a red sari with a handloom border, "such as a grandmother would wear," said Sulochana. I have noticed that goddesses with a streak of anger in them like to wear red.

Across the street from the house was a moderate-sized Vishnu temple, in a state of disrepair. The stone statues all had pieces broken off. "The Muslims did it," said Themozhiyar, Sulochana's brother-in-law. So the damage to the temple, I calculated, was three or four hundred years old. Who could say how old the temple itself was? They kept meaning to repair the temple but the money could not be raised, Themozhiyar lamented. It was just too bad, he said.

Broken up though it was, this temple was a peaceful place, peaceful and quiet. They kept it that way on purpose; the children were not allowed to play in the courtyard, or if they did so, they had to play there quietly. Every evening a bespectacled old Brahman priest sat on the temple's front steps, reading the daily paper, retreating into the calm, the serenity of the stone.

One other important temple stood in the village, the temple of the goddess Kanniyammā, also called the Seven Sisters (Kanniyammā was all seven, her priest explained). Her tiny shrine housed seven stones, all featureless and identical, lined up in a row. In front of the shrine stood a stone guardian that looked like a cross between the monkey-god Hanuman and a lion: muscular wrestler's body, a face that could have been monkey or could have been cat. Here wild and expensive festivals were held throughout the year: fire-walking ceremonies; glittery, funny, sexy professional performances of Kanniyamma's life story; costumed nighttime processions; alcohol-induced spirit possession; fireworks. A rival landlord sponsored many of these entertainments. At first, members of my Tamil family refused to take me to them, saying they were for the lower castes, for a deity that wasn't real. But later the women told me that they liked to go to these festivals; only the men wouldn't come. Finally they took me along.

Shortly after Kanakkamma married and moved into this village, her

Plate 7. Padmini, Mohana, Anni and the children watch a festival parade.

father-in-law died and the family broke up. Then there were no longer forty people in the household, but only two—Kanakkamma and her husband. Kanakkamma bore only one child, a son. At the time that I lived with the family, the son, in his late forties, was the nominal head of the household and a nominal head of the village. I say nominal, because in neither case was it clear that the reins were in his hands. That year (1980) he lost his post as hereditary village accountant because of state legislation decreeing that all hereditary village posts were to be abolished and village officers were to be appointed by the Chief Minister of Tamil Nadu instead. The news shocked the family. They said it was not a matter of income—the village accountant was paid only a hundred rupees a month—but it was an insult to them to be deprived of a hereditary post in this manner.

The changes that the family had undergone over the past generations were symbolized for me by two large portraits that hung on the wall in the main room of the house. The first was a photograph of Kanakkamma's father-in-law. He was a heavy man, with a stern expression on his cleanly shaved, bejowled face. His head was also clean shaven and his feet were bare, planted wide apart, firmly on the floor. He wore a silk waistcloth and a silk shawl over his right shoulder. He was seated in an elaborately carved chair, a staff held firmly in his right hand. There was a nāmam painted on his forehead. From the sharply focused portrait, he gazed keenly as an eagle into the eyes of the observer.

Adjacent was a picture of this man's son, Kanakkamma's husband. He was thinner than his father. He had a full head of black hair and a Victorian handlebar moustache, and he had on a pair of black, shiny, European-style shoes. He wore a white south-Indian-style waistcloth and a white, north-Indian-style shirt. Like his father, Kanakkamma's husband wore a nāmam for his portrait, but his hands were empty and he had what looked like a baffled expression on his face. The picture was out of focus.

No portrait had been made of Kanakkamma's son, Raghavan, so I don't know how he would have presented himself to the camera. In life he was a quiet, friendly man who spoke hoarsely when he spoke at all. He was thin and his face was gaunt. When he went out he wore rubber sandals, a short-sleeved white cotton shirt, and a waistcloth. He never wore a nāmam, even on festival occasions. The expression he wore was often a grimace, like that of someone squinting into the sun.

Kanakkamma's husband died when Raghavan was still a child. As he grew older, Kanakkamma became lonely for more children, and so she adopted into her household Padmini and Bhakta, two of her younger brother's six children. She also adopted Mohana, the child of her younger sister, who had died. Padmini, Bhakta, and Mohana were all somewhere between five and ten years old at the time. Shortly thereafter, the twenty-year-old Raghavan was married to Sulochana, Padmini's older sister, who was nearly seventeen. Padmini at that point was ten years old. Sulochana said that when she was a very small child, it had been decided that she would marry Raghavan. As she put it, "They made it 'certain' (*niccayam*), but that does not mean that the future marriage will happen without fail, it only means that they have decided to do it unless they change their minds later."

A year after Sulochana married Raghavan, she bore her first child, a daughter, whom they named Anuradha. Ten years passed before Sulochana's next child was born.

When Padmini was fifteen, she and another sister, Lalita, were married in a joint wedding ceremony to two brothers. Padmini's husband died. (This story will be told later.) When Padmini was twenty-one, the family married her to Themozhiyar. This wedding was arranged not by Padmini's parents, as the previous one had been, but by Padmini's older sister Sulochana and her husband Raghavan. Themozhiyar was not close kin to the family, but according to Sulochana, they felt he would make a good bridegroom for Padmini because he was a friend of the family's whom they knew well, he had no bad habits, he was a "good man."

The wedding was simple. There was no dowry. The ceremony was conducted by Themozhiyar's guru, a Saiva philosopher who lectured to a small group of friends and followers in Madras. Thus it was a "self-respect wedding," that is, a wedding performed without the mediation of

Brahman priests; this was the kind of wedding advocated by early leaders of the Tamil independence movement. Members of this movement saw Brahmans as the primary agents of north Indian hegemony in the subcontinent. Themozhiyar, through his guru, had been greatly influenced by this movement, and he brought his own version of its philosophy with him when he married. His deity was Siva, whom he considered the god of the south, in contrast to Vishnu, god of the north. "Praise to Siva of the southern land, praise to the lord of all lands" was the refrain of the worship ceremonies that Themozhiyar conducted. When he joined Kanakkamma's family, Siva became their god also.

THEMOZHIYAR

" . . . don't be sad, for the light will shine . . . "

Tirukkōvaiyār, 15.

Padmini and Themozhiyar lived for a few months in the house of Padmini's parents, but Padmini missed the place that had been her home for the past ten years, and they soon moved back to the house of Sulochana and Raghavan, where they remained. A year later, in November 1971, Padmini's first daughter Aṟivaraci was born. Less than three weeks after that, Sulochana delivered her own second child, Maṅkaiyārkkaraci. Another pair of children were born in 1974, this time only two days apart—Umapathi (Umapathi was her first son and last child) to Sulochana, and Arulmori (a second daughter) to Padmini. In 1978, again a pair of children were born, again only a few days apart—a son Jnana Oli to Padmini, and a son Sivamani to Padmini's cousin Mohana, who had married Padmini's brother and was often in the same house with Padmini. Themozhiyar commented tongue-in-cheek that he must have had a fertilizing effect on the family. Before he arrived, ten years passed without the birth of a child in the household. After he arrived, three double births took place. Each of his three children was born with a partner.

Themozhiyar lived with his wife's family, probably because at the time of his marriage he had no better place to go. Rents in Madras, where he worked, were high; he owned no land in his native village. He had an older brother and a younger sister, but he disapproved of his sister's spouse and of his brother's way of life, so he could live with neither of them.

According to Themozhiyar, his ancestors had owned a large quantity of land, but his father lost it all in lawsuits. For many people of the time, lawsuits were more a gambling game with high stakes than than they were a mechanism for righting injustice. Themozhiyar's father liked to gamble in this way.

Themozhiyar's mother died when he was ten. From that time on, he said, things were hard. In his early teens, angry with his father, he ran away from home and found work as a kitchen boy in Madras. Later, his father and his younger sister joined him there. According to Themozhiyar, he supported them both together with himself. He joined a union of restaurant workers. He said he used to grind batter until his hands were blistered and raw. He showed me a poem that he wrote at that time. It said, if someone sees your hunger and laughs at it, kill that man and drink his blood. He said those were his feelings then and he meant every word of the poem, but now he would not advocate killing.

In his home village, he had done well in school and someone had dubbed him Tēmoṛi, which means "sweet-talker" or "honey-talker" or "divine language" ("themozhi" is an alternate English spelling for tēmoṛi). The *-ār* at the end was a kind of honorific, evidently appended to the nickname by Themozhiyar himself. His original name had been Raman.

As a kitchen boy in Madras, he had studied in his spare hours, he said. He was not good at mathematics. He was frightened of English and never learned it. He devoted himself, therefore, to the study of Tamil literature. Some scholars from the Saiva Siddhanta Kazhakam, a large publishing house in Madras, took him under their wing and tutored him further. In particular, he became a student of a kindly man named Ramanath Pillai, a devoted scholar of Tamil Saivism. Pillai earned his living as a high school gym teacher, but he spent the better part of two decades writing a commentary to the long, cryptic, but in places very beautiful ninth-century Saiva text on immortality, Tirumantiram. For this commentary of over a thousand pages, the Saiva Siddhanta Kazhakam paid Pillai a small sum, supplementing his gym-teacher's salary.

How and when Themozhiyar "converted" to Saivism is a matter about which he spoke vaguely. Certainly Ramanath Pillai, who also officiated at his wedding, had much to do with cementing his faith. Of the various students that Pillai had, Themozhiyar was his favorite; at least, he was the most charismatic. When Pillai died in 1975, Themozhiyar assumed the role of guru to the small group of worshippers that Pillai had led in song and had lectured to every week.

Meanwhile, Themozhiyar had been increasing his own reputation and prestige via other channels. Through independent study, he earned the degree of Tamil Pulavar from Madras University, something like an M.A. in Tamil. For a while, he worked writing cinema songs. Then he got a managerial job in a large textile company. If he had stayed there, he said with something like commingled pride and regret, he would be earning a large salary now. But he quit so that he could devote himself to the study and teaching of Tamil Saivism.

Themozhiyar's marriage into the family brought in its wake many changes. They must have valued him highly to make, for his sake, the adjustments that they did, especially in view of the facts that he was not a close kinsman, and that he was living uxorilocally. He did contribute a city income, albeit an insecure one, to the household. It was a noble act to take the widowed Padmini as his first and only wife and to look after her. Otherwise, she would have been a burden to whichever of her siblings took her in, and indeed, as a young widow with no future, a burden to herself. But I believe that less down-to-earth considerations than gratitude and economic need were also involved in the family's restructuring of itself around Themozhiyar.

Like the stormy Lord Siva of South Indian myth, Themozhiyar, a Saiva, took his wife from a Vaishnava family. Like Siva, he did not get along with his in-laws. Padmini's parents disliked Themozhiyar. Her father (like Siva's own father-in-law) referred to him sarcastically as "that swami." Padmini's mother's mother said that there must be something wrong with him to marry without a dowry. If there had not previously been antagonism between Padmini and her parents, there was now. Sulochana and Raghavan sided with Themozhiyar.

In a house full of women, Raghavan now had a male companion. The women came to refer to Raghavan as Periyavar, "the elder [or big] man," and to Themozhiyar as Cinnavan, "the younger [or small] man." Periyavar was a term of respect, Cinnavan a term of familiarity. The two men now became a complementary and mutually dependent "set"—Raghavan the patient and indulgent older brother, Themozhiyar the impetuous and brilliant younger one. (Mythic models for this dyad are found in Siva's sons Vinayagar and Murugan, in the Mahabharata heroes Yudhisthira and Arjuna, and in the Tamil epic heroes Ponnar and Sankar. Themozhiyar and Raghavan knew these mythic figures. Were they semiconsciously following the pattern set by them? Or were the mythic brothers patterned after the kind of team that real-life older and younger brothers sometimes form?) By the seventh year of their union, Themozhiyar was already talking about breaking away and starting a place of his own, like a real younger brother, and Raghavan was trying to convince him to stay. Even though there was no question of a patrimony to be divided, there was a sense of a family core that should not be split up.

Themozhiyar called Raghavan "Annan," which translates "elder brother," and this is what we will call him henceforward, since, as is often the case in India, no one addressed him or referred to him by his "real" name. After Themozhiyar's arrival, Sulochana became Anni, "older brother's wife," to everyone, even her own children, who called her Annimma. Kanakkamma was Amma, "mother," to Themozhiyar; she was Attai, "father's sister," to the women. We will call her Attai. Themozhiyar himself was known as Ayya, "father, husband, lord," to all his friends and students, and the women of his household often used this term for him, so we will do so too.

KINGS AND ASCETICS

"Fierce one you belong to a cool bright land . . . "

Tirukkōvaiyār, 100.

Siva is the god of ashes and ascetics, a disreputable crazy god, destroyer of the world, dancer in fire. His consort is a wild, impassioned mother, uncontrollable, unpredictable, infinitely varied in form. Vishnu is the protector, the nourisher, maintainer of the structure, sleeper in water. His consort is bestower of riches, cow-like, never angry, never cruel, never free.

So Vishnu is the god of most Reddiars, for they, in their ideal-type, are landowners, men of the world, and proud of their riches. To 1980 Chingleput villagers, "Reddiar" meant "boss," not just anyone belonging to the Reddiar jati, but the head of a landowning family, a powerful man. For a young man of the Reddiar caste to say that he wanted to be "like a Reddiar" meant that he wanted to own as much land as he could and be as rich as he could and, most importantly, have others do his bidding.

The impression I received when I was alone with lower caste people was that Reddiars were more feared than they were admired. Laborers would tell me how badly they were treated and how little their landowning patrons would do for them. A Villi woman who worked for my Tamil family sang, "What do the Reddiars give us to eat? They give us big rats!" Another Villi woman jokingly asked Anni, "Did you give her [referring to me] any work?" Anni said, "No, she doesn't do anything but study." The Villi woman said, "If you have finished all your work, go to the Reddiar street and they will give you more." All laughed. This was when Reddiars were present. When they were absent, a Paraiyar man sang, "There goes the Reddiar walking over the bund in his white waistcloth. May he fall in the mud, break both his knees, and crawl all the way to his Vaishnava heaven." This did not sound so good-natured to me.

Reddiars prided themselves not only on their wealth but on their toughness and their readiness to fight. As members of the kingly class (*kshatriya varna*), they were also warriors. Even the unathletic Ayya knew how to do a fast dance with a staff that was supposed to ward off would-be attackers. According to him, all of the men in his natal family had been fighters, some of them killers. His father had nearly murdered two cousins who insulted his mother. His brother had driven off a gang of toughs who attacked him in a dark alley. Reddiar women could be brave, too. Anni had faced down a party of angry men who came to the house to find Ayya and beat him up (according to Ayya). A cousin whose husband had beaten her had turned and beaten him back. Then there was the tale of the old grandmother. Ayya and the women discussed among themselves their opinion that of all castes, Reddiars were the greatest scoundrels (*ayōkkiyarkaḷ*). But the stories that they told added up to a sense of pride in the ability of Reddiars to deal out a beating, as well as to take one.

The biggest battles that Reddiars engaged in, however, were not fist fights, but political contests with each other, landlord against landlord. In the village where we lived, which had a population of five thousand and so was nearly a town, there were two major factions, and our family was obviously on the losing side. The leader of the opposing faction had the allegiance of the lower castes, especially the Paraiyars, who were numerous and rapidly gaining in political consciousness. During the year of my visit, this leader sponsored two expensive festivals to the village goddess Kanniyamma, complete with goat sacrifices.

One evening, when a drama in honor of the goddess was being staged, this rival landlord invited us to come to his house and view the drama from his window. The women and children of our family went. The men did not. Ayya said that the mother goddess did not exist. She represented the ignorance of the people and he wanted nothing to do with her.

When we entered the house of the rival landlord, what I noticed first was the difference between his children and ours. His children were sleek and plump and well dressed. Their skin was smooth and pale. The young girls wore long skirts and had flowers in their thick, braided hair. Our children were small and bony; their skin was rough and sunburnt; their hair was thin. Umapathi's eyes were sunken and had dark circles around them. Arulmori's dress was several sizes too small; it had no buttons and the hem was torn out. It was the only dress she had. The women in the house offered us milk and sweets. I accepted, but the children refused, and sat silent and taciturn throughout the festival.

Our family felt at odds with the lower castes, but they were fighting a rising tide, while the rival landlord rode its crest. Ayya was building his rice mill on a piece of land owned in common by several hamlets. He said he had gotten permission from the hamlets to build there because it was only wasteland on which nothing grew. But now the Idaiyar goatherds were angry. They said he had taken away part of their grazing land. The other landlord told them that Ayya had been to America, had American sponsors, so he was certainly a rich man. Ayya told the Idaiyars that he was a poor farmer who owned only four acres, while some Harijans owned fifty (he did not mention that the family to which he belonged owned the maximum acreage allowable by law, though the Idaiyars must have known this). For days, Annan and Ayya went back and forth among the hamlets, trying the appease the angry Idaiyars. At last the dispute seemed to be settled. Meanwhile, a militant young Paraiyar farmer (Paraiyars are a large untouchable caste, most of whom are landless laborers) had purchased an acre of land adjacent to the few acres of chalky soil that Ayya had recently purchased and was cultivating. Ayya watched as truckload after truckload of topsoil was brought in from somewhere and unloaded on the Paraiyar's plot, a plot that he himself had hoped to buy. Rumor had it that the Paraiyar had gotten a government loan to buy the land. Ayya was angry. "The legislation is all in their favor," he said. "A Brahman boy who is at the top of his class cannot get a seat in a medical college, while a Paraiyar boy who is at the bottom will. You cannot even call a Paraiyar a Paraiyar. If you do, you will be arrested and thrown in jail." Nowadays Paraiyars were called Harijans, "God's children," the name Gandhi had coined to refer to all untouchable castes.

Our family undertook to turn the laws favoring Harijans to their advantage. Government assistance was given to Harijans who wished to purchase cattle, so the family bought a cow in the name of Munusamy, one of their hereditary Paraiyar servants. Munusamy tended the cow, and the family took the milk. But one day, Munusamy claimed the cow as his own, and the family was unable to get it back. When they told him they would no longer support him unless he gave them the cow, he chose to keep the cow, and moved away. "The Paraiyars of the village used to be loving and humble," said Anni, "but now they are starting to become arrogant, like the Paraiyars of the city."

Traditionally, on a certain festival day, the women of the family would spend the day cooking up dosais—rice pancakes— and would give one dosai to each of the laborers who worked for the family. Previously, Anni said, the laborers would come to the house and graciously accept their dosais. But now, she said, the laborers were insisting that one dosai was not enough, they wanted two. "By whose command," Anni asked, "do we work all day long preparing dosais for them? If they will no longer accept the dosais lovingly, we will no longer make them." So the custom was terminated.

But in truth there had probably never been much love lost between Anni and the servants who worked for her. She said, "Servant mentality (*vēlaikkāra putti*) never changes. No matter how much you do for them, no matter how much you say that you and they are one, if someone asks them what you've done for them, they will always say, 'Nothing.' "

There was one exception to this rule, said Anni, an old man who had worked for the family for many years. "He would always say to others, 'Our Reddiar is a golden Reddiar.' He used to bathe ten times a day. He wouldn't tolerate even a speck of dirt on his body." But he had died a year previously when a bus struck the bullock cart he was driving. "The man, the wagon, and the two bullocks were all turned into chutney. It was very sad," said Anni.

While the village Paraiyars were an increasingly threatening force in the lives of the Reddiar family, their opposites, the village Brahmans, were the objects of nobody's envy. The anti-Brahminical self-respect movement, the power of bhakti devotionalism which denied sacrality to social bounds, the secularism and atheism that were embraced with religious passion by many, these and many other forces made Brahmans no longer necessary as mediators between God and Man. Village priesthood had long since ceased to be a lucrative occupation for Brahmans, if ever it was one. Out of pity, the women of the household kept the family's hereditary Brahman priests on and fed them. The charity that in principle only flowed "down" in the form of gifts and clothing to lower castes, also flowed "up."

On the day of the Varalakshmi ceremony, a household celebration in honor of Lakshmi, goddess of wealth, consort of Vishnu, Anni had invited a Brahman priest to chant the names of Lakshmi, as the ceremony calls for celebrants to do, in Sanskrit. The priest arrived, a ragged, skinny, chicken of a man, with a huge tumor dangling in a pouch of skin like an oriole's nest beneath his throat. He entered the puja room and chanted something in Sanskrit-like syllables for about an hour, but it was evident even to me that he was winging it. Meanwhile the women and the children were in the main room, singing Māṇikkavācakar's "Sivapurāṇam," a Tamil hymn in praise of Siva, which they always sang when hymns were called for. (Ayya had brought the Sivapurāṇam into the household, and had installed it as the family prayer. Anni and those in her charge had learned it and recited it fervently.)

After the priest had left, I asked Anni if it was really necessary for him to come to the house and chant for the ceremony to be performed. Anni said no, but this was the way such Brahmans lived. Now times had changed and they had little to support them.

In this household's celebration of the Varalakshmi festival, I saw that issues other than those of sect and caste were at stake. In the morning of this particular day, for reasons I never learned, Anni was tense. As part of the celebration, she decorated the door of the house red and yellow in kumkum and turmeric. Why decorate the door? I asked her. "Because it is a woman," she answered tersely. She and Padmini and their twenty-year-old nephew Vishvanathan had made a pandal, a little house for the festival goddess, and had decorated it with dots of kumkum and turmeric, which they covered with mango and banana leaves, which they covered with paper flowers, which they covered with a silk sari. The decorations beneath were hidden by the decorations above—layer upon layer of mysterious armor. The goddess in the pandal was a pot decorated with gold-colored eyes and mouth, a coconut on top, a garland of *tāṛam* flowers and leaves around its rim, a necklace around its neck. Tāṛam flowers are never to be used at weddings, Anni had told me (they grow singly among spiky leaves so they mean lone self-protected womanhood, they have an aggressive smell so they mean excessive sexuality, snakes live in their bushes so they mean hidden danger), but for this ceremony she insisted they were important. Anni had asked Ayya to bring back tāṛam flowers from town and Ayya had replied, "Don't count on me (*ennai nampātē*)," in irritation as he walked out the door. Was it because he disliked the goddess? Or because it was a Vaishnava ceremony and he was a Saiva? Or something else? Anni had been sullen for the rest of the day, but the tāṛam flowers had been gotten from somewhere, and were used. It occurred to me, noticing how similar the pot-goddess was to images of the smallpox goddess Mariamman that I had seen, that perhaps Anni was celebrating this ceremony not as a tribute to Lakshmi, the ever-smiling wife of Vishnu, but as a tribute to the fiercer mother, the rival and mistress of Siva.

WAR

". . . On the mountain of our half-woman lord . . . "

Tirukkōvaiyār, 100.

The biggest transition the family had to make upon Ayya's arrival was the change from Vaishnavism to Saivism. Once, to see what he would say, I asked Ayya to explain to me why there had been in the past such antagonism between Vaishnavas and Saivas. What did it matter which god they worshipped? Weren't they all the same? Ayya answered that in ancient times, people worshipped God as mother and father together. Later they split them up and some worshipped the mother and some worshipped the father and they fought each other. Siva means light (*oḷi*) and the mother means darkness, greenness, fertility (*pacumai*), he said. Similarly, Vishnu (Tirumāl) stands for fertility, for wealth (*poruḷ*), for commingling (*mayakkam*), for compassion (*karuṇai*), all of which are characteristics of the mother.

Thus for Ayya, the conflict between Saivism and Vaishnavism was a conflict between male and female, or between what males stood for and what females stood for, between pure consciousness free of the burden of matter, and the pleasurable, dark, and rich mingling of substances.

According to Ayya, before his arrival this family was given to enjoyments and expenditures which it could scarcely afford. He said that Anni would often, on a whim, take a taxi to the movies, that she would spend money without keeping track of where it went, and that as head cook she would spend more per week on coffee than on food. Annan, he said, contributed his share to the wastage, going deeply into debt to build a huge brick warehouse which was only partly completed and had never been used. Ayya said that when he arrived he taught the family frugality and simplicity, though he admitted that they were still a long way from being completely reformed. Now an ascetic air permeated the household. Coffee was no longer consumed. Neither were eggs. The women wore few or no jewels. All the children of the family were taught Saiva hymns and wore sacred ash, symbol of renunciation. There were no grand celebrations. But a strong worldly undercurrent still was there. The women and children still celebrated Vaishnava festivals, and festivals to the mother, while the men abstained from both. Eggs were cooked for me in Ayya's absence, though I did not ask for them. The women even told me that they had secretly raised goats for slaughter, to raise household money.

As soon as the mother and the father became two, they had started fighting—so Ayya had said. As I watched the daily life of this household, it soon became evident to me that the battle between the male and female modes of existence was not waged exclusively on a mythological level. For there was a continual open struggle between the males and the females of our family. Moreover, it was an uneven battle, just as the cosmic struggles often are, for Annan avoided combat, and Ayya, the outsider, was left to contend single-handedly against the formidable alliance of Anni, Padmini, and Mohana.

For his part, Ayya would score points by saying that the women didn't feed him properly, that they were unhygienic, and that they were poor workers. He would ask for rice water and complain if they gave him anything else, then when they complied with his request he would complain that they gave him only rice water. He refused to bathe in the water from the well in the courtyard, saying that it was poisonous, but he scolded the women for not bathing before cooking everyday. He blamed Padmini and Anni for not keeping the house clean enough and said that they were responsible for the children's frequent illnesses. He also scolded them for laughing and playing too much.

The women were not without their answers. When Ayya was present they would argue vehemently with him. In his absence they would work to get me on their side. They invited me to play cards and dice with them and to go to x-rated movies with them (Padmini used this term), though Ayya said such things were immoral and a waste of time. It was never clear to me whether their invitations were joking or were serious. Sometimes I thought that they were trying to trick me into revealing that I indulged in what people seemed to think were typically American vices. Other times I thought that they truly enjoyed the idea of being naughty and doing things the men would disapprove of. Certainly, smaller acts of rebellion were a way of life for them.

Once, when we were picking vegetables in the garden, I came upon a preying mantis. I commented that among these bugs, the wife devours the husband. "That's just the way it should be," said Padmini, unsmiling.

Most interesting to me was their dispute over language. Both Ayya and Annan insisted that family members should always speak in proper, literate Tamil. Certain words and certain sounds were ugly to them; they were *koccai*, crude, low, inelegant, illiterate Tamil. But these were just the words and sounds that the women's speech was peppered with, and the women refused to change.

Just as some urbane Kentuckians hate fronted nasal vowels (the way hillbillies make "fire" rhyme with "hair"), Ayya hated fricatives, especially the *-cci* sound that came in the casual speech of the region at the end of many words. He preferred the smoother endings that literate speech was given to. But one of Padmini's most often used words was *etācci* ("whatever"). And Mohana, because of a gap between her teeth, had a slight lisp, which Ayya would mock. "Look how she says, '*Fāl, fāl*' [for *pāl*, 'milk']," he would say derisively. Mohana would only smile.

If a woman used the word *paṇṇi* ("made, did"), Ayya would scold her. "Only pigs (*panni*) say paṇṇi," he would say. He told the offender to use the word *ceytu* (a literate form) instead. And the woman would answer guilelessly, "I try, but I just can't remember," or more straightforwardly, "You say it your way and I'll say it mine."

It was Anni who was most likely to give the latter answer. Though she had memorized much Saiva poetry, and knew the literate forms well, in worldly life she made the use of worldly forms a matter of principle. So, when a guest came to the house, and I asked him, "How is your wife (*poṇḍāḍḍi*)," using a casual form, Padmini corrected me, saying that I should use the more proper word for wife, *manaivi*. But Anni said, "For Ayya we say manaivi, but in this house we say poṇḍāḍḍi."

Similarly, when I had asked Annan for a list of the castes in the village, he had called the village goatherds by the name Yatavar, a literate name identifying them with the cowherds of Krishna's youth. Anni had come up and said, "They're not Yatavars, they're Idaiyars. Everyone in the village calls them Idaiyars. If you teach her to call them Yatavars, no one will know what she's talking about."

The dispute was carried even into the naming of the children. The three girls born after Ayya joined the household each had two names, one given by Ayya, the other given by Anni. Ayya's names for them, formally bestowed at naming ceremonies after their births, were long, poetic names, signifying lofty abstract ideals—Aṟivaraci ("Queen of Knowledge"); Mankaiyārkkaraci ("Queen of Ladies"); Aruḷmoṛi ("Language of Grace"). The names given by Anni were informal, and were context-oriented, based on the circumstances of the child's birth. Arivaraci was Petti, "the elder," because she was born a few days earlier than her cousin, Mankaiyārkkaraci, whom Anni had named Cinni, "the younger." Arulmori was Varuṇi, named after Varuṇa the rain god, because on the day of her birth there were untimely rains. Interestingly, none of the boys was given such a casual, context-oriented name by Anni, although all of the children, boys as well as girls, were often called by shortened versions of their formal names (Arivu, Mankai, and Arul for the girls; Uma, Oli, and Siva for the boys Umapathi, Jnana Oli, and Sivamani).

The children called each other by the names Anni had given them, but if you asked any of them what her name was, she would answer with the name given by Ayya. However, Ayya chastised the adults for calling the children by the pet names given by Anni; through usage of the pet names, the "real" names would be lost, he said. He said a name should be such that every time someone spoke it, they would be reminded of some high principle.

The men and women of the household agreed on many general issues. They both felt that the family should be a "high" family, that it should be well thought of by the world, that it should be capable of feeding many people. But the men's and women's reasons for agreeing sometimes differed. For instance, both agreed as to the inferiority of servants and low-caste people, but the reasons men gave were mainly attributional, the reasons women gave were mainly interactional. Men said that servants drank, ate meat, spent money as soon as they got it on entertainment and food rather than saving and spending wisely, and lacked responsibility. Women said that servants sowed dissension in the family, were ungrateful, stole things, and lied.

These disagreements seemed to boil down to a few basic differences between male and female ideologies: men stressed purity and cleanliness, order, peacefulness, and high ideals. Women stressed physical togetherness, interdependence, and adaptation to circumstances. For the women, independence was not all that desirable, neither were purity and cleanliness tremendously important, neither were peace and quiet. Hence, Ayya often fled from the hullabaloo of the household to what he called his *dhyānamaṇḍapam*, his "meditation hall," the little house he had built across the lakebed from the village settlement. When he retreated there, Anni would plead with him to come back to the house, because (she claimed) she enjoyed her daily conflicts with him. She said that when Ayya wasn't around she felt as though she had nothing to do, the house seemed deserted, she finished all her work too easily. When Ayya was there she was happier, because it seemed as though she had a lot to do, and she never finished her work, for arguing with him on one side and working on the other. She loved this gregarious chaos.

But Ayya said that he didn't like the house to be like a "factory," making cooking into a big affair involving lots of people. It should be finished quickly and easily; he could do it alone if he didn't have work outside the house.

Ayya liked to point out that he was separate, not closely related to anyone in the household, and that he avoided the bonds of "attachment" (*pācam*). Anni said that she and other women liked get-togethers. They liked to work together, bathe together, eat together.

The difference was neatly symbolized at a large wedding that we went to. The men were all in one hall, all dressed in white, quietly listening to a concert. The women were all with the bride and groom in another hall, forming in their congregation a sea of multicolored saris, moving about, and "talking," Anni told me, "about kin."

Thus there was an agonistic relationship between the sexes, in truth an endless war, in this household, and not only there. The lines were drawn, the conflicting values clearly articulated. One might think that in such a situation men would choose to be more manly (whatever that might mean to them) and women to be more womanly; one would expect each side to wear its sex proudly, as it were. But this was not exactly the case. Instead the struggle between the sexes fostered androgyny on both sides, as though each sex desired to steal the other's thunder, or step across the line drawn around it by the other.

Ayya was a guru and he had had a guru. Though he loved this guru and nearly deified him, he refused initiation from him, thus causing the guru (who also loved Ayya) much pain. According to Ayya, the guru had said, "How would it be if a man and a woman lived together without marriage ceremonies? Undertaking a religious path without initiation is the same." In a certain way, the guru had wanted to marry Ayya.

Ayya was a preacher who taught about the ideals of Tamil womanhood as he saw them—softness, meltingness, subtlety, mystery, modesty. "As I teach," he said, "I become what I teach." To his followers, he exemplified many of the feminine ideals that he lectured about. Almost all of his followers were men, and some of them expressed an open homosexual interest in him. One of his longtime friends told him, "You are so attractive it's a shame you weren't born a woman."

The women of Ayya's household, by contrast, were far from his ideal. They, especially his wife, for all the goodness of their hearts, were loud, immodest, short-tempered, and unbending.

Padmini would bathe in the open courtyard where people from the outside could come and go, sometimes stripped to the waist. Anni argued with a lower caste male servant after her bath, casually dressing herself as she talked. When the women worked in the garden they would hike their saris and petticoats to above mid-thigh. When they were relaxing in the afternoon, they would lie on their backs with their legs apart, their knees bent back and their feet in the air, like puppies. With careless grace, they kept just the essentials covered.

Padmini was good at repairing the machinery in the rice mill. Ayya wept at the thought of her doing this hard work, but Padmini obviously enjoyed it. She was also good at supervising labor crews, striding among them like a queen, loudly ordering them about. When the foreman of one of the labor crews working on the rice mill came in for lunch, complaining that his men couldn't work because they hadn't gotten enough to eat, Padmini simultaneously argued with him at the top of her voice and served him a bountiful meal, interrupting her invective every now and then to ask politely if he would like more of this or that vegetable, in what struck me as a strange combination of hostility and hospitality, which somehow won him over. It was the same with the village servants. She would often work in the garden or the fields with young and middle-aged Paraiyar and Nayakar men, laughing with them and scolding them, teasing them about their eyesight, their incomes, their physiques. No one seemed to feel that she needed protection.

In contrast to the married women was Anuradha, Anni's grown daughter. Always smiling and soft-spoken, she never lost her temper and she scolded no one. When she played with the children she made them laugh, rather than (like her elders) beating them or teasing them and making them cry. She rarely went out, even to the garden or to weddings, she observed full menstrual seclusion, never assumed immodest bodily positions, always kept her body covered down to her toes, wore matching bangles and a brassiere. She had several years more education than her mother and her aunts—perhaps this accounted for the difference: she had

Plate 8. Anuradha.

been taught what a "civilized" (*nākarikamāna*) woman ought to be. Cleanliness, quiet, and modesty were values of the city. To appear civilized was important to many young people of the villages. Or perhaps Anuradha was practicing for the day when she would marry into a household other than the one in which she was raised, where the prevailing ideology might be different.

GROWING UP TAMIL

" . . . harder than anything to know . . . "

Tirukkōvaiyār, 2.

The children of our family were rough-and-tumble, disobedient, competitive, mysterious. None of them had any duties or chores in the household except to learn lessons, which they did poorly. When they were out of school they would tear around the house wildly or play in the dust of the temple yard across the street. But they never played with any of the other children of the village, and they never strayed beyond the invisible boundaries separating them from the forbidden parts of the world, which constituted most of it.

In the morning, when it was time for a bath, the older children would race to the bathing tank, the winner shouting in English, "First," the runner-up shouting, "Second." But they would all bathe together, the boys naked, the girls in their underpants. The toddlers would be there, too, playing with the water that happened to splash on their bodies, but the older children would take no notice of them. Later, an adult would bathe the young ones.

Sometimes the children would squabble. Attai said that it was children's nature (*iyaṯkai*) to fight. As they grew up, if they developed wisdom (*putti*), they would stop. Padmini had counseled me never to become involved in children's fights. I noticed that when adults did become involved in children's disputes, they did not undertake to determine who was right and who was wrong, but tried only to create an expedient illusion that would calm the child for the moment. When a small child cried because of an injustice perpetrated upon it by some older person, the caretaker would pretend to strike the offender, and the small child would be pacified, to the amusement of bystanders.

Not only the tension of conflict but the tension of desire would be resolved through the creation of illusion. Anni said, "When we take the children to town, they want to buy something. I will say, 'The things in this store are not good, we'll look in the next store.' And I will say the same thing in the next store, and so on until it is time to leave, and then I say, 'We must hurry or we'll miss the bus,' and so I get home without having spent any money for them."

None of the caretakers of the children ever said to me, "The world is deceitful, so while we are the world to our children we must be deceitful also." Yet I felt that the children of this household were raised on a diet of maya.

As the children grew older, the deceits grew more elaborate. So, for instance, once, as the adults were having lunch at the rice mill, Umapathi arrived with the other children. Ayya, for some reason, asked Umapathi alone whether he had eaten, and Umapathi replied no. Anni insisted that he had eaten. She punished him by standing him in front of the picture of Natarajan that sat on the altar in Ayya's retreat and demanding that he apologize, in the standard manner of apologizing to a deity, by crossing his arms and holding his earlobes and bowing up and down repeating, "I will not tell a lie." Umapathi did so, weeping. Then Padmini fed him alone a full meal. It appeared to me from the way he ate that indeed he could not have had a full meal that day, but Anni did not seem to recognize this. She told Ayya that Umapathi had gotten into the habit of lying frequently. They would ask him if he had done his homework and he would say yes, and they would look in his notebooks and find them empty.

A similar episode occurred with Umapathi's age-mate, Arulmori. She had bathed in the morning and wanted a clean dress, but the dress that had been laid out for her to wear had been used as a towel by Umapathi, and Arulmori's skirt and blouse, her only other outfit, were in a pile of laundry from the previous evening, waiting to be washed. Her mother Padmini shouted at her, "Moddai [the servant] washes clothes only in a crowd," indirectly scolding Moddai, who was on the other side of the courtyard washing dishes. Then Padmini said to Arulmori, "You can wear a dirty dress as a punishment for the mistakes you made in the past (*ceyta tappukku taṇḍanai*)." Earlier that morning, Arulmori had made a mistake in her homework, and Padmini had shouted at her until she wept. Anni had gently comforted her, saying, "Don't cry. If there is a mistake, you can correct it."

Such surprising events were daily affairs in the lives of the children. In general, a child could never know if or when or even upon whom the punishment would fall for a mistake that was made. One person would err and another would be punished for a mistake the other had committed in the past and thought forgotten. Or one would punish and another comfort. Always, in these cases, the punisher was the child's own mother, and the comforter somebody else. Or alternatively, the same person would punish and comfort, punish and comfort, until the child completely lost its bearings, and began to weep. Indeed, this was a favorite game for adults and older children to play with small children—to offer a plaything and then withdraw it, offer and then withdraw, offer and then withdraw. When the child broke down and wept, it would be cuddled and comforted, or else whisked away to enjoy some other amusement.

Somehow, the tears of a child were entertaining; they brought forth laughter from onlookers. Children themselves, finally, learned to laugh when they were scolded, at least some did. Their laughter would anger the scolder, and the scolding would grow angrier and louder, then the laughter, then the scolding, until at a climax the child would either run away, or suddenly burst into tears. Adult arguments would often reverse this pattern: people would shout back and forth at each other more and more loudly, until it seemed as though they might come to blows, and then suddenly a joke would be made and all would burst into laughter. In movies, tears and laughter were a stereotypic combination. There was something about the union of sharply contrasting feelings that appealed to people. For a Westerner, it could be very confusing.

Once I saw Mankaiyarkkaraci climbing a power tower. I yelled at her

Plate 9. Mankaiyarkkaraci.

angrily, "Have you got cotton between your ears? Come down from there!" She climbed down with what I took for a mocking smile on her face. I scolded her; she laughed; I scolded her; she laughed, then suddenly she was weeping. I felt remorse. I tried to apologize, to comfort her, but she continued sobbing. After that, for the rest of the afternoon, she refused to speak to me, and sat with her face buried in her hands, while I sat with her, first pleading with her to understand my point of view, then joking and trying to make her laugh. Sometimes her body shook, but with her face in her hands, I could not tell whether she was weeping, or pretending to weep, or laughing. As the sun went down, Arivaraci came to fetch her, and told me that Mankai would be all right. The next day it was as though nothing had happened.

Such was my relationship with the children. They seemed to me to be very like American children, up to a point. Beyond that point, they lost me, or rather, entangled me in webs I was surprised to find myself caught in.

Umapathi was the oldest boy in the family, the only son of the household head. He was much smaller and weaker than my own son of the same age, but much more bold, and he beat my son in footraces every time. Courage was expected of him. The other children would be comforted when they wept, for the other boys were babies, and the girls were girls. Only Uma had always to be brave.

Umapathi spoke in a gravelly voice, and both of his fathers, Annan and Ayya, were angry with him for using slang (*koccai tamiṛ*) and mixed language rhymes. Ayya had chastised him for a bit of doggerel he had made up: "I am sorry, *attai vīḍḍukkāri*." I thought that this was an interesting rhyme, because Uma had chosen a phrase from English that could not be translated into Tamil without great distortion (Tamil people never apologize so directly), and matched it with a Tamil phrase equally untranslatable (to gloss it "girl of my father's sister's house" misses its essential cheekiness), and had produced a meaningful jingle (a boy apologizing to his father's sister's daughter, the *murai peṇ*, the "rightful wife," for something—perhaps marrying another). Moreover the rhyme was good, and he had managed the end-rhyming characteristic of English verse but alien to Tamil, together with a suggestion of the initial rhyme characteristic of Tamil verse, even while the initial line was English and the final line Tamil. A great merger. But Ayya had criticized him severely for it. "Language is a living (*oru jīvan*)," he had said. "You must not chop it up (*tuṇḍākkakkūḍātu*)." Then Ayya questioned Uma, "Do you want to be high or low?" Uma was silent. Ayya repeated the question. Uma, with tears in his eyes, said, "High." But Uma, as the first son ("the only child, that is, the only *male* child," Ayya had called him, before Jnana Oli was born) had to bear so much, and had such a reputation for disobedience in the family, that I wondered how fully the question "High or low?" was really resolved in his mind.

Arulmori was called a "daddy's girl" (*appāppiḷḷai*). She used to swing on her father's clothes and hang on his body as though he were a tree, and Ayya would say fondly, "I like this Arulmori." By contrast, when Umapathi had tugged at his father's clothing, his father Annan had snapped back, "Fool!", though Annan was in general much more patient than Ayya. Arulmori was her mother's second daughter and nobody's son; not so much was expected of her and her life seemed less hard than Umapathi's. In one respect, Arulmori was the balancing other half of the rough-talking Umapathi: true to her name, which meant "language of grace," she spoke in clear, literate Tamil. Of all the children, she recited poetry the best, and she had a clear, musical voice.

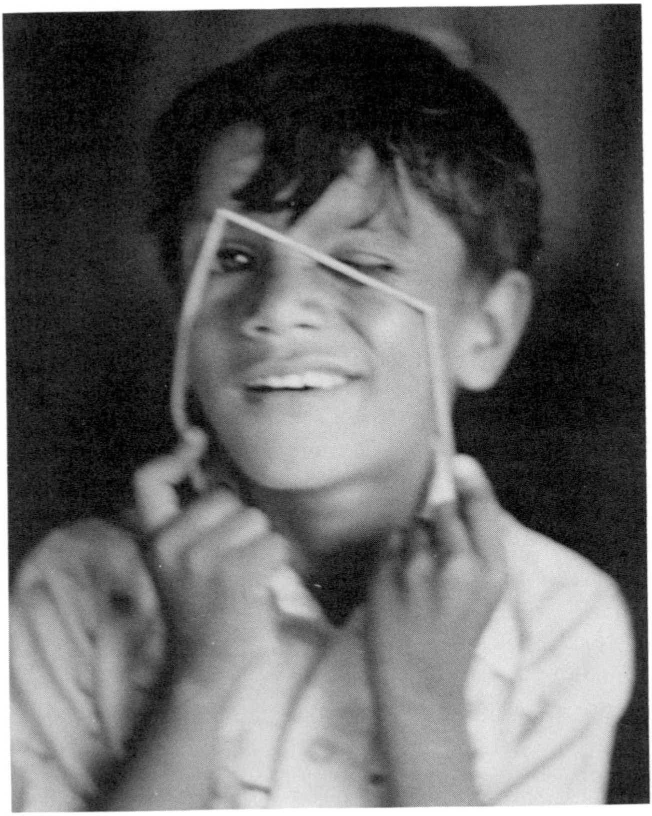

Plate 10. Umapathi.

But unlike her older sister and her younger brother, Arulmori had no same-sex age-mate, and hence (as we shall see they had) she had no real human mirror. She loved to dance with the shadow of her own body on the wall, so that when she grew older, her parents bought dancing lessons for her—a rare extravagance for this family. Like Umapathi she was alone and embodied her own opposite—good and bad, like Uma's high and low. She reminded me a little of a village goddess when one day she wiped my son's newly skinned knee hard with her thumb and smiling sweetly, gleefully, up at me, said, "Blood!"

GOING DOWN TAMIL

> " . . . as though one full soul drowning . . . "
>
> *Tirukkōvaiyār,* 307.

Anni ruled the household now. Her mother-in-law Attai had long since lost her power there. She was arthritic and could scarcely walk, and

Plate 11. Arulmori.

cataracts were growing over both eyes, but she could still see well enough to read the newspaper when she wore her glasses. She read it every day and reported to me the news from America and the Middle East. But the changes in her own world made her sigh. The attention the younger women paid her was cursory. They went their own way, which was not Attai's, and made no apologies. Attai remained always the image of patience and resignation, even while she bemoaned the structurelessness that now engulfed her home.

Across the street from the family house was the ancient Perumal temple, in ruins like the house itself. Ordinarily, the temple was closed and inactive, but one day a year, for the celebration of Krishna's birthday, they opened its doors. On this day Attai, who almost never left the house, would hobble across the street to pay obeisance to her old lord.

The age-long tensions between Siva and Vishnu, ascetics and householders, Brahmans and kings, were submerged now beneath the rivalries of the mother and the father, the worker and the owner. There were no Vaishnava–Saiva brawls, for the worshippers of both these gods now had stronger common enemies. But as the world decayed, it must have seemed to Attai that Vishnu the preserver was going under, while Siva, the god of paradox and apocalypse, triumphed. More than once, Attai lamented that all was mixed.

All the higher castes celebrated Krishna's birthday. On this day the Sivanaḍiyār Kūḍḍam ("The Gathering of Slaves to Siva"), a devotional group to whom Ayya lectured weekly, made a pilgrimage from Madras to the Tirumal temple on a hilltop near our village. On this day, said Anni, they became devotees of Vishnu, and people who ordinarily wore ashes, symbol of devotion to Siva, on this day wore the nāmam, she said. But I noticed that our family did not wear the nāmam, and I also noticed that Ayya and Annan were absent during the celebrations.

All day long, the children shouted "Gōvindā!" (a name of Krishna) with a drawn-out "Go" rising in pitch and amplitude, exploding in a triumphant "Vinda!" It reminded me of an American high school football cheer. The children loved the sound of it. A crowd of children in the village went together from house to house, carrying a pot in which they received from each house a handful of rice.

In the early morning, the Sivanaḍiyār Kūḍḍam also went from house to house, pulling a chariot, and singing, *"Kaṇēcan caraṇam, caraṇam Kaṇēcan"* ("Ganesan refuge, refuge Ganesan." Ganesan is the elephant-headed elder son of Siva.) By midday, several men and one woman were dancing before the chariot, possessed. One man was possessed by Murugan (Siva's younger son, god of war and beauty) and the surrounding crowd was chanting, *"Vēl! Vēl! Vēl!"* ("Spear! Spear! Spear!" The spear is one of Murugan's symbols.) A man dressed as Tirumāl ("The holy dark one," Vishnu, Krishna) with a garland around his neck, danced with the man possessed by Murugan. At the end of the dance, the two men embraced.

I missed many of the details of the festival—the variety of myths which fed it, the range of experiences which it produced. One fact about the festival was obvious. Like so many other festivals, it was a celebration of commingling.

On this day, as on all festival days, the first thing that the women of our household did when they rose was bathe. Usually they didn't bathe until late morning after the cooking was over and the children had eaten and gone to school. Then they would bathe individually, in the small enclosed bathroom. But today and on other festival days they bathed in the open, next to the well, all of them together. The women would not eat on this festival day until the food had been offered to the deity. Before the food offering, Anni laid a trail of pieces of camphor from the concrete projection of the front porch, through the front door, into the puja room where a plate of food lay. The camphor was lit by Anni and Padmini, with the children following. The deity to which food was offered was a nāmam drawn on the wall of the puja room, beneath the altar with Ganesan on it, the drawing of the nāmam flanked by drawings of conch and discus, Vishnu's symbols. As the food was offered, all the women and children with Anni leading sang the "Sivapurāṇam," as they had done for the Varalakshmi ceremony. The fact that these were festivals in honor of Vishnu, not of Siva, did not affect the choice of a hymn.

The little children were made to bow before the image of the nāmam. Then the older children did so, then Mohana, Padmini, and Anni. Attai was the last to offer obeisance to the nāmam. She remained on her knees, her body bent over, for more than a minute, as though she feared this homage to Vishnu would be her last. But perhaps it was only her age and her aching legs and back that made it difficult for her to move more quickly.

On festival days, it became evident that mixing was a goal in itself for our family—Vaishnava and Saiva, Sanskrit and Tamil, children and adults, male and female—all were joined in happy confusion. Festivals were a time for people to do things together—to bathe together, to build pandals and make special foods together, to worship together, to go about the village in processions together. But mixture was not a pleasure reserved for festival occasions. It was celebrated and renewed daily. The greatest amount of mixing took place in the morning, when all the people were in the courtyard, getting ready for the day. There were many jobs to be done at that time. The children had to be bathed, combed, dressed, and fed and their lessons listened to. Water had to be fetched for cooking, drinking, and bathing. Preparations had to be started for the main meal. Flowers had to be picked from the bush growing in the courtyard. The cow had to be washed. The house had to be swept. Myriad tasks were performed in the early morning, before the sun got high and the weather hot, before the children went to school and the men to the city. Some relatively stable division of labor might have been devised for this time, to avoid confusion and increase efficiency, but in fact there was nothing of the sort. The courtyard was the household's heart and meeting ground, governed by Anni, and she made it plain that order and efficiency were not her primary concerns. The most important thing was for people to be working together, noisily if possible, and with much moving about—both visual and audible tumult.

My notes for a morning, as I sat in the courtyard watching people go about their business around me, contain the following observations:

Padmini is helping the children with their homework. Some of them are crying. The old grandmother (Padmini's mother's mother) churns buttermilk. Anni cooks with the help of Modday the servant and then with the old grandmother's help. Annan dresses the toddler Jnana Oli. Padmini and Modday roughly bathe the children. Arulmori cries because she has gotten powder in her eyes. After their bath, Anni combs the girls' hair. Muttammal, the Paraiyar servant, sweeps and collects cowdung. Annan is on the front porch singing a hymn. The old grandmother and I pick flowers. Dogs eat the fecal mess left by Jnana Oli. Crows eat the other garbage. Padmini calls me to eat several times, but does not feed me yet. Eight-year-old Arivaraci and six-year-old Arulmori fight for hair ribbons. Anni helps Padmini bathe. Arivaraci picks up Jnana Oli. Attai advises Arivaraci and Arulmori regarding their fight. Moddai cooks dosais by herself. Her two-year-old daughter Ponni calls her but she does not answer. Muttammal waters and bathes the cow. The half-blind servant (a woman who does occasional work for the family) helps Padmini bathe.

On any given morning virtually anybody could be found doing virtually any of the tasks that needed to be done. The only hard and fast rule that I could discover was that Harijan servants could not participate in the cooking and serving of food, but they did everything else, and Moddai, the Nayakar servant, often cooked. I never saw the older men Ayya and Annan picking flowers or cleaning up, but Ayya claimed he had done both these jobs for his sister when he raised her, and once, when I had loaned one of my blankets to a Harijan man to sleep on, Ayya had made a point of washing the blanket himself, using large quantities of chlorine bleach. Another time he served me food with his bare left hand, after he had been eating with his right and there was no ladle and no one else to serve me. "For now, this will have to be my right hand," he said.

All boundaries were movable. In the course of a normal day, if no one else was available, Anni would clean the gutters, do the laundry and dishes, and dispose of the babies' messes. The old grandmother would make cowdung pies. The men would wash the children and chop the vegetables. As often as not, a task that was started by one person would be finished by another, whoever was handy. In terms of day-to-day activities, there was no sharp distinction between central family (those who had permanent rights in the household), peripheral family (relatives who were visiting but were not expected to stay forever), and servants. If there was a dish or two to be washed, a child might do it, or Vishvanathan might do it, or Anni or I might do it. If there was an errand to be run, Anni might send Vishvanathan, or a child, or her own husband. When there were vegetables to be picked from the garden, this job would be done by any combination of able-bodied people: children, adults, central householders, servants. A typical crew consisted of Padmini, Anni, Ganapathi Nayakar (a neighbor in his thirties), and Antoni (a Paraiyar laborer in his thirties). In the morning at 4:30 A.M., Anni would, without getting up, call

Plate 12. Ram Tilakam.

Modday the Nayakar servant, Ram Tilakam the Reddiar servant, and Anuradha her own daughter, to fetch the water from the pipeline, which was opened only at this time of day, while Anni herself went back to sleep. After they had gotten the water, the three young women would sit together in the dark and chilly courtyard, half awake, until dawn, when the rest of the household began to stir. When there was no pipe water and the women had to fetch water from the tank, Padmini, Mohana, and Modday would go. Padmini would carry one pot, Mohana two, and Modday three.

Thus it could be said that all the people in the household did the same work, but some of them did more. Likewise, they all ate the same food, but some ate less. Therefore, though there were no lines drawn between the tasks of different people, still there was an order which followed the gradation of people by age, by degree of centrality to the household, by caste, and by sex. The further down in this combined hierarchy you were, the dirtier, heavier, and more voluminous would be the work that fell to you, like sediment sifting to the bottom of a pond.

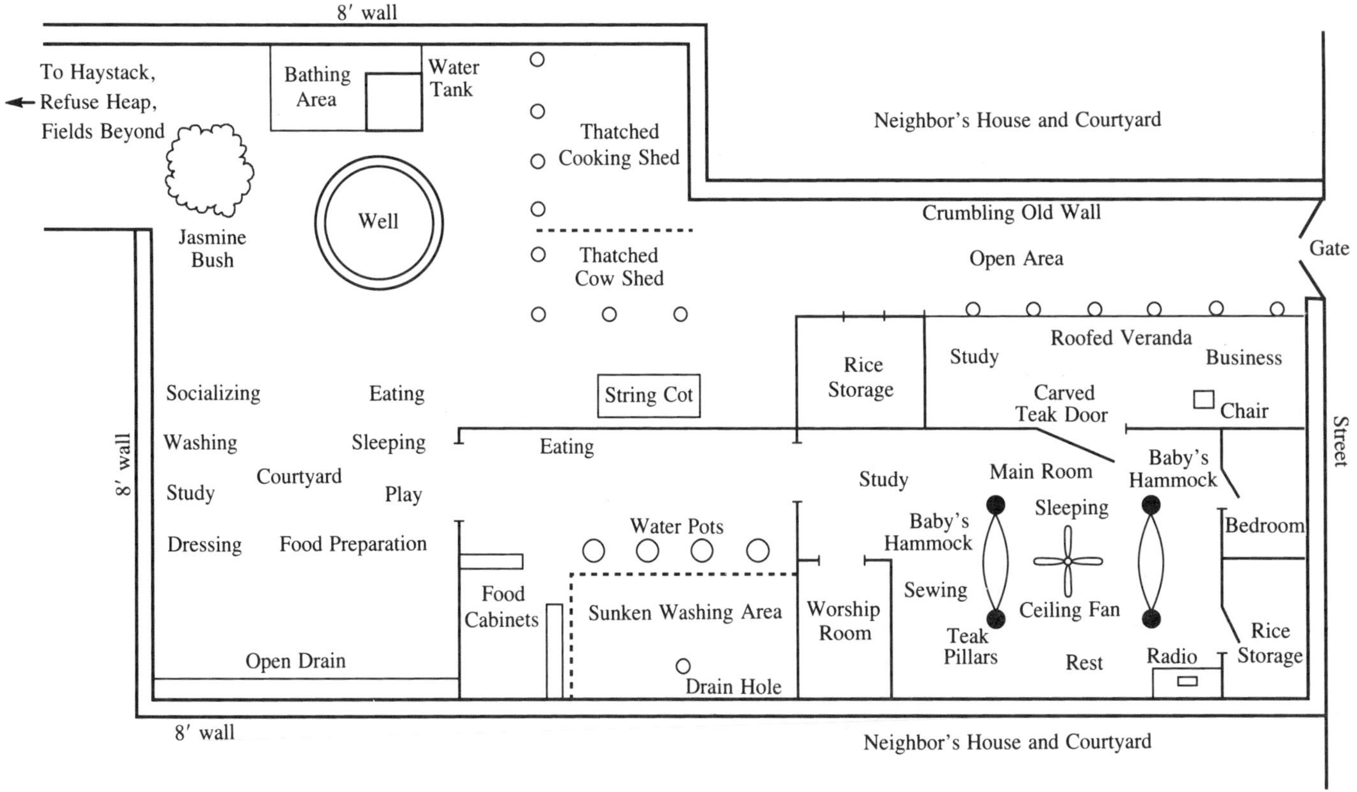

Figure 3. The family house.

Plate 13. Children playing.

POSTLUDE: HOUSEFLOWS

". . . where the honey fills the field . . ."

Tirukkōvaiyār, 100.

Households in rural Tamil Nadu, like the body as some Tamil people know it, are better seen as points of confluence than as "holds" in any stable sense. In them, many currents meet, mingle, and redivide. They are more turbulent and more dynamic than any of the streams connecting them.

In a Tamil village, doors and windows are almost always open. Except in wealthier places, most walls are crumbling; the narrow pathways that wind among houses are filled with the rubble of crumbled walls. Animals that no one owns—dogs, cats, rats, crows, monkeys, insects, reptiles—enter through the infinitely permeable borders of a family's dwelling space to receive the household refuse, or steal their share of the grain, or stalk each other. People depend on them, summon them for cleanup, even sometimes eat them. Offerings are made to crows. Lizards' comments upon conversations are heard with respect.

Most houses are constructed of mud and thatch, so that they are very impermanent. They must be rebuilt frequently or they disintegrate. Also, most houses are tiny, sometimes less wide than a reclining person is long. Many ordinary village families occupy more than one such shelter at a time, so that in effect their "house" is broken up and scattered over several neighborhoods. A poor man or woman taking a stranger through the village will point out several distinct locations, referring to each as "our house" (*nam vīḍu*). People easily shift residence from house to house, perhaps sleeping in one and cooking in another, living a kind of micro-nomadism, their seasons the times of day. Many people spend more time in the houses of neighbors than they do in their "own" house. Among friends, different houses could as easily be one house. Mobs of children surge through courtyards, restrained only, if at all, by the invisible walls of their elders' structured antagonisms—spats between families, caste prides and fears. Women sleep in their houses. Men stay with them, or else they leave and sleep with other men in the village center. Some people build their homes in the beautiful fields and orchards outside the village nucleus, but most prefer to keep the living village wrapped around them and twined through them, with others always very near. In empty places there are ghosts and snakes.

Within a village there occurs a perpetual daily ebb and flow of people through each other's living spaces. Superimposed upon this tide are the seasonal and generational fluctuations caused by visits of kinspeople to and from distant villages. A married daughter who lives with her husband in another village returns to her mother's house for her first parturition and often thereafter for months at a time. Children who quarrel with their parents go to live at the houses of other kinspeople for a while. Old people spend long periods of time in the households of their various children. In a landowner's household, poor distant relatives come to live, work, and be fed. Tenant farmers, laborers, and their families also come into their patrons' living space regularly, to perform any task they are called upon to perform, from removing dead rats to spending the night at the house as protectors of the women to rocking the baby asleep in their arms.

The confluent, turbulent, ever-shifting quality of the household would not be significant if it happened only for natural reasons. Tropical environments do encourage open windows and outdoor living and the growth and multiplication of many creatures. Anywhere in the world, walls will crumble. But confluence in the Tamil household, the close, tumultuous merger of lives, is taught and learned as a value, and this makes all the difference.

CHAPTER THREE

The Ideology of Love

PRELUDE: SURFACE AND DEPTH

On the surface is consciousness. Underneath is the unconscious, the deep wellspring, the knower who is hard to know, who can never know himself. This the way we think of it. The surface, having been crafted by the knower, is a face, a mask, an artifice, an obstacle, a lie. We have to get behind it, underneath it, to understand what is really going on. Because what is interesting is just what is hidden. If the surface interests us, it does so only because of its failures, because of the artfulness of its deception, which reveals the hand of the artist.

As anthropologists we are therefore simultaneously fascinated by and suspicious of everything the native tells us. Everything is significant, everything is revealing, everything is a lie. Our job is to lay bare the structure of the lies. In ethnology we seek to reveal to the world the nakedness of our informant, in its dazzling beauty, or in its ugliness, or in both. Somehow we convince ourselves, often enough, anyway, that this act of violence is an act of respect that benefits the native. At least we have shown the world that his nakedness is comparable to ours. At least we have shown the world what he really is, divested the world of its myths about him, even as we divest him of his own. But of course, we keep our own vestments on.

Let us try another metaphor. Let us not think of the person, the native, as a sphere, with a surface to be stripped off or gotten through to the real stuff, the contents. Let us think of consciousness, or better yet, culture (how do we distinguish between these two ethereal constructions of consciousness, or culture?) as an activity—culture/consciousness as an activity not done by one person, but done among people, leaving its traces in memory (which we shall admit is a mystery), which will be part of the matrix for the next cultural act, the next interaction. Let us say that culture is in the interaction. After all, where else would it be?

Then when we view things this way, we find that there is no surface or depth. Instead there is only the turbulence of confrontation, with ourselves as part of it, and this turbulence is the most interesting, because the most active, thing. It is where the rocks get carved. We can study the rocks later. Now let us consider the turbulence in which we together with others are swept up.

In all this churning, surface and depth are commingled. Now our aim is not to get to the bottom of things, but to stay afloat. Now what is most important is not what we or others are, but what happens between us—what others present to us, and how we receive it, and what we present, and how that is received by them, and what comes out of it all, continuously, what is being formed, the eddies, the patterns of waves.[1]

PROBLEMS OF TRYING TO DISCOVER WHAT PEOPLE MEAN

In this chapter I wish to describe some ways in which members of Anni's family attempted to demonstrate to me some of the principles that they regarded as important in the living of their day-to-day lives. I say "attempted to demonstrate" in order to stress the intentionality of their performances before me. One of the various things that they did, and that I believe they intended to do, as they ate their meals, swept their floors, recited their prayers, conversed with each other in my presence and with me directly was to convey to me certain information about themselves, about their relationship with me, and about their relationships with others.[2] Sometimes these intentions were conveyed to me directly, explicitly, in so many words. Definitions of terms for my sake, explanations of and comments upon behavior, one's own and others', to me as an ignorant stranger wanting to know, were common. More often, the intentions behind actions were conveyed to me much more subtly.

I use the term "ideology" here to mean the articulable, and at least sometimes articulated, ideas people have about why they do what they do with respect to each other—in this case, why they express or act out particular feelings or relationships in particular ways, or conversely, what the feeling behind a particular act is supposed to be. Ideology, then, is conscious formulation of motives and intentions. It is not "underlying" but in a sense "overlaid." This does not necessarily mean, however, that it is false.[3]

Plate 14. Jnana Oli and Ayya.

In living with this family one desire that I had was to learn what love was to them. I had come to believe that love was something that they thought about, or perhaps did not think about, but had "in their minds" in some way. They had the word *anpu*, which seemed to mean something very like English "love," and various related words, *pācam* ("attachment"), *ācai* ("desire"), *paṯṯu* ("devotion"). They had been exposed to many formal teachings expounding upon and extolling love, and they were surrounded, filled, and made into human beings by a culture that said in a thousand ways that love was the highest good. But how was I to grasp what love (or anpu) meant to them, and how was I to put it down on paper in a believable way? If I offer a woman ten rupees for an interview and she says to me, "Money is not important, people are important,"[4] to me that is a statement conveying more than a message about the relative value, in objective terms, of people and money. It is also a statement conveying information about the speaker, that she values people over money, and therefore (perhaps) that she is a loving person. But how do I know that the intention to convey the latter message was "there" "in her mind"? How do I prove it?

Ultimately, I can't, for no proof of another's intentions is possible. All I can do is assert that my interpretation of this woman's statement was one that would be accepted as a valid possibility by some Tamil people, because those other people had explicitly linked such statements with feelings of love. It is important to recognize, however, that the indirectness of this woman's attribution of lovingness to herself, the nonexplicitness of it, was essential to the conveyance of the message. In Tamil Nadu you can't directly say, with any hope of credibility, "I am a loving person," for the loving are also humble. All you can do is show it.

In the ordinary course of affairs, people did not often talk about love. They talked about what was to be cooked for dinner, or what one of the children had done that day, or whether they should start plowing now or later. Occasional indirect references were made to love. Even more occasionally, words for love and words of love were used. Yet acts of love, including acts done in words, were as common, and as wrapped in cultural significations, as eating.

In this account of love in the family I lived with, I have deliberately avoided trying to sort out the "sincere" expressions of feelings and intentions from the "insincere" ones. That would obviously be too hard a task. But I also cannot claim that my account of what I experienced is free of all subjective evaluation. I brought with me to Tamil Nadu my own, deeply rooted, culturally developed feelings about what love is and should be. These feelings ran head-on into the enactments of anpu that my Tamil friends presented to me. My idea of love and their idea of anpu took deceptively similar forms. My Tamil friends and I were attracted to each other partly for that reason. I thought that they loved me. They thought that I felt anpu toward them. But just at those times when I thought that there was some fundamental something that all human beings shared, and that I had found that something at last in Tamil Nadu, suddenly some small act would cast a deep shadow between us again, and once again they were strangers, whom I feared and mistrusted. I found myself thinking, time after time, "But *this* isn't love." Now, after years, I can answer myself with detached amusement, "Of course it isn't love, it's anpu." Somehow, back then, this relativistic answer never occurred to me.

The present account is not a description of anpu as seen "from the native's point of view." Nor is it a description of love as it is expressed in the Tamil context. It is a discussion of anpu as seen through the eyes of someone conditioned to look for love: partly my own creation, partly those other people's. I was strongly attached to this family, I cared what they thought about me, they changed me, now they are a little bit mixed in me. To whatever extent I have incorporated them into myself, to that extent this chapter speaks their feelings.

PROPERTIES OF ANPU

Containment (Aḍakkam)

Discovering the meaning of love to this family was rendered difficult by the fact that for them, love was by nature and by right hidden. Ayya had much to say on this, as on many other topics. Explanations of everything flowed so easily from him that I have had to clap my hand over his mouth at many points in this book in order to give others a chance to speak. However, I have included observations of his which were particularly revealing of his role in the family, or which were strongly borne out by actions and statements of other family members. Of the hiddenness of love, he said, "*Anpu aḍaṅki peruki ni̲n̲rum*" [sic], which could be translated, "Love grows in hiding." *Aḍaṅku* means "be contained."

A mother's love for her child—*tāy pācam*—the strongest of all loves and the most highly valued, had to be kept contained and hidden. Anni said that a mother should never gaze lovingly into her child's face, especially while the child was sleeping, because the loving gaze itself could cause harm to the child. (She told me this when she caught me gazing at my own sleeping child's face in just this dangerous way. When I told her it was our custom to let people lead their own lives, she said simply, "*Tappu* [That is a mistake]." After some time I learned that if you cared about people, you would interfere.)

A mother would avoid looking with love at her sleeping child because her look could produce *kaṇ ḍrishṭi*, "the evil eye," though for Anni it was not an evil force so much as a merely harmful one. Anyone could gaze at anything with appreciation, without the slightest malice, and harm could come to that thing. But for a mother to gaze with love at her own child was the most dangerous gaze of all. "*Tāy kaṇṇē pullātatu* [The mother's gaze is the worst]," said Anni and other mothers to me. Many women, like Anni, would show affection for others' children, through affectionate words and looks, but they avoided such shows of love for their own children, especially in public.[5] It was not the existence of mother love, but its concentration displayed through the eyes, that was dangerous.[6]

Mother love had to be contained, not only in the sense of being hidden, but in the sense of being kept within limits. Thus, almost all of the many women with whom I spoke on this topic said that mother's milk should not be given to a child for more than ten months, just as a child should not stay in the womb for more than ten months. Mother's milk was a special substance because it was mixed with the feelings of the mother and transmitted them to the child. In particular, mother's milk contained the mother's love. After a child passed the age of ten months, mother's milk would become very "sweet" (*inippu*) to him, and he would be all the more difficult to wean. If he kept on nursing, women told me, he would get "too much love." Then he would become fat and proud (*timir*) and beat on his own mother. Thus, letting love overflow its bounds could be harmful not only to the recipient, but to the giver as well.

(This was in contrast to Ayya's idea that mother love, like mother's milk, was a limitless good. Hence he said that a child should be nursed for "at least three years." He himself had been nursed for five. Anni, arguing with him, had said that a child would be a burden to nurse for so long. Ayya had replied, "Is the fruit a burden to the fruit tree?" And Anni had said, "After the tree had dropped its fruit, if you tried to tie it back onto the branches again, yes, it would be a burden." Ayya was delighted with this response, and recounted the story in his lectures.)

Other kinds of love had to be concealed in other ways. There was, for instance, the convention of mutual avoidance in public between spouses, a convention that Anni and Annan scrupulously honored, rarely even looking at or talking with each other, while Padmini and Ayya exhibited before others a relationship of total mutual abrasion.

It was not that sexual display itself was considered dangerous, or the movie theatres would have been empty. Nor were physical expressions of love forbidden. In everyday life, adult males and females who were not spouses could show loving affection for one another with a casual freedom surprising to me. (Padmini and Anni, for instance, like to lean on the shoulders of some of Ayya's visiting male friends, or lie near them and gaze fondly into their eyes as they sang their devotional songs.) But spouses, who were supposed to love each other most and to focus their sexual feeling entirely upon each other, were expected to keep both feelings hidden.

No one ever said that the sentiments of sexual love should not exist. Sexual pleasure (*inpam,* "sweetness") was not an evil force. It was one of the four goals of life; any normal human being desired it. Sexual pleasure was supposed to be gotten only through marriage. Marriage was not, as it is said to be in some countries, a strictly economic arrangement. An important part of marriage preparations in Tamil Nadu was going to "see the girl" (*peṇṇai pārkka*). The groom would be taken by some of his elder kinsmen to visit the house of a girl ready for marriage. Usually at this point the potential bride and groom, if they did not already know each other, were allowed at least to have a glimpse of each other, and the question of whether they "liked" each other (*piḍittatu*) or not was one of those considered seriously when the final decision was made.

The significance of that first glance is made much of in Tamil literature. For instance, in Kampan's Tamil Ramayana, Rama and Sita first meet and fall in love with their eyes. Souls are said to mix through the eyes. The first sight of the potential spouse is a kind of *darshan*[7]—a powerful emotional encounter and a transfer of spiritual and sexual powers. A woman could lose her chastity through such a glance—stories were told of daughters who had been killed by their fathers for letting their eyes meet those of visiting strangers. The eyes, like the sexual organs themselves, contained love, and the husband (*kaṇavar,* derived from *kaṇ,* "eye," and *avar,* "he") was the one to whom the eyes were given, followed by the heart. In the darkness of both, his image would be kept, as the wife (*manaivi*, derived from *manai,* "house") would be kept hidden within the house—in principle, out of love. Thus in our family, when people talked about "being like husband and wife" (*purucan poṇḍāḍḍiyāka irukka*), it meant being physically and emotionally very close and going to bed together at night. But any hint of the existence of such a relationship in public communications between husband and wife, or by one about the other, was avoided.

The custom of a woman avoiding mention of her husband's name was only part of a much larger set of conventions for hiding love. Not only was the personal name of the husband never used, but if possible he was never referred to at all. Only a very Westernized woman would refer to her husband as "my husband" (*en kaṇavar, en purucan*). If a woman had to refer to her husband, she would do so through a relationship he had with some other person, as "the father of so-and-so" or "the teacher of so-and-so." Some women would whisper and point when they wished to make reference to their husband. Others would refer to their husband by his caste name, as "my Reddiar." I asked Anni the reason for this convention and she gave her usual enigmatic answer to questions of this sort: "Habit [*paṛakkam*]." Other women cited a belief that if a woman uttered her husband's name, harm would befall him. One function of name avoidance, then, was to wrap the husband in a protective silence, whose nature and intent were nevertheless known to all.[8]

The husband was not the only one to whom reference was avoided. Some men would avoid speaking their wife's name, referring to her simply as *avaḷ*, "she." Ayya referred to his younger sister, with whom he had been especially close in childhood, as "the teacher in the town of x," where she lived, and it took me some time to realize that he was speaking about his own sister. A Paraiyar man of twenty, whose mother was only thirty-three, and whose father had deserted the mother and her children, carefully avoided all reference to her, calling her "so-and-so's sister" (naming his uncle) when he was forced to allude to her. Having been left as the man of his mother's house, this seemed his strategy both for expressing and for denying his closeness to her. Anni referred to a good friend of Ayya's, of whom she was very fond, as "brother from y," naming the man's village. Sometimes long-term friends claimed not even to know each other's names.

The custom of avoiding direct reference to the loved one was fuzzy around the edges. Only in the case of reference to the husband was this custom more or less strictly adhered to by more or less all women. In other cases, the application of this custom appeared to be a matter of the speaker's own will. It was a tool used for one's own purposes and not a ritual dictated by immalleable rule.

Another way of hiding love was to openly downgrade the loved one. Thus, if a woman bore a series of children who died very young, when another child was born it would be given an ugly name such as Baldy (Moḍḍay), or Nosey (Mūkku), or Beggar's Bead (Piccaimaṇi), to protect it. A beautiful child would have its cheek smudged with ink. If a child was highly valued, to directly display one's high valuation of it brought it danger, and so one had to make a pretense (which everyone knew to be a pretense) of not caring for it at all.[9] The same attitude could also receive less conventional forms of expression. So a mother who had borne and lost seven children (by her own reckoning) dandled the eighth, whom she had adopted, by the roadside, playfully asking it, "Are you going to die? Are you going to die? [*Cettuppōviyā?*]," tempting fate as though the child's life was of little concern to her.

It is possible that the custom among Paraiyar and other, mainly low-caste, women of singing and speaking of their husbands in the most critical, derogatory terms[10] was motivated, at least for some women, by the desire to protect the mates to whom they were in reality strongly emotionally bonded, or even, perhaps, by a desire to *show* that they loved their husbands and were protecting them. A similar motivation may have existed among the many men who made a habit of speaking harshly to their wives before others. "Don't reveal your treasure," said the poetess Auvaiyar. So a rich man, to protect his wealth, might dress in rags. If one regarded one's spouse as a treasure, one might best display one's regard by hiding it, as one kept a treasured wife confined. Thus, while the exterior of the relationship among spouses was almost universally mute, where it was not harsh, the interior of this relationship had sometimes an exactly opposite quality.

Habit (Paṛakkam)

Love was often described as a force that was tender, gentle and slow. A loving heart was a soft heart (*menmaiyāna manacu*). A heart that was not moved by the feelings of others was like a stone ("Make your heart like a stone," a village man told me, when a drunkard came asking me for money).

Food metaphors for the tenderness of love were many. Of all the different kinds of food, sweet ripe fruit (*paṛam*), whose coming into existence was a gentle and gradual process, was probably most symbolic of love. A mango (*māmpaṛam*) was like a breast. You kneaded it between the palms of your hands until the pulp was a creamy juice, then you cut a small hole at the tip and sucked the juice out. In the story of the temple of Paṛani, the goddess Parvati makes her two sons compete for a golden mango that she holds in her hand. The older son Ganapathi wins the contest, to the chagrin of the younger Murugan, but then Ganapathi hands over his mother's mango to his younger sibling, saying, "Little brother, to me, you are the fruit [*paṛam nī*]." In Tamil Nadu it is a sin to cut down a fruit-bearing mango tree, just as it is a sin to kill a pregnant cow. I cannot help but think it significant that the mango tree is called *mā*.

Love, or attachment, or a sense of oneness with a person or thing or activity, grows slowly, by habituation (*paṛakkam*). Unlike the term anpu, the term paṛakkam was used frequently in our household, and was an important and complex part of people's thinking and day-to-day theorizing about human behavior. Any addictive habit, such as coffee drinking or cigarette smoking, was a paṛakkam. Ayya was fond of saying that he had "no habits of any kind [*enta vitamāna paṛakkamē illai*]," a statement meaning that he had no physical addictions; but this statement also expressed for himself and for others in the family what they saw as a more general aspect of his personality, his lack of attachment (*pācam*) to any human being. He stood apart (*otuṅki niṯkiṟēn*) he said, and he self-deprecatingly claimed that he had no love (*anpu*) in his heart, either.

According to popular theory, a person could become habituated to virtually any state of affairs, and once a situation became paṛakkam to a person, that person would not only feel comfortable with it, but would seek it out if deprived of it.

Magazine and folk stories mocked human beings for their slavery to paṛakkam. One story told of a beggar woman named Kuṇḍammā whom a king fell in love with and married. The woman had been fat as a beggar, but as a queen she became emaciated. At last she told her husband, "Just leave me alone in a room with my food from now on and let no one watch what I do." The king agreed to her request and his wife again grew fat. But one day he spied on her through a break in the wall. She had divided her food into piles and was going to each pile in turn saying, "Please, sir, I'm hungry. Give me some food," before taking a portion of the pile and eating it. Her paṛakkam was to eat only food she had begged, and she could not change it.

Another story told of a woman who sold fish for a living. Once she was caught in the rain and was forced to spend the night in a flower vendor's stall. She tried to sleep, but she tossed and turned because the smell of the flowers offended her nostrils. So she took her own empty basket, which stank of rotten fish, and put it over her head. Surrounded by the familiar smell, she slept comfortably for the rest of the night.

These stories were repeated for amusement in our household, but they in no way exaggerated what the family members felt to be true. The idea of paṛakkam explained and justified the differences between people. There was no point in trying to create a better way of life for others because people liked and wanted whatever it was they were used to having.

Once Anni and I were walking down a road in Madras when we saw a hovel built under a bridge. "Even here people live their lives," she said. "Like us, a man and a woman and children. They have a good life. They don't have to answer to anyone [*yārukkum patil colla vēṇḍām*]. We who are in the middle, neither rich nor poor, must suffer many burdens. But as for them, if one day they get two rupees, they live on two rupees. If they get one rupee, they live on one rupee. If they get nothing, they go hungry for a day."

"But isn't it hard to go hungry?" I asked.

"It is just paṛakkam," said Anni. "If I eat at a certain time today, I will want to eat at that same time tomorrow. For them, going hungry is a habit."

What you looked like and what you did showed to others what your paṛakkam was, and hence, what *you* were. To counteract paṛakkam was difficult, so isolated acts were considered rare. If a man was seen entering a liquor store, he revealed that liquor was his paṛakkam. Black skin showed that its owner's paṛakkam was to labor in the sun. To spurn food at a wedding was to announce that your paṛakkam was to eat something better. To give a gift was to commit yourself to a paṛakkam of gift-giving. Young village men with urban aspirations said that they didn't *know* how to work the land; it was not their paṛakkam.

Most paṛakkams were acquired by exposure to and absorption of certain elements in the environment, but a paṛakkam was not a superficial overlay upon a personality. It went deep in and at a certain undefined point became that personality. So, for instance, northern Madras was regarded as a dangerous place, because the people there were violent. "Why are they that way?" I asked Anni. "Because fighting is a habit they have practiced and practiced and that quality has grown in them [*atē paṛaki paṛaki anta kuṇam vaḷarum*]," she answered. Through repeated practice, through paṛakkam, an action would become a quality (*kuṇam*) of the person.

So deeply embedded in the person was paṛakkam that it was not lost even at death. Babies brought certain paṛakkams with them into the world. That a child was born possessing certain knowledge (for example, how to suckle), and more importantly, that children of the same womb could have such different paṛakkams, was strong evidence for the reality of transmigration, of there having been previous lives. If a baby had paṛakkams, resembling those of a recently deceased kinsperson, people would surmise that that baby had that kinsperson's soul (*uyir*). Most babies were not assigned an ancestral identity in this way, and there were no apparent rules regulating this particular kind of rebirth: the soul of a male ancestor could turn up in a female baby, and vice versa, and it could be born to any woman in the kinship group. But this kind of rebirth was observed often enough for people to say that souls liked to be reborn among their previous kin if they had any choice in the matter.

Hence the idea of paṛakkam was in some ways like the idea of karma (*vinai, pāvam-puṇṇiyam*). It was, and was created by, action; it was embedded in the person and it was hard to get rid of; it was carried from birth to birth and could be passed on from generation to generation. But it differed from the idea of karma in at least one crucial way: without paṛakkam, love was impossible.

From one point of view, as I have tried to suggest, paṛakkam *was* love, or rather, it was the behavioral side of a reality that had also an emotional component, as weeping consists of both sorrow and tears. Paṛakkam was the reason for the growth of the feeling of love; love was the reason for the continuation of paṛakkam. To know somebody, to spend time with them, to be familiar or intimate with them, was to have paṛakkam with them. When you had paṛakkam with a person, just as when you had paṛakkam with a substance, that person became part of your system. This was why it was so important to avoid going near bad or untouchable people, it was important not even to talk to them, at least not too much or in too friendly a way—because they might become paṛakkam. And then, as the six-year-old Umapathi had told me, "You would become like them."

Paṛakkam implied friendliness, easiness, grace, because an action to which one is habituated can be accomplished smoothly, and people to whom one is habituated are not feared. Many people told me that villages were easier than cities to live in because in a village people had paṛakkam with each other, and in the villages people were kinder. "In the villages they mingle lovingly [*anpāka paṛakuvārkaḷ*]," it was said.

Harshness and Cruelty (Kaḍumai, Koḍumai)

Paṛakkam was gentle and easy because its action was slow. Gradually it built the powerful bonds of love. And love itself, powerful as it was, was gentle and tender. Tender feelings (*menmaiyāna uṇarccikaḷ*) flowed (*pāyum*) most easily between people. Only feelings of love could melt the heart (*manacai urukkum*).

But equally as it was tender and slow, love was cruel and forceful. Cruelty was a characteristic of love acted out more often than spoken of. However, some people said outright, "Love is very cruel [*anpu mika koḍumaiyānatu*]" or "Attachment is very cruel [*pācam mika koḍumaiyānatu*]," and I heard these two statements often enough to suspect that they, too, like the melting heart, were common formulae.

We on this continent consider love to be cruel in the sense that April is the cruelest month. Our highest flights are made in love, and we take our hardest falls there, too. Really, it is the disappointment of love that is cruel, but since love is almost always disappointed, happy love songs are not the norm. All of this is American common sense, I think.

But the cruelty of love had quite a different meaning to the Tamil family with whom I stayed. *Pācam,* the bond of affection, was cruel, like American love, because when the bond was broken, as always it had to be, the newly unbound person suffered pain. When you become habituated to something it becomes part of you, and when you lose it, part of yourself is severed. Hence the adage, *Peyyinōḍum pirital kaṣḍam*, "Even from a demon, parting is painful." Pācam was called cruel by a person observing a child weep as her mother went out the door. But anpu, in its meaning of a higher and unselfish form of love, could be cruel in its very enactment, in and of itself.

Part of the reason for love's cruelty was that, because paṛakkam was hard to overcome, it was sometimes deemed necessary to violently force people to do what was in their own best interests. When times or situations changed, people had to change also. Hence Ayya's sister Porutcelvi, in describing how lovingly Ayya had raised her after their father died, said, "He beat me to make me study [*aḍittu paḍikkavaittārkaḷ*]." Their father had not believed in female education, and Porutcelvi had become accustomed to avoiding books. Similarly, Anni, in attesting to the loving nature of an aunt who had helped to raise her, said, "She beat me to make me eat [*aḍittu cāppiḍa vaittārkaḷ*]," after she had become accustomed to denying herself food in another aunt's household. Beating children in the hope of getting them to study better was an everyday occurrence in this household, for small children's paṛakkam is to play, but as they grow, they have to change, and ripening (*paṛuttal*), as Ayya told me, is a painful process. Beating children to make them eat did not appear to be necessary, except when they were sick. When people were ill and their appetites were off, it was especially important to force food down their throats, even if they gagged and vomited it up again. "At least the essence [*cattu*] of the food will be absorbed," said Anni. Sickness itself could too easily become paṛakkam.

Acts embodying the cruelty of love could also and simultaneously be acts hiding its tenderness. Thus, physical affection for children was expressed not through caresses but roughly, in the form of painful pinches, slaps, and tweaks, which left marks or drew blood. Frightening a beloved child, like deceiving it, was also a favorite pastime. After my young son Daniel was stung on the arm by a scorpion, Padmini suggested that we buy a rubber scorpion and put it on his arm "to see what he would do." Yet since his arrival in the household Daniel had been pampered, and, for the most part, treated like a little king. In 1982, Mohana bore a second child, who in 1984 when I revisited the home was a rugged, bold, and healthy toddler. But she was for some reason terrified of a toy lion that someone had bought for her. Mohana and Padmini enjoyed showing the toy lion to the little girl and watching her scream. Yet the little girl was a family favorite, not like a scapegoat or runt. Why were the household darlings singled out for such exquisite torments? "It's a kind of love [*oru vakaiyāna anpu*]," said Ayya in response to my puzzlement at such practices.

Among adults, this "kind of love" took the form of heated noisy quarrels, which, however, blew over quickly and often terminated in laughter. "You don't fight with those you don't love," said Ayya, and after some time it dawned upon me that, inasmuch as love was in large part a matter of mutual habituation, or, as we would say, interaction, then perhaps intense love required intense interaction.[11] The true sign of love's absence might be the absence of any interaction at all.

That my guess was not entirely wrong was suggested by my observation of an argument that occurred between Anni and Ayya while I looked on. A cousin had come to the house to discuss a land dispute with Annan. In Anni's presence, the cousin had said an obscene word, and Anni had turned her back and walked away. After the cousin was gone, Ayya had chastised Anni.

He told her, "When I say things that I should not say, you tell me,

'Don't speak that way in this house.' The meaning of those words is, 'This is *my* house and I make the rules in it,' whether or not that feeling is in your heart. In the same way, when Padmini or Vishvanathan speak wrongly, you say, 'Don't speak like that in front of me,' But today, when a person spoke wrong words on the front porch, you simply left. If you scold the people of the house for speaking wrongly, you should scold outsiders also."

Presumably, Ayya was criticizing Anni for inconsistency or for lack of nerve. If *anyone* acts wrongly, he seemed to be telling her, you should have the courage to tell them to their face that they are wrong. You should not reserve your criticisms just for family members. At the same time (I thought) Ayya was doing to Anni exactly what he was scolding her for—because she was so close to him, he was singling her out for especially harsh criticism. Moreover, Ayya himself had been present at the scene he was now analyzing. Why hadn't *he* spoken up when the offensive word was said?

After Ayya's lecture (which was much longer than my paraphrase of it here) Anni had left, angry and hurt. Later, I asked Anni how she felt about what Ayya had said. She answered, "In this world, money is everything. Those with money feel no need to respect those without it. When someone from such a world brings ugliness like that inside, you can't chew it and you can't swallow it [*mennavum muḍiyātu muṛuṅkavum muḍiyātu*]. You have to just walk away. But within the four walls of the house, we are all one [*nālu cuvarile ellārum o<u>n</u>ṟu tān*]. If someone does something wrong [*tava<u>r</u>u*], is it right or possible to hide it [*ma<u>r</u>aik-kalāmā*]? We have a conscience [*manacāḍci*] and we must speak our minds." Thus to honestly convey one's disapproval of another's actions might be a sign of love for, closeness with, that other, even though it could be misread by someone as close as Ayya was to Anni.

When mothers made their children cry, not in anger but in playful affection, it seemed to me that some force other than a need for mutual openness was at work. Or perhaps I should say, set of forces, because childrearing is one area of life in which cultural, social, psychological, and biological patterns converge, and find simultaneous expression in single acts. We might count among biological forces acting upon the mothers in this family the omnipresent facts of scarcity and hardship in their world. You *had* to be tough, you had to be able to endure a lot, you had to be able to absorb insults with equanimity, you had to be able to bear without perturbation the sight of others getting what you knew you deserved, in order to survive with your mind intact in late twentieth-century India. To maintain your dignity, you had to be willing to give up even your life and the lives of your loved ones, as the story of the family deity instructed. Our family was better off than most, but food was still less than enough to go around. Toys, books, nice clothes—all these were luxury items. So mothers in our family saw themselves as training their children to be tough, and showed themselves in this light. Luxuries and soft treatment should not become paṛakkam, they said. When a small child learned to deprive itself, to say no to a tempting sweet, this development was reported with glee to others as a significant advance.

Related to the fact of scarcity was the necessity of sharing. The joint family was, in part, an adaptation to scarcity. One roof and one hearth were more economical than three roofs and three hearths. If you cooked for ten, as I was told, you would always have enough for eleven. But the great danger to a joint family was that it would fracture along the lines dividing nuclear units—each pair of spouses with their respective children. Love, which naturally (*iyaṯkaiyāka*) was given to one's own, had to be redirected across those lines. The stronger the love, the stronger the force that had to be exerted against it, to drive it outwards. Consequently, in our family, mothers deliberately spurned or mistreated their own children, forcing their own and their children's affection away from the closest blood bond. A mother might do likewise with a grown daughter, Ayya said, harshly scolding her so that she would desire to marry, and so that once she did, her heart would go to her husband and she would be happy.

For a child's own good, to "grow" a child, in the name of love or just for fun, a caretaker might cruelly provoke love's opposite. As I was sitting in the rice mill, reading poetry with Ayya, Padmini came running to me laughing. "Daniel hit me with a stick," she reported delightedly. "He took it out of my hand and hit me with it. I'm glad to see he's gaining a little courage."

Daniel, who now as I write these words is fourteen, recently entertained us at a party with a discourse on his memories of Padmini.

"I hated her. It seemed like she was always picking on me. Once I got so mad at her I broke the glass bangles on her arm and poked her with the broken pieces."

"What did she do?"

"She poked me back. I had tried before to break her bangles but I wasn't able to do it. But that day I was so mad I broke them all."

"Well, at least, Dan, she taught you something."

"What?"

"Anger makes you strong."

"Yeah, but it didn't do much good."

The Tamil family where Dan and I lived was a place of balancing forces, and so was the world as a whole. The world as it presented itself to the senses, the world of the here and now, was baffling, deceptive, full of maya. But as a totality and in the long run it all made sense, it all balanced out. This family believed in karma, believed that everybody had committed some sins in the past for which they would eventually suffer punishment. It followed that if you wanted to contribute to someone's future happiness, the best way to do it was to make them miserable in the present and get the inevitable punishment overwith. The story was told of a man who was forced against his will to kill a goat and grieved until the goat came to him in a dream to thank him for completing a curse that had been laid on a prince, to die the death of a sacrificial goat ten times before he could be reborn as a prince again. This had been the tenth death. The goat's murderer had been its unwitting benefactor. But if you thought about it, you realized that life was always this way.

One mother (not of this family) told me, it was wrong to make a child laugh because for every moment of laughter that the child enjoyed now he would have to suffer a moment of tears in the future. As in the case of mother's milk, sweet pleasures had to be limited, balanced by bitterness. If hardship was a habit and had come to seem sweet, so much the better.

Dirtiness (Aṛukku)

Without question, to the members of our family, anpu was a good and powerful force. One who had love was in a very real sense "higher" (*uyarnta*) than one who did not. A loving heart was a pure (*tūymaiyāna*) heart. But love was often at odds with the demands of physical cleanliness and purity (*cuttam*). It was not that love was intrinsically impure (*acuttam*) but rather that in the presence of love, conventional purity did not matter. This was the ideal of the ancient Saiva devotional texts, the ideal of bhakti, and the members of our family, especially the women, lived it to the fullest.

On a supraworldly level, love as pācam was a bond, and therefore an obstacle in the quest for purity, which meant the breaking of all bonds. Love as desire (*ācai*) was even worse, because it provoked restlessness (*alaiccal*), which prevented the peacefulness necessary to the maintenance of a pure heart. Ayya had tried to teach me these principles in his lectures.

But in regular life, things were viewed rather differently. A person could be praised for having "much affection" (*rompa pācam*). A calf taking its first steps would be described as "causing desire" (*ācaiyāy irukkum*), that is to say, being attractive. The trait in the calf, the feeling, the person who could feel it, none of these were wrong to be as they were. Indeed, something was wrong when the trait and the feeling were not there. The calf who was sick and unable to walk, the man who had no affection for others, these were not as they should be.

The term anpu could mean lustful infatuation (as in the case of the smitten demon, described below); it could mean clinging possessiveness (an old woman who accused her octogenarian husband of having five women a day was said to have had "too much anpu"). But more often it referred to a certain generosity of spirit, as well as of pocketbook. In this sense it was the opposite of ācai, though in its broader sense it encompassed the latter meaning also.

What anpu never meant was extrication of oneself from others or from the processes of life. Indeed to our family, and most of all to its linchpin Anni, it meant just the opposite. It seemed that Anni was engaged in a constant campaign to combat the forces of purity and to promote the forces of love. It was she who allowed the lower caste servants to help in cooking, defying the wishes of her mother-in-law. She herself engaged in food preparation even during her periods, mixing the tub of lemon rice with her bare hands. (Ayya had told me that if a woman during her period touched a growing plant, the plant would wither; if she touched a metal pot with her hand, the metal would corrode.) When Anni served me dinner, she would set aside the serving spoon and ladle the rice onto my leaf with her hand. When we went to visit a great Saiva temple and I carelessly forgot to remove my son's shoes from his feet before we went in, other people pointed and scowled, but Anni said, "It doesn't matter. Let him be." When, in an attempt to formally interview Anni, I asked her, "What are the most important things that a mother should know?", Anni's first answer was, "How to suck mucus from a baby's nose." Later, when my smaller son had dysentery, Anni was the one who washed his diapers.

One day, when I had finished eating, and Anni as usual had rushed to pick up my leaf, I said to her, "You must like bodily effluvia [*eccil*]." Anni answered that picking up another's leaf was an act of merit (*puṇṇiyam*). I said that if that was the case, Modday the servant must have a lot of merit. Anni said that she did. More often, however, when I asked Anni to tell me why she broke the rules of purity that I had thought all good Hindus followed, she would say, "These are advanced times when all are one and no one is alone."

In this household, the defiance of rules of purity conveyed a message of union and equality and was a way of teaching children and onlookers where love was. So, for instance, when Anuradha was eating rice with buttermilk, after she had eaten for a while and Jnana Oli (the two-year-old son of Padmini) and Sivamani (the two-year-old son of Mohana) appeared, she called Sivamani to drink some buttermilk: she fed him some rice from her plate with her hand and then had him drink some buttermilk from her plate. Then she had Jnana Oli drink some buttermilk from her plate, then Siva, then Oli, until both said "Enough." Then she herself drank down the rest.

Anuradha's feeding of the two little boys in this fashion accorded with the many deliberate attempts on the part of older people in the household to twin these children and foster love between them. Annan would often seat the two boys opposite each other on his two knees, with a single toy between them that he taught them to share. When the boys went out with their mothers, each woman would carry the other's son. The mothers themselves shared the kind of love that they hoped their sons would share. Padmini and Mohana, who had grown up together, went everywhere together, shared everything, and claimed to be "like husband and wife," often ate together from the same pot or bowl, alternating mouthfuls between them, in the same way that Anuradha fed their two sons. Watching me watch them eat like this one day, Ayya, standing by, knowing my fear of sickness, explained to me that eccil shared in love would not cause disease but would cure it. People who love each other will eat from each other's plates or leaves without thought of sickness. He said that he himself had never loved anyone that much.

Humility (Paṇivu)

Love was complexly implicated in expressions of pride and humility, servitude and domination, possession and renunciation. Through love, all these opposites were overturned. In acts of love, the humble became proud, the servant became master, the renouncer became possessed. Just as through love tenderness might be enacted as cruelty, so through love hierarchy took ironic forms.

In a typical bhaktic reversal of the symbols of high and low, Ayya had said in a lecture, "God is like a sandal, he is the foundation of all of us. God is like a broom, he makes the world clean."

But Anni had gone beyond him in the bhaktic elaboration of broom symbolism. Ayya and Padmini had quarreled and his anger with her had lingered. He had not spoken to her in days. The whole household was gloomy because of this. At the end of the third day, Anni had come marching up to him with a broom in her hand.

"I thought she was going to beat me with it," Ayya said later. But she had not.

"What is this for?" Anni asked.

"For sweeping," said Ayya.

"How often do we use it?" said Anni.

"Every day," said Ayya.

"What would happen if we didn't?" asked Anni.

"Dirt would collect in the house," said Ayya.

"All right," said Anni, "Quarrels are like dirt. They come into the house every day. Every day we have to sweep them away and start over."

Anni had used the broom, symbol of humility, as a symbol of forgiveness, forebearance, and patience (*poṟumai,* the strength to sustain, to endure, to bear up) as well as of purification, harmony in the household, and control.

Like the broom, sandals were a symbol of hierarchy, but their meaning as a symbol was reversible. To wear sandals was a sign of high status, wealth, pride, and in some circumstances, arrogance. To be without sandals, conversely, was a sign of humility. To be called a sandal, or to be beaten by a sandal, was a grave insult. Harijans could not wear sandals in the high-caste part of the village; human beings could not wear sandals in temples where the gods lived. One could not wear sandals in a field of growing rice; it would hurt the rice. One could not enter a person's home or go where people were eating with one's sandals on; to do so would be to show great contempt for the home or the food. The arrogance of the British was shown by their custom of going everywhere in their shoes.

Aside from such interactional considerations, there were attributional ones; in general people noticed whether one wore footgear, and if so, what kind. Yokels went without sandals; sophisticates did not. Laborers went without sandals; the educated did not. The poor went without sandals; the rich did not. Plastic or rubber sandals were much inferior to leather ones, but to go barefoot on the streets was lowest of all.

Yet wherever they went, Anni, Padmini, and Mohana never wore sandals. They were the only middle-class women I knew who publicly went barefoot. I offered to buy them sandals. They refused. I tried to go barefoot like them. They mocked me and said that my feet would not be able to bear the hot sand and gravel, and they were right. They also lacked other trappings of civilized womanhood, such as gold jewelry. Each of them wore one glass bangle on each arm. Between them they owned six or eight cotton and polyester saris, four or five silk ones (much fewer than some individual landless laborers). They preferred polyester clothing because, in Anni's words, "it works hard" *(uṛaikkum)* and was fit for a working woman. Cotton, especially homespun cotton (Gandhi's symbol of humility) tore easily said the women and was an expensive luxury.

When Padmini waited for the bus, she sat down on the bare soil, as only village women would do, and she teased me for standing, "as though you're being punished," she said. Such behavior fit into the ethos that

Padmini and her sister and cousin had worked out for themselves—they were simple *(eḷimai)* by choice; and they were protectors, not in need of protection. The spurning of sandals proved that they needed nothing between themselves and the sun-baked soil. When they went out, they walked with their backs straight and their heads held high, and they took long strides so that everyone could see their naked toes.

Ayya also often went barefoot. Friends would buy him sandals, and he would slip them off his feet on the train to Madras and then walk off leaving them behind. He lost umbrellas in a similar way. Finally he determined not to waste more money on umbrellas and sandals and went without either. His clothing consisted of two rectangular strips of thin white cotton—one a waistcloth which hung to his feet, the other wrapped around his shoulders. His friends and followers all wore shirts, trousers, watches—signs of status, education, and ties with the city. Only on important religious holidays did they dress like their guru, Ayya. In his younger days, Ayya said, he had also worn shirts, trousers, watch, and underwear, but one by one these symbols of social achievement had been discarded, and he, like the women, now kept little between himself and the world.

Poverty and Simplicity (Eṛumai, Eḷimai)

At the time that I lived with them, the family was poor. Extra clothing and jewelry would have burdened the household budget severely. Their quasi-ascetic behavior might be dismissed as an attempt to make a virtue of necessity, a concession to reality. But as it related to the ideology of love, their attitude toward poverty had more aggressive meanings. For by defining themselves as beyond the hierarchy established by wealth, they negated the values that legitimized this hierarchy and so (at least temporarily and to their own satisfaction) turned it on its head.

In Tamil Nadu of the 1980s, status games were played in great earnest by people at all levels of society, and wealth was by far the most important indicator of status. Families would commonly go deeply into debt for the sake of conspicuous display. For most families who had a daughter to be married, it was a matter of utmost importance that they celebrate the wedding as lavishly as they could and provide their daughter with a very large dowry. The custom of offering and demanding dowries had been outlawed as a social evil by state and central governments, but the law was unenforceable. Many young men saw it as their right to be showered with wonderful gifts on their wedding day. Poor boys as well as rich ones fantasized a postmarital paradise constructed of cinematographic delights. A prospective bridegroom looked forward to the day when he would have not only a jewel-bedecked wife by his side, but also a gold chain around his neck, a watch flashing on his wrist, a stylish wardrobe, a motorcycle, and more. Many parents, as well, measured the worth of a new daughter-in-law by the money and jewels she brought with her at marriage. If these gifts were less than what her in-laws hoped for, the girl would be held to blame, perhaps mistreated. To make matters worse, newspapers reported that "dowry-burnings"—in which young women were immolated by their in-laws as a way of punishing their parents for not coming up with the "promised dowry"— were occurring with increasing frequency. Though no one I met in Tamil Nadu was aware of any local cases of girls being murdered by their husbands or in-laws for the sake of money, still, the news reports from North India made everybody anxious. People felt compelled, therefore, to spend as much as five years' income on their daughters' weddings: the status of the family and the daughter's future were both at stake, they felt. Those who had little to spend in the first place were swept up (and cleaned out) by this tide, equally with the wealthy. As one Paraiyar man put it, "Now all the poor people are trying to celebrate their marriages the way millionaires do." For a boy not to demand a large dowry was to devalue his own family, but a groom's refusal of dowry could also be interpreted as a charitable and honorable act. For a father not to offer a dowry with his daughter, however, was to invite shame (*paṛi*), the one thing that Ayya, according to his own claim, feared most. The hardship that parents must undergo in order to scrape up a dowry for their daughter and marry her "well" is often interpreted as an act of loving sacrifice done for the sake of the daughter. Feelings of love and feelings of pride are both expressed through marriage expenditure, even though many who speak of it call it an evil.

But when the family into which Ayya had married sought a husband for the twenty-year-old Anuradha, they refused to offer a dowry with her. "When someone asks us, 'What will you give?' we say, 'We give only the girl [*peṇ tān koḍuppōm*],'" Ayya declared defiantly.

Without a dowry to offer, they had to search hard to find a suitable groom for Anuradha. I wondered if they would succeed. For those who fail, there are excuses: the daughter does not "want" to marry, no groom is good enough, the horoscopes never match. But these cannot counter the strength of opinion that a woman can never be happy without a husband and children.

Finally a groom was found for Anuradha, in far away Andhra Pradesh. It was a two-day journey by train. Frequent visits would not be possible. And the people in Andhra spoke a kind of Telugu that neither Anuradha nor her parents could comprehend. But Anni said the groom was kind.

Smilingly she reported to me that he doted on Anuradha so much he would never let her go anywhere without him (whether this was the whole story or not I would never be able to know). "He is poor, but he is a hard worker," said Ayya pleased.

In this context, money contrasted with higher things, with love, good character, pride, and as long as the family was poor, so it would be. "We are the poorest [among the landowning families of the village]," said Ayya, "because we give the most to others, and all the people know it. We are the most respected."

The family's relative poverty with respect to others in the village was proof of its moral superiority. In the same way, individuals within the family used their ability to do without to establish the superiority of their love. Anni said, "Whatever Ayya does not need, we do not need." Since Ayya did not drink coffee, she would not drink coffee. If Ayya refused to go to the cinema, she would also stay at home. If Ayya bought her nothing to wear, she would be content with her old clothes. There was something more than submission in her simplicity, for she undertook it in a spirit of hard-nosed boldness. Ayya called it *tairiyam* "nerve." It took some courage, he said, for Anni to maintain her practice of loving self-denial in public. When the women attended a wedding, barefoot and unadorned, Padmini escaped reproach. She was the wife of a man who had acquired the reputation of a renouncer, and it was only right (in the eyes of many) for her to become a renouncer also. But Anni was subject to scarcely concealed pity and scorn. A woman would glance at her, touch her own ears, nose, wrists, and throat, turn her palms upward, shrug, and project her lower lip, saying in the gesture language used for messages that should not be spoken aloud, "This pitiful woman has no jewelry." But Anni was not perturbed. Luxuries and sins were both, to her, *tēvai illai*, "not needed." Meanwhile, she indulged Ayya with yogurt and ghee, expenses that he had tried to give up but could not resist, while she herself never consumed them. Milk and its products were only for children, she said.

In the matter of renunciation of luxury, Padmini followed Anni and Mohana followed Padmini. It was a weakness, a sign of minority, to take more and show that you needed more. Just as it was a sign of growing up for a toddler to say, "No thank you," so it was a sign of being most grown up of all to deny oneself more than others. Anni, being most grown up of all the women, showed that she needed the least. She claimed that she would only wear saris that had been discarded by the younger women, because people would laugh at a woman "of our age" (mid- to late-thirties) if she wore a new sari. Anni said Anuradha showed that she was "grown up," *vaḷarntāccu,* on her eighteenth birthday, when Anni had typhoid, and Anuradha had wept, saying, "I don't want new clothes, I don't want a birthday at all as long as you are sick." To do without was a matter of pride, a matter of seniority or maturity, and most of all, a matter of love.

Servitude (Aḍimai)

Aḍakkam meant containment. It also meant control, both of oneself and of others. One also contained one's beloved. Containment and protection (*pātukāppu*) were both forms of binding (*kāppu*), which devolved from affection (*pācam*), itself a bond.

The reciprocal of aḍakkam was *aḍimai*, servitude, the state of being controlled by another, of being bound. Becoming aḍimai, like exercising aḍakkam, could be a powerful expression of love. But if aḍakkam entailed pride, aḍimai entailed humility (*paṇivu*). If aḍakkam meant having something to hold on to, aḍimai meant having nothing of one's own.

However as love turned acts of humility into acts of pride, so it turned acts of servitude into acts of dominance.[12] This reversal was particularly dramatic given the generally low esteem in which the family held servants as a class. Anni spoke scornfully of what she called "the servant mind" (*vēlaikkāra putti*). Ayya and others would also speak of the "slave mentality" (*aḍimai manōpāṇmai*—a term said to have been coined by C. N. Annadurai) of Indians as a cause of their current inability to rejuvenate their nation. Slaves and servants were the lowest of human beings and the most severely shackled.

But a slave of love was a different matter. A slave to the love of God possessed nearly unlimited power. In Tamil Nadu, and all over India, there are countless stories of devotees who, through their love of God, force God to do their bidding. And in human society, a servant of god was a recipient of the highest respect. Members of Saiva sects in formal discourse would symbolically abase, and elevate, themselves by calling themselves not "I" (*nān*) but "this slave" (*aḍiyēn*), while the guru who was nearly deified after his death would be called "the servant" (*aḍikaḷ*).

But the transformation of servant into master was not dependent upon reference to God or any sentiment of religious devotion. There was in our family a pronounced feeling that servants could easily gain the upper hand, a feeling exacerbated by the current shaky status of the family in village politics and the intercaste conflicts in which they were embroiled. There was an intuitive recognition of Sartre's dictum that in reality, the master is the slave. Thus when I said to Anni that I felt she was treating me like a queen, she replied, "A queen has no freedom."

However, the servitude of love, as it was practiced everyday by Anni, was more than potentially dominating; it was actually so. Her absolute control as servant was epitomized in her role as family food dispenser. It was she who decided who ate what and when, while if there was an order to eating, Anni ate last. There would sometimes be quantities of biscuits or fruit in the house, which Anni or one of the men would buy. No one would ever help themselves to them or ask for them. Instead Anni would dole them out, one by one. The children of the family were absolutely under her governance with respect not only to what and when and how much they ate, but from whom they were allowed to accept food.

Anni was notorious for her aggressive feeding behavior. It is a custom in Tamil Nadu for women to heap food on the plates of guests even after the guests are stuffed and vehemently refuse further servings. One gets accustomed to this and eventually one learns to stave off incoming servings by putting one's hand over one's leaf and saying "Enough," very loudly and with firm eye contact. But in this game, Anni was a more formidable opponent than most. Trying to keep her from slipping two more rice cakes under one's hands onto the leaf was a challenge of speed and dexterity. Friends would joke that they were afraid to visit the house because of Anni.[13]

I was often irritated by what I perceived as Anni's strong-arm style of solicitude, but at a certain point I came to learn that in Tamil Nadu, Anni's method might sometimes be the only way to get people fed. Anni, Padmini, Vishvanathan, Daniel, and I were on our way to a wedding. It was a five-hour train ride. We shared a compartment with a mother and her child, and a man and a child accompanying him. The child with the man was unwashed and poorly dressed. I asked the man if the child was his. He said no, it was a relative's child. The people in our party ate the food we had brought along. First Daniel ate, then I did, then Vishvanathan, then Padmini, then Anni. The mother and her child ate food that they had brought. The man had disappeared somewhere; the child that had come with him sat silently. Even when he was crushed between two sleeping adults, he did not speak or move.

Anni woke up the adults who were crushing the child. She coaxed the child to eat. When he refused, she called his guardian and told him to order the child to eat. Once started, the child ate ravenously. Then the other mother powdered the face of the child and asked if he had a mother. The child said no. Anni said you could tell by looking at him.

Opposition and Reversal (Etirttal, Puraṭci)

Love, as it was defined and enacted by our family, brought about reversals of all kinds. The closest bonds were concealed by denial of bonds, tenderness was transformed into cruelty, humility could be an expression of pride, servitude a means toward mastery. All of these reversals had their reasons, some of which were by no means culture-bound. Apparently reasonless reversals also took place. Nowhere could this activity of love be seen more clearly than in people's use of the word "mother" (*ammā*), the one word in the Tamil language more imbued than any other with sentiments of love.

As a term of address, ammā could be applied to the following people:

- One's own mother, or someone in the category of mother, such as mother's sister. So the children of the family called Anni "Annimma," and Padmini, "Pappimma."
- A superior female. For such a person, ammā was a term of respect and distance. Village adults wishing to show respect for me would call me ammā, even when they were older than me.
- A female of approximately equal status to, or lower status than, the speaker. Often in this case the use of the term ammā was part of hostile and sarcastic exchanges, as between sisters-in-law, or when a husband was scolding his wife.
- A male of equal or lower status than the speaker. When one addressed such a person as ammā, one was showing affection for him. So Annan often called Ayya ammā, and Anni addressed the male servants in her mother's home as ammā, in both cases with obvious affection. But this usage of ammā was one that occurred all over Tamil Nadu.

Conversely, *appā*, "father," was used as a term of affection for a female of equal or lower status than the speaker. The very intimate, even derogatory, terms *-ḍi* ("girl") and *-ḍā* ("boy") could be used in the same way, so that a man might address a woman whom he didn't know very well as "boy," to indicate brotherly friendliness towards her, while it would have been completely inappropriate, and very rude, for him to call the same woman "girl."

When I searched for an explanation for these customs, family members said they did not know. Ayya suggested that the reason was, "Love does not know head or tail." This struck me as plausible, given other aspects of the ideology of love in Tamil culture that I had learned. To show affection for someone, you demonstrated in a conventionalized way that you had forgotten what category they belonged to.

Mingling and Confusion (Kalattal, Mayakkam)

Love, then, mixed you up (*mayakkum*). A person who fell, as we would say, head-over-heels in love with another, was suffering, as it would be said in Tamil, from *mayakkam*, dizziness, confusion, intoxication, delusion. The same word was used to describe all these states. In all of them,

Plate 15. Daniel dressed as a girl by Anni, Padmini, and Mohana.

one lost one's ability to think clearly, or even to think at all. Then one could not be blamed for acting strangely. And one could easily be misused by others. The intoxication of love was notoriously dangerous for just this reason. A servant in a Brahman household jokingly said that a Brahman girl learns to sing so that when a potential suitor comes to visit and hears her voice in the other room "he will become confused [*mayankuvān*]" and marry her. Young men, and to an even greater extent, young women, were vulnerable to mayakkam, which could be produced by hypnosis or potions or spells as well as by the smell of certain flowers or, as above, by music. As a person grew older, especially a woman, she would be more resistant to mayakkam. Then she would be less in need of protection.

Love, through mayakkam, could make a person see exactly the opposite of what was there. The story was told in our household of a Saiva guru to whom an ignorant low-caste admirer, out of great love, offered a piece of raw meat. South Indian Saivas regard meat-eating as not only impure, but revolting. At the same time they imagine that the lowest castes especially relish raw meat. This is one thing that makes them low. But in the story the guru to whom this foul offering was made saw only the love, and blinded by this love to the physical realities of caste and taste, ate the meat as though it were a ripe piece of fruit, much to his less enlightened followers' disgust.

In a play shown in our village, the goddess Adiparasakti was created to destroy a demon. This goddess was huge and green, she bit her bright red tongue angrily, and she stomped about the stage wielding a sharp trident. The demon in the play took one look at her and was smitten with desire. He went home to tell his sidekick of the beauty of his new heart-throb. The sidekick at first was baffled. Then sudden comprehension lit up his face and he nodded and smiled like an eager puppy. "*Aha, ampu, ampu!*" he said, "Love, love!" ("Ampu," the sidekick's dopey rendering of anpu, also means "arrow." In this play, the pun was certainly intentional.)

Love as it was understood by our family not only reversed opposites, but erased distinctions completely. There will be nothing novel to Westerners in this idea; it is important only that we realize that for the Tamil family also, "mixture" (*kalattal*) was a consciously recognized attribute of what for them also was the overarching ideal of love. This was the meaning of Anni's reiteration that "we are all one," both here, "within these four walls," and now, "in these advanced times." People's presence with each other made them mix with each other, become used to each other, become one.

It was impolite, because it was unloving, to treat oneself and one's own with more favor than one allowed others, at least "within the four walls," in places where love should prevail. To discriminate was *ōra vañcakam*, "the deceitfulness of boundaries," that is, drawing lines. The most polite, most loving pronoun was the first person singular inclusive *nām*, "we" (including you). One used it, within the very innermost walls, when talking in one's mind to oneself. One used it when referring either to "my house" or to "your house." Both were called, politely, "our house." Anni elevated me to the status of her equal by often referring to "women of our age" (*nam vayacu*) and laying out the rules that we both should follow. It caused members of our family distress when I used the term "your children." All of them, including my own, were "our children," and if I needed to distinguish between them, I should refer to them by name. In the extreme, this mixture of yours and mine into ours became reversed again—mine were called yours, and yours mine. So when I wrote to Ayya's sister Porutcelvi that my second child had been born, she wrote back, "I can't wait to see my new son."

This kind of total mixing, the sharing and trading of homes, of children, of selves, was necessary for the existence of love. So Ayya offered an explanation of the Kaṇṇappan story, a story he returned to again and again, of a devotee so loving he tore out his eye to use as medicine on an image of Siva when he saw that the eye of the image was bleeding. Then the second eye of the image started to bleed and Kaṇṇappan reached for this own second eye, to tear it out like the first, when Siva stopped him. Ayya said, "This story proves that God has no love. Otherwise he would have recognized Kaṇṇappan's love from the first, and saved both his eyes, not only one. It was only after Kaṇṇappan placed one of his eyes on the image that God, seeing through Kaṇṇappan's eye, understood Kaṇṇappan's pain.

"In order for you to understand my heart, you must see through my eyes. In order for me to understand your heart, I must see through yours."

CHAPTER FOUR

Desire In Kinship

A NOTE TO THE READER

Getting through this chapter will take patience. Please have faith. Kinship jargon and diagrams can look forbidding from certain angles, and perhaps some readers, finding them here, may say, "Why is she doing this to us? What does this have to do with anything real?" I will try to explain.

Tamils and neighboring peoples have a very elegant set of ways of organizing their families and larger kin groups into patterned systems. Any person trying to understand South Indian culture must eventually come round to examining and trying to comprehend these elegant patterns of kinship organization. They connect with many things that are happening in the South Indian world.

The kinship patterns to be sketched in the following pages are, moreover, important to us just because an enormous amount has been written about them by Western scholars. These patterns are *attractive* to these scholars for some reason. One reason I would suggest, a sad one, is that we may, if we wish, study these abstract patterns just as such, as patterns, without ever having to deal with real people, their demands, their suffering, their embarrassing similarity to our less-than-perfect personal selves, the selves we try to conceal and transcend by means of our scholarly and artistic productions.

The second reason—a happier version, actually, of the first, sad one—is that these patterns have a kind of real beauty. I would argue that South Indian people create such patterns not only because they "work," not only because they perform some necessary social "function," but also because, in their beauty, they give their creators pleasure. And we, if we try, may find pleasure in them, too. Kinship patterns can be understood as objects of artistic appreciation, in the same way that mathematical proofs or car engines are, for some people, such objects. Opening the hood of a fancy sports car, some of us will see nothing but a confusing jumble of ugly machinery. Others, who understand such things, will be perfused with bliss. It is the same with kinship patterns.

In this chapter and the ones that come after, I try to show that kinship organization is as much a matter of feeling as it is of thinking, or, to use more scholarly words, that kinship is as much a matter of "affect" and free form "aesthetics" as it is a matter of "cognition" and social "regulation." I also try to show that there is a continuity between abstract patterns of kinship organization and the lived reality of actual people on the ground. To do this, I start with a discussion of the abstract aspects of Tamil kinship and move gradually back down to the concrete. This note is here mainly to cushion the shock some people may feel at the sudden ascent from the cozy heat of the last chapter to the lonely cold of this one. But be patient. Eventually we will come back to earth again.

SYSTEMS AND ANTISYSTEMS

". . . two forms there in the endless sea danced . . ."

Tirukkōvaiyār, 307.

The common denominator of most South Indian (and Sri Lankan) kinship systems is the presence of preferred or prescribed cross-cousin marriage: a man marries a woman in the category of his father's sister's daughter, his mother's brother's daughter, or in a few cases, his own sister's daughter. Some groups allow all of these possibilities. Most reported groups are said to practice marriage in one direction only: generally, a man may marry his mother's brother's daughter (this is called "matrilateral cross-cousin marriage"), but marriage with the father's sister's daughter is disapproved. Much less frequently, the reverse type of marriage, in which a man weds his father's sister's daughter ("patrilateral") is preferred.

Dravidian kinship terminology reflects and to a large measure helps to constitute what is called "Dravidian kinship" by defining categories of kin and by clearly displaying, through its own formal symmetries, the symmetries among these categories (figures 4, 5, 6, 7). The term "Dravidian" refers to a family of languages spoken mainly in South India. The Dravidian language family is entirely distinct both in structure and in presumed origin from the family of Indo-Aryan languages spoken in North India. The Dravidian kinship terminology varies somewhat from region to region in South India, but within a given region the terminology is the same regardless of what variant of the marriage system is preferred by a given

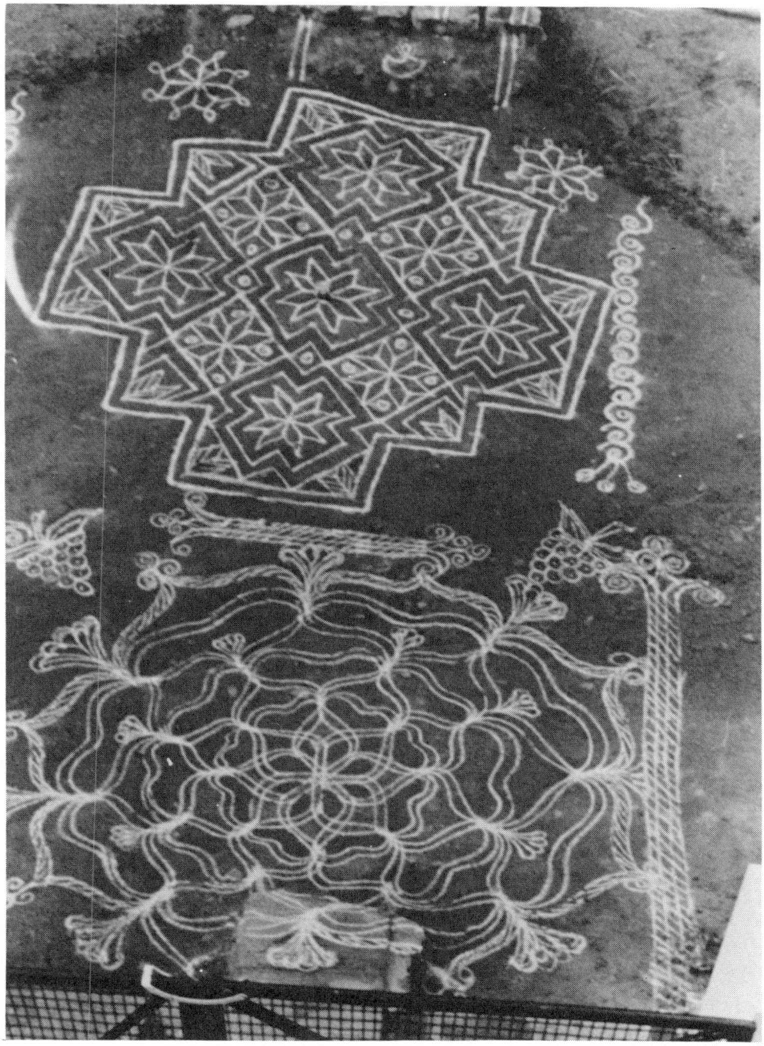

Plate 16. Kolams.

group.[1] Moreover, though kin *terms* vary from language to language, the overall semantic *structure* of Dravidian kinship terminologies remains essentially the same throughout South India. Hence, for instance, in most of the Dravidian terminological systems, a single term (e.g., in Tamil, *māman*) denotes mother's brother, father's sister's husband, and father-in-law; likewise, a single term (in Tamil, *attai*) denotes father's sister, mother's brother's wife, and mother-in-law; a single term (in Tamil,

Figure 4. Tamil kin terms.

pāḍḍi	Grandmother, spouse's grandmother, kinswoman of one's grandparents' generation.
tātā	Grandfather, spouse's grandfather, kinsman of one's grandparents' generation.
ammā	Mother, mother's sister, mother of any parallel cousin.
appā	Father, father's brother, father of any parallel cousin.
attai	Mother-in-law, father's sister, mother of any cross-cousin.
māman	Father-in-law, mother's brother, father of any cross-cousin.
akkā	Elder sister, female parallel cousin older than self.
taṅkai	Younger sister, female parallel cousin younger than self.
aṇṇan	Older brother, male parallel cousin older than self.
tampi	Younger brother, male parallel cousin younger than self.
purucan	Husband.
manaivi	Wife.
nān	"I." (Used in the diagrams here to designate self or ego).
maccān	Father's sister's son, mother's brother's son, male cross-cousin.
macci	Father's sister's daughter, mother's brother's daughter, female cross-cousin.
makan	Own son, son of same-sex sibling, own child's male parallel cousin.
makaḷ	Own daughter, daughter of same-sex sibling, own child's female parallel cousin.
marumakan	Son-in-law, son of opposite-sex sibling, own child's male cross-cousin.
marumakaḷ	Daughter-in-law, daughter of opposite-sex sibling, own child's female cross-cousin.
pēran	Grandson, kinsman of one's grandchildren's generation.
pētti	Granddaughter, kinswoman of one's grandchildren's generation.

Parallel-cousins and Cross-cousins

Relatives of one's own generation are all classed either as parallel-cousins or as cross-cousins, and are called by the appropriate kin terms. Cross-cousins are considered potential spouses. Parallel cousins are considered siblings, therefore not potential spouses. Whether a cousin is cross or parallel may be determined by looking at the linking relatives, that is, the line of people through whom one traces one's relationship with that cousin. Add up the number of primary cross-cousin links in this line (mother's brothers, father's sisters, man's sister's children, woman's brother's children) and the number of spousal links (husbands, wives). If the number is odd, the cousin is cross. If the number is even or zero, the cousin is parallel. My sister's husband's sister is my cross-cousin. My mother's brother's daughter's husband is my parallel cousin. My father's father's sister's daughter's son is my cross-cousin. My mother's father's sister's husband's sister's daughter's child is my parallel cousin. And so forth.

Another way of looking at this is to say that a cross is like a minus and a parallel is like a plus. Parallel times parallel equals parallel. Cross times cross equals parallel. Cross times cross times cross equals cross again. Spouses are cross and the children of opposite sex siblings are cross. Siblings are parallel and the children of same sex siblings are parallel.

maccān) denotes father's sister's son, mother's brother's son, and wife's brother; and a single term (in Tamil, *macci*) denotes father's sister's daughter, mother's brother's daughter, and wife's sister (the latter two categories are also often bifurcated into elder-than-ego versus younger-than-ego.) This shared semantic structure strongly suggests a system of bilateral cross-cousin marriage: in the ideal, two men exchange sisters in marriage, and their sons also exchange sisters, and so on down through the generations, so that the mother's brother's daughter and the father's sister's daughter are the same person. Real life, of course, seldom if ever matches this ideal. Indeed in Dravidian kinship it is necessary to speak not of two but of three levels of ideal versus reality: level A is the bilateral marriage ideal indicated by the terminology itself; level B is the preferred marriage pattern of a given group, which is usually unilateral and which therefore only partially fulfills the conditions set by level A; level C is the set of actual marriages which take place. For this third level, what statistical information is available indicates that among groups who use a Dravidian kinship terminology, actual cross-cousin marriage takes place less than 50 percent of the time, so that events taking place on level C only partially fulfill conditions set by level B.[2] The same statistical information shows, significantly, that when actual cross-cousin marriages do take place, they take place between very near cross-cousins much more frequently than among distant ones: that is, it seems that a man in South India is more likely either to marry his "real" mother's brother's daughter or to marry a stranger than he is to marry someone in the category of mother's brother's daughter who is nevertheless not close kin to him.[3] The statistical information is, however, quite incomplete, so that we may only take hints from it, not draw firm conclusions.

One crucial feature of Dravidian kinship is that it allows for the existence of matrilines or patrilines or both simultaneously, within a single

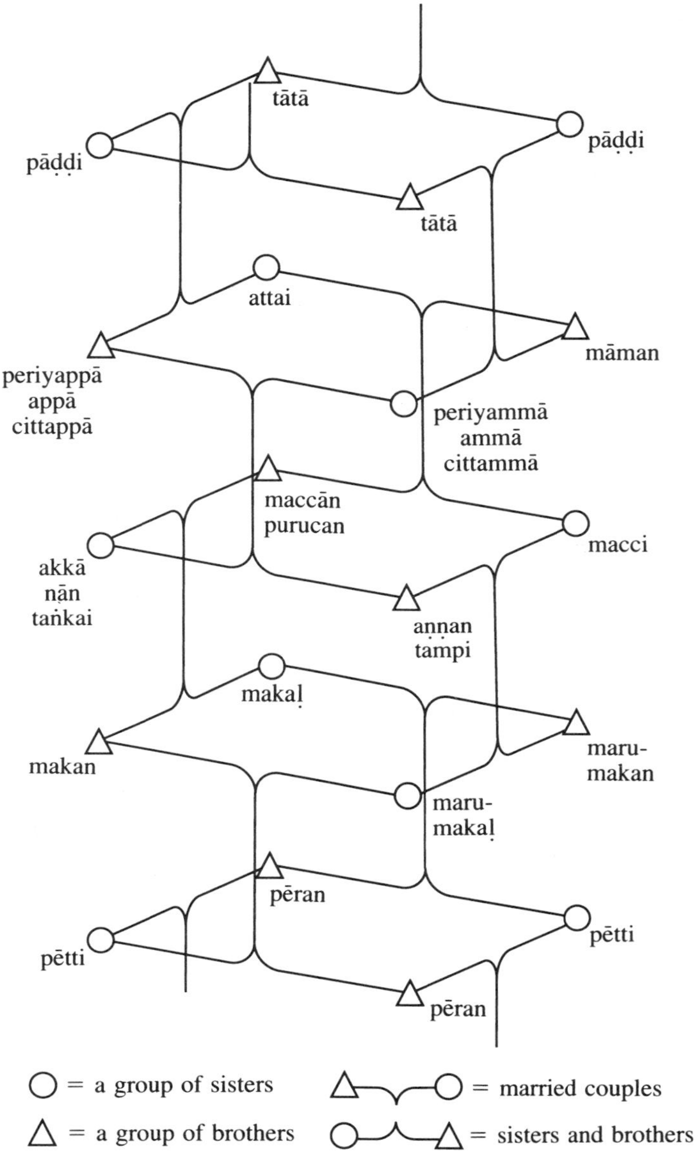

Figure 5. One image of the structure of Tamil kin terms: A closed circular pattern with radial symmetry (self as female).

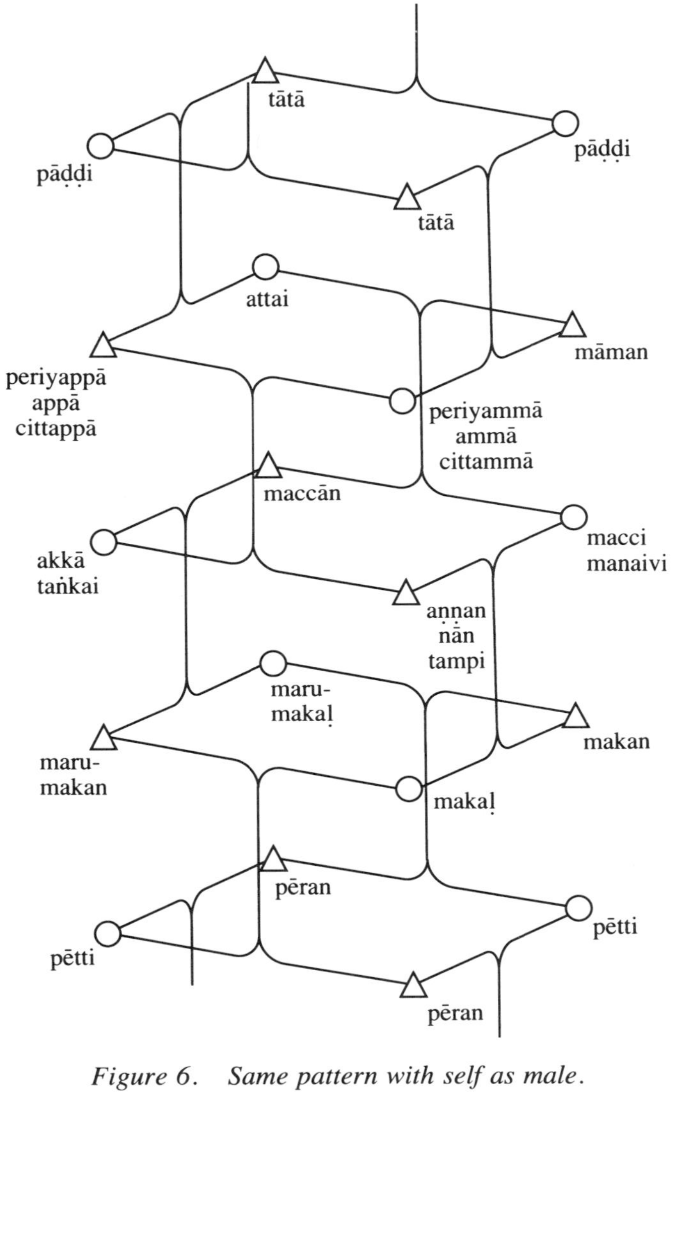

Figure 6. Same pattern with self as male.

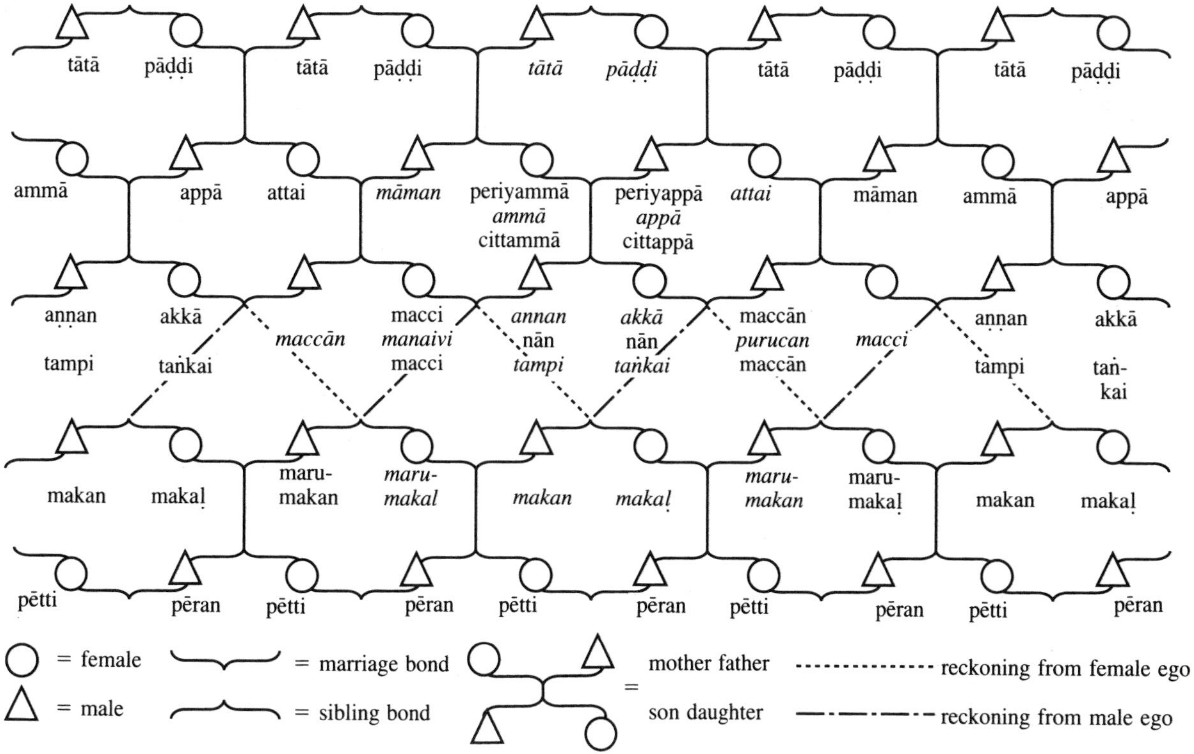

Figure 7. Another image of the structure of Tamil kin terms: An open repeating pattern with bilateral symmetry.

marriage system. Some South Indian groups are matrilineal and matrilocal. Most are patrilineal and patrilocal, but many of these are associated with "secondary," named matrilines. Even where there are no formally recognized matrilines, there often exist informal matrilineal groupings of women of up to five generations in depth who are divided by alternate generations between two households and maintain frequent and active contact with each other. The female side of a patriline, consisting of father's sisters and brother's daughters, may be equally solidary internally, and may also be solidary with the interwoven matriline.

Without departing from the fundamental pattern of cross-cousin marriage, a particular kindred group (in Tamil, *vakaiyarā*) may change over the years, or swing back and forth, or experience disputes among its members over choices between matrilateral or patrilateral marriage, patrilocal or matrilocal residence. Matrilateral and patrilocal marriages contribute to the solidarity of male and female patrilines by allowing all the members of a patriline to remain together within a single household, but through such marriages members of matrilines become dispersed over separate households (figure 8*a*). Matrilateral and matrilocal marriages allow for the continuity within a single household of male and female matrilines, but patrilines are spatially dispersed (figure 8*b*). Patrilateral marriages bring about similar conflicts between lines of men and lines of women (figures 9*a, b,* and *c*). These conflicts, involving families of three to five generations in depth, have powerful repercussions in the lives of individuals.

Over the years, European and American anthropologists have spent considerable energy in attempting to explain the persistence of the institution of cross-cousin marriage in places such as South India where it is practiced. Most of the explanations that have been developed are functionalist in that they see the practice of cross-cousin marriage as fulfilling some social function or human desire, thus contributing to individual or societal wholeness. Many are functionalist also in the sense that they regard the marriage system as bound up with other social and cultural institutions, such that a disruption in the marriage system would result in a disruption of other aspects of life as well, and vice versa. Holism—the idea that any given culture/society is an internally integrated system, complete in itself and self-maintaining—is a necessary presupposition of functionalist approaches in either sense of the word.

Anthropological analyses of Dravidian kinship, aiming, as they generally do, for elegant and precise causal explanations of social phenomena, are also characteristically essentialist and idealist in spirit. By calling them essentialist, I mean that each published analysis posits one essential

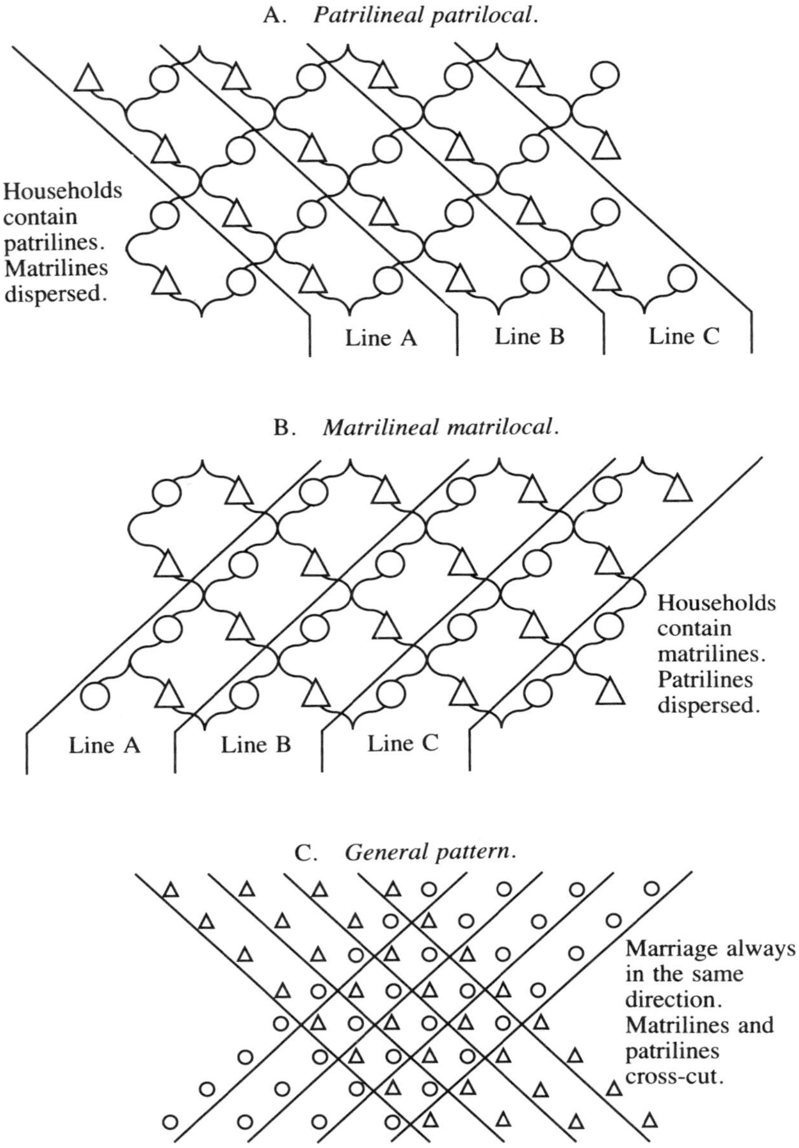
A. Patrilineal patrilocal.
Households contain patrilines. Matrilines dispersed.
Line A
Line B
Line C
B. Matrilineal matrilocal.
Households contain matrilines. Patrilines dispersed.
Line A
Line B
Line C
C. General pattern.
Marriage always in the same direction. Matrilines and patrilines cross-cut.

Figure 8. Ideal patterns of matrilateral cross-cousin marriage.

A. *Patrilineal patrilocal.*

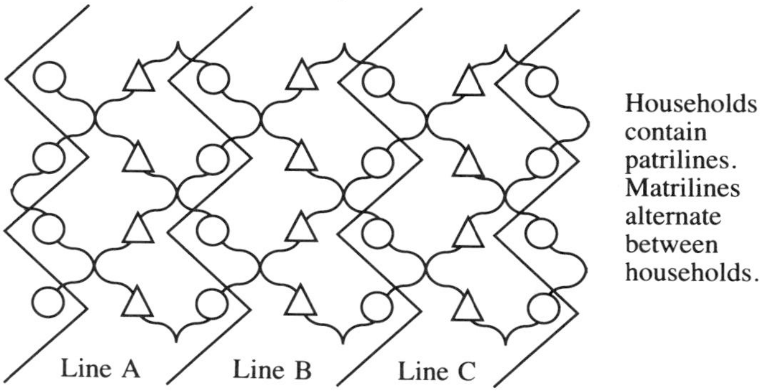
Households contain patrilines. Matrilines alternate between households.
Line A
Line B
Line C

B. *Matrilineal matrilocal.*

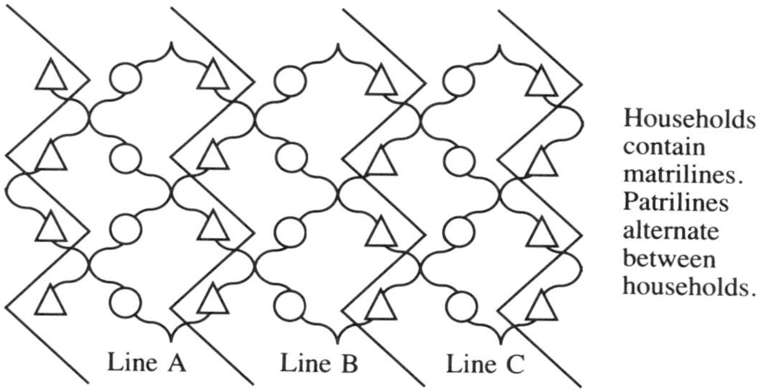
Households contain matrilines. Patrilines alternate between households.
Line A
Line B
Line C

C. *General pattern.*

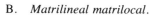

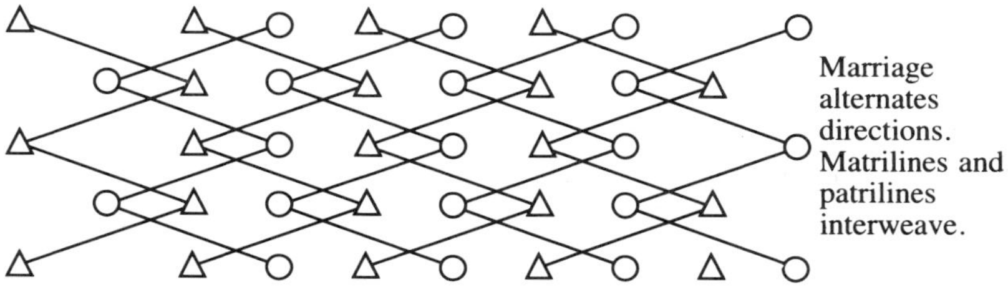
Marriage alternates directions. Matrilines and patrilines interweave.

Figure 9. Ideal patterns of patrilateral cross-cousin marriage.

explanation for the kinship system as it stands, one cause for the one effect, one reason for maintaining the institution which is equally valid for all participants in that institution, rather than allowing for the possibility that different actors in different social situations may engage in the same marriage game for a multiplicity of separate and perhaps even conflicting reasons.

By calling these same anthropological analyses idealist, I mean that for them, the behavior that is observed is considered to be an imperfect manifestation of a perfect pattern maintained in the minds of actors, replicated identically in the unconscious of each, or copied faithfully in the accepted ideology of each.[4] Just as functionalism and holism are mutually supportive forms of thought, so idealism and essentialism are mutually implicatory: all are monistic; all negate the plurality of wills and desires that make up actual human life.

Five approaches to the study of kinship in South India will be briefly considered here. Three of these are paths already taken: I choose to discuss them because they are the most well-trodden paths. The remaining two are paths we have yet to take: I choose to discuss them because my own approach, insofar as it accords with any general theory, is most in accord with them, and I think they may lead us in more fruitful directions than those that we have been following up until now. The five approaches may be labeled structuralist, culturalist, poststructuralist, Freudian, and post-Freudian.

Structuralist Approaches

The most famous modern analyst of South Indian kinship systems is Louis Dumont, whose approach to an understanding of these systems has evolved over several decades of fieldwork, writing, and heated debate with other Western scholars specializing in Indian kinship. In a recently updated version of some of his earlier theories,[5] Dumont argues that the Dravidian kinship system is at base an abstract organization of affinal relations between categories of kin. The central assertion of this theory is that not only relations of consanguinity ("blood" relations), but relations of affinity (marital relations), are considered by Tamil people to be passed on hereditarily from parent to child. These relations of affinity become realized, as it were, in ego's own generation, as relations of "alliance" between same-sex individuals. From his father a man inherits relations of alliance with the father's male cross-kin. Ego's father is in a relation of alliance with ego's mother's brother. Ego, as the son of his father, inherits its alliance with the son of the man to whom the father is allied, that is, with the son of the mother's brother. Ego marries his mother's brother's daughter as an affirmation of his alliance with this woman's brother. The institution of cross-cousin marriage, Dumont concludes, exists in order to reaffirm, generation by generation, this hereditary relation of alliance between categories of same-sex people.

Theoretically, as Dumont says, either categories of women or categories of men may be linked by alliance in this manner, but the examples given in Dumont's ethnography indicate that the maintenance of an ongoing relationship between lines of males is really what is at stake. Dumont stresses heavily that inherited alliance is a relationship between same-sex people only: a child of either sex inherits relations of "consanguinity" (i.e., relations with parallel kin) from its mother as well as from its father, but it inherits relations of affinity (i.e., relations with cross-kin) only from its same-sex parent. A man who inherits affinity with the men of lineage B may marry the sisters of those men, but the relationship that he inherits is a relationship with the men, not with the women. Heterosexual relations are thus completely bypassed as an element of the marriage system.

Also stressed in Dumont's schema is the principle that affinity in South Indian kinship is a relation between abstract, conceptual "categories" of people, not "groups" of actual people and certainly not pairs of individuals, such as "real" mother's brother (*māman*) and "real" sister's son (*marumakan*). In opposition to Radcliffe-Brown,[6] Dumont argues that the cultural relationship linking this pair of individuals is a matter of the categories they belong to and has nothing to do with the relationship of each to the woman who is mother to one and sister to the other. Indeed, Dumont asserts, in South Indian thinking a man is related to his mother's brother's daughter not through his mother at all, but through his father. It is thus a mistake to consider, he says, that the relation one has with someone in the category of māman is somehow an extension of the relation one has with one's "own" mother's "own" brother. Even though there is in Tamil a terminological distinction between the "real" mother's brother—(*tāy māman*)—and a "classificatory" mother's brother—(plain *māman*)—still for Dumont this is not enough to gainsay the view that kinship is primarily a relation of categories rather than of persons.

The essence of South Indian kinship, in Dumont's account, is the *idea* of affinity. This idea is an essence in that it is considered to be the single most important principle upholding the marriage system, allowing no rivals, and it is an essence also in that it is abstract. For affinity, as Dumont describes it, is not a matter of experienced personal relations between people. It is a general, invariant relation between, as he insists, categories. Actual experienced bodily relations, interpersonal relations, and especially sexual relations, are dismissed by him as trivial or nonexistent as far as the structure of the marriage system is concerned. Hence the notion advanced by culturalists that theories about conception can

Plate 17. Male cross-cousins cleaning their teeth together.

generate kinship systems is ridiculed by Dumont. Affinity is for him the fundamental, the only considerable, value.

Dumont's thought on kinship, original though it is, is not without roots. In particular, Dumont owes much to Levi-Strauss's *Structures élémentaires de la parenté*, in which Levi-Strauss argues that rules of exogamy (or, rules prohibiting intrafamilial "incest") exist for the sake of creating social solidarity among groups larger in size than the single family. Women are exchanged among families, rather than kept within the same family, so that the various kindred groups among whom such exchange takes place may be bound to each other by ties of affinity and so integrated into a larger unit. Hence, as regards their role in marriage institutions, women are much like words—they are tokens of communication and symbols of exchange. In a further elaboration of this theory, Levi-Strauss adopts an evolutionist approach to marriage systems, arguing that one institution can be expected to prevail over another if it contributes to greater overall social solidarity than does the other. Marriage systems integrate relatively larger or smaller groups of people, more or less tightly or loosely. The wider the group that is integrated, and the more tightly it is integrated, the more prevalent the system of integration will be. Matrilateral cross-cousin marriage is more prevalent than bilateral or patrilateral because matrilateral can encompass all available lineages in a single circular or hierarchical system. Bilateral marriage is conducive to intermarrying semi-isolates: two lineages trade sisters during each generation. Hence matrilateral marriage is a form of what Levi-Strauss calls "generalized exchanges"; bilateral marriage is a form of "restricted exchange." Patrilateral marriage is mediate between the other two systems: lineage A gives wives to lineage B in one generation and receives wives back from the same lineage in the next generation, thus the two lineages form a partial connubium, though each requires also to be affinally joined with at least one other lineage.

In *Structures élémentaires*, the topic of most concern to Levi-Strauss is the system of marriage rules, considered as an ideal, unconscious, collective mental representation. Underlying the account of social organization as the artifact of a set of collective representations is the conviction, stated explicitly by Levi-Strauss and inherited by him from both Durkheim and Boas, that the so-called "native point of view," that is, any particular individual's account of what is really going on in his own society, is a secondary rationalization—not a true explanation, but rather, something that itself needs to be explained by someone with a broader perspective on societies in general, namely, the ethnographer.[7] To a certain extent, Dumont appears to accept this premise concerning the falsehood, or at least insufficiency, of native explications of native life, inasmuch as his account of South Indian marriage systems posits a key collective representation, the notion of inherited affinity itself, which receives no formal or conventional expression in the Tamil language. Dumont does, however, credit conversations with Kallar elders (Kallars were the caste that he worked with) with enabling him to develop the theory that he does. If these elders, rather than Dumont himself, are the source of the notion of kinship as based on inherited affinity, several new questions arise. To what extent does the knowledge of these elders control Kallar social organization? To what extent is this knowledge shared by others? And in what ways?

Culturalist Approaches

Some recent theorists, notably Kenneth David and Stephen Barnett,[8] influenced by studies carried out in other parts of South Asia and the world,[9] have attempted to understand South Indian kinship systems in terms of native theories of how the essence of a person, or the "coded substance" of that person, is transmitted to other people. A central feature of such studies is the finding that in Tamil Nadu, rules regarding whom one may or may not marry are consciously legitimated by some informants on the basis of statements regarding how coded substance, or "blood," is transmitted, how it mixes with other coded substance, and how it affects people's ways of being and acting. Rules governing whom one may or may not marry, it is argued, derive from biological ideas concerning which substances are inherited from which parents, and how these substances are transformed during life.

In comparison with Dumont, so-called culturalists are more inclined, at least in their surface representations of themselves, to be respectful of "the native point of view" and to take "native" statements at face value, as direct expressions of the symbol system that motivates human action within the society in question. The trouble comes when there is a discrepancy among "native points of view," as of course there always is in India. Then culturalist ethnographers, inheriting from their predecessors the notion that any given "culture" is essentially unitary and univocal, tend to escape the muddle that a plurality of perspectives poses by being highly selective as to *which* "native points of view" they listen to.

Thus, Barnett and David's key informants provided them with wonderfully consistent, well-thought-out biological theories that accounted perfectly for the institution of cross-cousin marriage in South India. One such theory was that a person's "bodily essence" (*uḍampu* in Barnett's account), or "blood" (*rattam* in David's account), was passed on to a child from its father, and the spiritual essence, the "soul" (*uyir*), from the mother, so that you could marry someone who was not related to you only through males, or only through females, because then you would have neither blood nor soul in common with them—in effect, an ethnobiological theory of double unilineal exogamy.[10] Another theory postulated that, as in Bengal, a woman's bodily essence was considered to become transsubstantiated to that of her husband at the time of her marriage, so that she would not pass on to her child membership in her natal patriline. (Trautmann[11] finds that this theory was originally propounded a thousand years ago by the South Indian Sanskrit philosopher Madhava, in an explicit attempt to make South Indian marriage systems fit with the social codes enshrined in *dharmaśāstra*—a set of Brahman-authored texts written in Sanskrit in North India and dating from around 200 B.C. to 500 A.D. Dharmaśāstra outlines the principles of social order as understood by the texts' authors. Trautmann's finding suggests that the notion of transsubstantiation is, for South Indians, an after-the-fact justification of their marriage system rather than the reason for it.)

Textual origins or no, these theories are no doubt valid for the informants who offered them to the ethnographers questioning them. They also mesh with other aspects of South Indian ideology. At the same time, it must be pointed out that there are many South Indians who would vehemently disagree with the theories of conception and heredity described above, and would offer their own counter-theories, just as seriously held, which might account for cross-cousin marriage in a different way, or might fail to account for it, or might even contradict it.[12] What are we to do with these? And what are we to do with the many Tamil people who have no theories at all, and know of none, concerning the biological foundations of their marriage systems? Shall we write off these nontheoreticians as blind followers of traditions whose reasons are understood only by others?[13]

It is true that South Indian ideas concerning life processes are rich and do relate at many points to South Indian ideas concerning social processes. And there are many reasons to believe that for speakers of Dravidian languages, substance, action, and feeling are not such radically separate modes of reality as Westerners seem to find them.[14] But, given these vague generalities, particular points of view, particular expressions concerning the nature of life in South India are extremely diverse, and are not at all simple. Often, as they are presented to the ethnographer, they are fragmentary. Connections between system A and system B (e.g., marriage conventions and ethnophysiology) may certainly be found, but direct causal connections neatly pointed out by philosophically inclined informants for the ethnographers' sake are far from all there is. This does not mean that ethnographers should abandon interest in South Indian conceptualizations of life processes. Rather, it is suggested here that they should pay *more* attention to these conceptualizations in all their detail and variety, and *then* should begin to consider what they explain.

To return to the question of essences, many statements made among Tamil speakers about the nature of human beings suggest that it is wrong to assume that for Tamils in general, or for South Indians, the person has an "essence" at all.[15] It might be more productive for us to imagine, therefore, that Tamils, inasmuch as they have shared "beliefs" (another problematic category), tend to think of each person as internally variegated and distinctive because of the patterns of variegation that that person uniquely contains or displays. Moreover, the statements and actions of many Tamil people suggest that they think of these patterns as changing gradually over time, and from relationship to relationship, in complex and unpredictable ways—and that they think of them as having many sources. There are some traits that are gotten from the mother, some that are gotten from the father, some that are gotten from the environment—food, air, earth, water, stars—and some that are brought in from a distant time and place by the soul, *uyir*. If there is a most important component, it is surely this uyir, but of all the parts of the person, this is the part that is least bound to the laws of substances such as earth and blood. Uyir is breath, it is feeling, it is what makes a living thing move and grow, it is what makes *any* live thing be alive. When a man and woman make love, their very souls (uyir) mix in the places where they have most feeling; thus one may lose one's life in the act of making love. But the soul of a child is another altogether from those of its parents. The uyir comes from God, most people say, or from some past life, or from the air.[16] When the body dies, all the other components of the person remain. Only uyir is gone, cleanly and completely, to who knows where, having come in the first place from who knows where. Thus, the most common and honest answer that unschooled villagers give to the anthropologist's how and why questions about the way people are is simply, "*Ennattai kaṇḍōm?* [What do we know?]." People are as they are. Idle speculation about causes is arrogant and pointless.

Intellectual informants are often useful in such situations. Such individuals are able to elaborate fascinating theories for us on virtually any topic, just as there are Tamil poets who for a fee will write poems on any topic you choose to assign. We must respect these thinkers, for as natives, they are more qualified to explicate the native system of thought than we are. But they are a small, elite, and often (like us) an intentionally idiosyncratic bunch. They may make representations of the common man; but they do not represent him. The common man is not in the business of making representations; he is in the business of living. If we are trying to understand the way the common man lives on the basis of what the intellectual knows, we must try to find the common man within the intellectual and see how what the intellectual says relates to the actual living person that he is, rather than attending only to the content of his words. Precisely because the theories of Indian literati are so abundant and diverse, it is a big mistake to take any one theory emerging from the mouth or pen of an Indian thinker, or even many of them, and regard this theory as reflecting the true shape of Indian reality, or even part of it. Each theory is unique, and must be regarded as continuous with the unique personality that gave it birth.[17]

In advocating that we pay close attention to the details of what people say, I do not mean to imply that structuralism, which seeks the truth *behind* what people say, is invalid. To take statements at simple face value, without seeking their place in larger and less easily visible patterns, is not only not wise, it is not possible. Hence, the account I give below is at base structuralist, inasmuch as it is about patterns, relations between relations, and does not take isolated statements to be, in themselves, explanatory of whole institutions.

At the same time, in advocating a search for patterns that go beyond individual statements and actions and perhaps are given no overt form or symbol by those who maintain them, I do not mean to imply that the "cultural basis" (read ideational motivation) for marriage institutions is invalid. To claim this would in effect be to deny agency to people who live by such institutions. Rather, the suggestions I make above are offered as a warning that the meanings of kinship relations to people in a kin-based society are likely to be themselves complex, variegated, and not internally consistent. They are likely to be more like what we call feelings than like what we call thoughts. Their reasons are likely to be reasons of the heart.

Dumont's account of South Indian kinship discusses "affinity as a value." Culturalist accounts discuss the importance attached to the mingling of bodily substances. Both come close to, but skirt completely around, the issue of feeling or sentiment (*uṇarcci*) as a crucial one in Tamil thought and action about kinship. This is strange, for uṇarcci is a central concept in Tamil thought about life processes and is also far from marginal in any possible meaning of affinity to South Indians.

Both accounts also greatly downplay the significance of actual face-to-face personal relations, especially relations between male and female, in the operation of the kinship system. The nature of the *connection* between body and soul, vital to Tamils, to their understanding of their feelings and to their understanding of human relations, is similarly left untouched.[18] But kinship is not only, or even primarily, a matter of relations between categories of persons. Nor is it primarily a matter of relations between physical components of persons. It is, I would argue, primarily a matter of relations between persons, whole and actual persons. In their day-to-day associations with each other, they give the system being.

Poststructuralist (or Marxist-structuralist) Approaches

One helpful antidote to the idealism and naive holism of both the structuralist and the culturalist works discussed above is the poststructuralist approach to the study of social organization put forward by Pierre Bourdieu in his *Outline of a Theory of Practice*. His book cannot solve all our problems, but it does offer arguments that are very germane to the debate over South Indian kinship.

Bourdieu, like Dumont, has much in common with Levi-Strauss. He builds on structuralism and accepts many of its premises, but then he goes beyond it and tries to reveal and seek a remedy for its flaws. Bourdieu's most serious criticism of Levi-Strauss concerns the latter's reification of cultural "rules." Levi-Strauss, as is well known, created structural anthropology overtly on analogy with Saussure's structural linguistics and Chomsky's transformational grammar. Both Chomsky and Saussure sought to find the invariant mental structures or grammatical rules underlying and generating actual speech. For both of them, all the vagaries and unpredictabilities in the actual use of speech were epiphenomenal. Laws and rules governing the structure of a sentence or of a language at any given point in time, as well as historical change and "transformations" taking place between deep or universal forms and surface or particular ones, were all, for Chomsky and Saussure, quite beyond control and manipulation by the individual human actor.[19] The fate of human will and agency and the particulars of context they treated as beyond the confines of their discipline. Following their lead and bringing it to the study of culture, Levi-Strauss early claimed that "the demands of the rule as rule" are part of the basic structure (unconscious) of the human mind, which structure it is the aim of the ethnologist to uncover.[20] The rules of social structure and cultural order which Levi-Strauss sought to uncover were beyond time, even opposed to it.[21] The beauty of "traditional society" or of "pensée sauvage," in the view of Levi-Strauss and many others, is precisely that it is unconscious, wild, and natural like a pansy. It presents an exquisite order, but no named individual or group of people planned it: like Harriet Beecher Stowe's Topsy (whose persona reflects this Rousseauvian vision), it "jes' growed."

In response to this philosophy, Bourdieu now asserts that we are misled to consider social organization to be governed by unconscious and unauthored rules of which existing forms are imperfect realizations. Rather we must consider any particular human world to be a process of mutual creation of praxis and habitus. Habitus consists not of rules intrinsic to the human mind, but of patterns and tendencies which enter the fabric of bodily hexis (the body's invisible nets and snares) from childhood. Praxis is not the mechanical enactment, or failed enactment, of rules but consists of choices and strategies which are open-ended and indefinite in number, and which depend for their meaning and effectiveness upon the elements of uncertainty and surprise. In Bourdieu's view, rules of social organization do not "underlie" social praxis. Rather the establishment of social "rules" is itself a practical act, a political strategy carried out by particular agents and designed to legitimate a particular social order. In effect, Bourdieu's work is a Marxist rethinking of Levi-Strauss's dialectical but deliberately anti-Marxist structuralism.

The scenarios and strategies that Bourdieu describes as intrinsic to the real process of kinship (in Kabylia, Algeria, the place where he did field work) are agonistic, pluralistic, individualistic. His approach is opposed to what he calls the totalizing approach of structural-functionalism, in which kinship is represented as a total system, self-enclosed, predictable, with actors' uncertainty of other actors' responses to their actions treated as inessential to the operation of the system. A totalizing view, as Bourdieu describes it, is a disinvolved, bird's-eye view of a society, the view of an omniscient observer who already knows what is to happen as though all were predetermined, a view taken off the ground and out of the time in which actors live and make their choices. A totalizing view considers kinship as the working out of an overall plan which benefits only society-as-a-whole, which precedes and is the basis of praxis, and which has nothing to do with individual agency. Bourdieu suggests—and this is crucial for our argument—that the very notion of "society-as-a-whole" and of rules supporting the whole which have no specific origin other than that of the collectivity or of God may often be nothing more than the fabrication of particular interested parties who legitimize their hegemony by representing themselves as embodying the whole.

Bourdieu's approach to kinship leads us to ask vis-a-vis Levi-Strauss, whether the apparently integrative property of kinship practice such as mother's brother's daughter (MBD) marriage is really what causes this practice to endure longer and to be more prevalent than father's sister's daughter (FZD) marriage. Trautmann[22] points out that of the various possible forms of cross-cousin marriage, MBD marriage alone is in accord with the North Indian ideal of *kanyādāna* as outlined in the dharmaśāstra. The principle of kanyādāna ("gift of a virgin") specifies that one should give one's daughter in marriage as one performs a sacrifice to the gods, with no expectation of worldly return. Any kind of "exchange" of women between lineages would therefore be a less sacred, and so less prestigious, form of marriage. In modern Indo-Aryan communities, affines who are "wife-givers" are thus sharply distinguished from those who are "wife-receivers"; one should not give a wife to a lineage from which one's own lineage has received a wife, and vice versa. A family to whom one's family has given a wife is treated as superior to one's own family; a family from whom one's own family has accepted a wife is treated as inferior. Marriage is supposed to be consistently hypergamous.

Sanskritic North Indian culture in general has long stood as a prestige model for high-caste South Indians, for principally political reasons. The center of power on the South Asian subcontinent has long been the northern plains; the lingua franca for many centuries throughout the subcontinent was Sanskrit. It would therefore not be unreasonable to assume that the values of Indo-Aryan kinship have influenced the particular forms taken by Dravidian kinship in the south, conducing to a preference for MBD marriage, in which "the traffic in women" always flows in only one direction.

For South Indians, the principle of kanyādāna is much like the notion of transsubstantiation of a woman's bodily substance to that of her husband at marriage. Both principles align southern praxis with northern ideology but at the same time skew southern praxis in a certain direction. Both principles justify a complete severance of ties between a woman and her natal family at the time of the woman's marriage; both principles also justify the complete subordination of a married woman to her husband and his family.

As Leach and others have shown, MBD marriage supports relations of permanent, irreversible inequality among lineages; it conduces to a hierarchical organization of lineages and so adds weight to the principles authorizing caste hierarchy.[23] Such a practice—consistent with the production of large social units integrated by means of hierarchy, rather than with the production of small social units integrated by means of reciprocity—may be conducive to solidarity (therefore good for human beings) in Levi-Strauss's terms, but in Bourdieu's terms it is totalizing and the "solidarity" it engenders may be no more than an oppressive illusion. Why, we might then ask, should such a practice *naturally*, that is of its own accord, endure longer than one that is conducive to looser, less centralized forms of social organization? On the contrary, the latter might more reasonably be expected to have a natural survivability, the survivability of any acephalous or decentralized life form, in which if one portion of the system falls, the rest need not fall with it. If the more encompassing (and arguably for this very reason the more fragile) system is more prevalent, perhaps this is because, as a system which fosters hierarchy, it is very often in the interests of powerful parties to promote it. Perhaps when such powerful parties become less powerful, the most durable institution becomes the one that is most flexible, the one that allows for the largest number of alternative strategies of action—like a well-designed board game in which the rules are few and simple but the possible combinations of moves are many and complex.

Dumont's wide-ranging notion of "encompassment" takes on a different meaning when seen through Bourdieuvian eyes. To encompass, in Dumont's terms, is to include, as the whole includes the part. It is also to supercede in importance, as the interests of the society supercede those of the individual. Dumont argues that encompassment in both senses is a fundamental principle in South Asian society. Hence Brahmanical authority encompasses kingly authority because the Brahman represents the sacred whole of which the king's realm is only a part;[24] higher castes encompass lower castes because the higher are more pure and whole, the lower more impure and fragmentary;[25] in Bengal the wife encompasses the husband (bodily during intercourse) but the husband's patriline encompasses the wife (as a social being, for her whole married life), so the wife becomes part of the husband's patriline and its interests must supercede her own;[26] similarly in Bengal, the hierarchical love binding the joint family encompasses the egalitarian love binding the nuclear couple because the former is more inclusive, so love between husband and wife must be kept strictly circumscribed.[27] In South India it might be argued, following the same lines of thought, that the hierarchy of matrilateral marriage encompasses the reciprocity of patrilateral.[28] In short, for India overall, hierarchy encompasses equality, and the larger social unit encompasses the smaller, *unless*, as in the case of Brahmans within the caste system or patriarchs within a lineage, the smaller social unit is considered to represent the whole. But assuming a cynical stance we might ask, does all this encompassment happen because Indians as a collectivity value encompassment, or is it simply a matter of the more powerful making the rules? Do women and untouchables value encompassment in the way that patriarchs and Brahmans do? Why don't we ask them?[29]

Bourdieu's approach is useful to us because of its particularism and its action-orientation: it discourages us from reducing a culture to some set of presumably invariant and unanimously maintained collective representations, and therefore it encourages us to look more closely at the diversity of lifeways that actual people within a given society follow; it enjoins us not to dismiss this diversity as epiphenomenal.

Where Bourdieu fails us is in his inability to see the diversity within the human actor. For Bourdieu it seems that all action relevant to social structure (hence to kinship organization) is motivated by selfish calculation of political advantage.[30] It is for this reason, one presumes, that he is so skeptical of the notion of solidarity, for he sees only the one side of it—the hypocritical, oppressive side. It is good that we should be reminded that what we see as "diffuse, enduring solidarity"[31] is sometimes only tyranny in disguise. But we need also a way to understand the roots of this solidarity when it is real, when it consists of affective bonds between people, when it consists of actual feelings of love.

Freudian Approaches

If one searches for discussions of the affective elements of cross-cousin marriage, and especially if one looks for discussions of what this institution means in terms of the feelings that particular individuals in particular kinship relations have for one another, much of what one finds is partly or wholly Freudian in orientation. Freud himself, in *Totem and Taboo*, was the first to suggest that rules of kinship organization were a consequence of men's need to deal constructively with Oedipal feelings. Since then, Freud's thesis has been repudiated countless times by anthropologists, and yet Oedipus keeps reemerging in ethnographic studies of family and kinship, especially in South Asian studies, in increasingly sophisticated forms.[32]

It would not be useful to recapitulate in detail here the debates within anthropology over the relation of Oedipus to kinship. These debates center around questions of whether the Oedipus complex is real; if so, is it universal; are the feelings of individuals really at the heart of kinship organization; if so, do the unconscious and unacknowledged Oedipal feelings of individuals form part of public institutions such as those organizing marital alliances; are affective ties between individuals able to account for institutionalized relations between categories of kin; and so forth.

Regardless of the stand that one takes on these issues one must still confront the feminist objection to orthodox Freudian theory, which is that it regards women as fundamentally wounded (castrated) and diseased (hysterical). The application of Oedipal theory to kinship studies is likewise troublesome to feminists, in that it denies all agency to women. Men and their feelings are given all the credit (or blame, as the case may be) for construction of the kinship system. Are we not allowed to suppose that women and their feelings also had a hand in this construction?

Of course, from the point of view of feminism, structuralist and culturalist accounts of kinship systems fare little better. Levi-Strauss has been severely criticized for his characterization of women in marital exchange systems as essentially just pawns in the game. Dumont appears to be responding to actual or potential feminist criticism when he writes that relations of alliance are handed down from women to women as well as from men to men, but his exclusive reliance on male informants and his assumption of the primacy of male interests in the organization of kinship relations render the balance he posits superficial and ad hoc. Culturalists are still more sensitized to feminist interests, yet the kinship ideology they describe is on several key points problematic for women while suited to the convenience of men, and this bias appears to be accepted as natural by the ethnographers in question.[33] Bourdieu is to be credited for his detailed descriptions of female behind-the-scenes manipulations in Kabylia wedding negotiations, but his evident assumption that the desire for power is the one motivation behind all human activity may be criticized as fundamentally masculinist in tone. The failure of all of these writers to deal with the affective aspect of kinship relations has already been noted.

Exegeses of MBD marriage in terms of affect often take what might be called a quasi-Freudian approach. In this view, it is assumed that a man has a relation of affection with his mother and a relation of antagonism with an older-generation male in authority over the mother and/or over the younger male himself. Usually this authoritative and forbidding older male is the father, but sometimes it is the mother's brother. So Levi-Strauss predicted that in any society practicing cross-cousin marriage, a man would have either an antagonistic relation with his father and an affectionate relation with his mother's brother, or the reverse. The particular combination of lineality and locality (e.g., patrilineal and matrilocal) prevalent in the given society would determine which set of relationships would occur, and so would determine, in a society characterized by cross-cousin marriage, whether marriage was normatively matrilateral (marriage to MBD) or bilateral (marriage to either FZD or MBD).[34] Dumont applied this rule to Tamil marriage systems, only substituting patrilateral for bilateral marriage.[35] Similarly, Homans and Schneider posited a universal rule of kinship which stated that MBD marriage would be preferred in societies in which fathers had jural authority over their unmarried sons, and FZD marriage would be preferred in societies in which mother's brothers had jural authority over their nephews.[36] Much earlier than any of these writers, Radcliffe-Brown, in attempting to determine the value to the individual of MBD marriage in South Africa, suggested that it is natural for a man, when he forms a marriage alliance, to want to form it with someone who is like his mother—someone with whom he has a warm and friendly relationship. This person is the mother's brother. One extends one's affection for one's mother onto all of one's mother's kindred, in particular the mother's brother, and thence to this man's daughter, and so marries her.[37] Building upon this argument, Homans and Schneider suggest,

> As he visits his mother's brother often, ego will see a great deal of the daughter: contact will be established. As he is fond of his mother's brother, and as mother's brother and his daughter in the patrilineal complex, the Oedipus Complex if you will, are themselves particularly close to one another, he will tend to get fond of the daughter. Their marriage will be sentimentally appropriate.[38]

Radcliffe-Brown's "extensionist hypothesis," which posited that if one had an affective tie with an individual kinsman, that tie could be extended to all individuals in the same *category* of kin, follows from his fundamental premise that the basic building blocks of all social structures are *dyadic* relations, that is, one-to-one relations between individuals. This extensionist hypothesis is now generally rejected (perhaps wrongly so, in the Indian case at least, as I shall suggest below), but the same Freudian assumptions about relations between older and younger generation males and about relations between mothers and sons still remain in the more recent and sophisticated studies.

In all of these formulations, the affective relation between mother and child (whether son or daughter) is assumed to be invariant, and therefore not a factor in kinship organization. Likewise in all of these formulations, as in Freud's own opus, affect is not regarded as culturally constituted. The person to whom one directs one's positive or negative feelings may be seen to vary from society to society, but the quality of those feelings, the nature of their expression, the possibility that affect is no more the same throughout the world than is language—none of these matters is given much consideration by these analysts.

Post-Freudian (or Semiotic-Freudian) Approaches

A major anthropological criticism of Freud, as I have just said, is that he failed to consider affect or sexuality, even symbols of sexuality, as integrated into culturally organized symbol-systems. Yet this failure carries over into anthropological applications of Freud, even the remote applications considered above. This, added to the antifeminine bias, the antihistoricity, the determinism, the monotony, the intolerance of ambiguity and polyphony, the downright humorlessness that naive Freudianism shares with the other approaches considered so far, might lead us to despair of ever finding any theory that might assist us in developing a truly person-centered account of kinship (which, in case I failed to mention it, is what this chapter aims to do).

But let us not give up yet. There is one more approach to our problem that I wish to consider here. This is an approach which, to the best of my knowledge, has never been used by anthropologists at all; it is the work of the French psychoanalytic semiotician, Jacques Lacan. Like all other fancy theories, Lacan's work has its problems, not least of which is that it is almost impossible for the uninitiated to follow what he says—he deliberately made it that way, ludic old fellow that he was. Fortunately, a number of Lacan's feminist students have published lucid explications of his basic ideas.[39] With their help, through the stylish postmodern absurdities that riddle Lacan's work, I think we may find some real insights that may help us to better understand the dynamics of culture, kinship, and feeling.

I call Lacan post-Freudian because his ideas about human psychology are so different from what most people take to have been Freud's own. However Lacan himself saw himself not as rejecting or transcending Freud but as merely giving the most appropriate reading of him. In Lacan's view, the topic of Freud's analysis was not the psyche (whatever that is) but discourse, people talking. Hence Freudian theory properly belongs, for Lacan, not in the realm of psychology but in the realm of linguistics.

Lacan's work is already engaged with our own because it is informed by post-Freudian French ethnography, most especially by the work of Mauss, of Mauss's students Leenhardt and Griaule, and of Levi-Strauss. He is also familiar with many Indian texts, and makes reference to them in his writing. In some ways, he "thinks like an Indian," and he behaves like many an Indian guru, mingling the sublime with the absurd in ways that cause some people to laugh, drive others crazy, and enlighten only a few.

I must, therefore, insert a second warning to the reader here. Many serious people say they hate Lacan, because he invents strange-sounding words that make no apparent reference to anything in the universe that we are familiar with, and because often he is so deliberately maddening. He pulls the rug out from under us all the time. He is an academic trickster—the most unsavory kind of trickster there is—and worst of all (for some Americans) he is French.

Why then do I give him so much attention here? There are two reasons. First, because his vision of the incompleteness of the self has a number of interesting things in common with something we might call a Tamil world view, especially as this world view is expressed in Tamil kinship patterns. In other words, Lacan has hit upon some truths that Tamils have also discovered. People of different civilizations sometimes do this, cultural relativity notwithstanding. They harmonize with each other in interesting ways. Why should we not hear the music?

Second, the angel voices that Lacan conjures up may seem like hocus-pocus, but they are really no more so than any other academic theory. The hocus-pocusness of all academic discourse is in fact one of the main things that Lacan, during his life, was trying to communicate. Not that there is anything wrong with hocus-pocus: it can be fun, and even illuminating, but when we take it too seriously, it blinds us and it shackles us. Functionalism, structuralism, materialism, Freudianism, and all the rest of our theoretical viewpoints are all very useful but they are not ultimate Truth. In our "studies" of other people we must get beyond all these theories, we must get beyond Theory itself, if we are ever *really* going to understand those others. But getting beyond Theory is not as easy as it seems; it is no more easy than getting beyond Religion, getting beyond Language. We need someone to push us off of it, push hard. Well, a trying and crazy (but brilliant!) old man like Lacan might for some of us be just the ticket, if he can force us to deal with the difficult and the strange. For the worlds of people beyond our shores *are* difficult, they *are* strange, they *do* defy the categories that shape our comprehension. And yet they are not separate from our own world. We cannot ignore them; we have to learn to live not only with them, but in them.

Here I will end my sermon and return to my text. I try in the next few pages to give a clear and concise but faithful rendering of some of Lacan's ideas that bear upon the present enterprise—an account of Dravidian kinship. Despite my best efforts, I know that many readers will still find this section abstruse. So, if you really can't stand it, move on to the next section. Otherwise, bear with me. It will all soon be over.

Lacan does not see in the material of psychoanalysis universal pre- or transcultural symbols. For him, the self, like all other objects of experience, is linguistically constituted. Instead of calling it the ego or self, therefore, he calls this core of each person's identity the "subject," to emphasize its implication in grammar, its necessary opposition to some "object," and its "subjection" to the larger whole which is, among other things, language.

Being inherently a "part" of this larger hegemonic "whole," the subject/self is formed, in Lacan's view, not through processes of integration, but through a moment of fragmentation. The Oedipus complex consists, for Lacan, in the rupture of a primordial, static, imagistic, different kind of wholeness, the wholeness of a being looking into a mirror, the wholeness—in Peircean terms—of Firstness and iconicity, the original mother-child dyad. The rupture is effected by something from outside of this First wholeness; it is effected by an Other that is distant (as opposed to intimate), abstract (as opposed to tangible), arbitrary (as opposed to being its own meaning), and unattainable. This powerful and alien Other is called by various names: Logos, the Phallus, the Father, the Name of the Father, Language, Culture. At the moment of rupture by this Other, desire enters the self. The self now becomes Subject, for it now belongs to the father's world: the world of Saussure's Arbitrary; the world of Peirce's Law. The Subject gets a name and becomes a symbol, defined relationally and negatively. It feels itself to be a fragment, to be incomplete, to contain an absence. Language, the seeming whole to which the Subject belongs, in turn belongs to another, to *the* Other, the divine will of collective social authority. The Subject would like to appropriate this Other, and so redeem its wholeness, but this is not possible, for the Other both precedes and outlasts the self. Language is already there, and one is already defined in terms of it, even before one is born (and the more so after one dies). Even the unconscious, the foundation of the Subject, is nothing but "the discourse of the Other." The mother was an object in the sense of being something one could touch. The Other is an Object in the sense of being something alien, feelingless, objective. The closeness and ownness of the mother is replaced by the distance and untouchability of the Father.

The presymbolic vision of the self in the mother, or in general, in the self's earliest objects, is what Lacan calls *le stade de miroire*, "the mirror stage." The self imagines itself to be an image of an image (the baby sees the mother and himself in her). This vision is static and closed, an eternal, mutual reflection between two images. It is a mirage.

But, we are warned, the *quelque chose d'un*, the "something of oneness," the promise of oneness, that the phallus (or logos, or symbolic order) holds out is also a phantom and a fraud. "Meaning," the seeming goal and source of language, has no stability. It, too, is a matter of relations, arbitrary and contingent, always shifting. Thus meaning, that which is behind appearances, the "other of the other," which would be the self again, the true and whole self which knows and owns itself, can never be captured or appropriated.

The phallus, the distant, omnipotent paternal weapon that divides us from the image of ourselves in our mother is, then, nothing but language, the symbolic code or law. This code, like the Derridean "trace," perpetuates desire, sets up the illusion that there is something on the other side of what we perceive that will complete us.

Spurred by desire for wholeness, the Subject acts. It seeks to possess the Other (culture-as-a-whole, culture-as-given, culture-in-the-ideal), but it never can, because this Other is only an illusion. Still, the self keeps reaching for this illusory ideal. As long as it has this desire, it will keep reaching. Through its reaching for the wholeness of the phallus/code, it builds the human world. If its desire were fulfilled, if there actually were closure—a perfect culture—and if the self felt itself to become whole, then human life would end, everything would stop.

The phallic division of the self from the mother is "necessary" and "functional" says Lacan, because in a sense it gets us moving, it puts us into the semiotic order where the meaning that we are looking for is always somewhere else. However, we must watch out for this "necessary" and this "functional," because they serve the myth of oneness, and so they like it are frauds. In the final analysis, for Lacan as for Bourdieu, the appearance of oneness, the very ideas of "culture," of "function," of "whole," are authoritarian artifices, whose nonverity we must come to terms with.

There is a positive side to this philosophy, though, which Victor Turner, for one, approached in his notion of carnival. For Lacan what is real and not illusory is what he calls *jouissance*, a term that can be translated into English variously as "playfulness," "polymorphous sexuality," "bliss," or "female orgasm." This jouissance is neither an underlying code nor a transcendent principle, nor is it meaningful, nor is it unitary. It is not necessary in any sense; it is not a tool of communion or communication or the maintenance of any system. It is not even capable of being spoken about. It is just there, "constantly coursing over the surface of the body," not a complement or a completion, but a "surplus," a "supplement" and a "suppletion."[40] Most importantly, jouissance has nothing at all to do with "exchange" or "relations." Hence: "There is no such thing as sexual intercourse," declares Lacan.[41] Jouissance is a strictly private matter.

Most of Lacan's biological terminology, it should be stressed, is completely allegorical. In his interpretation of the Oedipus complex, Lacan is not concerned with the "real" father or the "real" mother or the "real" penis, but with a set of forces considerably more general, intractable, and abstract than these, for which forces such terms as "father," "mother," and "phallus" are only aides-memoire.

We can see in Lacan's ideas a rethinking of Freud's *Civilization and its Discontents* and *Totem and Taboo*. We can also see in these ideas the distant magnetism of Indian thought. The notion that the rupture of a transcendent male consciousness into the primeval maternal equilibrium causes the world to be created echoes Saṁkhya cosmology.[42] The Greek notion of logos, the unchanging, abstract, disembodied, divine law, is much like (indeed historically related to) the Indian *brahman*, the Word upon which the universe is founded, owned and controlled by a male elite.[43] Many Indian texts, from the Rg-Veda to tongue-in-cheek comments of present-day villagers, describe desire as a painful but creative activating presence in the world, just as Lacan does.

Lacan's rejection of the notion of exchange as a plus-value in the world of human relations is of course a direct response to Levi-Strauss's opus on kinship, as well as to Mauss's *The Gift*. Many feminist psychoanalysts have been attracted to Lacan's work because of his stress on female jouissance and on the goodness of its nonfunctionality; his criticism of ideas of "value" and "exchange" (including the exchange of women) as central to the meaning of kinship; his view that biological differences between male and female do not determine psychological differences between those labeled as masculine and feminine, but rather that biological features on the human landscape are merely arbitrarily chosen *symbols* marking the initial division between self and (m)other. For all these reasons, Lacan's work may prove useful to us in the present enterprise.

In a sense, Lacan's view does not contradict that of either Mauss or Levi-Strauss. The central principle of exchange, the principle that the transaction can never be complete, that culture consists in people denying their own completeness, men renouncing their possession of their own female half, their own mothers and sisters, so as to become eternally committed to an endless quest for wholeness through others—these principles are not negated by Lacan so much as they are described from an alternative point of view. Lacan's vision might be considered to represent the personal side of the social ideal that Levi-Strauss describes. The principle of exchange—which states that you must find the completion of yourself outside of what you already own, and that this process is never finished—integrates society (if it does do this) at the *cost* of a sense of perpetual *incompleteness* at any level lower than that of the whole society, including, and especially, that of the individual.

Lacan has in common with Bourdieu, beside his skepticism regarding the whole, an intensely agonistic world view. For both thinkers, there is a breach between a fictional totality called culture, rules, the symbolic, the system, and an actual, willful, sentient creature called the subject or self. For both thinkers this breach, and the uncertainty and incompleteness arising from it are what life is all about. Both thinkers are particularistic, antiuniversalistic, antiauthoritarian. For Bourdieu private strategies, for Lacan private sentiments, are at least as important as anything public or shared.

Also like Bourdieu, Lacan falls into the very trap he takes such pains to reveal. Bourdieu, as we have noted, never departs from his assumption that power relations are all that enter significantly into the construction of human societies. In this and other ways, his vision is as totalizing as some of those that he criticizes, for in attributing sole reality to power as a human motivation, he legitimizes those who pursue it, while rendering invisible all the rest. Similarly, Lacan, for all his critique of ideals, myths, and abstractions, never gets down to cases. He is himself a mythmaker, a formalizer and formulizer, a deliberately elusive and mysterious father-figure, founder of what has been called a "cult." He has become an exclusionist and an authority. He has become institutionalized. Ultimately then we must part ways with him as well—but not without having learned from him.

There will be many readers, I know, for whom the psychoanalytic-cum-semiotic view of the human condition outlined above will appear totally useless and spurious. For instance, if one believes that what drives human beings to act and to create is not some "spiritual" trouble but rather the material conditions of existence, namely, the need to subsist and procreate, then one must necessarily reject this and all other depth-psychologies as irrelevant to the social sciences. However, *if* one feels that Freud did touch upon some fundamental human truths that may illuminate some of the regions explored by cultural anthropology, *then* I would suggest that one should give consideration to the Lacanian reading of Freud, bizarre though it may appear. After all, Freud's ideas themselves would seem just as bizarre were we not accustomed to them. Especially if we are willing to admit that human creative energy greatly surpasses what is required for the purposes of subsistence and reproduction, that our creative energy is spent only partly in the service of strictly material ends and much more in the pursuance of other kinds of needs, and if we have observed that less material needs seem often to be pursued even at the cost of survival itself, then we may be able to accept as a working hypothesis that even something as seemingly utilitarian as a mode of kinship organization may be created and maintained by human beings largely if not entirely for artistic or existential reasons.

Synthesis of Theories

Building upon these considerations, we might describe Dravidian kinship as, first of all, a set of variant cultural creations all oriented around a single, unifying ideal, which ideal is never actually realized in practice. Yalman calls this array of related kinship systems "variations on a theme."[44] The notion that there *is* some basic theme from which the different Dravidian kinship organizations all spring seems strong. So Trautmann argues that there must have been in the past a single Dravidian kinship system, which one might call proto-Dravidian kinship, from which all present-day Dravidian kinship systems may be seen to derive.[45] This common ancestor may be reconstructed on the basis of properties shared by its presumed present-day descendants, in exactly the same way that a protolanguage is reconstructed from the modern members of a language family, though none of the modern descendents replicates all the properties of the protosystem. Trautmann posits that the unified proto-Dravidian kinship system he reconstructs was a historical reality. But of course he would not claim that we could ever know this for sure. In a sense, the unified protokinship system, like a unified protolanguage, is a fiction or myth. It may be that Dravidian, for as long as "it" has "existed," has *always* been a *family* of languages with certain attributes in common, and was *never* one single language.[46] In the same way, Dravidian kinship may never have been one single system, but always, as it is today, a set of variant systems, no one of which matches the "protosystem" of bilateral cross-cousin marriage which the semantic structure of all of them seems to presuppose. Perhaps it would be better, then, to speak of "meta-Dravidian kinship" rather than of "proto-Dravidian kinship." Or perhaps

Plate 18. Paddi churning buttermilk: a form of jouissance.

we could think of Dravidian kinship in terms of Wittgenstein's famous notion of family resemblances, except that here the various related systems, rather than drawing upon a common pool or collection of features, instead draw upon a common *structure*, so that the illusion of an overarching, or underlying, or ancestral unity is great.

Secondly, the Dravidian kinship ideal is a *linguistic* construct: it is a set of words organized in a tight, symmetrical pattern, and defined in relation to one another. This pattern is in some respects like a poem; its symmetry gives it a certain aesthetic appeal. Ego or self is an intrinsic part of this pattern, occupies a particular place in it, and is defined in relation to the other terms.

A key, though hidden, feature in the pattern of Dravidian kinship terms is marriage. The organization of kinship terms makes no sense unless a certain kind of marriage is assumed. Ego takes his or her proper place in this pattern, then, by marrying. (Marriage is by far the most important ritual in Tamil Nadu, by far the most important event in the life of the individual there.) By marrying, ego upholds and seeks to appropriate the tradition created by his or her ancestors; by marrying, ego becomes part of convention; in Tamil Nadu, when ego marries he or she enters fully into this central part of the Tamil language (symbol, to Tamils, of their entire cultural heritage). At the same time, when ego marries, he or she (especially she) is broken away from the world of the mother, the primal world of shared bodies, which comes before words. That marriage is indeed perceived by many Tamils as just such a break from just such a world will be documented amply below.

It might be imagined that in Dravidian kinship organization, one leaves, at marriage, one kind of unity (the world of the mother, knit together by physical acts of love) to enter into another (the world of the social whole, knit together by the language of kinship). But the harmonious, symmetrical ideal unity held forth by Dravidian kinship terminology is manifestly an illusion. It is not just that the marriage-system mapped by the terminology is only sometimes realized, so that we have the usual gap between words and praxis, between cultural norm and statistical fact. Instead, for any particular Dravidian kinship community, there stands a third factor *between* the perfectly ordered semantic ideal built into the language and the partly chaotic empirical world of actor's choices. This third factor is that community's particular set of marriage *rules*, which legislate that marriage shall be enacted within the community so as to maximize the temporal power and religious prestige (the two are often interconvertible) held by the community's senior males. The rule of *kanyādāna* plays a key role here.

Under the rule of kanyādāna, marriage becomes defined as a father's sacrifice of his daughter to the invisible (*aḍṛṣṭa*) world.[47] The fruit of such a marriage must not be the kind that can be enjoyed in this world that we live in now. In principle what is being upheld through kanyādāna is dharma—the invisible moral order of the universe (similar to Lacan's idea of the-name-of-the-father). In fact what is being upheld is the prestige of the father who gives away his daughter in such a marriage—in exchange for the wealth he expends in dowry and elaborate marriage festivities, he receives (in Bourdieu's terms) a large pile of "symbolic capital."

Under the rule of kanyādāna, marriage for the sake of bodily and emotional *pleasure* (*kāma*) is renounced. This renunciation, unlike the other, is quite real, but here it is not so much the father, as the daughter and her bridegroom, who (unwittingly) make the sacrifice. To the extent that marriage follows the rule of kanyādāna, *and* to the extent that it is enacted as part of a system of exchange, to that extent pleasure (jouissance) is factored out of it.

But here is the third and final point that must be made about Dravidian kinship: regardless of whether they get it or not, South Indian people, both male and female, *expect* pleasure to be a fruit of marriage. They also expect personal and emotional completion and fulfillment to be provided to them *through* the marriage system. People may rebel against a particular marriage, but they do not rebel against the principle of cross-cousin marriage as they do, for instance, sometimes rebel against the principle of caste hierarchy. Cross-cousin marriage is an *option,* a matter of choice, in a way that caste hierarchy is not. If you marry a stranger that stranger *becomes* your cross-cousin. The kinship system, unlike caste, bends to accommodate the heart's desire, or seems so to bend, promises the hope of joy, or seems so to promise.

The statistical evidence that South Indians prefer in real life to marry either a nonrelative or a close cross-cousin (that is, someone whom they know personally and with whom they may have a longtime bond), making little of the option they have of marrying a distant cross-cousin, hints at the way in which the institution of cross-cousin marriage is taken as an affirmation of personal ties, more than just a reproduction of categorial affinities. For modern South Indians, cross-cousin marriage is, among other things, a *romantic* ideal. They reach for this ideal, and yet they rarely if ever achieve it, in part because it is always mediated for them through the rules of temporal power, the rules of interested exchange.

The Approach Taken Here

My aim in the remainder of this chapter and in the chapters following is to work toward an understanding of some of the meanings and causes of Tamil kinship institutions as they are revealed through expressions of sentiment taking place between actual people. For instance, we will consider what one particular woman says to and about one of her sisters-in-law on the topic of how this sister-in-law is considered to feel and how she makes others feel. Certain "myths" about kinship will also be discussed. These myths are not treated here as abstract codes, for they are in all their realizations, that is, in all their tellings, very particular expressions of particular sentiments held by particular people. The meanings of a given story—what is important in it, why it is told, what moral imperatives may be derived from it—vary greatly from person to person, from telling to telling.

In this approach, then, I attend as much to the private as to the shared, as much to the particular as to the universal. In stressing the private and the particular, one runs the risk of being accused of anecdotalism, and of one's informants being accused of atypicality. But it is necessary to deal with the apparently atypical in order to recognize that there are infinite strategies, infinite ways of playing the game, and to see that it is not the code but the praxis, not the iron rule of the ideal but all the failed attempts at its embrace, all the imperfect embodiments of its illusory phantom nature, that keep the game going.

The main point I will try to make in this chapter, then, is that the continuation of a particular institution such as cross-cousin marriage may be posited, not upon its fulfillment of some function or set of functions, but upon the fact that it creates longings that can *never* be fulfilled. It is possible to see kinship not as a static form upheld by regnant or shared principles, but as a web maintained by unrelieved tensions, an architecture of conflicting desires, its symmetry a symmetry of imbalance, its cyclicity that of a hunter following his own tracks.

A secondary point I wish to make concerns the question of "extension" of sentiments from one kinsperson to others—for example, the idea that one might feel for all the men classified as brother the same sentiments one feels for one's "real" brother, "by extension." This idea has rightly been rejected as a total explanation of marriage institutions. It obviously leaves too much unaccounted for to say that cross-cousin marriage is practiced because an individual may fulfill his desire for his mother by marrying his mother's brother's daughter, or someone in that category. However, in considering kinship as simultaneously a linguistic system and an organization of affect, I think that we would be equally in error to reject out-of-hand the possibility that sentiments, like ideas, may be channeled by means of words. It is important not to overlook the fact that in many parts of India, including Tamil Nadu, the selective use of kin terms is a powerful way of conveying, igniting, or engendering certain sentiments. One may apply a particular kin term to someone who is not in the genealogically "correct" relationship to one as a way of expressing a kin-based feeling toward them. Conversely, when a certain term is applied to a person, convention dictates that appropriate sentiments be expressed, inappropriate ones suppressed. A dramatic example of the affective impact of kin terms occurred recently during the Sikh-Hindu riots in Delhi, in which a group of Sikh men was prevented from murdering a group of Hindu women by being told that these women were their "sisters."[48] Less newsworthy, but still moving, instances of the affective use of kin terms occur often in everyday life. A woman in her fifties weeps because a neighborhood girl addresses her as *akkā*, "older sister," a term she has not been called by since her marriage. A man drunkenly making his way home encounters a woman he knows on a lone street; the woman backs away fearfully; the man replies, "How can you be afraid of me? I am your little brother [*tampi*]"; the woman loses her fear and continues on her way. In a film, a man risks his life to save that of a woman he has just met, crying out with great emotion, "If you are the sister of so-and-so, then you are my *macci* [MBD]." In a folksong, a man repeatedly asks a woman for something to drink. First she responds by calling him "older brother"; he says, "I don't mean that." Then she calls him "younger brother"; again he says, "I don't mean that." At last she calls him *māmā* ("mother's brother," a term of address for a potential marriage partner or a lover); then he says, "That is the water I want."

Examples such as these could be multiplied indefinitely. Some detailed cases of the affective uses of kin terms will be given in the text below.

The notion that face-to-face relations between individuals are in some way the foundation of social structure also deserves reconsideration, especially if we are allowed to reintroduce the diachronic dimension into the study of social systems and to think in terms of how each person as he or she grows from infancy to adulthood learns to conceptualize and to act within the social structure. We can easily imagine a child learning the meaning of the term "older sister" first in relation to a particular individual, and then learning to apply this term, with the feelings that go with it, to other individuals, and finally to whole categories of people. But the association of this term with a particular dyadic relation will always be, in both a temporal and a semantic sense, primary. Whenever I use the word "sister," somewhere in the back of my mind there will always be evoked an image of the first person I ever called by that name.

Individuals in what we might call a potential kin relationship with each other—say, very distant "sisters"—might choose to realize and enact this relationship, or they might choose not to. If they choose to enact it, they may do so in many different ways. If they never see or hear of each other, their sisterhood may not exist for them. But people who are engaged with each other in some way, people who must face each other daily or who require things of each other, *must* have some emotional stance toward each other. When individuals are so engaged, their ability to act in their mutual interest, or alternatively to defend themselves against each other's incursions, hinges upon the sentiments they have for each other. These sentiments in turn are given shape by what they call each other. Complex feelings may be evoked by a familiar word, as much as they are by a familiar face.

We Americans like to think of true feelings as free and spontaneous. The idea of "conventional sentiments" seems almost oxymoronic to us. It rankles us, seems phony.[49] Could a man *feel* that a woman is his sister just because her position in the social structure causes her to be classified as a sister with respect to him? Tamils, like us, often chafe against the artifice and hypocrisy of relationships established by the force of convention instead of by choice.[50] And emotional dissimulation certainly exists among them just as it does among us. In spite of all this I would still suggest that Tamil people can and in many circumstances do "really feel" such structurally enjoined sentiments. Emotional patterns developed in childhood among close kin are brought into play repeatedly throughout an adult's lifetime. People replay their first loves and hatreds again and again through countless successive relationships. The patterns are not the same worldwide, but for each person, there are such patterns. I would suggest that in Tamil Nadu it is just this set of patterns which are conventionalized (i.e., overtly recognized and deliberately shaped in certain ways) and given the names of kindred. As soon as a Tamil child can understand words, it is taught, together with the names of body parts, the appropriate terms for its kin.[51] It is also taught in a multitude of crude and subtle ways how to feel toward those kin. (The terms a small child is taught to apply to people are chosen to suit the emotions the child is taught to feel toward these people. The child learns genealogy much later.) How, then, can childrearing practices fail to have a strong effect upon the deployment of kinship strategies among adults? For it is just in childhood that the material for strategies, what we are accustomed to call "culture" and what Bourdieu renames "habitus," enters the body.

In sum, this chapter makes two arguments. First, the continuity of a kinship strategy such as cross-cousin marriage may be attributed to a dynamic of unresolved tensions and unfulfilled desires as much as to the fulfillment of some function or the resolution of some conflict. Second, we can see kinship strategies as played out from the emotional habitus acquired in early childhood within the domestic family. The tensions and desires about which I shall speak all have their origins in the household and in childhood.

The approach may be regarded as a feminist approach because it stresses the importance of the particular, the private, the affective, and the domestic, and because it considers the relations between males and females, and children's experience of these relations, to be largely constitutive of the social order. We have seen that the Dravidian kinship system is generally treated by cultural theorists as a cognitive structure, and by social theorists as a political one. At issue, on the one hand, are conceptual relations among categories, and on the other, relations of wealth and power among adult men. When the same system is considered in terms of its emotional consequences, and in terms of its effect upon the lives of women and children, then we may see what should be obvious in any case, that marriage patterns strongly interact with childrearing patterns, and that these patterns just as strongly influence, and are influenced by, the affective and political bonds that join the two sexes in battle or in love.

Tensions between groups

1. Matrilateral—tension between matriline and patriline as interest groups.
2. Patrilateral—tension between males and females as interest groups.

Tensions between individuals

1. Father's desire for continuity versus son's desire for independence.
2. Daughter's desire for continuity versus mother's desire for independence.
3. Love between opposite-sex siblings versus compulsory bond uniting spouses.
4. Informal adoption negating the boundary between kin and affine versus formal marriage reasserting this boundary.

Figure 10. List of cross-cutting desires in a Tamil household.

TENSIONS AND HARMONIES

The Exchange of Children Is as Important as Marital Exchange

People are shared among families, and the sharing renewed, through marriage. When people are shared, they share their physical lives—they see each other constantly, they work together, they listen to each other's talk, they share food, they touch often, they make love. But the physical sharing is important mainly because of the feelings that go with it, especially love, whose growth such physical sharing engenders. Marriage is a ritualized, public, and formal sharing of persons and the materials of life among families, in which men of the kinship group are expected to make the final decisions regarding who is to marry whom, what materials will be exchanged, when, where, and in what manner the wedding will take place. There is another kind of sharing of persons, private and informal, which is yet perhaps just as important as marriage, and perhaps more so, in establishing bonds of love. This is the sharing of children among women.

That the sharing of children among women is an ancient custom in Tamil Nadu is indicated by the presence in Tamil Sangam love poetry of the figure called *cevili tāy*, the foster mother of the heroine. In this body of poetry, only seven characters normally speak, so it is safe to say that even two millennia ago, when this poetry was written, at least the ideal of foster motherhood was of great cultural significance. The foster mother is represented as having as much affection for the young heroine as the girl's own mother, who also speaks from time to time in these poems. Modern pundits state emphatically that the foster mother was not a hired wet nurse. Also important is the *tōṛi*, the girlfriend of the heroine, not her sister, but so close to her that sometimes they seem to be the same character, speaking in the same voice. Modern pundits consider the tōṛi to be the daughter of the foster mother.

In modern Tamil Nadu, it is common for a woman to take into her house the child or children of one of her kinswomen and raise them as her own for a time. There are no rules regarding how, or why, or for how long, or with whom, this should be done. Sometimes the children are orphaned or sometimes the adopting woman is childless, but this is by no means always or even usually the case. Economic considerations are not cited by adopting women as reasons for adoption. Inheritance rules do not change by dint of informal adoption, and the child's own mother is not necessarily any poorer or richer than the adopting one (the children of poor relatives are sometimes taken into the house as servants, but this is a different matter).

Why, then, do modern women adopt each other's children? Altruistic considerations seem to be foremost. A Paraiyar woman with seven children of her own adopts the four children of a distant kinswoman who has been killed by her (the kinswoman's) husband. The children are too young to work and add to the family income. The adopting woman takes them in at the risk of her own life, and becomes ill, possessed by the spirit of the children's dead mother, when the father forcibly takes them back. The wife of a rickshaw driver who has borne seven children and lost them all in infancy adopts a girl baby found abandoned in a temple. She shares the little girl with two of her husband's sisters, the child spending several months a year in each woman's home. The wife of a college professor takes into her home the children of her brother and daughter, so that the children can attend better schools. A Brahman widow and her young daughter live in the home of the widow's married sister. Also in this home live the children of the deceased daughter of the adopting woman. And in our family, the widowed Attai adopts two of the daughters of her brother and the orphaned daughter of her sister, because her own son is grown and she wants children in the house. The three girls had been adopted by other aunts prior to their adoption by this one. All of the adopting women I have mentoned here belong to castes that reckon descent patrilineally and are virilocal. Most interestingly, in many cases, the adopting woman is the child's *attai*, father's sister, so that a girl may be raised as a daughter by the woman who later becomes her mother-in-law.

Thus many children in Tamil Nadu grow up with more than one "mother" and experience more than one household as home. The transitions can be jolting. Children may cry pitifully when their own mothers leave them behind. But they may also develop a deep fondness for their foster caretakers, which they carry with them into adulthood. For female children, the system of child-sharing combined with the system of cross-cousin marriage has as its most obvious consequence the likelihood that a girl will not experience such a radical break in the continuity of her life at the time of her marriage as will her North Indian counterpart. Instead, there will perhaps be a series of small breaks occurring earlier in life, which may nevertheless be strongly felt by children less than seven or eight years of age. In a Tamil family, as I have observed above, the first words a child is taught are kin terms, together with names of body parts. It is important to get them right, to know from the start who is in what relation to oneself. Oscillation between households might contribute to the sense of contextuality inherent in kinship relations. A child felt as a sibling early in life might later be known as a spouse, or potential spouse.[52] Under good conditions, membership in several households, including the households of affines, might make a child feel more at ease in the world. But for many small children, there is manifest anxiety associated with the boundary between kin and affine, a boundary that often coincides with the boundary between households. Such psychological boundaries may have to be crossed more than once as part of the general process of growing up.

Four Important Bonds

The bond between generations, the bond between siblings, and the bond between spouses, are likely to come in conflict with each other in any kin-based society. At certain times in his or her life, these different kinds of bonds are likely to pull an individual in different directions. As one bond grows closer, another may stretch and break, and someone may be left out in the cold. The trick is to have as many bonds as possible and keep them all in harmony with each other, not let any of them break. In Tamil society, for those who do not value conflict, the absence of any bonds at all is one ideal. Positive bonds on all sides is another.

Within the nuclear family, four relationships seemed to be especially important to the Tamil people whom I knew. These were the mother–daughter, father–son, husband–wife, and brother–sister relationships. When I say that these relationships were important, I mean that individuals often expressed feelings of strong love for their opposite member in any of these pairs, and that they also often expressed strong anxiety about the actual or potential breaking of their bond with this person. Conversely, the same bond might be perceived as a powerful shackle and its rupture longed for. In Tamil, the term *pācam* denotes both affection and forcible confinement, as of an animal for sacrifice. Among kin so bonded, longings for freedom and longings for continuity cross-cut each other. In all four of the relations considered here, there were good reasons for both kinds of longing. In all four cases, both the love and the fear, the attractions and the repulsions, invested in the bond received stereotyped cultural expression. Here I will describe some of the feelings associated with each of these bonds in turn, then I will go on to suggest how the institution of cross-cousin marriage, with the particular meanings that South Indians ascribe to it, builds upon the tensions among these bonds, the anxieties and the unfulfilled or dashed desires that each of them gives rise to. The tensions and anxieties, it will be seen, spring from problems that are by no means confined to South India. The pattern of their harnessing, however, is perhaps uniquely South Indian, inasmuch as it is linked to South Indian kinship organizations. I do not mean to suggest that the emotional tensions sustaining these four bonds constitute *the* foundation of cross-cousin marriage in South India, only that they together form one reason for the continuance of the kinship process, one set of forces propelling the cycles through which it moves.

A Man Sees His Son as a Continuation of Himself
(The father longs for continuity, but the son longs for independence.)

The purpose of getting married, according to village men with whom I spoke, was to have offspring, heirs (*vāricu*). These were people who would carry on the lineage, take care of one in one's old age, work the land that one passed on to them, and see that one was properly buried and remembered in yearly rites after one died. Daughters, however much one cared for them, could not contribute to one's continuity in this way. "They stay with you for ten years and then they're gone," said a number of fathers. Ironically, the consensus among both male and female parents was that daughters were more loving than sons, if there was any difference at all among them along this dimension. Daughters would welcome their father into the house. They would ask, "Have you eaten?" Sons would just say, "Oh, it's you."

But sons, and the love of sons, were crucial, because sons were proprietors of the two substances in which the selfhood of a village man was most invested—his land and his seed. It would be difficult to overestimate the emotional significance of owned land to men who worked it and whose fathers had worked it. From this land came their food and in it their bodies and their ancestors' bodies might be buried.[53] There could be no greater symbol of the substantiality and continuity of one's own body than the paddy field with its precise but easily broken boundaries and the precious supply of water running through it, easily stolen, easily lost. To sell one's land was not only to lose one's livelihood, but to lose the foundation of family pride for generations past and future.

As for seed, that is to say, human seed, semen, cultural constraints prevented me from interviewing men whom I didn't know very well on this topic. Fortunately, male anthropologists have done this job for me, and there is also no dearth of textual references to this topic.[54] Though ideas vary, there seems to be almost universal agreement among Indian men that semen not only makes babies but also is or contains a fluid more vital than any other substance in the body, so that to "lose" an excessive quantity of semen is a life-threatening event. Semen as a substance is very closely associated with the idea of the soul that survives after death (*uyir, ānmā, jīvan*) and in many contexts is identified with it. Though it is often said that females too possess semen, the identity and activity of this female seed is mysterious. It is sometimes said to be menstrual blood, which is a substance of a very different nature from male semen. In general, when people talk about semen (*vittu, intiriyam, jīva sakti*), they are talking specifically about the male ejaculate. The people who express concern or anxiety over what happens to their semen are males.[55] Thus sons receive and carry on the seed and soul-stuff of their fathers in a way that daughters cannot.

Beyond the land and beyond the seed, the spiritual fate of the father is in the hands of the son. In lower caste priestly and shamanic families (Ampalakkarars, Paraiyars, Velars) around Madurai, the family deity is passed on through possession or dreams or the choice of the father to the most worthy or eldest son or grandson. In some households, the family deity is all but forgotten, but in others, this deity is a vital presence with whom the head of the family strongly identifies and whose will is sought whenever there is a family crisis. When it comes in dreams, it might come in the form of the deceased father or grandfather.[56]

The son not only continues the father's spirit, he has the capacity to be both its liberator and its protector. It is interesting in this regard that the most popular male gods in Tamil Nadu—Kannan, Murugan, Ayyappan, Pillaiyar—are all children, sons, the majority of whose worshippers are men. A main function of these deities is the removal and forgiveness of sin and similar burdens. Hair, that fertile pollutant, is offered to Murugan. Some men grow beards and heads of long hair to shave off and offer to him. Then, some say, it is as though all the unhappiness they have experienced during the time the hair was growing is lifted from them. On

Plate 19. Annan and Jnana Oli supervise transplanting.

pilgrimages to the mountain temples of Murugan, devotees may carry large decorated structures called *kāvaḍis* attached to their bodies with fish hooks. The structure is intended to make the devotee similar to Murugan's vehicle, the peacock. The devotee removes this heavy burden and offers it to Murugan when he reaches the mountaintop shrine. Similarly, there is an annual, men-only pilgrimage to the mountaintop shrine of the boy-god Ayyappan. The devotees must endure much hardship before reaching their goal. They are said to be following in the footsteps of an evil elder man who tried to take the young god's life and subsequently repented. As they travel up the mountain, the devotees chant "*Caraṇam caraṇam Ayyappā* [Refuge, refuge, Ayyappa]." A song incorporating this chant is expremely popular in modern Tamil Nadu.[57]

Pillaiyar, too, may be a forgiver or remover of sin. Pillaiyar is the elephant-headed god. His name means "son" or "child." For reasons I do not know, worshippers commonly greet Pillaiyar by means of a conventionalized gesture of apology—they cross their arms, tug their ears, and slightly bend their knees up and down several times. Pillaiyar will forgive them for whatever wrong they have done. He will also remove the obstacles to their happiness, whatever these may be. Whenever an enterprise is begun, Pillaiyar must be worshipped first.

One of the most important deities in the village near Madurai where I worked was called Vinai Tīrkkum Vināyakar ("Vināyakar who ends karma"; Vināyakar is another name of Pillaiyar). He was supposed to have lifted a curse from the village which was causing all the children there to die. The man who told me this god's story, and who was a great devotee of Vinai Tīrkkum Vināyakar, was one whose only son had killed himself because the father had not consented to let him marry the woman that he loved. This father also confessed to all that he had beaten his wife during her pregnancy with this son and so considered himself to be the cause of her subsequent deafness. I believe that the father was seeking his son's and wife's forgiveness, and removal of the burden of his sorrow, through his worship of Pillaiyar. This would be an apt penance, for Pillaiyar himself in the story of his origin was murdered by his father.

Pillaiyar is the prime example of an Indian mythic type that A. K. Ramanujan calls the Indian Oedipus.[58] In Indian Oedipus stories, rather than the son murdering the father, the father murders the son—and then repents. In the origin story of Pillaiyar, Siva's wife Parvati decides she wants a child of her very own, who will be answerable only to her. She creates Pillaiyar out of her own bodily substance. The little boy then does as she says and prevents Siva from interrupting her during her bath. In another version of this myth, he sleeps with her. Siva jealously beheads him. Parvati is so enraged that she threatens to destroy the whole universe. Contrite and terrified, Siva seeks a new head for his wife's murdered son. All he can find is an elephant, so he takes its head and installs it upon the son's body, so reviving him. The wife and son forgive the father, and all is well again. Pillaiyar is made chief of Siva's armies, but he remains celibate throughout his life. One of his tusks is broken off. Some interpreters say this broken tusk represents the sacrifice Pillaiyar made to his father.

Was the old man in the village who worshipped the sin-removing Pillaiyar hoping both for forgiveness and for some kind of restoration of the son whose marriage he obstructed and whose death he caused? I can say only that the story of Vinai Tīrkkum Vināyakar together with the story of his son's death and his wife's deafness were the three he chose to convey to me, in a single narrative, as the key events in his life.

Another man told me the story of his own near-death experience with the god Ayyappan. His father had been forced to sell his land during a famine and had meagerly supported the family laboring for the same landlord to whom he had sold out. This father, who the son said had been more loving towards his sons than their own mother was, had died suddenly of snakebite. The eldest son, the narrator of the story, was left with several very small younger brothers to take care of. He felt that he could not afford to marry and have children of his own until he had raised all of these brothers.

After some time, he became ill with a stomach disease. Over the months it became worse. After unsuccessful attempts at treatment by village herbalists and local doctors, his caste elders ordered him to go to the government hospital in Madurai for treatment. He put his faith in one of his younger brothers, who had studied through the fifth standard, "to do the correct things" at the hospital. This younger brother had him admitted, and the doctors there ordered that he be operated on immediately. He was certain that he was going to die and worried what would happen to his body. But he told his younger brothers not to take his corpse back to the village but to have it buried somewhere near the hospital, for too much money had already been spent on him, he felt. "Then," he said, "not wanting to go out for nothing, I called upon Ayyappan, to put my sins upon him." To his great surprise, however, he woke up and recovered from the operation. He credited Ayyappan with saving his life.

As this man told his story, all the events of his life seemed to center around threats to the continuity of the patriline: the forced sale of the family lands, the sudden, devastating loss of his father, his anxiety lest he be unable to marry and have sons of his own, his concern for and dependence on his younger brothers, his belief that his body would not be returned to the ancestral land, and finally, his sense that the burden of single-handedly taking on the responsibility of the family before he himself was fully grown was more than he could bear. I feel, though I cannot prove, that his turning to Ayyappan in the hour of his expected death, asking Ayyappan to shoulder his burden, symbolized his hope that the patriline not be dropped.

People in Tamil Nadu take gods very personally. That is why they worship them. In the cases described above, the feelings of fathers about sons are opened up to us. Sons can free the souls of their fathers, by forgiving them, or by taking away the burden of their sins (here is another example of karma being passed on from ancestors to descendants). But the son has to exist, to have been born and not to have died, in order to take on the burden. Moreover, it is a matter of the son's own choice, whether to accept the burden or not.

Men have good reason to be anxious, first, lest they have no sons, and second, lest their sons abandon them, unshoulder the burden of their land, their lineage, their sins. The land, at least, is likely to be broken up, the integrity of it lost, if a man has more than one son. Hence the continuity of the father is in double jeopardy. For fathers always want their sons to remain together, to keep the land undivided, but sons, more often than not, end up dividing it. Quarrels between sons are harmful to the family spirit. This fact was very graphically illustrated in the village one day when Naccan, a young Ampalakkarar priest, angrily shattered the clay image of his family deity, because after the death of his father he had not received as large a share of land as he had expected. Right after this, he separated from his brothers, establishing a separate household. In shattering the deity he shattered the memory of his father, completing, in this act, the destruction of the patrimony.

A Woman Sees Herself as a Continuation of Her Mother
(The daughter longs for continuity, but the mother longs for independence.)

Parallel to the father–son bond is the mother–daughter bond. This bond, too, is felt to be both vital and vulnerable to breakage, but whereas in the relation between father and son it is the father who most fears loss of continuity, in the relation between mother and daughter it is the daughter who fears this loss.

In Tamil poetic discourse, both oral and literary, a common image for a young woman is the vine (*koḍi*). It is said that her body is as slender and graceful as a flowered vine. But the vine also is an image of continuity between generations, especially generations of women, recalling as it does the umbilical cord, and the processes of flowering and fruiting, important metaphors in Tamil culture for female sexual maturation (which is called "blossoming," *pūttal*) and birth-giving. So a female agricultural laborer sings in a lament to her lost mother, "We blossomed on your vine," and the phrase, "O mother who bore me" is a constant refrain in these laments, which were the most commonly sung songs among lower caste women in the two widely separated villages where I heard and recorded folksongs.[59]

Marriage, when the daughter leaves the household of her mother, is a cutting of the vine. Hence the famous opening words of the song of Nallataṅkāḷ, "*E<u>n</u><u>r</u>aikki kalyāṇam eṅkaḷ iḷankoḍikki* [When will be the

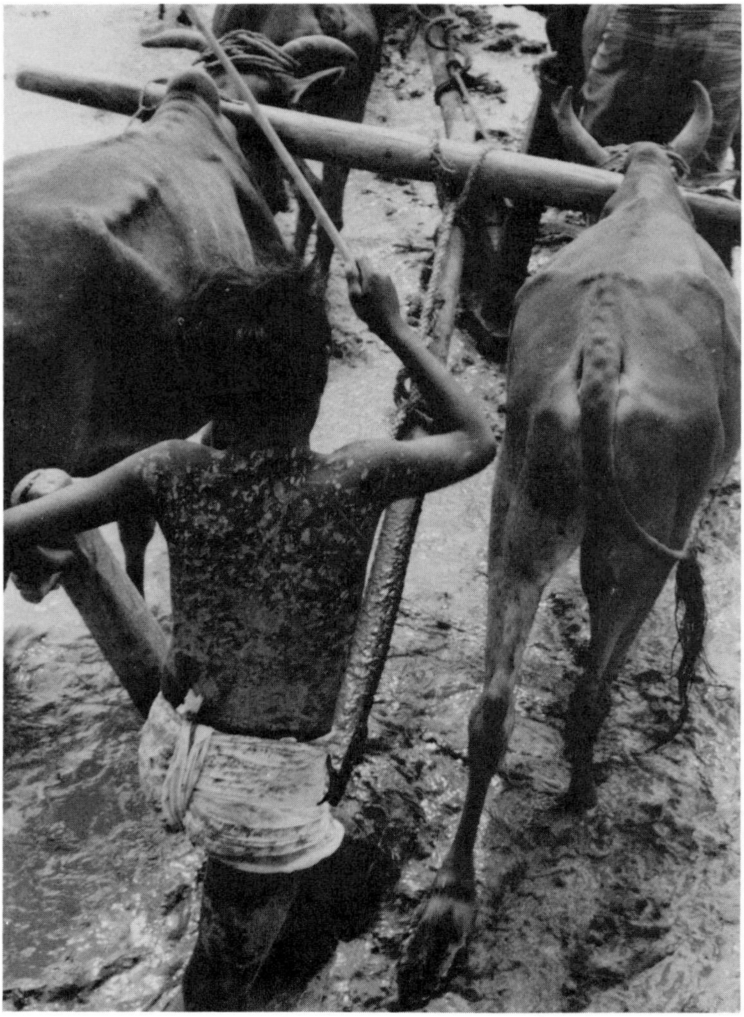

Plate 20. A boy ploughing.

wedding of our tender vine?]"—recited to me by Anni—are powerfully ominous. Her wedding coincides with the death of her parents. When she is told she must leave for her husband's house, she angrily tears off her ornaments. Consequent upon her wedding, she starves with her children and is refused reentry into her mother's home. When her oldest son tries to prevent her from killing herself and her children, she answers him, "They will laugh at us motherless children."[60] To have one's ornaments torn away, to be cut off from sources of nurturance, to be excluded from one's home, all of this is the meaning of a girl's being cut off from her

Plate 21. Women transplanting rice seedlings.

mother. In some versions of the Nallataṅkāḷ story, she is literally dismembered. To be cut off from the mother is equivalent to being oneself cut to pieces. Many women in Tamil Nadu identify with Nallataṅkāḷ. All know her story.

A girl finds her place of origin in the loins of her mother, which may be described as a garden, and she identifies her own womb and genitals with this place. So in one lament, the singer complains to her brother, "Have you forgotten my pomegranate garden, the place of your birth?" The two great landmarks in the sexual growth of a girl, her first menstruation and her first parturition (and often subsequent parturitions also) take place in the house of the mother (*tāy vīḍu*). It is important to note that a girl's natal home is always called her "mother's home," even though in actual fact the house usually belongs to the father. Similarly, the place of origin of both males and females is the *yōni* of the mother (this contrasts with the Greek formulaic metaphor of a person "springing from [a man's or god's] loins"). For Tamils, the belly of the mother (*tāyinuḍaiya vayiṟu*) is the place from which one came, and the place to which one goes for comfort is her lap (*maḍi,* "fold"). A grown woman with children of her own may lie with her head in her mother's lap with no sense of shame. Adults do not lie with their heads in their fathers' laps in this way.

A child can become separated from the mother through the death of the mother, or, if the child is a girl, through the child's marriage. In some laments, the death of the mother and the marriage of the daughter are

Plate 22. Padmini and Anuradha decorate the altar of the goddess Lakshmi for the Varalakshmi ceremony.

treated as equivalent severances. Then "seeking mother" (*ammāvai tēḍi*) becomes a natural activity, no matter what degree of maturity the child has supposedly reached, no matter how distant the world where the mother dwells. In laments, the dead mother is "hiding" or "gone to a foreign land," and the daughters are left seeking (compare this to the Greek myth of Demeter, where the mother seeks the daughter).

The term *ammāvai tēḍi* is a formula, a cliché, in Tamil Nadu. In the mid-seventies a magazine story with that title appeared. There it was written that all human souls on departure from their bodies seek their mother, and all good souls find her, appearing to them in whatever form she took on earth. The boy-god Murugan is a helper in this story, settling in the lap of his own mother, the great goddess, and appealing to her on behalf of all the mother-seeking souls. Males as well as females seek the mother after death.

In life it is the girl who is most likely to be separated from her mother, especially while still a child, because marriage is normally virilocal, and girls are younger than boys when they marry. Not only when she is still a child, but when she is a mother, or even a grandmother herself, a woman may still make visits to her natal home, "seeking her mother." Thus it happened that one young woman, married to her mother's brother, came to the town of her birth to visit her mother, only to find that their paths had crossed on the way. The mother had gone to the daughter's house to see *her* mother (the daughter's mother-in-law). The young woman said with a smile, "I came seeking my mother and she's gone seeking her mother." This young woman was more fortunate than many, in that her mother-in-law was her own mother's mother. This family, though it was patrilineal, also sheltered a strong and active matriline; all the daughters continued throughout their lives to seek the advice and comfort of their mothers in times of crisis.

Patrilocal marriage contributes to the continuity of the patriline, but it causes a break in the continuity of the matriline, and this break is felt especially keenly by the daughter who is cut off (albeit only partially and temporarily) not only from the mother but from the entire natal home and family. The mother stays in the place she was, and she may have other children to console her, but the daughter has no other mothers. So a daughter may feel herself to be shattered by her marriage. Conversely, a return to the mother's home may be felt by the daughter as a reuniting of herself, with herself. Surely, the break in continuity with the mother is one meaning of the several major myths about females shattered or dismembered as a consequence of marriage of the allied action of males (Māriamman beheaded, Kaṇṇaki and Mīnākshi debreasted, Nallataṅkāḷ and Siṅkammāḷ cut up into parts). In the village near Madurai where I worked, the clay image of the goddess Mantaiyammāḷ is broken to pieces on her festival day, which is also her wedding day. A similar idea may lie behind the representation of many village goddesses, for example, the "seven sisters," as physically plural, though one in spirit, and sometimes also in name. Kanniyammaḷ in Themozhiyar's village is such a goddess. In her shrine are seven small identical stones, which are her. On the other hand, her festival day celebrates not her wedding but her return to the house of her mother. And her myth tells not of her shattering, but of the merger of the sisters into one figure who is their own mother. The mother saves the world by destroying a demon who wants to marry her. And the sisters defeat their husbands by proving, in this united action, that the female force in the universe is superior to the male. Thus in this myth, continuity among females triumphs over the hetero-erotic forces threatening it. Usually, though, it is the other way round.

I have suggested here that daughters are more anxious about the break in mother–daughter continuity than are mothers. This is because the daughter has more to lose. Whereas a father seeks his own continuance through his sons, a mother does not, I would argue, seek such continuance through her daughters, at least not to such an extent. The reasons are several. In the first place, a mother does not ordinarily pass land on to her daughters. The garden of the yoni is entirely metaphorical. In the second

Plate 23. The village priest anoints the lion of the goddess Kanniyamma.

place, though a woman may achieve spiritual immortality, she is not dependent upon the existence of daughters, or any offspring of her own, in order to reach this state. Patrilineal households may have female house deities. These are, minimally, those who have died unwidowed, "still with flowers" (*puvōḍakkāri*); even if they die unmarried, they will be honored among this collectivity of saints. When they die, they become again like children, I was told. Children's garments are offered to them to wear, for they are again as free and as pure as children. Living women in laments express envy for the dead mother's freedom—but one does not have to have been a mother in order to become free. Women who have died in childbirth, women who have died heroically, satis, all of these may be specially honored and deified. The great South Indian goddess Kaṇṇaki was a woman who died childless, in agony after her husband's murder. Similarly the Madurai woman Siṅkammāḷ, murdered by her brothers, and likewise the Coimbatore woman Taṅkāḷ, who dies in suicide with her brothers, both become goddesses after their death and live forever in heaven as well as in the hearts of their many worshippers.

Daughters are not needed for the immortality conferred by martyrdom.

Men desire offspring for the purpose of future continuance. Women desire offspring more for the rewards of the present. If a couple has no offspring, or only female offspring, the woman will be blamed by her neighbors. If a couple has many children, especially many sons, the status of the woman will be enhanced. Sons will be expected to support both parents in their old age. If a couple have only daughters, they are more likely to spend their old age alone.

Large numbers of children bring status and increase the chances of future well-being, but the bearing and raising of them is a hardship for women. Thus women are much more likely to want to limit the size of their families than are men. Voluntary tubal ligations are much more common in Tamil Nadu than voluntary vasectomies. Women may fight with their husbands over their right to be sterilized. But a woman will rarely allow herself to be sterilized unless she has had at least one son. And if a woman must choose which child to feed, she will feed her son and let her daughter go hungry; hence, even in Tamil Nadu, more boys live to adulthood than girls.[61]

We may tentatively conclude that mothers do not value daughters as highly as daughters value mothers, or as highly as fathers *and* mothers value sons. However daughters value mothers very highly. Hence, while men (and some women) worship young, childless male deities and seek refuge in them, women (and some men) are more likely to worship the goddess as mother and seek refuge in her in that form. More than anything else, the mother is a protector. So the refrain of a popular song to Māriamman pleads, "Except for you, there exists no one to protect me, Māri-mother [*unnai vīḍa yārum illai ennai kākka Māriattai*]." Women gather and sing this song.[62]

It is clear that Tamils perceive each of these two vertical bonds, mother–daughter and father–son, as problematic. On one end of each bond, there is an intense desire for continuity. The other end of each is lukewarm, and there are strong forces threatening continuity on both sides. The maintenance of either bond is possible within a South Indian family; to keep it strong is something one might realistically long for; one will have observed that it remains strong in some other families. But unbroken continuity of *both* lines simultaneously, a matriline and a patriline within the same household, cannot be easily maintained. In the most prevalent form of marriage, marriage of a man with his mother's brother's daughter, maintenance of continuity within both lines is essentially impossible.

The mother–daughter bond and the father–son bond may be imagined as two parallel threads, woven across by two other threads perpendicular to the first two but parallel to each other: the brother–sister bond and the husband–wife bond. These two bonds also pull against each other. Here we will consider first the nature of the brother–sister bond.

The Bond Between Brother and Sister is Strong but Must Be Denied

Childhood erotic adventures between siblings probably occur among people everywhere. The feelings associated with these adventures get variously transformed, rechanneled, or repressed by different cultures in different ways. For instance, in the United States and Europe, the so-called latency period, during which girls hate boys and boys hate girls, discourages contact between opposite sex children, though secret erotic exploration during this period also is not entirely eliminated. Separation of siblings from each other and exposure to many unrelated children in school contexts is another of many Western customs which discourage sexual contact among siblings, without incest taboos ever having to be explicitly taught. In other societies, children may be taught about incest prohibitions and shamed out of incestuous contacts at an early age, and/or girls may be married in early puberty and physically separated from their brothers, so that sibling puppy love never has a chance to blossom into full-fledged adult eroticism. Whatever the shape of its repression, however, the fact is that for many human beings, the first erotic partnership is formed with a sibling.

This is not to say that the first erotic *feelings* are directed toward a sibling. In all cases where the mother is the primary caretaker, the mother can only be the first object of a child's desire, and even among scholars who reject much of Freudian theory, there remains little doubt that infant sexuality is a reality. One has only to watch any baby nursing to be aware of the intensity of feeling involved in this act. Erotic feelings on the part of mothers while nursing are described with horrified fascination in Indian folktales while they are discussed as "natural" in American parenting magazines.[63] Evidence continues to mount that repressed erotic love for the mother occurs in many places throughout the world, including in particular South Asia, even if such repressed love is not "universal" in some absolute sense.[64]

In searching for psychoanalytic understandings of South Asian familial eroticism, I have found Karen Horney's reformulation of Freud to be more useful than Freud himself.[65] Horney agrees with Freud's idea that the mother is the first object of erotic desire for both male and female children; she departs from Freud by suggesting that it is not necessary for a female to repudiate her identification with the mother and her desire for her in order to attain normal psychosexual development. Horney goes on to suggest that womb envy on the part of men may be the source of the myth that females are castrated and envy the physical penis. Lacan's reworking of Freud will also be useful to us here, especially his emphasis upon the feelings of longing and incompleteness of the subject/self that ensue upon the wedding of the subject to the System.

In India, erotic feelings for the mother on the part of both males and females are perhaps stronger than they are elsewhere. The reasons why this might be so are a matter of debate,[66] but the manifestations of these feelings in Indian superstructure and behavior are too massive to ignore.[67]

In Tamil culture, love for the mother is strongly encouraged. Erotic love for the mother is, of course, strongly repressed. However, an interesting bit of Tamil ideology (perhaps borrowed from the Victorian British?) claims that children before puberty have no sexual feelings. Hence close physical relations with the mother are allowed up until that time. Many adults, especially men, remember having been nursed for years, even to the age of five or beyond.

What does all this mean for sibling relations? If desire to possess the mother is especially strong in India, we might expect sibling rivalry to be especially intense. But there is no evidence that this is the case. Indian children are often reported by Western observers to be more cooperative among themselves than their Western counterparts.[68] Part of the reason may be that children's rivalry for the mother abates when they discover each other as potential, secret sexual partners.

In the case of older brother and younger sister, such a discovery and transferrence would be especially likely to occur. For the boy, a younger sister, being female offspring to his mother, could be seen as a duplicate of the mother, only, being smaller, she would be less threatening, more accessible, and more amenable to control by him. For the girl, an elder brother, being a protector, could also be seen as a form of the mother, only, being male and other, he would possess added fascination.

In support of these latter transferences, Tamil mythology creates a stunning isomorphism between the brother–sister relation, the sister–brother relation, the mother–child relation, and the husband–wife relation. There are many local shrines containing one large rock and seven small rocks. In different shrines these are interpreted variously as (1) a mother (Nallataṅkāḷ) and her children, (2) a brother and his younger sisters (Pattiniyamman), (3) a sister and her older brothers (Siṅkammāḷ in Mēlur near Madurai; the siblings in the Auvaiyār story told below), (4) a husband and his wives, and (5) a wife (Tirōpati) and her husbands.[69]

I am suggesting here that intense erotic love for the mother might under some circumstances be converted to intense attachment between brother and sister. A belief in the reality of the blood bond, in the powerful emotional significance of having emerged from the same womb (*cahōtarar*) would contribute to this attachment. Never being fulfilled, the brother and sister's desire for each other will never be spent. It will remain chaste and eternal, but pervaded by pain. Each will feel sacrificed—the one a martyred protector, the other a martyred innocent. In quest of a cultural ideal, through a vision of wholeness embodied in the kinship code, each will seek to recover the other. But only in death, out of time and beyond the code, will they find this recovery possible.

The bond of deep longing joining brother and sister, and the idealization of this bond, are attested in many places throughout Tamil Nadu. In the next chapter, an example from life of this bond of longing will be narrated. Similar examples of a culturally sanctioned powerful emotional tie between brother and sister are reported from North India[70] and Nepal.[71] Certainly it is not a uniquely Tamil invention. The historical taproot of this feeling (for it is deeply rooted) might even be traced to Proto-Indo-European kinship and poetics.[72] But in Tamil Nadu, where dramatic intensity of feeling vivifies all art as well as many household dramas, the tragedy of the brother–sister bond receives a wide range of remarkable expressions.

In a recent essay, Indira Peterson has brought together and analyzed a number of accounts of the diverse formal enactments and representations of brother–sister love in South Asia.[73] Peterson's material includes myths, folktales, proverbs, rites, movies, and novels. This material is drawn from throughout South Asia, but Peterson focuses on Tamil Nadu. A theme Peterson finds running throughout both North and South Indian material is the sister's possession of "magical" or "sacred" protective power over her brother. This balances the protective power that the brother exercises over his sister in the social realm, so that the relationship between brother and sister is overall one of reciprocity. In several myths, the sister's protective power takes the form of clairvoyance: she is able to perceive hidden dangers threatening her brother and so protect him from them. The power of the sister is hidden or covert in a second sense as well, Peterson finds, in that it often gets downplayed, or interpreted out of existence, in villager's exegeses of the stories in which this power is revealed. This hiding of sisterly power is especially apparent in the North Indian village of Karimpur, where Susan Wadley studied women's songs and rituals.[74] There, a rite in which the sister ties a protective band around her brother's wrist is interpreted by villagers as the sister acting in her own behalf, seeking to obtain her brother's protection of her, rather than acting altruistically to protect him. A *kathā* told in conjunction with this rite is similarly reinterpreted by the villagers. In this story, "at the time of her brother's wedding a sister saves her brother from eating poisoned food, protects him from magical thorns—despite the ridicule of the wedding guests—and ultimately stands guard over her brother and his wife on their wedding night, managing to kill a snake which creeps in to bite the brother."[75] Karimpur villagers telling this story interpret it as a model of the sister "worshipping" the brother and exhort all other sisters to follow her example. For North India, Peterson concludes, "the notion of women as powerful beings is underplayed or suppressed in the ritual as well as in the social realm, perhaps because it is seen as potentially disruptive to the stability of actual social relations between brothers and sisters, not to mention between men and women in general."[76]

By contrast, in South India, the sacred power of sisters over brothers, and indeed of women in general, is more overtly recognized.[77] The institution of cross-cousin marriage has much to do with this recognition, for in South India, as we shall see presently, the marital tie is clearly represented in important ancient and modern stories as a continuation of the sibling tie. Further, in such stories, the woman is portrayed as the center of the family, the main unifying force within it, the point of conjunction between otherwise disjoined human beings.[78] Thus Beck argues that the "kin nucleus" as it appears in South Indian mythology is not a married couple nor a male head-of-household but is a female with her father, brother, husband, and sons.[79] The nucleus of this nucleus appears in the great temple of Mīnākshi in Madurai, in which Mīnākshi, owner of the temple, stands at the center flanked by her husband Siva and her brother Vishnu. Minākshi remains eternally at a point of conjunction, precisely between the two males, because in her story, her wedding is celebrated but kept short of completion every year.[80]

As Peterson observes, the brother–sister bond is "*the central focus of the south Indian kinship system and marriage* and no doubt influences the sister's self-image and the brother's image of the sister at all levels of the psyche."[81]

Peterson discusses three major Tamil myths, a novel, and a movie whose central topic is the brother–sister bond. The first of these is the *Auvaiyār Katai*, a story told in conjunction with a ritual of protection performed by women for their brothers. This ritual, the *Auvaiyār nōnpu*, is supposed to be performed in secret, with no men present (although men can know *about* it), and men are not supposed to hear the story. Peterson, following Reynolds,[82] reports that only low-caste women perform this nōnpu, but I have found that high-caste women also relish telling the Auvaiyār story, and also like to keep it secret from men.

Auvaiyār was an unmarried woman poet of the Sangam era, celebrated for her didactic verse. In the story, Auvaiyār teaches a younger woman to bring posterity to her seven brothers "by ritually eating substances and objects symbolic of death and evil omen. She helps the brothers get married and herself marries a king. When the brothers are once again struck by poverty because of their wives' negligent behavior, the sister intervenes, teaches the nōnpu to her sisters-in-law, and restores them to their prosperous condition."[83] Here the priority of the brother–sister bond over the husband–wife bond is clear. Also evident is a tension between *nāttanār* and *nāttanār*, sisters-in-law, sister and wife of the same man.

This tension is the focus of the story of *Nallataṅkāḷ*, "Good Little Sister," and here even more clearly the sister's bond with her brother has both moral and spiritual priority over the bond with the wife. In this story, Nallataṅkāḷ and her brother Nallatampi ("Good Little Brother") are raised together and love each other so dearly that they are inseparable. When she comes of age, Nallataṅkāḷ is given in marriage against her will to the king of Kāsi, to whom she bears seven children.

> When a great famine afflicts Kāsi, Nallataṅkāḷ decides to seek her brother's aid; busy with a royal campaign, Nallatampi sends his sister home to his wife Muḷiyalaṅkāri ("Inauspicious Witch"). Muḷi insults Nallataṅkāḷ, starves her children, and throws the woman out with her children. With the help of shepherds, the distraught Nallataṅkāḷ finds an abandoned well; she throws all her children into the well, and herself commits suicide by jumping in after them. When Nallatampi comes looking for his lost sister, he finds the well by means of the *tāli* (wedding necklace) and *paṭṭai* (an ornament given to women by their brothers) which she has left outside the well, and which, having been turned into a rock at Nallataṅkāḷ's command, are visible only to him and the woman's husband. The brother cremates the dead bodies and promises to avenge his sister. Going home he arranges for the wedding of his son. At the wedding he denounces Muḷi as a murderess to his own son, and engineers a horrible death for Muḷi and her relatives. When Nallataṅkāḷ's husband arrives, Nallatampi informs

> him of all the events, and the two brothers-in-law commit suicide. Siva and Parvati revive the brother, sister, husband and the seven children. Nallataṅkāḷ demands and receives the boon of being enshrined in a temple and tank in Kāsi, while her sister-in-law is turned into a stone, to become the laughing-stock of travellers. The two brothers-in-law, rejoicing, ascend to Siva's heaven, Kailasa.[84]

A third major myth in which the sister–brother bond is the central theme is the long Tamil epic, *Aṇṇanmār Katai*, recorded and analyzed by Brenda Beck.[85] The name of this epic, *The Story of the Older Brothers*, perhaps reflects a recent (North Indian influenced?) attempt to mask the importance of women in Tamil culture, just as the other major Tamil epic, *Cilappatikāram*, whose most powerful figures are all women, is nowadays named *Kōvalan Katai* (*The Story of Kōvalan*), after the heroine's rather weak-willed and ineffectual husband.

Beck gives to *Aṇṇanmār Katai* the English title, *The Three Twins*, because the epic is not only about brothers, but about two brothers and a sister, born together as magical triplets, who accompany each other through many adventures. The sister, Taṅkāḷ, has a clairvoyant connection with her brothers, Ponnar and Caṅkar, so that when they die, she learns of their death in a dream, finds their bodies in the forest, temporarily revives them, and then dies and rises to heaven with them. Taṅkāḷ never marries; Ponnar and Caṅkar do (Taṅkāḷ helpfully cremates their wives when she learns of her brothers' death). Beck shows that the epic in its entirety shows a repetition of certain relations over the generations; in each generation a powerful female aids the heroes; with each succeeding generation this female becomes smaller and more specific: Great Goddess Parvati, regional goddess Cellattā, local goddess Kāli, mother of the heroes Tāmarai, sister of the heroes Taṅkāḷ. Each of these magical females, Beck says, blends into the others above or below her. Perhaps, therefore, we may speak of a kind of mythic matriline as forming the backbone of this epic. However the main point to be stressed here is that *Aṇṇanmār Katai* represents yet another piece of Tamil literature of widespread and enduring power whose main import is the celebration of the brother–sister tie.

When we come down to modern times and modern art forms, we find the same themes expressed, if anything, even more clearly than before. Here the best I can do is quote Peterson's beautiful translation of a passage from a Tamil novel of 1968, Nila Padmanabhan's *Talaimuṟaikaḷ* (*Generations*). I reproduce this passage here just because it gives us a very precise "native exegesis" of the biological-cum-emotional heart of

Tamil kinship. In this passage a brother faces his sister for the first time after determining to rescue her from a life of lonely widowhood imprisoned within her father's house:

> . . . perhaps these two hearts met and communed with each other in that immortal moment when face met face, and eyes embraced eyes.
>
> In those silent moments, no words passed between them. They felt a kind of joy sweep over them, as if, simply through the exchange of glances, each heart had shared with the other all its sorrows, troubles, and hopes for release. It seemed as though the most ingenious edifices of language and phrase, the most intricate dexterities of conversation, handed down through generations, through eons—it seemed as though in the eternal flow [*piravākam*] of that soundless [*anasvara*] moment, all these were blunted, rendered useless, smashed to pieces, when they confronted the steady torrent of that wordless moment. . . .
>
> How wonderful!
>
> Tiravi was overcome with wonder at the powerful experience of deep feeling, an experience that he could not quite take in. "Is it possible that, just because the seeds of our life, our bodily substance, our very blood, and our birth itself, came out of a single source, we are blessed with the transcendent vision of uniting with the other in feeling, of intuiting the very thoughts of the other?"

Each "intuiting the very thoughts of the other," the brother and sister find that their oneness of body (*uḍampu*) is transformed into a oneness of spirit (*uyir*); as in *Aṇṇanmār Katai*, those born together willfully die, shed their bodies, and mount to heaven as spirits together. For all the words that are given to its expression, this oneness of brother and sister is "soundless," it "smashes words." The oneness itself "handed down through the generations" makes all the weight, the tradition of these generations, invalid. The longing of brother and sister to reunite with each other can only happen when they step out of the terminology, the eternal tradition, the symbolic world created by their ancestors, which holds them apart even as it is built on the love which binds them. Peterson comments,

> In the affective vision of the brother–sister relationship in the south as well as in the north it is the enduring love between two human beings born out of the same source and

> the same soil that is ultimately stressed, the Tamil case being different chiefly in this respect, that here there is a tremendous consciousness of the sister as a sacred being, and of the brother and sister as the primordial, nuclear pair.[86]

Peterson does not mention at this point the other great difference between South and North India which affects the brother–sister bond, namely, that in the south, brother and sister may marry their children to each other. But she concludes her paper with a cinema song from the 1960s, which shows more clearly than any other piece of "data" one might produce, how in the Tamil ideal, siblings live in their children, and in uniting their children, unite their own lives again.

The film, *Pācamalar* (Flower of Affection) is about a brother and sister separated against their wills. The song is a lullaby, sung simultaneously by the brother to his baby son and by the sister to her baby daughter. They sing about marrying the babies to each other. Two important technical details should be mentioned here: first, the song encourages a reversal of the norms of kanyādāna and dowry-marriage, by suggesting that the boy will offer wealth in exchange for the girl's hand in marriage. Second, the kind of marriage the protagonists here sing about is "within the rules" (the babies are cross-cousins), but it is not the "normative" kind of cross-cousin marriage. Most commonly, mother's brother's daughter marriage is "preferred." MBD is the kind of marriage which, when it becomes patterned and institutionalized, fosters nonreciprocal relations among lines of kindred and "integrates" larger numbers of people. This is also the kind of marriage which is in line with the principle of kanyādāna. But the other kind of cross-cousin marriage, the kind sung about here, may be in some ways more satisfying, in that it approximates more closely the ideal set up by the terminology, it allows for true reciprocity between siblings over the generations, and it transforms the sibling bond into the spousal bond without crossing sexes: the sister returns through her daughter, the brother through his son. Perhaps for this very reason, patrilateral marriage is discouraged.

The song is called "*Malarntum malarāta malar*" (Flower Both Blossomed and Unblossomed or Half-blossomed Flower). The title I think refers both to the nature of the baby and to the nature of brother–sister love. Peterson translates the song thus:

> O child slumbering like a half-blown flower,
> O wild goose who blossoms
> like the dawn turning into day!

Soft breeze rippling through the river,
caressing the vine!
O Tamil poetry, born on Potikai hill,
reared in Maturai city!

Brother: You were born to win many battles
with your elephants and armies
you were born to marry your aunt's [*attai*] daughter
and live in joyful love!

Sister: He'll give you a gold watch and diamond necklace,
he'll ask for your hand—
your uncle [*māman*] will give much wealth,
he'll offer the whole world,
in exchange for the sister's [*taṅkai*] daughter's hand
in marriage for his son!

Sister: Shall I tell you of how my brother brought me up
like a darling daughter,
sheltered me under his wing?
Shall I tell you of the unimaginable misfortune
which separated us?

Together: We were born together, joined like the eye and
the pupil,
like the pupil and the image within!
Though the earth and sea and sky should come to
an end,
we shall not forget our love,
nothing can break our bond!

In later chapters we shall see how such thoughts enter into the lives of ordinary people.

The Bond Between Husband and Wife is Conflictful but Difficult to Sever

Whatever the sources of its strength, the sibling bond is primordial. It comes before any bond with an outsider. In some matrilineal societies, including some South Indian ones, the brother–sister bond retains priority throughout life. A man's home is his mother's and sister's home. Brothers and sisters cooperate. Husbands come and go. Hence in a traditional Nayar household a woman had many quasi-husbands and one "real" husband whom she met only once in her life. All of the husbands were peripheral figures. Only her relations with her brothers were of genuine significance.

In many patrilineal societies, on the other hand, even though the brother–sister bond has temporal and emotional priority, it is expected to give way to the husband–wife bond. To the suppression of erotic ties (if they exist) is added the severance of economic ones. A woman after marriage leaves the household of her mother and her brother and joins the household of her husband. If she is dependent upon the labor or landholdings of a man to support her, her husband or his kin must provide it. Hence in parts of North India, a woman after marriage is considered to be literally no longer of the same blood as her natal kin. In central Uttar Pradesh a rule of village exogamy combined with a rule prohibiting marriage with any close kinsman make for a relatively clean break between a girl and her natal family at marriage and help ensure that her loyalties and dependencies after marriage will be on her husband's side. This is not to say that in North India a married woman does not desire to return to her natal home, or does not have chances, even frequent chances, to do so. But marital conventions are so arranged that a woman's natal ties are clearly secondary to her marital ones, and a woman's husband is clearly dominant over her.

In most of Tamil Nadu, however, the brother–sister tie is neither clearly severed at marriage, nor is its emotional priority over other ties translated into social priority. The blood bond remains, and is affectively the strongest bond, but the marital bond is supposed to take precedence over it in cases where the two bonds conflict.

Meanwhile, the nature of the bond between spouses is vague, neither clearly hierarchical nor clearly egalitarian. On the one hand, the ideal of chastity and devotion to the spouse is entirely a female ideal, entailing a wife's subordination to her husband. On the other hand, it is not unusual to find men espousing a "feminist" point of view on this matter. So for example, one old man, advising a young man on his imminent marriage, told him, "Think that a goddess is entering your home." On the level of ideology, either the male or the female may be regarded as superior, depending upon who is talking, and under what circumstances. In practice, an egalitarian household policy appears to be common. When I asked villagers who made the important decisions in their households, more than half of both males and females said that husband and wife made them together.

In part because (and to the extent that) many of them are wage earners, wives in Tamil Nadu often will not accept a subordinate role with respect to their husbands. As wage earners, women laborers with whom I spoke regarded it as unfair that they received smaller daily wages than their husbands. They were quite vehement on this issue. They considered the work they did to be equal in value to the work of men.

Within the household, as well as in the domain of paid labor, there was a strong spirit of rivalry between many women and their husbands. Wives would not automatically accept submission. Neither would their husbands. Neither was it easy for wives and husbands to keep out of each other's way, sharing a household as they did. Consequently their relationship was often, from what I was able to observe, disputatious. Nevertheless, at all levels of society, lifelong monogamy and fidelity to the spouse were the ideal, though some honored this rule in the breach more than did others. Even among members of untouchable castes, who are often reported to be more lax than higher castes as regards marriage rules, divorce was not easy. When I asked one young Paraiyar woman whose husband had deserted her and her children why she did not divorce him and remarry, she replied, "It would bring down the caste." Others of her community concurred.

Neither could a man easily break the tie with his wife. In a single village, I heard of three cases of men murdering their wives, and one case of a man committing suicide, because their wives stood in the way of their marrying another woman. Murder and suicide are desperate ways out of a situation from which there is no other escape. While the prevalence of such violence does not support the idea that women in South India have relatively high status, the fact of wife-murder does suggest that the marital bond is taken seriously: only death can sever it.

In the ideal, both the husband and the wife should remain faithful to each other, regardless of the hardships involved. According to one Paraiyar elder, if a couple come into conflict with each other, the other members of their kindred group should help them work things out. Only if a wife is totally insane and uncontrollable should she be sent back to her parents' home, and then only as a last resort. Even if she lives "like an animal in the forest," he said, her husband should put up with her. Women, in the same way, told me that if their husbands were unreasonable, they had to simply not think about it, "not make a big thing out of it [*pericākkakkūḍātu*]," as they said. The adage, "*Oruttar porutta, iruvar vāṟka* [If one can bear it, both can live]," has high salience for such people.

The eternal conflict between spouses is abundantly reflected in Indian mythology, especially Tamil, which debates the issue of male versus female superiority back and forth endlessly on a cosmic level, in the form of battles and contests between deities or demons and their real or would-be mates. Siva and his consort(s) are especially given to such confrontations, but other deities also get into the act often enough (e.g., Rama and Tadaka, Arjuna and Alli, Kanniyamma and the buffalo demon). The rivalrous relationship between spouses contrasts with the cooperative relationship between brother and sister, so that battles for supremacy between brother and sister occur rarely if ever in Tamil myths.

The Spouse Usurps the Place of the Sibling

Both in mythology and in real life, it is painful for a sister to watch another woman become mistress of her mother's house and of her brother, more painful still if it appears that the beloved brother is deceived, and the home closed off, by the newcomer. So Nallataṅkāḷ complains to her older brother, "My mother would herself have invited me into her house, but I don't know whether your wife will do the same."[87] Similarly, a Paraiyar woman sings in a personal lament to her brother, "I go back to the house where I was raised, and find that your wife has set two mongrel dogs to guard it."

By the same token, it is painful for a brother to watch his sister become the possession of another man, more painful still if the man appears to abuse her. There have been at least two very popular Tamil movies on this theme: *Pācamalar*, mentioned earlier, and *Taṅkaikkōr Kītam*. In *Taṅkaikkōr Kītam* (*A Song for My Sister*), released in 1980, a boy struggles as a day-laborer to raise his younger sister, put her through college, and marry her wealthily. In dreams and in waking, he is obsessed by her image. But because of a misunderstanding, after her marriage, she disowns him. Meanwhile, a villain plots to rape the hero's sister's husband's younger sister and put the blame on the hero. The hero saves his sister-in-law by shooting the villain, while the dying villain blows the hero to smithereens with a hand grenade. The closing credits are highlighted by shots of a young boy playing with an even younger girl in an idyllic green pasture.

This movie played for months to theaters packed with sobbing crowds. The theme of the older brother martyred for the sake of his younger sister seemed to strike a nerve in many people. The theme of the cast-off older brother occurs in different form in the myth of Madurai Mīnākshi's wedding. Mīnākshi's older brother Aṛakar (a form of Vishnu) travels to her wedding with Cuntar (a form of Siva) but returns in anger when he is told that the wedding has been started without him. (Coincidentally, the names of Mīnākshi's husband and brother both have the same meaning, "Beautiful Man," in Sanskrit and Tamil respectively).

The story of Aṛakar in turn has local variants, for example, the story of Ponnar-Caṅkar as told to me by a Paraiyar shaman north of Madurai.

According to this shaman, Ponnar-Caṅkar, the patron and possessing deity of the shaman, was a deity in chains. "Why was he in chains?" I asked. "He had to be kept in chains because he was such an angry god," the shaman answered. "Why was he angry?" "Because he couldn't go to his sister's wedding." "Why couldn't he go to his sister's wedding?" "How could he," concluded the shaman, "when he was in chains?"[88]

Strange as the circularity of the shaman's story may seem to us, it reflects with a certain accuracy the bind that ensnares the older brother who loves his younger sister: eternally bound by his passion for his sister because he can never spend it, unable to spend it because of the way in which he is bound to her, he will never be able to break free.

Spouses, meanwhile, are bound in an opposite sense. Though their relationship may be hostile, because of the ideal of fidelity it is difficult for them to sever connections with each other. Indeed, the very fact of their being forcibly bound to each other may induce hostility between them, as we see in the West also. (Plato's *Dialogues* have been translated into Tamil, and several Tamil men told me, with assent in their voices, that Socrates said of marriage, "It's like a fort. Those who are out want in. Those who are in want out.")

Ayya referred to marriage as *ceyaṯkai puṇarcci*, "artificial union." Love that "happens by itself" he called *iyaṯkai puṇarcci*, "natural union." He even likened wives to *porutpeṇḍīr*, "women who live for money" (i.e., prostitutes) because they trade their sexual services for material protection. The massive exchanges of wealth that take place at weddings contribute to this cynical view of marriage, which view is not a novel one in Tamil Nadu. Ayya got his analogy between wives and prostitutes not from Germaine Greer but from the eighth-century Tamil text *Tirumantiram*. The tenth-century text *Tirukkōvaiyār*, more sympathetic to female sensibilities, similarly criticizes the way in which, "like pearls and conch shells, young girls are sent everywhere, anywhere, to be ornaments for men's bodies."

The elements of force, self-interest, and artificiality characterizing marriage contrast with the spontaneity and altruism of the brother–sister bond. Peterson cites proverbs and songs from all over India celebrating the "purity", "unselfishness," and "joy" of this bond.[89] Of folksongs sung upon a bride's return to her natal home, Peterson notes, "the focus of these songs is not the obligatory aspect of the [brother–sister] tie, but the natural, mutual love of the siblings."

In short, one pattern that emerges (with many variants and exceptions) from an examination of sibling and spouse relations in Tamil culture seems to be this: that brother and sister develop a strong affectional bond

Plate 24. Padmini at the doorstep.

for each other but are not allowed to share a life, while spouses are expected to share a life regardless of the degree of their compatibility. The spouse may become in some ways like an unwanted sibling, competing for superiority, for goodness in the eyes of the world, for the favors (such as money) that the world has to offer. And the sibling may become like a desired but forbidden mate. Emotionally, the sibling and spouse relationships seem to switch places back and forth. While in social action, each is kept strictly separate, in the mind, each is easily converted into the other.

In mythology, this interconvertibility of sibling and spouse relationships is clearly apparent. So, for example, in the epic *Cilappatikāram*, an episode occurs in which the husband and wife Kōvalan and Kaṇṇaki are asleep on the road to Madurai. Two ruffians come along and ask their protector, the Buddhist nun Kavundi, who they are. The nun replies, "They are my children." At this, one ruffian comments, "Have you ever noticed how brother and sister often act as though they were husband and wife?" In the mind of Kavundi, the spouses have been turned into siblings. In the mind of the ruffian, these "siblings" are turned back into spouses again.

In the Aṇṇanmār Katai studied by Beck, the heroine Taṅkāḷ and her brothers Ponnar and Caṅkar are incarnations of the goddess Parvati and her brother Vishnu; but they are *also* incarnations of the Mahabharata heroine Draupadi and her five husbands the Pandava brothers. I have already suggested that in the Aṇṇanmār Katai, the descent-by-incarnation of Taṅkāl from a series of goddesses is a kind of mythic matriliny. If this is so, we may see in the Aṇṇanmār Katai a shadow of the generational alternation of siblings and spouses which Dravidian kinship in its idealized form represents.

A modern singer takes up the theme of sibling-turned-to-spouse when she laments to her older brother, who has forsaken her (so she feels) for his wife, "Have you gone with Madhavi, and have you forgotten my pomegranate garden, the place of your birth?" Madhavi was a courtesan for whose sake Kōvalan deserted Kaṇṇaki. The singer is implying that the wife is like a prostitute, while she herself (the singer, the sister) is the true and original wife, and the rightful representative of the mother.[90]

Sister and wife of the same man, then, are coequals. Often in both myth and life they are bitter rivals and enemies (though sometimes, as we shall see later, they are just the opposite of this). Brother and husband of the same woman are in a similar relationship. If, either the brother–sister bond were less strong to start out with, or the husband–wife bond were looser or more easily dissoluble, we might not find the sibling and spouse relationship in mirror opposition, as we do. Whatever its causes, however, this opposition is a powerful presence in many people's lives.

CONCLUSION

". . . the meeting place that will never reach its end . . ."

Tirukkōvaiyār, 307.

Dravidian kinship terminology is a highly patterned, symmetrical, and indeed aesthetically satisfying verbal system. If the terminology reflected *precisely* the organization of human beings on the ground, then all the tensions described in this chapter would be resolved and all the desires would be fulfilled. Matrilines would not conflict with patrilines, women

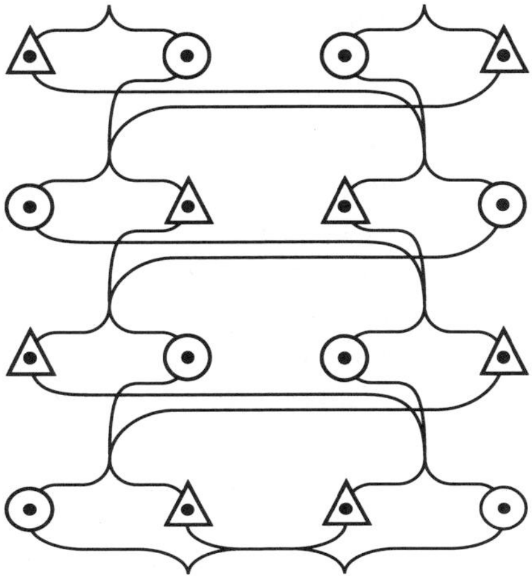

Figure 11. Ideal pattern of bilateral cross-cousin marriage.

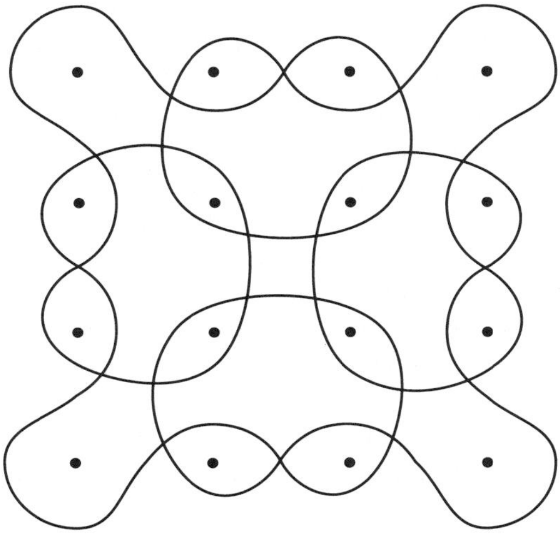

Figure 12. Kolam. *A design drawn by women on the threshold of the house in the morning, when all is well with the family. One of many.*

would not conflict with men, the bond between siblings would not conflict with the bond between spouses. A single small family, two lines of women, two lines of men, two pairs of siblings, two pairs of spouses, would meet all its own needs forever. Patrilines and matrilines would parallel and reinforce each other. Father–son continuity and mother–daughter continuity would harmonize. These harmonized continuities, in turn would harmonize the bonds between siblings and spouses. A father would continue in his son and a mother in her daughter, and then, when the children of siblings became spouses, the siblings themselves, in the bodies of their children, would reunite as marriage partners. Spouses would bear siblings, siblings would bear spouses, and the separate continuities of matrilines and patrilines would merge.

I have tried to show that in Tamil Nadu, there are strong expectations that each of these different continuities will be maintained; the expectations for harmony are perhaps reinforced by the aesthetic symmetry of the terminology system.

But in real life, as we know, this terminological system is not acted out perfectly, indeed it could never be. Rather it occurs in various partial manifestations, each of which approximately fulfills some people's dreams, but completely baffles others. The baffled dreams are not thereby killed; rather their unfulfillment leads to a sense of injustice—A sister thinks, "My brother *should* have stayed loyal to me, but instead, by favoring his wife, he betrayed me." Or a husband thinks, "My wife *should* do as I say, but instead she coddles her brother." Or a father thinks, "My daughter *should* have married my sister's son, but instead she eloped with a boy on her mother's side, and so she betrayed my obligations to my affines." Or a daughter thinks, "My mother *should* have kept me near her, but instead I was sent far away." Complaints like these, in just such words, are common, even though the offender has acted within the overall rules of the game, only stressing the fulfillment of his or her own desires.

On the ground are such people with their various longings, supporting the continuation of the kinship ideal by investing their different personal dreams in it, but in that very process pulling against each other, making the possibility of each other's total fulfillment all the more remote. As long as this ideal answers to the desires that have been written in their bodies since childhood, they will keep reaching for it, and as long as they reach, its various imperfect manifestations will continue to be born.

CHAPTER FIVE

Siblings and Spouses

PRELUDE

Like husband and wife, brother and sister share a womb, and share a home. Brother and sister are born from the same womb (*uḍan piṟantu,* "born together"; *cahōtarar*, "same womb"). Into one womb, husband and wife pour the strength of their lives. From this womb springs their mutual future, their continued life. The son is the father's seed, the daughter the mother's vine—the same seed, the same vine, spouses before, siblings after, and in the next generation, spouses again. Girls marry at twelve, bear at thirteen. Generations succeed each other rapidly. The daughter's first pregnancy may precede the mother's last. Lives blossom and fade quickly. Children reap the fruit of their parents' sowing; karma goes from father to son of the same seed as easily as from body to body of the same soul. My parent dies, my child is born, the same soul with the same habits, the same laugh, male then, female now, later either. Thus blood lines and soul lines intermingle.

> PORUTCELVI
> ". . . my breath and soul is he who
> is the heart-crystal . . ."
>
> *Tirukkōvaiyār*, 5.

Of all loves, the most tragic love is that shared by orphaned older brother and younger sister. The brother who raises his sister is both her parent and her spouse. His shoulders are too small to carry her lightly. He spends his childhood's energy to keep her. With the help of his toil, she becomes a full woman, then she flies away, with nary a backward glance, leaving his nest empty. So the story goes, from the brother's side. The sister sees it differently. She is driven from her natal home, her mother's home, her home, by the evil new woman who steps into her brother's heart. To the strong love of siblings, marriage is always a betrayal.

Porutcelvi is Ayya's sister. She is about five years younger than he is. When I meet her, she is in her late thirties. She lives in a tiny one-room house in a town south of Madras, where she works as a schoolteacher. Her only child, a teenage daughter, lives with her. Her husband is in the merchant marine and is away from home most of the time. His picture hangs over the doorway. Porutcelvi's house is clean and in good repair, but it has no water supply. Porutcelvi has to hire a woman to bring water in pots from the river some distance away. When I arrive, she asks me what I would like to eat, and I tell her whatever she has on hand—dosais would be good. She has no dosai batter in the house, so against my protestations she sends to a local restaurant for dosais and is disappointed when I don't eat them all.

In a corner of the house hangs a collection of fashionable saris. Porutcelvi presses me to accept one of them from her as a gift. I decline, explaining that I would have no use for it in America. Before I leave she convinces me to accept a black waistcloth heavily embroidered with gold thread—a Muslim man's wedding apparel. I can make it into a skirt, she says. Later I learn that this was the garment her husband wore on their wedding day.

In the evening, she walks with my little son in her arms until he falls asleep. While I visit others, she lies down beside him, to comfort him in case he wakes up. Later, she takes me to visit her friends, politely inquiring about the customs of our country, discoursing on the customs of her own. She asks me to repeat for her the marriage vows that Westerners take. She lectures me in limpid, scholarly Tamil about God's care of the soul. God is like a mother, she says, gently guiding the childlike soul down the right path, punishing it only to keep it from going astray. In the morning and in the evening, she performs a worship ceremony in her home, singing the hundred lines of Māṇikkavācakar's "Sivapurāṇam" in a clear, strong voice that rings through the Muslim neighborhood where she lives.

Like Anni, Porutcelvi was renamed by Ayya. The name given her at birth was Lakshmi, the Sanskrit name of the goddess of wealth, Vishnu's consort. Lakshmi is a very common personal name for women throughout India. But at some point, Ayya had translated his younger sister's name into Tamil (*poruḷ* in Tamil means wealth; *celvam* also means wealth; her short name, Celvi, is a common one for Saiva women in Tamil Nadu). The name her brother gave her is the name that she now goes by.

During hard times, says Porutcelvi, her mother comes to her in

Plate 25. A village bride.

dreams, to comfort her. When her mother was alive, Porutcelvi did not have so much affection for her, she says, but Ayya did. There were three of them, the oldest brother, Ayya (Porutcelvi calls him Annan), and herself. Their mother became pregnant again when Porutcelvi was very young. A few days, as Celvi remembers, after the birth of a female child, her mother came running to her and told her that by dawn the next morning she (the mother) would be dead. She died that night. Ayya fell on top of the corpse sobbing, so great was his sorrow.

Even from childhood, says Celvi, or at least as early as she can remember, Ayya had great bhakti. From the age of fifteen, or perhaps earlier, he would undergo attacks of *iraipattu* (seizure by a deity). There would be *atircci* (shock), he would tremble uncontrollably so that no one could hold him, and run out into the street. His brother would run after him and bring him back. After that, it took him an hour or two to return to his senses.

Ayya is by nature a very angry person, says Celvi. That is his *piravikuṇam,* the quality he has had since birth. She said that once when they were children in their home village, he and his brother climbed a tree and were playing in it. The older brother tackled Ayya. Ayya climbed down from the tree, went to his grandmother's house, got some clothes and money, and went to Madras. He did not come back. Celvi, learning of this, sat down on the steps of the village tank and wept. Their father said to the older brother, "It is your responsibility to go and find him." The brother went, and he, too, did not return. Celvi and her father went to Madras to look for them. In the Saidapet police station, they found the older brother. He had been working in a restaurant. Ayya had found a job making tali strings.

Their father and their first older brother were both very cruel; one could not expect love from them, said Celvi. The father believed that women should not study—that was the belief of those times. But Ayya, by his own labor, grinding rice batter and sewing, had put her through school. Celvi, Ayya, the older brother, and the father had all lived together in Madras. The father worked and Ayya also worked, earning twenty-five to thirty rupees a day sewing, which was quite a lot of money in those times.

However Ayya is, she is that way too, says Celvi. Whatever he believes, she also believes. He has become more famous than she, only because he has studied more. If anything happens to Ayya, she knows, and if anything happens to her Ayya knows. There is a kind of connection between their hearts. The oldest brother is not connected with them in this way.

I ask Celvi, what does she think are the conditions that caused her brother to be as he is? She talks for a while about the importance of the company of good people (*nallār cuṛal*). Then, mysteriously, she relates the life story of the Saiva saint Cuntar, who had reached Kailasa and the feet of God but had descended from the mountain once, noticed two girls, and thought them both beautiful. For this lapse, God punished Cuntar by making him be born on earth again. The two girls became his wives. Cuntar wept, "How can I ever regain your holy feet, now that I have lost them?"

Celvi wrote a poem to Padmini, Ayya's wife. Before he was married, Celvi said, Ayya knew only physical pain. When you take a soft fruit and repeatedly beat it, what will happen? So it was with Ayya's heart after his marriage. She said she wrote this poem when she observed Ayya and Padmini fighting and could not bear it.

In love he did not grow
He grew love, and held it.
He cherished work. In the world
He lived as a great man.
In school he did not study but
He sang garlands of songs.
To words he gave the soul of words. In high
Words and deeds he dwelt.

He lived respected by the learned. Even in dreams
The learned he respected.
His feelings he protected; imperishable
Discipline he guarded.
He hated his kin; in justice
He fed his own.
You gave him your tie—O God—
He grew the bond.
Why did you make him your kin? Why
Did you hurt his tender heart?

Pācattil vaḷaravillai—avan
pācattai vaḷarttuk koṇḍān.
Uṟaippaiyē pēṇivantān—ulakil
uttamanāy vāṟntu vantān.
Paḷḷiyil paḍikkavillai—ānāl
pāmālai pāḍi vantān.
Collukku col uyir koḍuttān—uyar
collilum ceyalilum avan iruntān.
Kaṟṟavar matikka vantān—kanavilum
kaṟṟavarai matittu vantān.
Uṇarvukaḷai kāttu vantān—aṟiyāta
oṟukkattai kāttu vantān.
Cuṟṟattai veṟuttu vantān—nērmaiyil
cōntattai māntiruntān.
Pantattai nī koḍuttāy—iṟaivā
pācattai avan vaḷarttān.
Uṟavai ēn koḍuttāy—menmai
uḷḷattai ēn nōkaviḍḍāy?

Of Porutcelvi, Ayya says, he does not worry about her. She has enough self-confidence to look after herself. Besides, she has made her own choices. She married a man of whom Ayya did not approve.

Once, according to Ayya, he went to spend the night at his sister's house. Her husband was not there. Late at night, in the rain, the husband came and knocked at the door. Ayya said he called out, "Who is that knocking in the middle of the night?" The husband, hearing Ayya's voice and fearing to enter (since it is wrong to be out at all hours) did not answer but slept in the rain. In the morning, when Celvi saw this, she said to Ayya, "Don't you want me to be with my husband?" Because of her saying this, Ayya says, he will no longer enter her house. "I will not stand between you and your husband," he reports that he said. She, who knew him well, was wrong to think that he would not let her husband in the house.

"I raised my sister from the time she was three until the time she was

Plate 26. Ayya relaxes in Peruveli.

twenty-two," Ayya said, "About nineteen years. I carried her on my shoulders, I combed her hair and braided it and put flowers in it. If a parent raises a child so lovingly, and then sees someone beating the child, how painful it will be for the parent. So I saw her husband strike her, and when I saw that I went to strike her husband, but she stopped me, saying, 'Who are you to come between a husband and his wife?'

" 'That's right,' I thought, 'Who am I?' The words ring a thousand times inside my heart."

PADMINI

". . . for you are like the tiger-town,
o bright-browed one . . ."

Tirukkōvaiyār, 126.

By all accounts, both Padmini and Ayya were hot-tempered people, and they were at their hottest in their showdowns with each other. Padmini provoked Ayya, for whom verbal elegance was a sacred value, by addressing him sarcastically as *swami* and unrespectfully as *nī*. Ayya provoked Padmini by saying things like "All women are dogs," or "I see that bed loves you so much it won't let you go," and mocking her emaciated body. During that year, in my presence, they were constantly at each

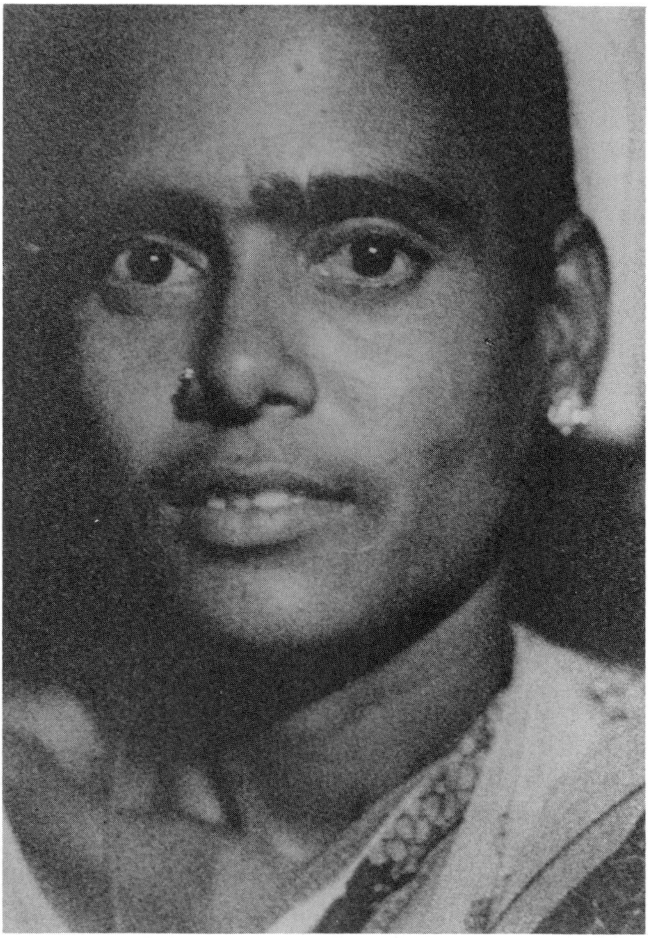

Plate 27. Padmini.

other, so that I wondered how either of them could stand it. Other members of the family also expressed distress at their quarreling and angry natures. But they said that Padmini and Ayya had always been like this. In fact, in the past, they had been worse.

In Ayya's case, no explanation seemed needed; anger was just a quality he was born with ("his *cupāvam,*" said Attai; "his *pir̠avi kuṇam,*" said Porutcelvi). But for Padmini's angry nature, they sought explanations, perhaps because she was in the house with them more. An uncomfortable silence fell over the family when Padmini lost her temper, scolded an adult, beat a child or servant. Attai said, distressed, that no matter how much they told her that it was wrong to get angry like this, when they told her, she would pout and her anger would not go away. Anni said, angry herself at the time, that Padmini lost her temper often because she always thought she was right and would never defer (*paṇiya*) to others.

Padmini, besides being short-tempered, was very thin, and people saw a link between these qualities of hers. Because she was thin and weak, she had a short temper. Because she burned herself out in anger, she grew thin. According to Padmini's mother, both the anger and the thinness began at the time Padmini had typhoid, when she was twenty-one years old. She showed me a photograph of a plump and smiling little girl—Padmini at the age of ten.

As Padmini came through the noonday sun alone one day, bringing him lunch, Ayya said he was worried about her, she was growing even thinner. He said he had spent thirty rupees to buy medicine for her. He said that getting so much money out of him was like sqeezing water from a dry cloth (and he wrung his veshtie tightly in angry illustration); he made so much effort for her and then she ate only one or two pills and left the rest.

Padmini, having arrived, hearing this, said that she didn't take any medicine, for there was nothing wrong with her.

Ayya said that he worked hard to see that the family was well taken care of; if they wouldn't take care of themselves, what was he to do?

But from my point of view, Padmini was only mirroring Ayya, for he also refused to take medicine, or to rest when he was ill. In the same way, though he said he thought she should wear gold jewelery, she refused, because she had decided to be "simple" (*eḷimai*) like him. Ayya valued hard work and thought of himself as a hard worker, but he wanted his wife to stay at home. Then after he (against her expressed wishes) had constructed a rice mill, she (against his expressed wishes) went to work in it. Her defiance on one level could be seen on another level as admiration, support, and trust.

The idea that there was something hidden in Padmini, and yet that there was nothing hidden, preoccupied Ayya. He often said, "She harbors nothing in her mind," meaning no secrets, no grudges, every thought immediately spoken and gone, every wish immediately expressed and forgotten. But he also liked to say of Padmini, "She is like a jackfruit." The jackfruit has a very sweet, sticky inside covered by a hard, spiky shell. Thus to Ayya, Padmini was the same inside and outside, and yet she was different.

Such ambiguities pervaded their relationship. When, in Ayya's mind, Padmini did wrong, and he criticized her, and she wouldn't listen, he would punish himself (and, indirectly, her) by fasting for days. He said that he was punishing himself for making her persist in her wrongdoing by telling her not to do it. The distinction between the wrongdoer and the victim, the punished and the punisher, was completely lost. Thus in his punishment, he bound himself to her.

Padmini would criticize Ayya and disobey him, but when others joined her in the attack, she would rush to his defense. For instance, she said that immediately after Jnana Oli was born she had decided to have a tubal ligation, though Ayya had said he did not want her to, because she was already so weak. She asked the advice of her obstetrician, a woman. The obstetrician said that she could certainly have an operation if she wanted one. Padmini said that after the operation, she had felt something like a large hard ball in her belly. She was afraid to tell Ayya because he might scold her. I told her I thought it would be wrong for a husband to scold his sick wife. Padmini answered, defending him, that he would never attack her when she was ill; he would only say, "I told you so." When Ayya was absent, Padmini would never criticize him, beyond lamenting that he criticized her. She would only disparage and fight with him when he was around.

Ayya treated Padmini reciprocally. When she was absent, the things he said about her were highly laudatory. He made her sound almost mythic in her wifeliness.

A story he liked to tell his new friends concerned the manner in which he had gotten married. He said that as a young man he had never wanted to get married; he wanted only to lead the life of an ascetic. But well-meaning friends wanted him to marry and, to humor them, he had gone around with them to visit the various eligible girls they had in mind for him. One of these girls was Padmini. Later he had forgotten all about her and all the other girls, he said, but she had remembered him. After having seen him, she had vowed to marry no one but him and had herself adopted an ascetic way of life, in imitation of him. She had surprised her parents by saying, "I no longer want gold bangles; earthen bangles are enough for me." Though her parents tried to get her to marry others, for seven years she had remained steadfast in her resolve to consider no other bridegroom. When she had reached the age of twenty-one, still unmarried, Attai and Anni had gone to a great Saiva festival to beseech Ayya to marry her. They had worn sacred ash, and they had approached him, unknowingly, at a sacred time and in a sacred place by the temple. Attai had wept, prostrating herself before him, and had told him that if he refused to marry this girl, she would remain forever unmarried. Moved by Attai's tears, Ayya had consented to be Padmini's husband.

I would never be able to find out how much of this story was "true" in our sense of the word. I think it had a certain truth of the heart. It echoed the story of Siva and Parvati's courtship, and I think it was important to Ayya that his marriage be thought of in this way. Anyway, Siva and Parvati also had their spats. But nonmythic history sometimes moved in on Ayya's memories and forced him to revise them.

When I visited Padmini's parents in Malaiyanur, I was sitting by myself on the porch, and a child asked me if I would like to see some family pictures. I said yes. The child went into a back room and brought out a stack of old photographs. Among them was a wedding picture: two teenaged brides, flanked by two very ugly bridegrooms. Standing between the two brides was the four-year-old (by my estimate) Anuradha. One of the brides was Lalita, Padmini's slightly older sister, who still lived in Malaiyanur. The other bride was clearly Padmini herself. A neighbor had entered, and I asked her who the man was standing next to Padmini. In hushed tones the neighbor said, "That was Padmini's husband. He is dead."

I was surprised, because in all my questioning of the family about its history, no one had ever hinted at this first marriage of Padmini's. How many other events of the past had been concealed from me? When I returned, I asked Ayya about the photograph. This is the story that he told me at that time:

When Padmini was younger, she was introduced to Ayya as a potential bridegroom. Ayya himself was not interested in marriage and forgot this incident, but Padmini remembered and got the idea that she would marry only him. Anni and Annan, with whom she was living, also wanted her to marry Ayya. Ayya agreed to do so. Meanwhile, however, Padmini's parents had other plans. They had heard that a certain family was very wealthy, and they had decided to marry Padmini and Lalita to two brothers in this family. Annan and Anni, not wishing to oppose Padmini's parents and feeling that the decision should rest finally with them, had let the parents have their way. They had asked Ayya if he would come to the wedding and Ayya had said certainly he would come. But when he arrived and saw the bridegroom, his mind began to burn. It was clear to him, he said, that Padmini's bridegroom was very ill with tuberculosis. When Padmini saw Ayya, she had begun to weep. Then Ayya knew that she did not want to marry this person. He sent word to someone saying, "Don't think it is because I was to marry Padmini that I say this. The bridegroom is very sick. For the sake of both her health and his, he should not be allowed to come near her. If you don't believe me, take him to a doctor and do what the doctor says."

Ayya said that he was furious with Padmini's parents for risking her health for the sake of money. As soon as the ceremonies were over, they took the bridegroom to a doctor, and the doctor said that the groom should go immediately to the hospital. He did not spend even the wedding night with Padmini, said Ayya. Padmini knew not even one day of married life with him. He remained in the hospital while Padmini returned to Anni's house. The groom was not an evil man, said Ayya. The events that occurred were not his fault. He died within a few months of the wedding. After that, Padmini got typhoid. There was talk of sending her to Lalita's house where she could earn her keep as a servant. Then Ayya had married her. (By my reckoning, there was a hiatus of at least four years between Padmini's first and second weddings.)

I asked Ayya why he hadn't told me previously that he had married the widowed Padmini—from my point of view, this was a fine thing that he had done. He said, no, it was a very small thing. Why was I making so much of it? He said that he had already told me about this event, but that he had told me in a hidden way.

I wondered what Ayya was referring to. About a week before, he had been talking about the desirability of widow remarriage. He had said that lower castes allowed a woman to marry a second time; higher castes should also. "If a girl is married at fourteen and widowed at nineteen, can we expect her to stay as she is? Is her only desire to put food on people's plates? Having no husband, she will find love somewhere, and bring the family shame. In the household, the only men will be her brother, her father, and the servant. She will embrace the servant. Rather than letting this happen, it is better that she be allowed to remarry."

Ayya said that he had known such a girl. A man had been asked to marry her but had said to Ayya, "How could I marry a woman that another man has known?"

Ayya had said to the man, "You think she is the only one who has been with another man? How do you know that a previously unmarried girl will be so pure? She most likely has had a lover, too. The only difference is that you know about this one, you don't know about that one." Thus Ayya said that he had convinced the man to marry the widow.

When Ayya had told me this story, I had not given it much thought. Now it occurred to me that perhaps this story was the one through which Ayya had told me the truth "in a hidden way." Perhaps the man he had talked into marrying a widow was no one but himself.

We return now to the scene in which Padmini is bringing Ayya his lunch, and Ayya is criticizing her for not taking her medicine.

For about three days, Ayya himself had been ill with a bad case of diarrhea. He was weak and dehydrated. They had finally convinced him to visit the house of the doctor, where he had defecated in his clothes, but still he would not take his medicine, the same medicine he had forced me to take when I was ill with the same disease, and which had quickly cured me.

Saturday night Ayya spent alone in his ashram. When we visited him Sunday morning he said smilingly that he had lain awake during the night thinking about the fact that when you are well, everyone stays around you, but when you are sick, and really need someone near you, no one is there.

Padmini came in the morning and again in the afternoon, bringing him lunch. An argument mounted between Padmini and Ayya, Ayya voicing his most common complaint, that Padmini spoke harshly (*kaḍimaiyāka*) and saying that at least when she was serving food it should be sweet (*inimaiyāka*). Padmini responded, "How am I supposed to speak when as soon as I come in the door you say you don't care whether I come in or not." The argument escalated, with Ayya still criticizing Padmini. "Any work you do, you should do right; any work I do, I do right," he said, until Padmini was in tears and Ayya announced that he was leaving for Madras, though he was still quite ill. Padmini grabbed his bag to keep him from leaving. Ayya grabbed it away from her. Padmini blocked the door; Ayya took her by the shoulders and pushed her to the floor. Padmini appealed to me, "What have I done wrong? You have been here three months, have you seen me do anything wrong?" She looked at Ayya. He said, "Do I have to tell you?" His eyes were lowered.

I asked him, "What kind of a teacher [*āciriyar*] are you?"

"I am a small man [*ciṟiyar*], as you can see," he replied, "a very small man."

But only when I threatened to return to America did Ayya agree to stay. Padmini went to the rice mill under construction nearby and sat down weeping. I went to comfort her.

Padmini said to me, "He says I have a sickness and should drink medicine. I have no sickness. The reason I am thin is that I have no peace of mind. My husband says I'm no good, my sister says I'm no good, my uncle says I'm no good, my brother says I'm no good."

Ayya came bringing a blanket and a pillow, smiling, and said ironically as he looked at me with my arm around Padmini, "This is a beautiful sight." He told Padmini, who was sitting in a corner weeping, that if she must cry, she must do it properly, lying on a blanket. He said to me, "There are some things a man should not talk about." I said, "Don't talk about them then." Ayya said, "At least when making love and serving food a woman should be sweet." Padmini was silent. He continued to talk. At last Padmini was asleep, lying on her side on the blanket, her thin body curled around her husband's knee.

I left them there in the rice mill. They returned to the ashram after some time. Padmini fed me the rest of my lunch, then left. After she left Ayya said to me, "I have given you a chance to see Padmini's true nature, what happens when her feelings come strongly [*viraivāka*]. As I told you, she harbors no evil thoughts."

I said to him, "Her heart is higher than yours."

"That is right," he said, "A good artist, a good actor, must be able to go very low, as well as very high." He said that he had put on this performance for Padmini's sake.

MOHANA

". . . come back gently into your old home . . ."

Tirukkōvaiyār, 126.

Ayya's other sister is Mohana. She is his sister not by shared descent but by marriage, being his wife's father's sister's daughter. But though she is not his blood kin, he feels responsible for her. He doesn't worry about Celvi, he says, but he worries about Mohana, because Mohana does not have the will to do battle for herself.

Mohana's mother was the youngest of five children. The father of Anni and Padmini was born immediately before her. After she was married, she was told that she would never be able to bear children, and she was childless for fifteen years. During this period she adopted Anni, her older brother's first daughter. Anni says that this aunt had an angry nature, like Padmini. But she raised Anni lovingly, like a daughter, beating her to make her eat, and Anni reached the age of twelve not knowing how to do any kind of housework.

After fifteen years of childlessness this aunt gave birth to Mohana. Nine months later she was pregnant again. After a full-term pregnancy, she died in childbirth. The baby also died.

Anni, now twelve, returned to live with her own parents. Mohana's father remarried. But he was not such a loving man, says Anni, and the new wife did not care properly for the children.

Kanakkamma, Mohana's mother's older sister, was widowed. She had one grown son, and she desired to have other children in the house. So she adopted Mohana, together with Padmini and Padmini's younger brother Bhakta. The three of them were very small children at the time. When Anni reached the age of seventeen, she was married to Kanakkamma's son. Padmini and Mohana continued to grow up in this household, raised by Padmini's older sister Anni and her husband. When Padmini married, she continued to live with her husband, Ayya, in this same household, because Ayya had broken off all ties with his natal kin and was a good friend of Anni's husband. It was Anni and her husband who had chosen him to be Padmini's spouse.

When it came time for Mohana to marry, she expressed a desire to marry Tambu, one of the brothers of Anni and Padmini. Thus she would be able to maintain ties with the household in which she had been raised, though she would have to live in the home of her parents-in-law, Anni and Padmini's parents. According to Ayya, Anni and Padmini tried to dissuade Mohana from marrying Tambu, because Tambu had many bad habits and could not be expected to be a responsible husband. But Mohana insisted, and so they let her have her way.

Two years after she was married, Mohana gave birth to Sivamani. The delivery was hard. Ayya blamed Sivamani himself. "When delivery is difficult," he said, "it's a bad sign. If a child starts life by giving his mother trouble, he's likely to give her trouble forever."

Sivamani was not a healthy baby, and he came at a bad time. "It was raining heavily," said Anni. "Padmini had just given birth [to Jnana Oli]. I had typhoid. We all thought that Sivamani was going to die."

"He would throw up everything he ate," said Padmini, "large quantities of vomit. And he wouldn't open his eyes. We carried him through the mud and rain to the bus stop. We took him to big doctors all around Madras, but he didn't get better. We all thought he was going to die. Finally we took him to see our family doctor. He put some Terramycin on a piece of cotton and rubbed it on Sivamani's eyes. Soon his eyes opened. The doctor prescribed white goat's milk, boiled and strained three times, and rice water, for him to drink. Now Sivamani is fine. Our doctor is a golden doctor."

As she told this story, Padmini thwacked Sivamani on the back. He toppled over and she kissed him. "Don't you ever do that to us again," she said. Sivamani laughed.

Ayya said, "Padmini's brother [Sivamani's father] has a sore on his penis. It has become infected and he is going to have to have an operation. I know what that disease is. You may have noticed that Sivamani has a very short penis, as though it had been sawed off. When he grows up, he will have trouble. That is because of the disease he got from his father. His sickness after he was born was also a result of this. When I told this to the family, they all became angry with me. So I didn't say anything else. We ourselves bore the expense of Sivamani's treatment. We took him from doctor to doctor. Shouldn't a father help care for his newborn son? Sivamani's father said, 'It doesn't matter to me whether he dies.' When we took Sivamani to our own doctor, the doctor was irritated. He said, 'Why didn't you bring him here first?' Anni and Padmini were ashamed and said, 'We went to the places one is supposed to go.' He examined Sivamani and looked at the medicine the other doctor had prescribed and said, 'He is giving him *this*?' He also said, 'Because of a fault in the father, the child also has this fault.' He said it in a civilized way, not spelling out the trouble directly, because Anni and Padmini were there. Padmini and Anni said, 'The younger one [their name for Ayya] said it was a disease caused in this way.' The doctor smiled at me and said, 'You have understood the matter correctly.' "

Mohana's duty as an honorable woman is to live with her parents-in-law and help them with work in the house and fields. But she spends as much time as she can in the household of Anni and Padmini. Tambu comes there occasionally too. When he visits, he is like a ghost. People act as though he is not there. Most of the time, only Mohana will serve him meals.

Mohana comes to Ayya to talk with him about her husband Tambu. Tambu is a petty thief. When he visits the home he takes money out of people's bags. "Anni has not spoken to him in how many years?" asks Mohana, rhetorically. But when Tambu enters the hospital for his operation, Padmini visits him daily and brings him meals. Ayya is furious. He says it is a waste of his own hard-earned money to feed a man like Tambu. Padmini's answer is simple. "Tambu is my brother," she says. "If he is sick in the hospital, how can I not feed him?"

When Mohana was orphaned, her parents left her eight acres of land in Malaiyanur, the village where her parents-in-law live. Tambu uses part of the income from this land to support himself. Because he will not assist with the agricultural work or contribute any income from outside employment, his own parents no longer allow him to stay in their house. He has built himself a rough mud hut next to his parents' house. He sleeps there sometimes, when he has nowhere else to go.

Meanwhile, Tambu's parents have sold two acres of Mohana's land and plan to sell more. What they have not sold, they cultivate, keeping the income for themselves. When Mohana is in her parents-in-law's house, she is alone with them and her brothers-in-law. She is not able to confront them all and demand her land. If she refuses to sign away more land to them, life will be made difficult for her in their house. If she decides to settle permanently in Anni's house, Tambu will take it as a sign that he, too, can permanently settle there, and it will be very hard to get rid of him.

Ayya says that Mohana's only recourse is to fight with her parents-in-law, get her land back so that she will have an income of her own, and live by herself in a separate house in Malaiyanur. Ayya says that if he were

Mohana, he (she) would leave Tambu and marry someone else. Mohana has seen a movie in which the wayward husband eventually straightens out because his wife is patient and forebearing. Mohana hopes that if she is patient, Tambu will reform as the movie husband did. Ayya says that she will learn to hate that movie.

Ayya says further that if Mohana decides to fight for her land he will support her, but it is a decision that she herself must make. He will not decide for her. He has learned from bad experience with his uterine sister not to try and intervene between husband and wife, unless the wife herself puts up a fight and asks for support.

A heated discussion takes place, with Anni and Padmini on one side, Ayya on the other, and Mohana weeping in the middle. Anni says that Mohana must fight with her parents-in-law to get back her land, but that she cannot do it without the support of Ayya and Annan. Ayya says that Mohana must decide for herself what to do. She does not need her brothers' permission to act. Anni continues to press him. Finally, greatly agitated, he says, "If you want your land and they won't give it to you, whether it is your father-in-law or God, we will come there and fight for you."

The next day, Anni, Mohana, and I set out for Malaiyanur. Neither Ayya nor Annan comes along. A long discussion takes place between Anni and her mother. Her father sleeps nearby, evidently unconcerned about the conversation. Nothing is resolved. Anni and I leave Malaiyanur the next day, while Mohana and Sivamani stay behind.

When they are together in Anni's house, Mohana and Padmini play and joke together often. Mohana, less confident than Padmini, is Padmini's shadow, following her example, playing her straight man. One evening, Padmini slips her arm around Mohana's waist and summons me. "Decide," she commands, "which of us is the greater beauty." I inspect their ears, their fingernails, and the backs of their necks, and proclaim a tie. Padmini protests, "That woman is very black and she has a gap between her teeth. You judge unfairly." Both of them grin widely.

Padmini says that as children, she and Mohana used to play husband and wife. I ask her how a female could play the part of a husband; Anni comments that she has asked the same thing. Padmini does not answer, but tightly embraces Mohana and declares that she will marry her today. Mohana giggles.

Padmini and Mohana like to lie side-by-side in the afternoon or evening, sharing a narrow bed, sharing a pulp magazine, sharing whispered secrets. "I know what you're doing," says Anni, with a note of disapproval in her voice.

One day in the garden Padmini says to Ayya, "Last night when no one was there I crept up on Mohana who was sleeping and put my arms around her and she screamed."

Ayya sometimes criticizes Mohana and Padmini for "playing too much." He often mocks Mohana's mild lisp. He says he feels a "burning" (*ericcal*) when Padmini and Mohana spend twenty-four hours a day together and Padmini won't be separated from Mohana even briefly, but he says he would feel the same jealousy if Padmini spent too much time with her mother, and he makes no more of it.

Padmini and Mohana's husband–wife game, carried with them from childhood, is more than just a game now that they are adults. Mohana is in many ways like a real wife to Padmini. She humors her, delouses her, accepts her jokes, admires her, never criticizes her. When there is extra work to be done, Mohana does it. When there is a decision to be made, she passes it up to Padmini or Anni. There is a very clear hierarchy among the women in this respect. Yet in other respects, they are equals, or even images of each other. Ayya often speaks of Padmini and Anni as though they were a balanced set, each complementing the other. But in their own eyes, Padmini and Mohana form a team, while Anni is a match for Ayya. Padmini and Mohana are built the same, and all their clothing is shared. When they go out, each carries the other's child. In the evening, each puts flowers in the other's hair.

Their eating together is a strange and beautiful ritual. They wait until all the others are finished, then they put the leftovers in a pot and Padmini mixes them up with her hand. They sit down facing each other, with the pot between them. Padmini takes a handful of food, shapes the food into a ball in her palm, and puts the food-ball in her mouth, then she makes a ball of food and puts it in Mohana's mouth, then Mohana does the same. There are no "manners." They wolf down great mouthfuls. One would say that they were eating like animals, except for the rhythmic and balanced way in which each feeds herself and the other. They do not play the game of trying to get each other to eat more than their fill. When one says "Enough," the other leaves off feeding her. When both are done, each woman licks the other's fingers and her own.

One afternoon as Anni is leaving for a wedding, Mohana and Sivamani arrive from Malaiyanur. Padmini greets Mohana, not with bubbling joy but with an exchange of news. Mohana has a drink of water, then Padmini feeds her by hand, making balls of rice and vegetables and putting them one by one into Mohana's mouth. Padmini has just eaten, so Mohana does not feed her.

Sivamani and Jnana Oli stand staring at each other. Annan takes one on each knee, places a toy truck between them, and kisses each in turn. He sits with the children on his knees, while Padmini and Mohana talk. Then the older children rush in and all grab Sivamani at once, pulling him this way and that. At last, Padmini picks up Sivamani and walks away with him in her arms.

PATTERNS

Nāttanār and *nāttanār,* sister and wife of the same man, may be the most bitter rivals or they may be the most intimate friends. Padmini and Porutcelvi compete for the affection of the same beloved man. They despise each other. Padmini and Mohana are bonded to a man who steals from both of them. They are lovers. Of course, the situation is not really as cut-and-dried as this. Each relationship that a person belongs to affects each of that person's other relationships. And there are kinds and degrees of influence of bond upon bond. The form that a web of kinbonds takes varies according to the personalities at the nodes. So personality structure and kinship structure are also interlinked systems.

Males and females form opposed interest groups, just as do different lineages, just as do different generations. The strong feelings joining members of one sex are said to have a bodily basis, just like the feelings joining sibling to sibling (*ratta pācam,* "blood bond"), or parent to child (*peṯṯa uṇarcci,* "birth feeling"), or wife to husband (*pāluṇarcci,* "sexual feeling"). Females are said to be all of one caste (*inam*). Their bodies are the same. There are feelings that only they know. They sometimes form alliances against men. As competitors for the same prizes, they sometimes fight one another.

It may be that the core ambiguities of family life arise at the points of collision, or intersection, between different kinds of love bonding different kinds of people. When the blood bond and the sexual bond divide a single person, then that person may well question his own identity. When the bond within a sex crosses the bond between sexes, androgyny may result. When the parental bond and the sexual bond cross, tender and murderous feelings may merge. And yet all these various bonds, far from being kept separate, are drawn dangerously or (as the case may be) deliciously close by South Indian cultural patterns. In the matter of kinship, as in many other matters, the people of Tamil Nadu seem to relish walking close to the edge.

CHAPTER SIX

Older Women and Younger Men

ANNI

". . . he who is hidden,
whom the gods do not know . . ."

Tirukkōvaiyār, 5.

It often seemed that the net of love was cast beyond the closest person, perhaps, as with parents spurning their children, in order to keep the circle of love wide, or conversely, to create an illusion of indifference or to divert attention away from the true, more inner love. The person that Padmini loved most, said Anni and Attai, was not Padmini's own husband, Ayya, but her māmā—"mother's brother" as she called him, though technically he was not this—Anni's husband. In the whole family, this "māmā" was the only one she never scolded, they said. As for Anni, in front of me she paid little attention to her husband and devoted herself to the care of Ayya.

"*Aṇṇi, aṇṇan, aṇu, aṇukkam,*" said Ayya, "Brother's wife, brother, the subtle, drawing near," so creating an etymology for the name of the woman he called Anni. "My Anni loves me better than my wife," he said.

To Anni, Ayya was *koṛuntan,* husband's younger brother, younger sister's husband. Koṛuntan is close to *kuṛantai,* "child," and might best be translated as "the tender one," for in her husband's younger brother, a woman may find a tender friend, one who can be her baby, while in his older brother's wife, a man may find a woman who is like a mother, sister, and secret wife. So an old man who labored in the fields for the family used to sing as he was drawing water, "Anni, Anni, you bring water to my brother to cool his thirst, won't you bring the same water to me?" And there is a proverb which says, "My older brother's wife is my half wife, and my younger brother's wife is my own [*Aṇṇan manaivi arai manaivi, tampi manaivi tan manaivi*]" But when I asked Ayya if there was a traditional love relationship between an aṇṇi and her koṛuntan, he looked stunned, horrified. "No matter what happens, I will never reveal my secrets," he said.

The respect and closeness that Anni and Ayya felt for each other were evident. They enjoyed conversing and debating with each other. From what I could see, more words were exchanged between them than between any other two members of the household. Often they went shopping together. Then they would walk along the street chatting. Sometimes they would go to the city together. Then on the long train ride to Madras, Anni would tell Ayya every detail of all the things that had happened in the household while he had been at work. When Ayya went alone to Madras, Anni would wait up at night for him to return. When he arrived she would serve him dinner and they would stay up conversing long after all others were asleep. After lunch Anni and Ayya would lie together in the afternoon in the main room talking, their heads sharing a pillow, their bodies perpendicular to one another. At night, too, they would sometimes sleep side-by-side. Neither Anni nor Ayya was ever seen reclining with any other person, male or female. Each stood somewhat apart and alone.

Anni took her name, the name that even her own children called her now, from her relationship with Ayya. Him she would call "Aṇṇan", "older brother," or "*Ayyā,*" which means "lord" or "father" or "husband," thus confusing many who first met the two of them together. "How can you call him *Aṇṇan* when he calls you *Aṇṇi?*" people would ask. Anni would answer, "*Paṛakkam.*"

Before he set out to Madras to give a talk, Anni would help Ayya prepare his lesson. Only she knew by heart all the hymns that he sang during worship and had tried to teach the family. When Ayya was planning to give away a notebook of poems he had written, Anni protested. She wanted at least the songs written in his own hand—lovesongs he had composed not long after entering the household.

It was because of Anni's great lovingness, said Ayya one day, that he had married into the household in the first place. He praised her unschooled wisdom. "She watches everyone from a distance," he said, "and she knows everything that happens. She is wiser than me. The only difference is that she hasn't studied and doesn't use lovely words like me, otherwise people would be taking lessons from her."

When I reported to Anni what Ayya had said, she became embarrassed and denied it, but in fact, Anni often entered into the lessons that Ayya taught and became through him, transformed by him, a teacher in her own

Plate 28. Sivamani, Arulmori, and Daniel.

right. When he spoke in his lectures, as he often did, of "the women in our house," he was speaking principally of Anni. "Women in the house are like *ñāniyarkaḷ,* people of holy wisdom," he said. "That is why we call them *maḍappeṇḍīr*." (*Maḍam* means innocent, and maḍappeṇḍīr are innocent women. But *maḍam* also means monastery, the place where supposedly holy men dwell.)

Ayya told his listeners what Anni had told him about the broom. He told them what she had said about the fruit tree. He told them about a time he had gotten a thorn in his foot. "Don't you have enough sense to keep out of thorn beds?" Anni had said as she had dug at the thorn. But Ayya had yelped in pain as she dug and Anni had said, "All right, let it work itself out."

"And later it did come out by itself," said Ayya. "Thus Anni taught me that God removes our sins gradually, to avoid causing us more pain than we can stand. God comes in many forms," he concluded, "Why can't God come in the form of one's aṇṇi?" Thus Ayya's friends called Anni "our guru's guru" in a manner that was only half-joking.

Ayya's favorite poet, next to Māṇikkavācakar and Tiruvaḷḷuvar, was the nineteenth-century Saiva saint Ramalingar. He conducted a series of lectures about this saint and dreamed, he said, of being "the Ramalingar of this century." In the legend of Ramalingar's life, he is a social misfit, so tender-hearted that he weeps for a stone, raging against the evils of the world, the most terrible of which is flesh-eating, scorning human company, spurning conventions, fleeing marital love, a great poet with no schooling. Throughout his life he remains a precocious child, orphaned and alone, with no one to understand him or take care of him, except for his older brother's wife, who shelters him in her home, feeds him, and protects him from the world. "Like me, poor Ramalingar had a loving aṇṇi," said Ayya.

Ayya would often contrast Anni's wisdom with his wife's simplicity. He described Anni's activities as *pakkuvam*, a word meaning ripeness, fitness, cookedness, in the proper time and place, to the appropriate degree, but also (interestingly) hiddenness, sneakiness, opportunism. This was a quality that Padmini lacked. Thus, in discussing the contrast between the two of them, Ayya would say:

"Anni appears to work hard, but quietly [pakkuvamāka] she takes care of herself. Padmini doesn't."

"In our household, when someone serves us, it is the custom to give something in return. Padmini gives unlimited amounts. Anni gives within limits."

"Anni is patient. Padmini wants everything when she wants it."

"Anni hides information that might show her to be dependent upon others. Padmini hides nothing."

"When I ask Padmini to do something, she either does it or she refuses. Anni says she will do it, then quietly [pakkuvamāka] she does the opposite."

"Watch out for Anni. If there are a hundred people in a crowd, she will know if one of them is hiding something."

Clearly for Ayya, Anni understood the nature of the hidden. She knew what others were hiding, and she herself knew how to hide things. Her behavior, therefore, was rarely straightforward. Padmini rebelled; Anni submitted. But one felt that Padmini's rebellion arose, in part, from a frustrated desire to please her husband. Even when she did please him, he would conceal his pleasure under anger, real or feigned, and so manipulate her. Anni, in contrast, controlled Ayya by serving him.

Unlike Padmini, Anni would not buy a new sari for herself, nor—although she would wear old saris passed on to her by younger women—would she accept the gift of a new sari from anyone but Ayya. Such a policy was a strong statement of devotion and humility, but it was also a challenge to Ayya, her loving adversary. When I asked Anni why she wouldn't wear the sari I bought her, she said that she was waiting for

Ayya to buy her saris, it was his duty to do so, and he was to buy two at a time, so that she could change them.

Similarly, Anni would never go to a movie without Ayya, even if the whole rest of the family was going. She would instead make her pleasure contingent upon his decision and plead with him to go, "so that the whole family can be together."

Most interesting to watch were the feeding games that took place between Ayya and Anni.

"The Elder One is patient," said Anni. "Whatever you serve him, however you serve him, he will eat. But Ayya has to be served correctly, or he will pick up his leaf and hurl it away. Correctly means everything has to be right there—buttermilk, ghee, rice, salt, lentils—so that he will be served fast, otherwise he will get up before you serve him.

"But Ayya knows how to serve himself. The Elder One doesn't. Even if everything is cooked, the Elder One doesn't know how to serve it to the family. Ayya will cook it and serve it."

Ayya said that it was Anni's "job" (*vēlai*) to feed him, and feed him properly. He often complained to Anni, to his friends, and to me that she did her job poorly. She would fix him buttermilk and he would say that he was sick and wanted only rice water. So she would fix him rice water and then he would tell her that she was too lazy to fix decent meals. She would complain about how exacting he was but always she strove to cook to his taste. Daily she cooked for him, as for the rest of the family, and brought him food. Unless she left him alone with it, he would refuse it, saying that he didn't like that kind of food, that it was not good for him, that he had a stomach ache, that he wasn't hungry. Anni would argue and coax for a while, insisting that the food was fine and good for him. If he still refused to eat she would force feed him as though he were a recalcitrant child, holding the back of his head with her left hand and bringing a ball of food to his mouth with her right. He would keep his lips tightly shut until the last second, when he would open his mouth, and in went the food. Then he would chew it and swallow it. In this way Anni became his mother, servant, and controller.

Anni's aggressive servitude, her striking combination of devotion and force, could unite with Ayya's proclivity for creating bonds of pain through self-and-other punishment, to create unimaginably complex emotional equations, dramatically displayed before large audiences.

Anni told me the following story. Ayya told it to me independently later. Their versions were surprisingly similar.

Shortly before the full moon of Cittirai, the most important festival day of the year for this family, Ayya got another thorn in his foot. This one did not work its way out but became infected, and his foot became painfully swollen. On full-moon day, the swelling grew worse, and the foot was too sore to walk on. By evening Ayya concluded that the pain was too severe and distracting for him to conduct worship ceremonies for the crowd of a hundred or so people who had come for this festival. He therefore devised a treatment for himself. A solution of kerosene and salt was to be heated to boiling, and a sharp knife heated to red-hot. Then the knife was to be plunged into the kerosene solution and stabbed into his foot, "where it hurt the most." All of Ayya's family and friends were there, but none was willing to administer this drastic treatment to him, except Anni. As she proceeded with the treatment, Ayya was trembling with pain. His friends were weeping, and one of them cried, out, "Stop! He doesn't need medicine." But Anni had continued until Ayya himself directed her to quit.

Pain in the foot might have had a special meaning for Ayya. Anni told me that when he was a small child, his mother punished him for eating green rice by branding him three times across the foot with a red-hot iron. Then, unable to bear the sight of her child suffering so, she wept. Ayya remembered his mother as the very incarnation of love and patience, and thought of her death as the greatest loss of his life, at the memory of which he still sobbed uncontrollably. Now Anni was the one who punished out of love, and Ayya said of her in passing, "Only Anni knows my mind."

VISHVANATHAN

". . . he frees us as befits our hearts . . ."

Tirukkōvaiyār, 22.

Vishvanathan was a distant relative—Padmini's sister Lalita's husband's older brother's son—making Padmini his *citti,* "little mother," or mother's younger sister. Being a poor relative, and young (in his early twenties), Vishu was a quasi-servant. But he admired the big landowners, and hoped to achieve wealth and status of his own someday. Even more than owning land, he wanted to own and drive a bus or truck, for these were valiant occupations, as well as lucrative ones. "You need courage to drive a bus," he said, gazing into the distance. He wanted Ayya to buy him one.

Vishu was to Padmini as Ayya was to Anni, but Padmini was less roundabout and subtle in her management of Vishvanathan than Anni was with Ayya. Whereas Anni and Ayya were equally matched, Padmini dominated Vishvanathan absolutely.

She was always solicitous of his welfare. If he had to run an errand in the rain, she would dress him up in a great rubber slicker. If there were

Plate 29. Anni and Jnana Oli.

special items of food available, she made sure that he got some. When she became supervisor of the rice mill, she had him stay there with her; their two toothbrushes hung side by side on the wall there. When he lay down to rest, she would put a pillow under his feet.

Ayya cast angry glances at Padmini when she did such things. Luxury foods such as fruit should be reserved for children and guests, he said. Padmini would answer, unperturbed, "Everyone should be served equally."

But Padmini would also mercilessly tease Vishvanathan. So for instance one evening after dinner when Vishvanathan was there, Padmini loudly asked me whether I wanted a banana like a grandfather or a banana like Vishu. I said I didn't understand. Padmini said, "A banana like a grandfather is soft and squishy, but a banana like Vishu is firm and hard." Poor Vishvanathan slunk shamefacedly away.

Often Padmini would scold Vishvanathan and beat him on the back, as she did with the children and female servants. Vishvanathan would say nothing. The other family members would be silent. When Vishvanathan said that he wanted to leave this family, with which he had lived for six years, Padmini told him that he could never survive on his own, that he would certainly fail, that he was just like a little child. She was so angry that she refused to serve him lunch.

Ayya told Padmini not to keep scolding over and over. He told Vishvanathan that he could take all the money he needed and go, but he should not come back. (Later he told me that he was just saying this to make Vishvanathan try harder to succeed.) Meanwhile Padmini was angrily silent. Ayya told Padmini to give food to Vishvanathan. Padmini refused. So I served him, then Mohana took over from me.

But Vishvanathan later said, of his various cittis, Padmini was the best. Though she beat him, she fed him regularly and didn't make faces while feeding him. When Padmini's sister Lalita served him, she would make a face, and in her house he would only get two meals a day.

Vishvanathan had a mother's brother with a daughter of marriageable age in whom Vishvanathan was interested, but the uncle would not marry his daughter to Vishvanathan, because Vishvanathan was so poor. According to Vishvanathan, this uncle also was once very poor. He had only a small patch of land that he worked. One day he climbed a power tower and grabbed the wire in order to kill himself. He fell senseless to the ground. Vishvanathan's father came and nursed him back to health. Then he gave him a ring off his finger and told him to go and somehow live. The uncle got a good job in a factory, and after that grew wealthier. But he soon forgot his debt to Vishvanathan's father.

When Vishvanathan was still a child, his father died, and at that time, Vishvanathan's father's brother, Lalita's husband, appropriated the land that Vishvanathan's father had left. Vishvanathan sometimes spoke of getting back the land that was rightfully his, and Padmini and the rest of the family here encouraged him, though it would mean a break with Lalita and her husband, and also physical separation from Padmini herself.

"If this household helps Vishvanathan too much," said Ayya, "—there is a kind of talk in this country—Lalita's husband will speak wrongly about us. He will say that we are opposing him, or helping Vishvanathan oppose him just by assisting Vishvanathan. Still, we will help Vishvanathan. People in our household will not turn anyone away hungry."

One day Vishvanathan disappeared from the house without saying a word to anyone. He was gone for several days. No one seemed worried.

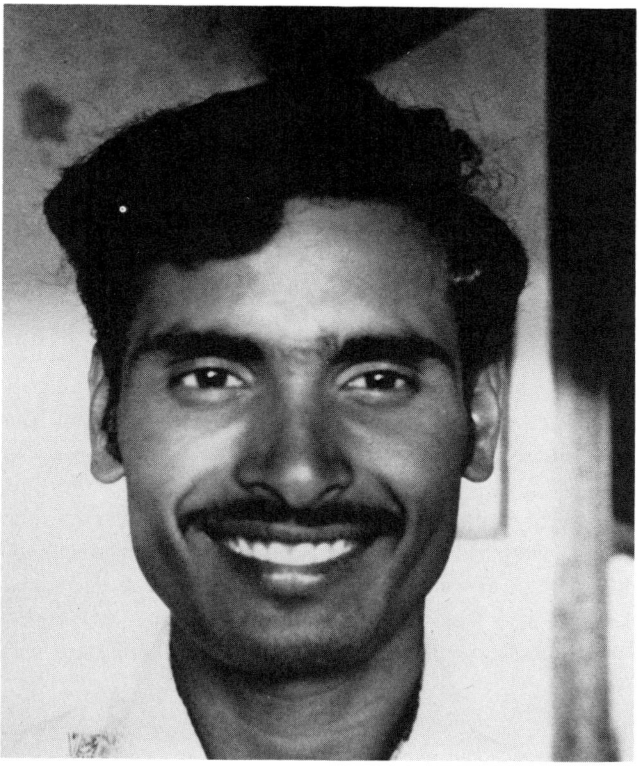

Plate 30. Vishvanathan.

Somehow they knew that he was going to his father's brother's house to claim his land. When Vishvanathan returned, Padmini, angry with him for leaving without saying anything, would not speak to him for a day. She only spoke to him when he was leaving again that evening. This time he was leaving "permanently." As they waited at the bus stop, both Padmini and Vishvanathan were weeping. "Why are you so angry with me that you didn't speak with me for so long?" Vishvanathan asked. He was obviously more hurt by her day of silence than by any of her beatings.

That day as she served Ayya lunch, Padmini had also been weeping. She was worried about where Vishvanathan would eat. Her sister wouldn't feed him properly; where he was staying he would get only two meals a day; he had never cooked for himself; he needed strength to cultivate his new farm (he had been given two acres, two bullocks, a pump, and half a house site). Padmini begged Ayya to give Vishvanathan money. Ayya refused and they quarreled bitterly. Padmini departed still weeping. After she left, Ayya commented, "It is the habit of everyone in our household to give something in turn for service. But when Padmini gives, she gives beyond limits. She wants everyone to be together; she does not like separation. She will cry when you leave, too," he said (but she didn't).

The next evening I asked Padmini if her mind had cooled from the sorrow of parting with Vishvanathan. She said, no, it would take a few days. "That shirt that we have seen a thousand times," she mused sadly. (Vishvanathan had only one shirt. Its flashy pattern seemed as much a part of him as his face.) What really made her sorrowful, she said, was the way that when she beat him, he never fought back. She said he had no courage (*tuṇivu*); he was like a child. She grieved at his going off into the world like this, though she knew it would enable him to gain courage. He had never cooked for himself before. Her sister's husband would not treat him well.

My surprise at Padmini's sorrow was increased when I learned that Vishvanathan's departure was not really permanent. He had said he would return again in a few days, and in fact he did, and subsequently spent more time at this house than in the village where his land was. And Padmini continued to scold him and feed him as she always had.

CHAPTER SEVEN

The Lives of Children

Childhood is made much of in Tamil Nadu. People love to decorate their walls with pictures of little babies, to worship child gods, to create literary images of children in many different genres, and to play with children—not, as with some of us, because they believe that the child requires this kind of attention, but rather, it would seem, just because the adults themselves enjoy it.

But Tamil adults with whom I spoke said little to me about their own childhoods, even when pressed. They said that they couldn't remember those days long past. They also had little to say when I asked them how they reared their own children. Questions such as, "What does a child need most?" or "How do you raise a child?" or "What must a parent do for a child?" or even, "How do you show love for a child?" were all interpreted materially. "Clothes, jewels, books, food"—these were the stock answers that I got when I fished for discussions of the emotional needs of children. To raise or grow a person (*vaḷarttal*), I found out, meant above all else to grow them materially. Adults would speak of patrons who increased their wealth as the people who had "raised" them.

If you ask an American what a child needs most, the answer is likely to be "love." Money, Americans will say, is not as important as love. But when I asked Tamil women and men if you could give love without giving money, their answer was an emphatic, "No!" On the surface of it, this contrast is ironic, since in fact Americans give their children vastly more of what can be bought with money that most Tamil parents are able to give their children, while Tamil children are the recipients of much more whole-hearted affection than American children usually get. My hour-long interviews with relative strangers failed to capture the kinds of realities that were taken for granted.

Personalities in Tamil Nadu are astonishingly diverse. Even within one family there are great variations. For this and other reasons, I have not attempted to do the kind of study that correlates features of childrearing practices with properties of adult personalities. I have also not attempted to do a developmental study—that is, to locate the minds of particular children at some particular point on a scale of a social scientist's devising. I have also not tested or probed the minds of the children I met. For the most part, I have tried to be like a naturalist, observing my beings of choice in the wild, trying not to scare them away.

In the descriptions and interpretations that follow, it will be seen that I give at least as much attention to the actions of adults as to the actions of children. What I am interested in are the meanings of particular events both to the adults and to the children who participate in them—the meanings of interactions as total patterns. Since adults are much more powerful than children, they have a much stronger hand in shaping interaction than children do. I interpret adults as teaching through interactions and children as learning from them. Also, I interpret most of the teaching that I see as more or less deliberate, though it is often hard to draw the line between conscious and unconscious teaching. I do not posit, however, any one-to-one correspondence between particular communicative acts and particular meanings conveyed.

In my descriptions and interpretations of events involving children, I try to take account of the fact that each child's personality is unique and each child's experience of life is unique—though I know that many *aspects* of each child's experience are also experienced by other children in India. What I am trying to do might be called a configurational study of experience—I want to see how the different components of a particular child's experience fit together into a pattern and lend meaning to one another, whereas with another child, the same or similar components might be parts of a different overall pattern and take on different meanings. So, for instance, children all over India get weaned in a sudden and bitter fashion, but I believe that the *meaning* of the weaning experience might differ greatly from child to child, according to the configuration of meaningful experiences in which it is set (e.g., the presence or absence of a younger sibling who is nursed after the older one is weaned, the quality of other kinds of food available to the child, the characteristics of other caretakers beside the mother, their relationship to the mother and to the child, the personality of the mother, whether the child is male or female, and a thousand other "variables"). It is also important to remember that each child brings with it into the world a distinct set of cognitive and emotional patterns and tendencies, which also must help to shape the meaning–configurations that are formed in the child's mind. An emotion-

Plate 31. Annan with Jnana Oli and Sivamani.

ally volatile child and a "laid back" child, for instance, might process similar experiences in quite different ways. Here again, all I am arguing is that we should not attempt to homogenize the world, especially the Indian one. We must consider ways in which this world proliferates variant dharmas and makes them fit together.

From the beginning of their lives, children in our Tamil household were involved in complex enactments of love, but their involvement was different from that of adults, since they were being taught the rules of these performances, even while they were being used by certain adults to send messages to others. The small child, who on the one hand was trying to establish a sense of himself or herself as an entity, and on the other hand was trying to be part of the life going on around him or her, learned early the principles of theatrics—the disguising and blurring of true relations and identities, the sudden dramatic transitions from one emotional extreme to the other, the multiple ironies. It seemed to me that behind all these deceptions, illusions, and inversions, each child treasured a secret identity, which he or she would mysteriously guard. How successful the child was, both at theatrics and at guardianship of the self, depended ultimately on what truth came through the drama—how hard or how gentle were the beatings, how many the chances for secret kisses, how much the milk that entered the belly.

JNANA OLI

> ". . . our child with his spear-bright eyes . . ."
>
> *Tirukkōvaiyār*, 339.

Jnana Oli was the child of Padmini and Ayya, their third and last child, their only son. At two he was a sensualist, and he was proud. When I picked him up he would lie in my arms arching his back and throwing back his head, his eyes half-closed, his lips half-parted in a dreamy smile. When I offered him a biscuit he refused it with a wave of his hand. From the beginning of our acquaintance he let me bathe him, and he let me carry him when he felt he needed to be carried, but all the time that I was there he never accepted the food that I offered. Sometimes when I called him he would turn and walk away. Sometimes, unbidden, he would take my hand.

Often, the smiling women of the household would ask Jnana Oli to perform. "Do a dance," they would say, and Jnana Oli would dance, stamping his feet up and down and wiggling his small body, amid a wide circle of admirers. "How does grandmother walk?" the women would ask. Jnana Oli would bend forty-five degrees at the waist, put his hand in the small of his back, and hobble around in a circle. "Say 'Salutations!'" He would fold his hands and speak the word. "Ask, 'Have you eaten?'" He would ask. He knew many words for a two-year-old, and he had a wide repertoire of body language.

The older children did not often carry Jnana Oli or play with him the way street children did with small brothers and sisters. All of Jnana Oli's caretakers were adults, and there were many of them: his own mother Padmini, his mother's sister Anni, her husband Annan, his own father Ayya, his mother's brother's wife Mohana, his mother's father's sister Attai, his cousins Vishvanathan and Ram Tilakam, the servant Modday. Anni delighted in having Jnana Oli list his caretakers in rank order, from most favorite to least. Sometimes Jnana Oli's mother was in first place, sometimes the head of the household, Annan. All of these caretakers adored Jnana Oli. All of them together had given him the pet name Oḷikaṇṇā, "Oli darling," and it had stuck and become his regular name. Yet, but for their use of this name, all of the caretakers expressed their admiration in markedly different ways. He was like a little magnet that they formed a pattern around, each part of the pattern unique, yet the whole symmetrical. His personality incorporated this pattern.

Anni was Jnana Oli's most subtle teacher. Sometimes she would sit in the afternoon with Jnana Oli on her lap, one hand cradling his head, the other cupped over his penis, talking with him. When he said something charming she would squeeze his penis gently, as one would squeeze a friend's hand, in a sudden small burst of affection. Oli, when he napped, lay face up with his hands folded in the same easy way over the same tender place, sheltering it in his sleep.

Anni's lessons had many meanings, and they involved a large component of benevolent deceit. For instance, when she asked Oli to rank his caretakers, she taught him that he had some control over his social world, inasmuch as it mattered whom he loved most, and he was free to dispense his love at will. But in truth he was very little in control of the social organization of the household, and the hidden lesson of the ranking game was that, just as he had the power to assign a value to others, his value was a function of other people's need to be valued by him. He was good, and even superior, because others sought his love, but without them, where would he be? As in the matter of the trusteeship of the penis, self-containment was sometimes just an image of containment in others.

Relationships, whether of enmity or of love, shifted, and were transformed into their own opposites, as bitter turns into sweet and sweet into rotten in the course of things ripening. One could not take it for granted that a feeling was as it had been. So relationships and feelings had periodically to be reexamined and renamed. Anni told me that children had a custom. One child would say to another, "Green fruit or ripe fruit [*kāyā paṛamā*]?" making a fist with the index finger and pinky extended for *kāy*, "green fruit," and only the pinky extended for *paṛam*, "ripe fruit." When there was a fight between people, they were separate, like forefinger and pinky, and the relationship between them was hard and sour, like a green fruit. But when they were friends, they were one, like the single pinky; their relationship was sweet, and whatever passed between them would go down easily:

> One day, Jnana Oli announced to Anni that Padmini had hit him. "Are you kāy with your mother?" asked Anni.
>
> "I am not kāy," said Jnana Oli.

Anni said, "Will you make what your mother said kāy to you [*ammā conna pēccai kāyā viduvāyā*]?"

"I will not leave mother kāy [*nān ammā kāy viḍa māḍḍēn*]," said Jnana Oli.

Anni said to me later that what Jnana Oli was trying to say was, "I will not abandon mother [*nān ammāvai kay viḍa māḍḍēn*]." (The word *kāy* with a long *ā* means "green fruit." The word *kay* with a short *a* means "hand." *Kay viḍu* is to take one's hand away, leave off, let go of, abandon.)

Thus Jnana Oli was tricked by Anni, for in the act of proudly saying no and making the manly proclamation, "I will not abandon mother," he relinquished his pride and forgave his mother, agreeing that what she had said to him, even in anger, he would swallow as though it were a ripe fruit.

Often it was obvious that Anni did not mean what she said, as when she picked up a thorny stick and said smilingly to Jnana Oli, "May I prick you with a thorn?" He laughed as she lightly touched him with it. Such loving threats of violence were many. With Anni they gradually faded into actual punishments for actual misdeeds. When Jnana Oli had a temper tantrum, she took a large stick and tapped him on the bottom, then banged the stick loudly on the floor, then picked him up and comforted him. He seemed barely to notice the stick. Ultimately, Anni's "punishments" of Jnana Oli never went beyond threats, yet she triumphed over him, not because she provoked fear in him but because she was so skillful in the creation of double messages that through them she could maneuver him in any direction she chose. The resolution of her debates with him could often be taken in more than one way, so that both Jnana Oli's pride in himself and sense of dependence upon her might be enhanced during a single interchange:

When Jnana Oli picked up a stick and made a threatening gesture with it, of a kind that adults habitually made toward him, Anni observed him and said, "Naughty. Say naughty, mother. [*Tappu. Tappummā ceppu.*]"

Jnana Oli was silent. Anni picked up the stick, and with the same threatening gesture that Oli had made, repeated her command. Oli still refused, standing defiantly with his hand on his hip. Anni whipped his hip with the stick then instantly swept him onto her lap and cuddled him, saying in affectionate mock-anger, "So you put your hand on your hip (*kay iḍupile poḍḍiyē*)." Then she said, "Who hit you? Did Arivaraci hit you?"

Jnana Oli muttered something like "manamana-manamana," poutingly. His sister Arivaraci, sitting nearby, interpreted what he said, "You did it yourself. [*Nīyē ceñcē.*]"

Jnana Oli climbed down from Anni's lap. Anni picked up the stick and brandished it, above him, commanding, "Say, 'Naughty, mother.'" Jnana Oli began to cry fearfully. Anni picked him up and cuddled him, then sat down with him in her lap. She said, "If you don't say, 'Naughty, mother,' I will go away. Shall I go?"

Jnana Oli said, "Go."

Anni said, "Where shall I go?"

Jnana Oli said, "Go to the house."

Anni said, "I'll go to the house if you don't say, 'Naughty.' "

Meanwhile, Oli's father on the sidelines was commenting to me that Oli was right to refuse, and that Oli in his stubbornness was just like himself (the father).

Anni repeated her threat. "I'll go the house. Say, 'Naughty.' "

Finally, Jnana Oli said, "Naughty, mother. [*Tappummā.*]"

Subsequently, Jnana Oli hit his two-year-old cousin Sivamani with the same stick and knocked him down. Sivamani wept. Anni asked what happened. Arivaraci said, "Jnana Oli knocked Sivamani down and after that they began to fight." Anni said nothing but returned to her conversation with Jnana Oli's father.

The order "*Tappummā ceppu* [Say naughty, mother]," that Anni gave Jnana Oli was elliptic and vague. By itself, the term "tappu" is mild. It is often glossed in English as "mistake" because it suggests an absence of malevolence on the part of the wrongdoer. The appended "-mmā" can mean many things. As applied by people like Jnana Oli to people like Anni, it is an expression of dependence, a plea for love, a cry of fear and longing. As applied by people like Anni to people like Jnana Oli, "-mmā" is a casual, affectionate term of address. When Jnana Oli repeated "Tappummā [Naughty, mother]," to Anni, he might have been accepting her indictment of him, or he might have been handing it back to her. As the statement was phrased, both possibilities were left open.

The ambiguity of Anni's message to Jnani Oli was compounded by her act of brandishing the stick at him to make him repent of the act of brandishing the stick, and the act of turning a whipping suddenly into a cuddling. Thus Jnana Oli learned a flip-flop lesson: brandishing the stick is half wrong and half right, wrong on one side but right on the other. Context and relations entirely determine the moral significance of the act.

Beating was not wrong in itself, nor was weeping a sign only of sorrow. Sorrow was only the proximal meaning of tears, but they had distal meanings, and distal meanings beyond those. So Attai sang a lullaby for me, that she had sung to all the children she had raised:

> Lullaby, lullaby, who hit you and made you cry?
> Water trembles in your weeping eye.
> Lullaby, lullaby, the river will be high,
> The elephant will rise from its bath.
> The pond will be high,
> The horse will rise from its bath, lullaby, lullaby.
>
> ārārō, ārārīrō, yār aḍiccu nī aṛutāy?
> Aṛutu kaṇṇu nīr taḷumpum.
> Ārārō, ārārīrō, aṟu niṟampirukkum,
> Ānai kuḷiccērum.
> Kuḷam niṟampirukkum,
> Kutirai kuḷiccērum, ārārō, ārārīrō.

Many Tamil lullabies ask the same question, "Who beat you and made you cry?" There must have been a beating, it is implied, for there to be a weeping. And in this lullaby, still more is said: on the far side of the weeping, someone will find joy.

Jnana Oli's mother, Padmini, was more volatile than the calm and philosophical Anni. She could lose her temper in a flash, unexpectedly. When Jnana Oli accidently knocked over a pot of sambar, Padmini grabbed him under one arm, carried him into the next room, and beat him for five minutes while he screamed. (Later she told me that she had to beat him because the hot sambar might have burnt him and he had to learn to be more careful.) Her expressions of affection, like the ventings of her anger, were private and intense. I found her sometimes alone with Jnana Oli in the back room of the house, kissing him and caressing him. She would stop when she saw me, as though I had caught her doing something wrong.

Indeed there was a sense that the love between mother and son could grow too strong. Hence Mohana and Padmini often took over care of each other's sons when they were together in the same household, and Mohana was allowed to joke with Jnana Oli in a way that was forbidden to Padmini:

> Like most small boys, Jnana Oli had only one shirt for a garment. One day it tore and he took it to his aunt (*attai*) Mohana to mend. Mohana told him that she would only mend it for him if he would marry her. Oli, to whom Mohana had often proposed marriage, but who had

always refused until now, solemnly agreed, and Mohana took his shirt and mended it.

When I (always addressed by the children as Peggymmā, the way Anni was called Aṇṇimmā and Padmini Pappimma) tried to join in this game, asking Jnana Oli not to marry Mohana but to marry me, Anni turned to me with great seriousness and told me that a woman in the category of mother should never propose marriage to a child.

Jnana Oli was weaned at the age of one year, as were all of the children in his household, by bitter neem juice being rubbed on his mother's breasts. Now, at the age of two he received cow milk, one cup in the morning and one cup in the evening, and the degree of anxiety he showed with respect to the cup of milk was surprising, considering his composure in other situations. In the evening, when he saw the cup of milk coming, he would cry in fear, but he drank the milk without a struggle. In the morning, he accepted the cup of milk willingly but cried when they temporarily took it away to wipe his mouth. With this vital food alone he had no choice; making sure he drank his milk, and drank it all, was a matter of deadly seriousness to the women of the household. Milk was very expensive, and it was the only source of concentrated protein that Saivas allowed themselves (indeed, *caivam* in Tamil means "vegetarian" more than it means allegiance to a particular god). The older children and adults in this family did not get milk at all but had occasional helpings of diluted buttermilk or, much more frequently, went without. For any child, the experience of sweet mother's milk given on demand suddenly followed by such a bitter weaning must have imbued the idea of motherhood with contrasting meanings. After this, the daily forced feeding and forced withdrawal of cow's milk by any of several mothers could only have strengthened a sense that duality was an essential attribute of love.

Like her sister Anni, Padmini taught Jnana Oli the value of closeness to others by threatening to withdraw this closeness. And conversely, Oli learned that he could elicit interaction by stubbornly withdrawing himself. But Padmini pushed this game further than Anni and introduced the element of jealousy, more painful than a thorn:

Jnana Oli had been throwing daily temper tantrums. People responded by carrying him from one place to another and offering him playthings, but daily he became more difficult to satisfy. After one such bout, his mother embraced his cousin Umapathi and said, "Umapathi is my darling; you are not my darling." Jnana Oli angrily stalked away and refused to talk to anyone for one and a half hours. When he returned, he found his mother again lying by Umapathi's side. He

> turned on his heel, went back to the side room, and refused to speak to anyone for the rest of the afternoon—about three hours. His aunts Mohana and Anni tried to get him out of his pout, but no matter how they called him, he would not budge. They talked about this episode later with delight, especially marveling at his perseverance, that he could maintain a pout for so long.

In contrast to the women, Annan handled his nephew Jnana Oli in a more or less straightforward, consistently kindly manner that was neither playful nor combative. My strong impression was that he was intentionally trying to teach Jnana Oli, through his own example, to be patient, gentle, and unselfish. But, unfortunately, the more patience Annan showed, the more impatient Jnana Oli became.

In the middle of the night, when Umapathi awoke and had to urinate, his father Annan was the one he called to go with him, and Annan went. When Jnana Oli also woke and cried, Annan tried to comfort him as well, rocking his hammock, telling him to chant *namacivāya* ("the name of Siva," a mantra). I asked Anni in the morning if Annan had done this for all the children when they were small. Anni said yes. When Anuradha and Ayya's sister's daughter were babies he used to carry one in each arm and sleep on his stomach with one arm over each.

Often Annan would twin Jnana Oli and his age mate Sivamani, one on each side of his body, as Anni said he had done with the girl children. Seating one little boy on each knee, so that they faced each other, he would play with them. Or after they bathed he would pat them both dry at once, nuzzling them both gently with his chin.

But during the months when I was in the household, I saw that Jnana Oli demanded increasingly more of Annan's attention, and the less aggressive Sivamani had to content himself with other diversions, such as playing with the servant's daughter Ponni, whom Jnana Oli ignored. By this time, Annan had superseded even Padmini in Jnana Oli's ranking of favorites.

The situation soon got out of hand. Annan was in the habit of bringing home toys and biscuits to be shared among the children, but particularly desirable objects were monopolized by Jnana Oli. So it was with a set of plastic blocks that were introduced into the household: they became the focus of day-to-day ranking games. The servant's child Ponni could not even touch the blocks. Annan built a truck out of them and tried to get Jnana Oli and Sivamani to play with it together, but somehow Jnana Oli ended up having it all to himself. Earlier, when the older children had played with the blocks, Arivaraci had cleaned them up. Now Jnana Oli dumped them out of their box, howled, and summoned the beleaguered

Vishvanathan to put them back. "*Vicaṇṇā, vāri pōḍi,*" he said, "Brother Vishu, scoop them back." Vishvanathan complied.

Annan, the village accountant, was on the front porch discussing some important piece of business with a group of men. Jnana Oli came out onto the porch crying, telling Annan to come and build a toy truck for him. Annan went inside, built the truck, and came back out. Jnana Oli followed him. One of the men gave Jnana Oli some biscuits. Another proceeded to make a building for him out of the plastic blocks. Mohana came out on the porch and carried the protesting Jnana Oli back into the kitchen. Jnana Oli soon reappeared on the porch. This happened several times. Annan tried to humor Jnana Oli, carrying him around, giving him more biscuits. Before long, the men on the porch were gone. Annan rocked Jnana Oli to sleep in his hammock. While Jnana Oli slept, Annan sat on the front porch chanting Saiva hymns in his hoarse tenor. When I looked again, Annan was asleep on the floor inside while Jnana Oli swayed sleeping in the hammock above him.

Attai commented to me that Jnana Oli often had fits of stubbornness (*piḍivātam*). People had to carry him around, but no matter what they gave him, he was not satisfied. She said that his father also had fits of stubbornness. Sometimes he refused to eat for ten or twelve days. "Why?" I asked. "Because people will not do what he says," she answered. I asked Ayya if this was true. He said yes. If people would not do what he said, then what he said must have been wrong. Then he had to punish himself because it would not be right to expect others to punish him, he explained.

Though Jnana Oli had not yet achieved such skillful and refined expressions of stubbornness, all of the people in the house agreed that he was following in his father's footsteps. Ayya noted proudly that Jnana Oli was reaching the point where he knew no fear. He was developing the spirit of resistance (*etirppu uṇarcci*). If someone hit him, he would hit back. He would even hit his own mother, Ayya said.

Proud though he was of his only son, Ayya was little involved in the everyday care of Jnana Oli, and Jnana Oli at this stage showed little overt interest in him. They did not avoid each other, but neither did either go out of his way to be with the other. It is doubtful, however, that Ayya's backstage comments about Jnana Oli's fighting spirit were lost on Jnana Oli.

If we are to believe what Ayya said about his relationship with his own father, this "spirit of resistance" was something that Ayya, in his turn, received from above. His father had a reputation for violence and was feared by all, said Ayya. Moreover, he was born under an evil star.

Consequently it was very difficult for him to find a wife and he ended up marrying a woman of a different division of Reddiars, a marriage that in those days was against caste rules.

The father and the son failed to see eye-to-eye on many matters. The father smoked tobacco and ate meat, two customs the son abhorred, and Ayya claimed that he often said to his father, "All of the bad things that you do, I will not do. The family will not fall because of me. It will be a great family."

Ayya said that he studied against his father's will and worked hard to build up a collection of books, which his father burned. His father tortured him by binding him to a stake, whipping him, and leaving him to stand in the sun. According to Ayya, his father fought against injustice but was not himself unjust. "But he did unjust things to you," I said. "He did those things out of ignorance," answered Ayya, "not knowing that they were wrong."

His father's aim, said Ayya, was to raise his children to be good—not to steal, not to lie. "Like myself, he was a loving person, but he did not show his love externally. He always spoke to us as though he were angry."

After Ayya's mother died, his father sat in one spot for four days, weeping. "If he had had no love, would he have wept like that?" Ayya asked. Subsequently, the father was more gentle with his children. He bathed them himself and fanned them on hot nights. As he lay dying, his last words to Ayya were, "Be careful."

Ayya bore little resemblance to the father he described. As I have mentioned earlier, he attributed to himself, and others attributed to him, many "feminine" qualities. But he admitted to having beaten Padmini in the past, "to punish her for having beaten the children." Of this past habit, he repented. The temper remained. He himself had little patience with children, including his own; occasionally he would smack them for the smallest of trespasses, such as putting a hand in his way when he was sewing. For slightly greater errors, the punishments he meted out might be more severe. According to Anni, two years previously the children had stolen a broken padlock and traded it for ice cream. Ayya punished them by beating them on the backs of their hands with a stick and making them keep their hands outstretched while he did this.

In connection with such punishments, Anni stated that both Jnana Oli and Umapathi had a "good habit." If you told them to shut their mouths, they would shut them and keep them shut, even if you beat them until it hurt. None of their sisters could do this.

Thus, Jnana Oli had in Anni, Padmini, Annan, and Ayya four very different kinds of parents. But in his dealings with each of them he might have discovered, repeated in so many different ways, a similar message: that love, the giving of self, and pride, the containment of self, are both desirable, and each is inseparable from the other. With Anni, acts of autonomy and dependence, defiance and acceptance, might be elicited, encouraged, or rewarded by a single word or gesture smoothly merging opposites: "Naughty, mother [*tappummā*]," or "I will not abandon / will not leave as a green fruit [*kāyviḍamaḍḍēn*]," or the arm that in one sweep both whipped him and lifted him into the comforting lap. Anni taught contextual variation of the meaning of an act such as the wielding of a stick, so that the child holding the stick and standing on the boundary between a context in which its use was forbidden (an adult whom he was not allowed to beat) and a context in which its use was permitted (a child whom he was allowed to beat) might experience himself as the space in which a thing became its opposite.

Visual and verbal puns, contrasts, and grammatical ambiguities abounded in Anni's dialogues with Jnana Oli. Her play with him delighted in hidden meanings: love hidden beneath anger hidden beneath love, so that it became impossible to know which was the real and which the mock emotion. The transition between the extremes of reward and punishment was so gradual that the boundary dividing them, if it existed at all, was imperceptible.

With Padmini, intense anger and intense affection appeared in sharp and sudden contrast to their surroundings, upon the same face; and jealousy was aroused, the contradictory experience in which both anger and love are provoked, collide, and merge. Jnana Oli's response to his feeling of jealousy, withdrawal from interaction as a way of provoking interaction, was similar to his response to Annan's devotion.

Annan's relentlessly patient affection compelled Jnana Oli to oppose him; the more Annan placated him, the more Jnana Oli demanded placation. By complementation he became the opposite of this man, his "distant father," who was in fact so loving, intimate, and humble. And his own father, encouraging his defiance from a distance, guided Jnana Oli to be, like himself, both defiant and distant. Hence the son who rebelled against the punishing father could end by honoring this father with the highest kind of love: the mirroring of the father's own spirit. For such a son, acceptance of punishment—refusing to flinch while being beaten—was a matter of pride, as well as of love. Later Jnana Oli might learn, as his father had learned, to punish himself as a way of punishing others. To internalize the punisher was to throw his punishment back at him, simultaneously becoming and returning the image.

Another kind of mirroring was taught by Padmini and Annan together, who often treated Sivamani, Jnana Oli's agemate, as though he were Jnana Oli's double—Annan by physically pairing the two boys on the left and right sides of his body; Padmini (with Mohana) by exchanging them.

Jnana Oli at the age of two had great autonomy. He could take or leave any person he pleased, he could break rules, he could make new meanings. Within the walls of the compound, amid so many people, he was completely mobile and yet completely constrained, never alone with himself but always engaged with someone. Like an electron running through a crystal, he was always part of somebody's orbital. Never was the nature of the matrix in which he moved more evident than at mealtime. One morning I made the following notes:

> The women were eating their morning meal, seated in a circle on the floor. Jnana Oli sat at Padmini's left, with his legs crossed. He went to Attai, then to Anni. He sat in Anni's lap. Anni tried to feed him an idli, but he refused. He went to Attai's lap, then back to Anni's lap. Anni began to feed him rice and sambar.
>
> Sivamani was sitting to Padmini's right. Padmini gave him some food on a plate. He fed himself. Anni fed Jnana Oli a drumstick [a vegetable]. He refused the second one. She went back to feeding him rice.
>
> Padmini tried to feed Sivamani but he refused. She put the food into Jnana Oli's mouth instead. Attai put a ladleful of sambar on Sivamani's plate. Jnana Oli got up and picked up the pot of buttermilk. Padmini held the pot while Jnana Oli drank from it. Jnana Oli came over to me. He leaned against the door to the central room. He was holding in his hands a small shred of plastic, which he was holding while people fed him. While Sivamani fed himself, Jnana Oli, exactly the same age as Sivamani, never touched the food he ate with his own hands. The servant Ram Tilakam passing through the doorstep pinched Jnana Oli's cheeks. He sat by himself in the doorstep talking to no one in particular.
>
> Anni, having finished eating, arose and walked toward the courtyard. Jnana Oli followed her. He stood in the doorway to the courtyard. Anni returned with an armful of dirty dishes. Jnana Oli sauntered back to the circle of women still eating and stood there. He went to Anuradha and put his hand on her shoulder but received no response. He went to Mohana and put his hand on her shoulder. No response.
>
> Sivamani arose. Ram Tilakam took him by the wrist and led him to the wash place. She poured water over his hand.

> Padmini fed him buttermilk out of the pot. Sivamani commenced playing with the dirty pots. Anni took them and stacked them. Ram Tilakam wiped his face.
>
> Anni told Jnana Oli and Sivamani to go to the main room. The two of them went there, Jnana Oli in the lead. Anni put them both in their hammocks and swung them. They were sitting up in the hammocks; neither seemed ready to sleep. Anni lay them on their backs and continued to swing them.
>
> Mohana came up, slapped Jnana Oli hard on his bottom through the hammock, and gave the hammock a hard swing. Jnana Oli whimpered, "Sourpuss [*muñci*]." Mohana gave Sivamani a swing, then stopped the hammock and leaned over to whisper to him.
>
> Jnana Oli said to Anni, "Aunt Mohana pinched [*Mohanattai kiḷicci*]." Sivamani said, "Mother pinched [*Ammā kiḷicci*]."
>
> Jnana Oli and Sivamani remained awake. Anni was reclining on her belly on the floor talking to me. Sivamani climbed down from his hammock and lay between her legs with his head on her bottom as a pillow. Jnana Oli watched from his hammock as Padmini played with my son. He climbed down from his hammock and lay with his head on a pillow near Mohana. Padmini lay down with him and cuddled him. She told me to write in my notebook that she was cuddling Sivamani.

Jnana Oli had a plurality of mothers. Many laps cradled him, many hands fed him. He slipped without friction in and out among them as though they were all interchangeable. And they themselves aimed to be equally loving toward him and all the other children of the house, though of course this ideal could not be realized to perfection. Thus his own mother was embarrassed to be caught cuddling him and called him by his cousin's name. This was the plurality of love—his own mother, hidden among many duplicates, himself duplicated in others, a matrix of mirrors that had a certain magic, enabling as it did this small boy to live his life both very bound and very free.

SIVAMANI

> ". . . having found such a friend . . ."
>
> *Tirukkōvaiyār*, 19.

At two, Sivamani would have seemed healthy, except for his puffy eyes and swollen belly. He dimpled when he smiled. He could dance like

Plate 32. Jnana Oli.

Jnana Oli. In this household, Sivamani was so mixed with Jnana Oli, and with Jnana Oli's siblings, that he got in the habit of calling his mother Mohanattai, "Aunt Mohana," while he was there, because all the other children called her that. He was one with his cousins, he was outnumbered by them, he was their shadow (they were not his).

He differed from them, and in particular from Jnana Oli, because he did not belong entirely to this household. Together with his mother, he had to spend at least half of every year in her mother-in-law's house, where he was the only child and there was no one else to play with. During much of this time, Mohana was kept occupied tending the fields of groundnuts that belonged to her mother-in-law, and Sivamani was left to his own devices. The village was much more remote from the city than the village of his cousins, smaller and vastly quieter. The altitude was higher and the weather chillier. During the rainy season, several rooms of the house would be an inch deep in water. Moreover, the food in this house was different. In Sivamani's cousins' house, there were milk and ghee. In his grandmother's house, there were neither. Mohana laughed at the memory of him asking his grandmother for ghee. He had become accustomed to too much luxury, she said.

One day, after Mohana and Sivamani had been staying at the home of Anni and Padmini for some months, Anni returned with them to the home of Anni's parents, Mohana's in-laws. I went too. It was a day-long trip, by bus and oxcart. When we arrived at the house in the late afternoon, Sivamani was very grouchy, frequently crying, and he grew grouchier as the evening wore on. He wanted to eat a banana and was refused it, and he cried at that. He wanted to play with the water in a bucket and was not allowed to, and he cried at that.

At about seven in the evening the family sat down to eat. Sivamani, standing apart, looked around at the dark walls of the room they were in, the shadows flickering from the lantern, and suddenly burst into a wail. Anni said to Sivamani, "Go out and get Anuradha and Jnana Oli [whom we had left far away in the other village] and tell them to come and eat." I told Anni I thought that probably Sivamani was crying because he missed his friends back at the other house. Anni agreed. Sivamani went out into the hall as Anni had directed, looked around, then realizing that he had been tricked, wailed even louder than before. Anni picked him up and carried him out to the front porch to comfort him. Mohana laughed uproariously.

Thus Sivamani was taught what Jnana Oli was taught, to value others by considering their absence. But whereas Jnana Oli was taught by means of threats that were never carried out, Sivamani was taught through unrealized promises. Jnana Oli thought that he was in control of his world, especially of other people's comings and goings and of his own. But Sivamani could have entertained no such illusions. Jnana Oli swam at will through the fluid but stable medium of his family. Sivamani had to spend much of his life with no such medium to swim through. His grandparents, like his father, cared little for him. Subsequently, in their household, his mother would attempt suicide. She (and Sivamani?) had gone for days without eating, and her parents-in-law had not even noticed, she said.

When Sivamani was living again with his cousins, a dramatic thing happened. Padmini and Mohana went with their children to a festival, and somehow Sivamani got lost in the crowd. "We gave Sivamani to a little boy from the village to carry," said Padmini, "and when we looked, he was gone. Mohana and I searched everywhere for him. We were weeping. Sivamani would be hungry and that little boy wouldn't know what to do. After two hours, we found him in a choultry [a shelter for pilgrims] near the temple." Lost in a crowd of strangers for two hours Sivamani had been terrified. Would Jnana Oli have been entrusted this way, in a festival crowd, at night, to the arms of a half-known child? What might it mean, to be allowed to fall out of the nest?

Perhaps Sivamani would forget this incident. Still, there were daily small reminders to him of his medial position—in but not in, equal to Jnana Oli, but then, at crucial moments, not. People would treat Jnana Oli and Sivamani with similar rough affection. Oli they would strike or pinch. Siva they would knock over. Jnana Oli would be angry and would strike back when he was struck. Sivamani could not push an adult down. When he was pushed over, he would laugh, as his mother laughed. For in effect, he had inherited his mother's status—a status determined as much by affect as by structural position. Sivamani's mother Mohana was married to Jnana Oli's mother's brother Tambu. Following the same pattern, when the children grew up, Jnana Oli might marry Sivamani's younger sister. Indeed when Sivamani was four he did get a younger sister, who was better cared for than Sivamani himself had been in his toddlerhood. Perhaps this was because when the little girl Minakshi was born, her mother had broken with her parents-in-law and become permanently a member of her cousins' household, where wealth was increasing and life in general was better. Perhaps Minakshi was well cared for because she was the last child of her generation born in that household, everybody's baby. Or perhaps she was favored because there were thoughts that she might someday become Jnana Oli's wife. If this happened, Jnana Oli would become a "wife-taker" with respect to Sivamani, and a cut above him structurally as he already was emotionally. As life shook down now, when the boys were just two, Sivamani's role with respect to Jnana Oli was that of beloved sidekick, eternal second fiddle. Thus, matched though he was by the adults with his affine Jnana Oli, Sivamani was distraught when the servant Modday disappeared with her ragged and hungry little daughter Ponni. "For Ponni was Siva's best friend," said Mohana. "He loved to dance with her."

One evening after dinner, Mohana swept Sivamani onto her lap. Sivamani took her face into his small hands and kissed her on both cheeks and on the chin. I told Mohana that I thought Sivamani was not looking very healthy. Mohana said that his belly had gotten very big but his arms and legs were like matchsticks. She was smiling, but it seemed to me that she was worried. When the children sat down to eat, Mohana fed all the other children while Sivamani, hungry, whimpered but said nothing. Finally Anuradha served Sivamani. After Sivamani had finished eating, he got up. Padmini thwacked him on the back in her usual affectionate way. Sivamani lurched forward, then fell backward. Mohana laughed out loud. "He's like a little truck with a heavy load," she said, "a big heavy load up front." She laughed until the tears rolled down her cheeks.

ARIVARACI

> ". . . something broke this girl . . ."
>
> *Tirukkōvaiyār*, 6.

Arivaraci was Padmini's oldest child. She was born three days before Mankaiyarkkaraci, Anni's second child. The two girls were often addressed or referred to jointly as Arivumankai (Jnana Oli and Sivamani were also paired in this way, as Olisiva). Since Arivu was born first, she was nicknamed Petti, "the big girl," while Mankai was called Cinni, "the little girl." There was, however, no difference in size or status between the two girls as far as I could see. Mankai was the more aggressive of the two. Arivaraci's formal name meant "Queen of Knowledge." Mankaiyarkkaraci's formal name meant "Queen of Women." The latter was the name of a heroic queen of long ago, who through her bravery saved an army. Arivaraci's name was unique, coined by her father.

"Shortly after Mankaiyarkkaraci was born," said Ayya, he wrote a song. He did not directly say that he wrote it for his own infant daughter, his first child. Perhaps he wrote it for both of the baby girls:

> Smiling flower! Ripe fruit!
> Gift-giving smell! Sweet taste!
> Substance of the open secret!
> Image of abundant grace! Golden light!
>
> Cool moon coming with the south wind!
> Song-flower growing in the sweet tongue!
> Holy grace dancing in the meeting ground!
> Star light resting in our hearts!
>
> Sweet sound harvested in music!
> High secret blossoming in the ancient tongue!
> Great treasure born from the soil!
> Light-giving holy lamp bonded to the family honor!
>
> Good smell wafting from a flower!
> Lovely jewel ripened in a raindrop!
> Great yield reaped from the land!

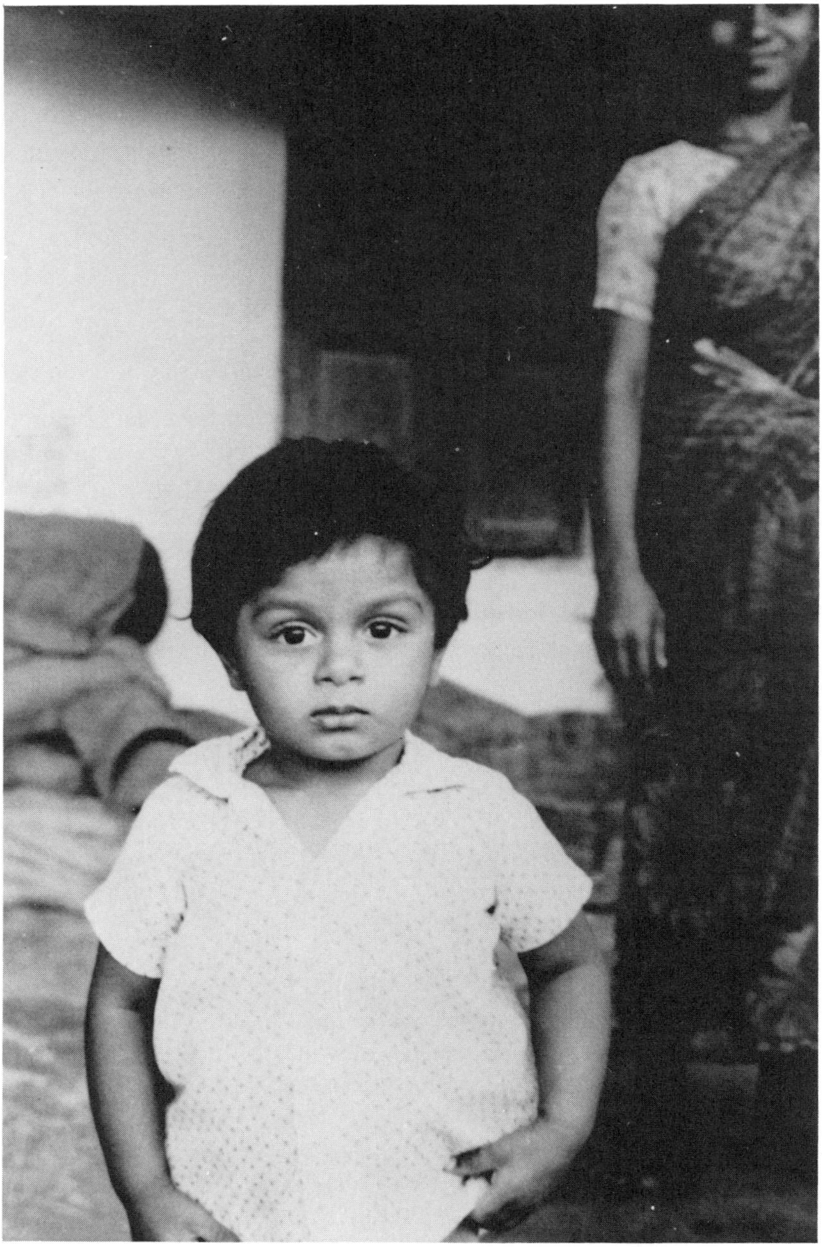

Plate 33. Sivamani.

Gem of grace sprouting out of goodness!

Light of grace dawning from silence!
Body of wisdom! God food!
Vine of the family, born
In the friendship of souls!

Cirikkum malarē! Ceṛuṅkaniyē!
Cīrtaru maṇamē! Tīñcuvaiyē!
Virinta maṟaiyin niṟaiporuḷē!—Aruḷ
Vaḷattin polivē! Ponoḷiyē!

Teṉṟalil vanta kuḷirnilavē!—Tīn
Tamiṛil eṛunta pāmalarē!
Maṉṟil āḍum tiruvaruḷē!—Eṅkaḷ
Manatil amarnta cuḍarviḷakkē!

Paṇṇil viḷainta innicaiyē!—Paṛan
Tamiṛil malarnta māmaṟaiyē!
Maṇṇil piṟanta perunitiyē!
Māṇpuṟa oḷiviḍum tiruviḷakkē!

Malaril maṇakkum naṟumaṇamē!—Maṛai
Muttil mutirnta eṛilmaṇiyē!
Nilattil viḷainta perumpayanē!—Mana
Nalattil iḷaitta aruḷmaṇiyē!

Mōnattil utitta aruḷ oḷiyē!—Vān
Mēkattil utirnta maṛaiyamutē!
Ñanattin vaḍivē! Nallamutē! Uyir
Naḍpil piṟanta kulakkoḍiyē!

Such had been Ayya's dreams of a daughter.

Arivaraci was different from the other children in the family. They were saucy and daring. She strove to be good. She would sweep the house, scrub the dishes, run errands for her parents. While the other children were playing, she would stand apart, or she would join them for a while and then leave them early to go home. In the early morning, while the other children slept, Arivu would be up, helping the servants fetch the water. She was the one who performed the daily worship ceremony to Ganesan. Under her breath, she would curse herself for tiny mistakes.

Except for Jnana Oli, all of the children in this family were thin and often ill, but Arivu was the thinnest and was sick the most. Whenever she traveled with her family to a festival or marriage or to visit friends, she would get a fever. She would get pains all over her body but especially in her legs and feet. Sometimes she would lie down in the evening crying. In a manner characteristic of all the children in the household, if someone asked her why she wept she would just keep weeping, without giving an answer. Others would answer for her, or no answer would be needed.

When she wept like this, her grandmother Attai would take her feet in her lap and rub them.

In the morning before school the children would all recite their lessons. At the end of each lesson in the schoolbook, there would be questions. Padmini would read a question and the child would chant the answer in a monotone. The child was required to repeat the text word-for-word. Arivu would often stumble. When she did, Padmini would taunt her and beat her on the face until she wept. This was hard for me to watch. I asked Ayya why Padmini punished Arivu so. Ayya said that Padmini wanted Arivu to be a great scholar, and this was her way of accomplishing it.

Anni said that of all the children, Arivaraci had received the most beatings. "Why?" I asked. "Fear," said Anni. Padmini beat Arivu to make her study, said Ayya, and this made her fear school and fear that the teachers would beat her, too. When she saw the teacher, who was a big man, said Anni, she was afraid to go to school, and every day she had to be beaten. She was so terrified that they had to drag her there, and then she would run away. Now she was terrified of being late. Arivu did not study as well as Mangai, said Anni. She was just not as smart.

Sometimes, when she was little, Arivu would get a fever and they would take her to the doctor. When they said the word "doctor," she would be afraid and start crying. Then Padmini would beat her. When she was being beaten, she would wet her pants out of fear, and they would beat her to make her stop.

To show that she was Saiva, devoted to Siva, Arivaraci wore sacred ash, a sign of desire burnt and cooled to eternal barren purity. Saivas are renouncers, ashes the final mortification of the flesh. Arivu would spread the ashes over her forehead, taking great care that they should be even, filling in the gaps with touches of her finger. Sometimes, using them like talcum powder, she whitened her whole face with them. Worldly desires merged with release from the flesh.

PONNI

> ". . . by whose origin the unblessed sicken . . . "
>
> *Tirukkōvaiyār*, 5.

> ". . . Enter, for this is your home . . . "
>
> *Tirukkōvaiyār*, 399.

Modday was a servant of the household, belonging to the lower caste of Nayakars. All the other inhabitants of the household, including the two other indwelling servants, were relatives. Although she was of a lower caste, Modday was never excluded on grounds of "purity" from any of

Plate 34. Arivaraci.

the household activities. She often cooked for the family, and she ate from the same plates as the family.

Nevertheless her life was hard. She ate her one meal a day at 10 P.M. She rose at 4 A.M. to get water, carrying on her head and in her arms ten to twenty gallons at a time. She did almost all the family laundry, washed almost all the pots and pans, cleaned the drainpipes, and performed many miscellaneous tasks. Anni and Padmini addressed her in loud voices with words steeped in vitriol. They never spoke to her gently, they never joked with her. I had seen other lower-caste servants, Paraiyars, much lower in the caste hierarchy than Nayakars, talk back to Annan and Anni—answer loud and angry words with loud and angry words. Modday evidently did not have this option. I never saw her try to argue.

Modday's two-year-old daughter, Ponni, wandered about crying or masturbating, or slept alone in a corner of the floor, covered with flies, while her mother worked. She looked sick. Her belly was more swollen than Sivamani's, her arms and legs more thin, her hair was falling out, she drooled constantly. Observing that Ponni's condition was deteriorating, Anni at last took her to the doctor's "for a blood test." The doctor, a close family friend, prescribed a concentrated protein solution. I believed, as the doctor through his prescription had apparently tried to signal, that Ponni's main problem was insufficient nourishment. I confronted Anni and Ayya with my distress. I told them that they were keeping me fat enough with all the ghee they poured on my meals. This was not how I wished to be repaid for the money I gave them. Surely, at least while I was there, they could afford to feed this tiny child adequately.

Anni responded by telling me that Modday was a good worker but she had too much pride (*timir*). They took her in when she was a child of nine from a household of her own caste that was not treating her well. When she came of age, the other household found a husband for her and married her off. She ran away from him to live with another man. After some months she returned to the house battered and emaciated. Her husband had beaten her. She would not return to him. An old man was with her. The old man said that she had left her husband for a rickshaw driver, then left the rickshaw driver for someone else.

The family took her in again, said Anni. After about a month, they found that she was pregnant. They tried to convince her to have an abortion, but she stubbornly refused.

For the birth, Anni had taken Modday to Chingleput Hospital. (Anni, Padmini, and Mohana had had their babies in a nursing home in Madras. They said that the doctors at Chingleput Hospital had a reputation for murdering patients. It was a very scary place.) Anni said that after Ponni was born, Modday had the habit of asking for Ponni the same things that the other children in the house received. It is the custom in all houses, said Anni, for there to be differentiation between the child of the servant and the child of the master. Modday should have known this, and she would find out if she went to work in other people's houses. There, she would not be allowed to eat off the same plate as the family; a separate plate would be kept for her. Here, it had been ten years since they had observed even that distinction.

Nine months after Ponni had been born, her father had appeared at the house, asking to take away Modday and Ponni. Up until then he had not made an appearance, said Anni. Modday said that she did not want to go with him, she wanted to stay in this house. The family said that since they had paid the two-hundred-rupee expense of having Ponni born in a hospital, they would not let Modday and Ponni go unless he would repay them that amount. Maybe then he would understand the seriousness of mar-

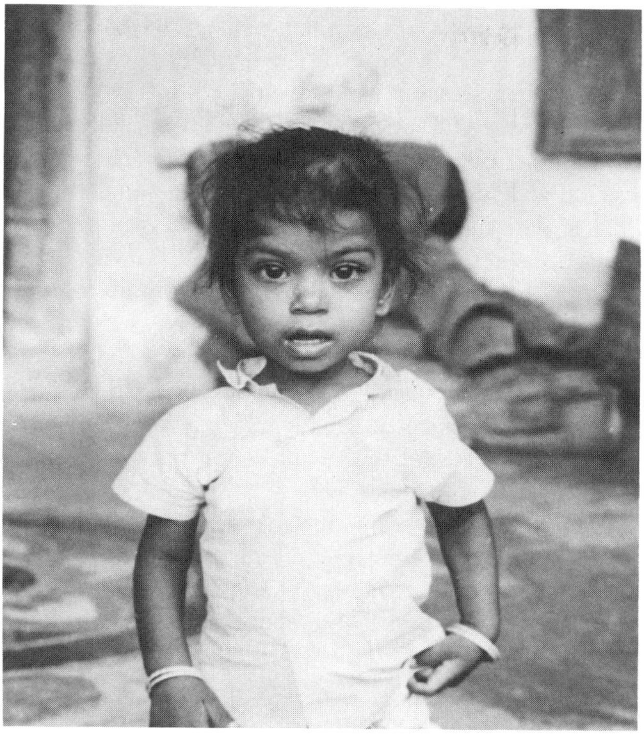

Plate 35. Ponni.

riage. This demand frightened him away, said Anni. He left and never returned.

Ayya told me that all the children in the household were treated equally. Ponni was sick because she ate dirt. His own daughter Arivaraci had had the same problem, and she had been the same way. They had bought medicine for Ponni, but Modday herself wouldn't give it to her. If Ponni was treated differently from the other children, it was her own mother's fault. What motivation would they have for not giving Ponni milk, when they gave it to the neighbors for free?

Ayya said that Modday herself separated Ponni off and demanded to raise her in her own way. They would not interfere with a mother raising her child. Besides, he said, when their own children were thin and not fully nourished, in a household of fifteen with an income of eight hundred rupees a month, they had taken in this pregnant woman, when everyone else had refused. Would I have done the same? Angrily I said, if the child is in your own household, you should not allow her to become like this.

If you don't have the means to take care of her, you shouldn't have taken her in in the first place. Ayya gazed at me silently, incredulously, tears in his eyes, and then answered, "Maybe you're right."

Later I pondered, could it be that Modday herself was responsible for the starvation of her own child? Carrying her burden of laundry at noontime across the wide dry lakebed, Ponni trailing behind crying, Modday would hurry to deposit her load at the house, then run back to pick her daughter up off the hot sand. She would pin flowers, when she could get them, into Ponni's thinning hair. She would steal moments from washing dishes to play with Ponni. On one hand, Modday was sometimes harsh with Ponni. When Ponni picked up a plastic block, Modday took it from Ponni, put it in Jnana Oli's hand, and said unsmiling to Ponni, "Go. You go." But on the other hand, when Ponni and Sivamani were playing together, Modday, now smiling, taught Ponni to say "Go" to Siva, and threatened to snatch Siva's penis away.

Modday would also tease Ponni the way the other mothers teased their children. At night, when Ponni was crying, Modday pointed to an airplane flying overhead and said to her, "See! There goes an airplane! Go catch it!" Ponni ran a little in that direction and then stopped short and started crying. Modday drew Ponni close to her, smiling, saying, "It doesn't matter. Don't cry," gently.

Later that evening, Ponni ran up to me. I sat her in my lap and offered her a piece of fruit. Modday signaled me from across the courtyard to stop. Then she crossed the courtyard with a load of dishes, stopped beside me, and said, "Don't pick up Ponni and put her in your lap, and don't feed her fruit. Those habits will come to her and they will scold me." I asked if it was all right to play with Ponni without picking her up, and she said yes. Then she whispered, "What they tell you is all lies. It is very hard . . ." and stopped because Padmini was coming near. Padmini asked her what she was saying to me. Modday said, "I told her not to pick Ponni up." Padmini told me that I should not give bananas to Ponni because they were bad for her, she could not digest them. A few days later, Modday and Ponni were gone. The family told me that they had run away. After a month, my son reported to me that Modday and Ponni were working at another Reddiar house just down the road. But I never saw them again.

I realized that from one point of view, what Modday had told me had been right. Why make Ponni happy now, if denial of that same happiness later would only make her cry. She might as well learn now that nothing would be hers to have forever. I remembered the philosopher Patanjali's adage, "Even in pleasure, there is the pain of knowing it will end." But Modday had never heard of Patanjali. And all I knew at this point was that I had no answers.

CHAPTER EIGHT

Final Thoughts

> After having recited the last verse of *Tirukkōvaiyār* that he was to read to me, verse number 399, Themozhiyar paraphrased it: "The heroine has been temporarily deserted by her husband for the sake of another woman. The heroine is god [*civam*]. The other woman is the world [*ulakam*].
>
> "One day, the other woman comes to visit the home of the heroine. She does not know what she will find there. The heroine welcomes her, and offers her everything she has. She says that they stand in the same place, therefore they are true kin of the body [*meyyuṟavu*]. The home of the one is the home of the other, the child of the one is the child of the other. The heroine does not say to her rival, 'Go away, the child born of my body belongs to me.' She says, 'This child is yours.'
>
> "Shamed [*veḷki*] by the generosity of the heroine, the other woman hides her face and departs. But to say that she hides herself means she will stand naked. To say that she goes away means she will return."

It remains now to give an accounting of what has been described in the chapters preceding, a catalogue of patterns.

In the introduction to this volume, three themes were mentioned as threads intended to bind together the whole. The action of mutual expectation between India and America, or between any two different perspectives, was one theme; the relation between ideal and experience was a second; ambiguity and the sacred was a third. These three threads are tightly woven together: the sacred is an ideal manifested ambiguously in experience; it is born in the thought that arises between two separate consciousnesses—male and female, East and West, wild and cultured, human and divine. No one being may hold it within himself. Another name for this exceedingly complex reality may be love.

We may focus on any one aspect of this truth with many names. It is difficult to focus upon all of it at once. In this book I have tried to focus on the very quality that keeps it out of focus, its inherent ambiguity. I have tried to say in different ways in all the preceding chapters that ambiguity is not something to be gotten rid of, even in a scientific analysis of human behavior. Ambiguity is crucial to all kinds of understanding between human beings. Every event has more than one meaning, and will as long as more than one person lives on the earth. A related assertion would be that the need to love is as important a force in human society as is the will to power. Power wants to destroy or consume or drive away the other, the one who is different, whose will is different. Love wants the other to remain, always nearby, but always itself, always other.[1]

Of course these assertions go far beyond the material of my text. I make them in order to indicate the flow to which I would want this text to contribute its small momentum.

Coming back down to the scope of events discussed in this text, we may consider a kind of repeating order suggested by these events. Maintaining our focus upon ambiguity, we may notice that, in Tamil culture, there exist some similarities in form between certain kinds of poetic ambiguity and certain kinds of psychological ambiguity. It is possible that ambiguity in both these areas serves similar, unifying functions, poetic ambiguity allowing for the unification of disparate cognitive patterns, or world views, psychological ambiguity allowing for the unification of disparate emotional patterns, or personalities.[2] In both cases, of course, what is being discussed is communication—idealized communication on the one hand (the performance of Tamil poetry), ordinary communication on the other (the conveyance of personal views and feelings in prosaic contexts). A list of similarities between poetic and psychological ambiguities can even be drawn up. I do not try to pretend here that my catalogue is in any way exhaustive, or that there is any kind of perfect parallelism between Tamil poetics and Tamil family life. But certain parallels are there.

It will be seen that all the patterns of ambiguity I describe below have to do with defining the relationship between self and other. The question of what is me as opposed to what is you is in general precisely what is left up in the air. Hence it would seem that, as life proceeds, what happens to the self is neither individuation (i.e., increasing differentiation of self from others) nor internal integration (i.e., crystallization of a stable sense of self), but rather a continuous *de*crystallization and *de*individuation of the self, a continuous effort to *break down* separation, isolation, purity, as though these states, left unopposed, would form of their own accord and freeze up life into death.

In passing, it may be observed that some of the decrystallizing patterns of communication commonly employed in Themozhiyar's family are very similar in form to what are called, in Freudian terminology, defense mechanisms. It would perhaps not be surprising to find that the same tools that are used to defend the boundaries of the ego in one culture are used to dismantle these boundaries in another. But I leave it to other researchers to follow up on this possibility.

MIRRORING/TWINNING

Repeatedly in this family, a pair of children or adults would be linked with each other by themselves or by others and defined as balanced and equivalent: equal in some ways, opposite in others, a matched set, mirror images, twins. The names of such a pair of matched personalities might be merged into a single compound word when people called them or spoke of them, as Olisiva or Arivumankai. They might have matched nicknames, such as Periyavar ("the elder man") and Cinnavan ("the younger man"), or Petti ("the big girl") and Cinni ("the younger girl"). If they were born at the same time and place, as were Arivaraci and Mankaiyarkkaraci, even their full names might echo each other. Twinned children of the same sex were dressed alike. They were also often physically paired on the right and left sides of an adult caretaker's body, and when they were carried, their respective mothers exchanged them.

When people discussed the personalities of children who had been twinned, they molded them into mutual complementarity. According to adults' accounts of them (and the children's behavior was roughly in accord with these accounts), Mankai was smarter, bolder, more aggressive, and younger; Arivu was duller, more timid, more obedient, and older. Jnana Oli was proud; Sivamani was humble. Arulmori was a sweet speaker, a graceful dancer, and a father-charmer; Umapathi was a rough speaker, a tough fighter, and a rebel. The definition of children within a household as each other's balancing partners is not a process unique to Tamil Nadu. American mothers describing their different children are inclined to do the same thing. Children growing up together create themselves in opposition and complementarity to one another. In the Tamil household, however, this process was not merely noticed but enhanced and encouraged in many ways.

In the Tamil joint family, also, twinning processes were not completed in childhood but were continued into adulthood or might even commence there. Adults would twin each other as they twinned sets of children, comparing and contrasting, pair-by-pair. Ayya was "the younger one," the skillful and impatient; Annan was "the older one," the patient and unskilled. Anni was the wise, who knew and kept things hidden; Padmini was the simple, who spilled everything out. Mohana was Padmini's "wife"; Padmini was Mohana's "husband." Mohana was timid and couldn't stand up for her rights; Celvi was bold and could. The combinations were endless.

What purpose did twinning serve? We might answer by asking, Did it need a purpose? When Anni conversed with me in the afternoon, describing the contrasts she saw between Annan and Ayya, there was no information that needed to be conveyed. Anni found pleasure in creating a symmetry through her words; this kind of conversation was the poetry she made.[3] She would have disavowed the lofty title "poetry," the pleasure she would not have disavowed. The feeling of harmony among people, of many different harmonies, the harmony of many people working on a simple task that could have been done by one or two, even the harmony of a good fight, this aesthetic feeling was treasured by Anni. Life itself was art for her. Where we find cultural patterns, seemingly so natural and artless, in terms of bare survival so extravagantly purposeless, in the finely crafted tapestry of Tamil kinship systems, for example, could people like Anni have been at work?

But in worlds beyond our own, where, as Boas long ago discovered, ornament and utility are not separate categories, poetry can also serve a purpose.[4] So let us return to the question, What purpose did twinning serve?, and answer it differently.

If the feelings of those who were twinned in the Tamil household were at all like those of people born as biological twins, who often feel that they are scarcely separate individuals, then we might hypothesize (rather banally) that twinning fostered solidarity within the family, the more so if each person had more than one "twin" and all were involved in a network of complementarities. The cross-cousins Mohana and Padmini, structurally rivals, were in their feelings like yin and yang—each the complement of the other, neither complete in herself but each finding her completion in her partner, closely mingling their identities as they shared food from the same pot and mothered each other's sons. When one member of such a pair looked across at her opposite, she might well ask, is that person me, or not me? And there would be no clear answer. And she might have many opposites, and therefore many faces she called "me."

The defense mechanism twinning most resembles is what Anna Freud called "splitting," a state in which a person experiences, in mixed form, two attributes that she would rather keep separate, and so assigns them, in fantasy, to two different persons or entities—the giving breast and the withholding breast, the loving mother and the devouring mother. In Anni's family, the twinning process seemed almost to reverse this mechanism. Two initially separate people were rendered complementary and then merged. The most-merged personalities (and so the least autonomous) were therefore those of adults.

The poetic device that twinning most resembles is rhyme. Perhaps it is relevant to our argument that in colloquial Tamil, there are many rhymed or otherwise matched-by-sound word-pairs that are used formulaically to denote the two extremes of some category (e.g., *ānai–pūnai,* "elephant and cat"; *māṅkai–tēṅkai,* "mango and coconut"; *tuṇi–maṇi,* "clothes and ornaments"; *mēḍampaḷḷam,* "hill and valley"; *āḍumāḍu,* "goats and cattle"; *māman–maccān,* "uncle and nephew"; *ammā–appā,* "mother and father"; and so forth). Hundreds of such pairs exist, they come up often in conversation, and there is even a productive process for creating a pseudo-mirror for some term (replace the first syllable of the term with *ki*, as in Vishvanathan's coinage, *Bournvita–kinvita,* to denote a miscellaneous collection of breakfast drinks he had to prepare). The creation of mirror-pairs is thus a linguistic as well as an interpersonal device with wide currency among Tamil speakers. Moreover the linguistic device, the creation of matched names, is an important part of the psychological strategy of twinning pairs of people.

COMPLEMENTATION/DYNAMIC UNION

It happens often that a person performs an act in order to get a certain response, but instead, the opposite response is forthcoming. Then, instead of changing her way of behaving, the first person repeats the original message, even more strongly than before, and the original negating response is repeated, more strongly than before, so that, for instance, the more I reach out to you, the more you withdraw, and the more you withdraw, the more I reach out. After a time, both people know that their actions will elicit responses that are the opposite of those they seem to desire, and yet both people persist in just those actions, so that it seems they are trying to elicit the very behavior they ostensibly are trying to oppose.

Some examples will make clear the nature of this pattern: Anni tries to persuade Ayya to eat; he refuses. She persists, but the more adamantly she persists, the more stubbornly he refuses. She knows that if she left him alone, he would eat of his own accord; he knows that if he ate just a little, she would cease to harass him. Yet they carry on their gustatory wrestling match, as though the struggle itself was something they valued. Or again, Arivaraci weeps at the thought of going to school; Padmini beats her to make her stop weeping; Arivu weeps more loudly, and Padmini beats her more. Or again, Jnana Oli demands attention from Annan. Annan plays with him in hopes of appeasing him, but the more Annan plays, the more Oli demands. Or again, Jnana Oli goes into a pout. The women beseech him to join them, but this only causes him to pout more conspicuously, and so forth.

This way of acting is very similar to what Bateson calls complementary schismogenesis.[5] There are some important differences, however, For one, Bateson's schismogenesis is the creation of no human agent, it arises spontaneously, as when I spill blue paint and you spill yellow, neither of us sees the other, and the green paint that is formed is the consequence of no one's plan. Participants in Bateson's schismogenesis do so blindly, not realizing the direction in which their behavior is leading them, whereas in our Tamil family, it was evident that participants in what I call complementation knew exactly what they were doing. Second, for Bateson schismogenesis was a destructive process, hurting people and driving them apart, whereas in our family, the process of complementation had distinct rewards; this was why they engaged in it. Chief among the rewards, surely, was maintenance of engagement, continuation of the relationship in a dynamic mode that would have been curtailed if someone had done the "right" thing and the conflict, whatever it was, had been resolved. Thus Anni did not want to finish her work as quickly as possible, did not want to have no one to argue with, for quiescence and solitude felt bad to her. Perhaps they were too much like death. To maintain the tension and so keep the engagement alive, to give the engagement a goal, a teleology as it were, and to keep this goal forever receding, is a specific Tamil strategy, much like the Romantic Quest still shaping much Euro-American behavior,[6] but with the crucial difference that the European valorization of lonely striving for union is replaced in the Tamil case with the striving for perfect balance within an already realized union of agents, a union whose continued life is composed of this very striving, the tension and movement generated by imbalance. Tamil people consciously work to keep alive this living union, by never allowing balance to be achieved.

One institution exemplifying the valorization of dynamic union is Tamil money-lending etiquette, in which people intentionally never settle accounts completely one way or the other but always add one rupee extra to their repayment, so that there will always be reason for the two parties to the exchange to meet and do business again. Ayya's refusal to end his lessons on the final verse of a poem followed the same principle. But the prime example of this tendency to keep union alive through the maintenance of unresolved tensions is the "Dravidian kinship system" (or better, the mutually reinforcing patterns of marriage, child-rearing, emotional organization within the household, and political organization within the kindred, which are played out in a great many ways by people involved in South Indian life). Dumont's main assertion about this "kinship system," as I read him, is that it is maintained precisely for the sake of a constantly renewed, never-completed engagement between two parties ("categories of kin"), hence the title of his book *Affinity as a Value*. What I have observed in Tamil Nadu supports Dumont's conclusion that Tamil people arrange their lives as they do and subscribe to certain ideals of human organization largely because they are motivated by this desire to maintain a living affinity, an imbalance constantly moving toward but never resting at balance. I depart from Dumont in believing that the foundation of "Dravidian kinship" is not *only* the intellectual–aesthetic satisfaction derived from contemplating the symmetry of relations between categories; nor is the meaning of Dravidian kinship the perceived necessity (on the part of some) to create a viable power structure within the South Indian context; nor does the encompassing, consuming capacity of a hierarchical system of social organization entirely explain why certain people in South India feel constrained to call certain others by certain names, marry certain others, sustain certain others. Behind the millenia-old perpetuation of Dravidian kinship, fueling it, giving it momentum, there also burns longing between actual human individuals, longing aroused in part by the experiences of childhood and in part by mythic and ideal patterns that people seek to live out but which, in their actual lives, they can never fulfill. Longings pull against longings, ideals against ideals, the act of seeking fulfillment only intensifies the desire, so tension is maintained and the pattern of complementation repeated indefinitely. When I marry my child to my brother's child, I do not satisfy my longing for my brother but only set the stage for a similar longing to emerge in the next generation.

A number of Tamil poetic devices correspond with, or enter into, processes of dynamic union between living persons, ideals (categories of persons), or groups. We must recall, first of all, that the symmetry of the "Dravidian kinship system" is more than anything else a *terminological* symmetry[7]—that is, it establishes a certain order in the world by calling certain beings by the same name and so effecting a partial identity among them, or by calling attention to this partial identity and thus rendering it more cognitively salient. When I call both my mother's brother and my father-in-law by the name *māmā,* I recognize, by so naming them, that in some respects I may regard them as identical. But one fundamental, perhaps universal, poetic process is the establishment of identities through naming, that is, through metaphor. Take a poem by Rilke that begins, "Spring has come again. The earth is like a child that knows poems by heart"; having established this identity, Rilke's poem continues talking of the earth no longer as though it were *like* a child but as though it *were* a child: "For the vexation of long learning, she gets the prize . . . " Having learned this poem, we may come to think of the earth as of a class with female children and may always call it "she." If a metaphor "takes" in this way, a poetic order is established in the world, and we may be more inclined to treat the earth in some of the same ways that we treat a living female child. So it is with Dravidian kinship terminology. If this terminological system is not the origin of identities between father-in-law and mother's brother, it is an important means of rendering those identities salient and making them part of a perceptible, larger pattern. The pattern established by the symmetry among words for kin lends an order to behavior as, in general, poetic features of language (such as metaphor) lend an order to life.

We are talking not only about metaphor, however, but about complementation, or dynamic union, as an effective poetic process in Tamil life. Such a process cannot be illustrated through a set of words taken out of time, as the set of "kinship terms" in Tamil, but can only be observed in linguistic or other acts taking place in time—specific sentences, poems, or conversations, or specific marriages or life histories or kindred histories. We have already considered a few nonverbal (or only partially verbal) microevents illustrating complementation in the life of the Tamil family. If we consider more fully verbal events, we stand more squarely in the realm of pure poetics, and in this realm, in Tamil, we may observe the same general valuation of the struggle, the desire never to reach balance though constantly striving for it, that we find in day-to-day Tamil life.

Here we will consider just one example of complementation in Tamil poetics, Porutcelvi's poem found early in chapter 6. Outside of its context, there is nothing "remarkable" about this poem, written by a schoolteacher assiduously following all the textbook rules of poetics as she writes and, at the same time, giving voice to particular strong, culturally sanctioned feelings that she holds. In this poem, Porutcelvi employs a number of devices that are either so common as to be almost mechanical in Tamil poetry or which are actually obligatory there, occurring not only in written poetry but in virtually all Tamil oral poetry (that I am aware of) as well. The important point to note here is that all these devices have the effect of maintaining tension, forestalling resolution.

In the first place, lines are paired. Each pair of lines is linked by enjambement—metrical units do not correspond with grammatical units; before a metrical line is ended, a new statement is begun; the listener must wait for the beginning of the next line to learn how this statement begun earlier will end—and then the ending in most of Porutcelvi's couplets turns out to be a paradox (e.g., "He renounced his kin. In justice / He fed his own"). Suspension, in the form of enjambement, is traded for tension, in the form of paradox, and so the poem proceeds, couplet by couplet. Both paradox and enjambement are basic poetic strategies in Tamil.[8] Porutcelvi is following well-trodden paths when she uses them as she does.

Second, in each pair of lines there is strong initial rhyme, weaker internal rhyme, and never any end-rhyme, so that at the end of any couplet there is no strong sense of closure. This absence of end-rhyme is characteristic of all Tamil poetry. In part it is an artifact of the grammatical structure of Tamil, which specifies most basic grammatical categories by means of suffixation and so limits the possibilities for interesting end-rhyme. In Celvi's poem, each couplet ends with the same suffix, *-ān* (masculine singular ending—she is writing about her brother), except the very last couplet, which ends in *-āy* (second person singular ending), so that the poem leaves the hearer with a markedly unsettled feeling. Moreover, the ending of this poem is a question, an angry challenge demanding a response, "Why did you make him your kin? Why / Did you hurt his tender heart?" One actual human being addresses another in this poem: Porutcelvi is speaking directly to her brother's wife Padmini. She is not forgiving or explaining, she is accusing, putting her accusation in the form of a question. Matters are not settled, a response is demanded, and only an angry response is possible. So the internal tension of the poem, never resolved, is merged with the irresolvable tension bonding the sisters-in-law in lifelong enmity.

SEQUENTIAL CONTRAST

There are stories in Hindu mythology, as in Chinese Taoist philosophy, of dreams that exist within waking that exist within still more dreams. I am a king who dreams he is a pauper, who dreams he is a king, who dreams he is a pauper, and so forth, until I do not know which is the waking reality and which the dream. The point of such stories is that both dreams and waking are equally real.

As in so many Indian tales, which like to play with the boundary between dream and waking, theater and actual life, sacred and profane, so in Indian visual art there occur many double-entendre images, in which, for instance, lotuses alternate with stars, or birds with fish, or female symbols with male ones. The onlooker can see one pattern and then the other, in sequence, but can never resolve them into one, or see both at one time, or decide, finally, which is the "real" figure and which the "real" ground. The mind flashes back and forth. The effect is like that of a strobe light.

I have tried to show that in Tamil marriage patterns as they are enacted over successive generations, the opposed relationships between spouses and opposite-sex siblings may enter into a sequential alternation of this sort, so that generation by generation, the spousal relation and the sibling relation (or more generally, relations of "affinity" and relations of "consanguinity") are transformed back and forth into one another endlessly.

In face-to-face interactions, the sequential alternation of opposite feelings or relations happened often in our Tamil home when adults dealt with children, as when they teased them by alternately offering and withdrawing a toy, or alternately punished and comforted them. Adults among themselves likewise enjoyed alternating between emotional modes we would call extreme and contradictory. To hang on to a single feeling was not a moral imperative for them.

The working of karma, as presented in Attai's lullaby or in the justifications offered by Ayya and Anni for deprivations and punishment, also showed this kind of pendulum pattern. Proximal sorrow would surely turn into distal pleasure, present happiness into future pain, and then one step further, it might change back again—an endless round.

Again, these Tamil pendulum patterns were reminiscent of Chinese Taoism in that opposites were shown to depend upon one another and to generate one another: the seed of kinship was contained in affinity, the seed of reward in punishment, the seed of quiescence in activity, the seed of tears in laughter, the seed of laughter in rage. Hence there could be no permanent separation of opposites. One could not stay permanently angry with the punishing mother, because she soon became the loving mother. A sister would not be permanently parted from her brother, because their children might wed. Living in a troubled world, at very close quarters with others, one learned to accept the bad with the good. We need only set our own spatialized images of opposition and contrast into time to see that all rhythms are transformations and reverse transformations of states into opposite states and then back again, repeatedly. It was part of the style of this Tamil family—one of their "habits," as they would say—to dwell upon such rhythms. This is perhaps one reason why poetry, with its very pronounced alternations and intricate flowing contrasts, was so important to them. Song is an art form in time; it cannot sustain unbridgeable oppositions.

PROJECTION/INTROJECTION

Ayya was a master at this—as, for instance, when he punished himself as a way of punishing his wife; or when his father distanced him and he in turn distanced his father, and then Ayya himself came to distance his own son and that son in turn distanced him; or when observing his son's disobedience, he referred this attribute back to himself. Who was the agent and who was the patient? Who was doing what to whom? Who was mirroring whom or learning from whom or reacting to whom? It all became obscure. By bouncing their feelings off each other in this way, people became bound to one another, even through hostility.[9] They populated on another with their own feelings, it seemed to me, and they populated themselves with the feelings of others. Like mirroring, projection was a means through which personalities developed not singly but interdependently, shaping themselves to one another.

Habits and personality traits were transferred laterally, just as they were handed down through the generations. The patterned organization of kin helped channel the projections. Ayya would compare his two "sisters" with each other, projecting onto one what he had learned from the other. Anni compared her various "aunts" in just the same way. Jnana Oli and Sivamani had an affinity for each other that they inherited from their mothers. Sisters-in-law infused each other with anger and with sexual expectations. A son was expected in some way to embody his father, a daughter to embody her mother. Anuradha was patient like Anni, Jnana Oli was stubborn like Ayya, Arivaraci was nervous and thin like Padmini, Sivamani was expected to have sexual troubles when he grew up because his father had overstepped his sexual bounds, Ponni was despised because her mother was despised.

The "origin" of some particular habit or trait in the family—who first had it, who passed it on to whom—would be impossible to determine. Jorge Luis Borges has a story about this: the narrator sees a bit of godliness in an otherwise despicable acquaintance, a particular bit of kindness or a shine in the eyes; he wonders where the acquaintance got this admirable trait, who he learned it from; he traces it back to a friend of the acquaintance, then back from there to a friend of the friend, and so continues his network analysis until he gets all the way back to God.[10]

Personalities in the Tamil family also have a divine component, or better to call it mythic. We have seen, for instance, how the rivalries between the men and women in our family mirrored the divine rivalry between the gods and the goddesses, and how each side even called upon this divine rivalry for justification and support of its cause. A suffering woman may compare herself to Nallataṅkāḷ; a conflicted woman may be devoted to Māriamman; a man torn between family life and asceticism worships and emulates Siva; a man who believes he destroyed his son and now seeks the lost son's forgiveness worships Ganesan.

When we reach the realm of mythology we return again to poetics. Myths, like poems (I mean now Tamil poems, especially unwritten ones) are unique in each performance, as each personality is unique, but originality is no more desirable for a myth or poem than isolation is desirable for a person. They are made of transformed pieces of each other. When we read a Tamil poem or hear a Tamil myth, only rarely do we know, as we know in Porutcelvi's poem, for instance, exactly whose spirit animates it. There is so much intertextuality in South Indian stories, so much projection into and introjection from other texts, so much borrowing and lending, that it is meaningless to try to draw lines between texts or to say what is the "authentic" version of some tale. As we speak of "intertextuality" among poems or myths in South India, so we may speak of "interpersonality" among human beings there. Considered in himself, a lone man has no meaning. He is suffused with the feelings, the spirits and substances, of those who live near him, and they are suffused with his. We Americans place so much faith in the boundary drawn by our skin, that thin physical membrane, that we build our whole concept of personhood there. Most Indians, as we have known for a long time, do not,[11] so they seem strange to us. Because, for them, their living within one another is a concrete, physical fact, we cannot grasp what they are to themselves. We try to enskin them, "encompass" them, pin them down and control them, with our theories. The more we fail to face their ambiguity, the ultimate unboundedness of their being, the less we are able to see them.

INTERNAL CONTRADICTION/CATEGORY MEDIATION

Consider the law of the excluded middle: a thing cannot be both *A* and not *A* simultaneously. This is a principle of logic, but it is often taken to be a property of the natural world. For instance, we have a deep conviction that a person must be either male or not male, and not male means female. Anything else is an anomaly, a monster. If some of us (I mean now Americans) defy this convention—if some men "act like women" and some women "act like men," or if some men and women adopt "unisex" clothing styles or in one way or another actually "change their sex," it is because those men and women do not believe in the validity of "male" and "female" as culturally defined opposites. There are no essential, irreducible differences between male and female as human types, such people feel.

In the Tamil family, also, as we have seen, there were androgynous personalities—women who deliberately acted against the image of femininity, men who deliberately acted against the image of masculinity. Ayya claimed he was a woman born as a man. Padmini took over many masculine tasks. In general in South India, androgynous personalities are many, both in myth and in life. More than a few women plow their own fields, though the plow is known by all as a symbolic penis. Transvestism among men is very common, and even "normal" boys can get away with dressing up like girls, just for fun, and learn to move their bodies in convincingly female ways. Siva is a hermaphrodite; pictures of Krishna make him look like a girl.

Does this mean that masculine and feminine are not valid categories to South Indian people? Are the women who plow or the men who dress up as women questioning the essential opposition between male and female? No. Indeed, androgynes are the very ones who make the most of this opposition, who most articulately express or most convincingly enact the belief that male and female are opposed cosmic forces, as different from each other as black and white, as powerfully charged as earth and sky in a lightning storm. Indian androgynes are not asexual, nor are they ungendered. Certainly, the androgynous personalities in the household that I lived in were far from sexually neutral; they also expressed strong loyalty to their gender and its principles, for the values of the two genders differed. Rather than attributing grim and unbending sexual differentiation, or denial and repression of sexuality, to Indian peasant culture (our own projections, certainly), we might consider the proliferation of androgyny there to be one aspect of a pleasure in sexuality in its original polymorphous nature that we ourselves miss, together with an intellectual enjoyment of paradox, which, also, we fail to share. This is not to say that sexual oppression, and repression, do not occur in India. But too often, this is all that ethnographers see.[12]

In the Tamil household, intermediate kin-types were something like androgynes—that is, they were *A* and not-*A*; they fulfilled a desire for the impossible. By intermediate kin-types, I mean kin-types that fell between the great polar categories of parent, child, sibling, and spouse and mingled their contradictory attributes. A man's *aṇṇi,* his older brother's wife, could be something of a mother to him, something of a sister. *Māmān,* the mother's brother, and *maccān,* the older sister's husband, could be something of a brother and something of a father. *Nāttanār*, the brother's wife, could be a female husband. Many of the intermediate kin-types, such as daughter-in-law, sister's son, brother's wife, also had the added connotation, secret spouse. All kinds of combinations occurred, including hybrids of male and female, sibling and spouse, own and older generations. These hybrid relationships were generally not discussed as such, nor were they explicated for the ethnographer inquiring after rules, perhaps because, like the equally omnipresent androgyny, they involved departures from ideal types, or like Anni's cooking procedures, they entailed flexions of rules of separation that the ethnographer had read about and carried with her, as partially assimilated values, into the "field." Nevertheless, such hybrid roles and relationships were enacted openly in the day-to-day life of the family. If one stepped a little beyond explication, they were there for all to see.

The context-relativity of behavior sometimes meant that a person, crossing contexts, became a temporary *A*-and-not-*A*, an embodiment of seemingly incompatible properties, like Padmini having to act simultaneously the roles of hostess (generous and kind) and mill owner (tough and tight-fisted), graciously and politely serving the labor supervisor and, at the same, loudly arguing with him regarding how much to feed the workers. Or like Jnana Oli brandishing the stick with which Anni had "beaten" him, half of him aggressing freely, the other half of him submitting to punishment for threatening such aggression. Or like Sivamani changing houses, confused as to whether he was in his cousins' house where he would be indulged, or in his grandfather's house where he would be neglected—his confusion deliberately increased by his mother and his aunt.

Little children, as we have seen, could be caught and confused by contradictions, but older people could use them to advantage. Because unlikely combinations of culturally defined categories or properties were allowed, there was room for a greater range of possible personalities, there existed a greater range of possible relations into which one could enter, and there remained available a greater range of possible modes of being that one could assume without having to worry about maintaining consistency. Hence one escaped a certain internal tyranny; one was not bound too closely by any one rule of the self.[13]

HIDDENNESS

The meaning (*poruḷ*, "substance") in a word is likened in some Tamil poems to the light in the eyes, the heat in the fire, the scent in the flower, the spirit in the body—a subtle power guarded by the form, hidden by it, difficult to grasp. Thus, much high Tamil poetry is not straightforward, its perceptible surface is a play of illusions, it seems to be saying many different things, no one can know for sure what is inside.

In our study of this one Tamil family, we have seen many acts of deliberate irony, many ways in which feelings were hidden by giving form to their opposites, while at the same time, the hiding of certain feelings was so conventional that in the very act of hiding them one communicated their presence to others.

Ethnography in such a situation becomes a problematic exercise.[14] For there are many times when the "truth" that lies behind the "form" (we never can escape our own folk-ontology) is not at all clear. If one asks a man what his monthly income is and he says two hundred rupees, it might in reality be ten thousand (for then he would certainly conceal his treasure), or it might be two hundred as he claims (for then he will have nothing to conceal). The look on his face will not give him away. Or if one asks a woman if her husband is good to her and she says no, she may be lying (protecting her treasure) or she may not be. There is no way of knowing for sure.

In the life of our Tamil family, the hiding of true feeling sometimes took conventional forms, sometimes unique ones. To protect a child against death by calling it an ugly name was a conventional act. To disguise one's concern for its health by laughing at its swollen belly was a more particular way of doing the same thing. (And a genuinely despised person might also be called by an ugly name or laughed at, as was Modday.)

As for conventional forms, they could assume a wide range of personal meanings. The convention of avoidance and overt hostility between husband and wife sometimes embodied a hostility that was real; sometimes it concealed a deep affection; sometimes it did both. The convention of denial of overt affection between mother and child might harbor many sentiments ranging from a desire to protect the child from external evil, through a desire not to spoil the child, to true self-hatred projected onto the child. An attitude of servitude toward a person might be assumed as a sign of true submission, or as a means of achieving dominance and control, or as both. An attitude of humility could be assumed as a sign of pride. An acceptance of bodily impurity might signify perfect purity of the heart. Seemingly cruel behavior might grow out of a feeling of love.

Why do Tamil people hide their feelings as they do? Certainly not for the reasons that we hide ours—to maintain autonomy, show independence, avoid commitment, prevent rejection, protect ourselves from pain.

If one is to believe the bhakti poets, the pundits, the cinematographers, the healers, the singers in the fields of Tamil Nadu, Tamil people believe in abundant feeling, in letting it flow through the body and out through the points of contact between human beings into the hearts of others.[15] Why then, do they also conceal it?

The reasons Tamil people have for the custom of hiding true feelings are probably many. As a convention, as a form, this custom may turn up in many places because of its very capacity to perform many tasks, to take on many meanings. I have argued that many conventions in Indian culture are maintained because of their polysemy, their rich ambiguity. If we maintain this frame of mind and then step up to a higher level, we may see that ambiguity itself is a convention of this sort, a form with many possible functions, an act (or a type of act) with many possible meanings.

But I think that the hiding of feelings in Tamil Nadu is generally not meant as a cutting off of communication. It is not intended to make the would-be knower of the feelings go away. Like all the other forms of ambiguity discussed here, it encourages relationships to become and remain in a dynamic mode. It establishes a tension that binds self to other. "Generosity only encourages greed," a Tamil proverb says. But Tamils do not, for this reason, renounce generosity. To those whom one loves, one gives without limits, and one expects their demands to be limitless. The giving is not done to end the taking but to start or keep going an endless, dynamic bond.

In much the same way as giving increases desire, hiding encourages further seeking. In the West, as we know, the artful concealment of some body parts is done with this goal in mind. In Tamil Nadu, a similar kind of seductiveness sometimes is the force behind the hiding of feelings. The pout, the extremes of self-punishment and self-denial, the refusal to eat, the refusal to state the cause of one's tears, the harsh treatment of one's own child, all of these acts invited embraces, indulgence, inquiries, attention. In a playful manner, to say a startling thing or to behave in a preposterous way, set people speculating about the truth inside, made them realize that they had not yet fathomed all the complications within the other, got them interested in exploring again. "I know you. Who knows me? [*Unnai nān a<u>r</u>ivēn. Ennai yār a<u>r</u>ivār?*]," said Ayya in a letter, quoting the poet Māṇikkavācakar. "I am a mysterious man [*Nān oru marumamāna manitan*]," he said, using his own words. But was not everyone this way? "To know the whole of a person is a very difficult thing," he said. "All we can really know of a person is our relationship with them. We make a mistake if we think that is all there is."

PLURALITY AND MIXTURE, BOUNDLESSNESS AND REVERSAL

Love to the Tamil family, as we have seen, was *kalattal*, mixture, and *mayakkam*, confusion, what Victor Turner called carnival and communitas, ideas that he, and we, surely got from Tamils, as well as from Rajasthanis, Marathis, Ndembus, Cajuns, Chiapans, and many other people around the world whom we still do not know very well.

In our Tamil family, the blurring of boundaries took the form of daily reversals, some commonplace, some thought up on the spur of the moment, of whatever "real" relations were expected to be, and all of this was done, people would say directly, out of love. Calling people by the wrong kin term, by the wrong gender, calling your child "my child" and my child "your child," and calling a house that belongs to me but not you (or you but not me) "ours"—all these were examples of loving category reversal between pairs of people who loved, or might love, each other.

But love went beyond pairing. Ultimately, as we have seen, it negated pair-bonds, especially exclusive ones, and embraced everybody. Then it took the form of the confusion of plurality, when one lost one's identity, and one's loved one's identity, in the crowd. Weddings and festivals, whose main point seemed to be the colorful and totally chaotic aggregation of huge numbers of people, were communions exalting plurality, and so, to a lesser extent, were mornings in the courtyard and mealtimes. The most strongly maintained value of Anni's household was the value of communal plurality, in which all that stood for self and other, mine and yours, was deliberately, creatively, repeatedly overturned. No single rule was absolute, no single order held eternal sway.

The endless sea, the world full of countless creatures, the universe full of countless worlds, the epic that goes on forever, the book whose expansion takes several lifetimes, the quatrain all of whose meanings can never be told, the syllable that contains all truth, the family that always has room for another child, the religion that always has room for another god, the person made out of others, who are made of still others, the one human being whose full nature can never be known—these are just some of the boundless domains recognized in South Indian culture. How do we grasp them? How do we make them our own?

In the end, perhaps we will just have to realize that some things are ungraspable and unownable. We cannot find the "key" to Indian culture, or to any one of its boundless domains, or even to one of its individuals. Isn't it clear by now that the more we try to master, the more we will lose?

Perhaps we could take a methodological cue from Sivamani—try to be a part of things, weep when we get hurt, and go on trying. It may help if we can learn to accept the reality and the power of chaos—the unpredictable, the uncontrollable, the contradictory, the illogical, the unexplainable. It may be that chaos works best if our goal is truly ahimsa—to let all the living live, to let each one speak and see in its own way. We do not want to consume all others, leaving nothing but our own self. If our own particular vision of truth can take its place among the multitude, then really we will not have done so badly. We may even learn to keep life going, "in these advanced times when all are one, and no one is alone."

Epilogue

When Keith and I returned with the children to Tamil Nadu in 1984, Daniel was ten, and our second son Abraham was two going on three. Themozhiyar's family had left their old house in the village and had moved to a large apartment in the nearby town of Chingleput. Sivamani and Jnana Oli were attending a Catholic school there, not for religious reasons but because in the opinion of their parents the Catholic school would give the boys the best education available in that district: most importantly, the Catholic sisters would teach the boys English. A good knowledge of English would enable them to get good, well-paying jobs when they grew up. The school uniform the boys wore every day consisted of a clean white shirt and trousers and sturdy leather Oxfords.

In the four years since our previous visit, Jnana Oli had grown sweetly shy and studious, while Sivamani had become tough, aggressive, and athletic. Arulmori at the age of ten was gangly and foal-like and had come to resemble her mother Padmini. Arivaraci and Mankaiyarkkaraci, both thirteen, had metamorphosed into poised and graceful young women. Arivaraci now was the more confident of the two. She liked my sparkly crystal earrings and traded her goldplated ones for them.

Among the children, only Umapathi seemed to be the same person, a layer of sauce and foolhardiness thinly concealing his vulnerable young heart. On one occasion he tried to get Abe to climb out on the steep roof with him. I think he was angry with Abe for something. It would have been a fifty-foot fall.

The adults were all the same as they had been except for Attai, who had lost her eyesight and also had broken her hip, so that she could neither read nor walk and was in pain all the time. Her son, Annan, had had to choose between an expensive hip operation for her and a private educa-

Plate 36. Aruljnanapperuveli.

tion for the two young boys (neither of them his own son). For the sake of the future and for the strength of the family, he had chosen the latter. While Themozhiyar was in the distant town of Madurai helping me with my new project, he received a telegram from Annan saying that Attai had passed away.

Keith returned with Dan to the United States in August of that year, because his own mother was very ill. I returned with Abe in late October. A year after that, Keith and I separated permanently. Now Keith occupies the house that he built in 1979, with a little help from Themozhiyar and from me. Dan and Abe are doing fine, though as they grow their memories of India fade. Abe seems a little more American than Dan, a little less androgynous. Today (February 1, 1989) I got a letter from Themozhiyar asking how this book is coming along, and saying he would like to see me one more time before he dies. I guess I should go back there sometime soon.

Notes

PROLOGUE

1. I hope that this prologue is not too off-putting. My aim in writing it is to provide some kind of sketch of the philosophies impinging upon me as I write this book, and of the shape these philosophies have taken in my mind, since they do very much affect what I say and how I say it. If my statements seem obvious to some American readers and opaque to others, perhaps they will still be useful to scholars in distant times and places—especially scholars in India—who might want more information concerning the strange academic climate in which this work and others like it have been able to grow.

2. On the dream of wholeness see Durkheim 1933/1893; Sapir 1924. On the loss of wholeness see Marx 1890/1932; Freud 1890; and again the same work by Durkheim.

3. Jakobson 1960.

4. Levi-Strauss 1969a/1964.

5. Boon 1982, 253.

6. Clifford and Marcus 1986.

7. On code as tyranny, see Bakhtin 1981. On the value of discord, see Kristeva 1984. On the fragmentation of the self, see Lacan 1968. On the nonexistence of meaning see Derrida 1976. On the term "post-modern" see Turner 1985.

8. The term "logocentrism," coined by Jacques Derrida, refers to a belief that there is some underlying, perfect, unified truth that contrasts with the imperfect, plural, world of experience. In theology it is the belief that God is One and is different from the world; in psychology it is the belief that the soul is one and is different from the body; in linguistics it

is the belief that the code is one and is different from what actually gets said (or, somewhat more naively, that meaning is shared even if the "words for" things are not). It has been argued in various ways by many people that a kind of idealism, a desire for perfection beyond what is ever attainable, is engendered by logocentrism. Some think that logocentrism is a specifically Christian affliction. But it is present among Hindus, too. Parallel to Greek *logos* is Sanskrit *brahman,* which means, like logos, both Word and God, and is mirrored in the perfect soul or self:

> Verily what is called space [*ākāśa*] is the accomplisher of name and form [*nāmarupa*]. That within which they are is the word [*brahman*]. That is the immortal, that is the self [*ātman*].
>
> (Chandogya Upaniṣad 8.14)
>
> For where there is duality, there one sees another . . . there one speaks to another . . . there one understands another. But where everything has become just one's own self, then whereby and whom would one see? . . . Whereby and to whom would one speak? . . . Whereby and whom would one understand? That self [*ātman*] is not this, not that [*neti neti*]. It is unseizable, unattached, unbound.
>
> (Muṇḍaka Upaniṣad 1.1.6)

In modern India, as in the West, folk wisdom continually reaffirms that God is one though appearances are many, that each person contains an inherently perfect or perfectible soul that seeks union with this God, and that "the world" (Sanskrit *saṁsāra,* Tamil *ulakam*) is a condition from which it is necessary to escape. The idea that certain words or texts, such as the Vedas, embody eternal truths, is also a binding concept of Hinduism in its many forms. Thus Westerners and Indians start out with certain shared premises that are fundamental to both civilizations but are not human universals and which surely affect in important ways the kind of communication that takes place between Western ethnographers and their Indian informants.

9. On pluralistic societies, see Leis 1970; Marriott and Inden 1977; and a host of others. On plural (spirit-possessed) individuals see Obeyesekere 1981; Claus 1975; Lewis 1971; and many others. On the plural quality of spoken language see Hymes 1974; Schegloff 1981; Tannen 1984; Ochs and Schieffelin 1984. On other people's ideas of the self, and the self as a nondiscrete entity, see Mauss 1938; Schneider 1968; Geertz 1974; Carrithers et al. 1985; Marsella et al. 1985.

10. Tedlock 1983.

11. Wagner 1975; Boon 1982.

1: WHAT LED ME TO THEM

1. I am not the first person to challenge the validity of such labels for Indian culture. For works reexamining the concepts of "tradition" and "the traditional" in India, see Rudolph and Rudolph 1967; Singer 1959, 1972; Appadurai 1981*b*; Parry 1982; Dirks 1987; Preston 1982. For works questioning the notions of "purity" and "hierarchy" as reigning principles in South Asian society, see Marriott 1976*a, b*; Marriott and Inden 1974, 1977; Mencher 1974; Gough 1972; Appadurai 1986. For works demonstrating the inappropriateness of the labels "other-worldly" and "nonmaterialistic" to Hindu world views, see Waghorne 1985; Daniel 1984; O'Flaherty 1984; Preston 1982; Mencher 1974; and Gough 1972. For refutations of the notion of Hindu womanhood as profane, benign, and powerless, see Wadley 1975*b*, 1980; Peterson 1986; Marglin 1985; Beck 1982; Hart 1973. For discussions of the nonrigidity of Hindu culture, see Ramanujan 1980; Appadurai (forthcoming); Singer 1972. This list contains only a small sample of the numerous scholarly works that challenge Western stereotypes of Hindu India. That attacks on such stereotypes continue to be mounted only shows that they are far from dead. Often blanket characterizations of Hindu society contain interwoven stereotypes and antistereotypes. For instance, Louis Dumont in many of his works describes Hindu society as a world in which the individual is subsumed to the collective, and the aims of the profane (*artha,* "power") are subsumed to the values of the sacred (*śuddha,* "purity"). All of this reinforces prior Western stereotypes of the passive, other-worldly Hindu. Yet in arguing that Indian caste hierarchy is built upon the loving ideal of encompassment and is perhaps more suited to human social nature than is Western competitive egalitarianism (hence the title of his book *Homo Hierarchicus*), Dumont breaks with the old Western vision of Hindu society as intrinsically oppressive and inferior to the West. Similarly, George Hart shows that in ancient South Indian culture women, far from being considered the weaker sex, were regarded as the bearers of formidable powers that men had always to look out for. Here Hart breaks an old stereotype. But then he goes on to argue that women in South India had to be severely oppressed just because they were considered to have such powers. The penalty for a woman's free expression of her sexual feelings would be death, or worse. So we are left again with the old image of the Asian woman as totally under the thumb of man, a slave with no recourse to *real* power in the world.

2. On the Great and Little Traditions see Redfield 1957; Marriott 1955. On the study of Text and Context see Blackburn and Ramanujan 1986.

3. For examples of heroes and gods as persons who live see Dumont 1959; Harper 1957, 1963; Claus 1973, 1975, 1979; Inglis 1985; Moreno 1985; Blackburn 1986; Obeyesekere 1981.

Dumont 1959, 72–74 describes one example of the contextual particularization of the sacred through spirit possession:

> It is true that the spirit of a man [of the Saoras of Orissa] who died of smallpox loses its individuality as it becomes merged into the smallpox spirit. This spirit, although it appears as an individual spirit, is in turn made up, at least in part, of the spirits of all the people it killed; it is a collective being called by a single name. . . . What the Saoras are essentially dealing with is not a collection of individual spirits but a vast and complex, essentially multiple spiritual being from which apparent individualities detach themselves as the occasion demands. . . . The spirits of the hills are individuated in connection with the surrounding cultivating villages . . . The tutelary spirits are individuated in connection with the individual shaman whom they marry. The spirits of the dead remain individual essentially in connection with the people of their lineage. . . .

In the same way, we might say that in Tamil Nadu, each spirit, each divine personality, each story becomes individuated with respect to particular contexts, particular events in particular people's lives.

4. Story told in O'Flaherty 1975.
5. See Kapferer 1983; Yalman 1963.
6. Hudson 1978; Harman 1986.
7. O'Flaherty 1973.
8. Kapferer 1983; Yalman 1963.
9. Beck 1981; Dimock 1982.
10. Beck 1981.
11. Hiltebeitl 1988.
12. Hart 1974; Babb 1975.
13. Yalman 1963.
14. Bennett 1983.
15. Gough 1955; Fruzetti 1982.
16. Marglin 1985.
17. Nicholas 1982.
18. Ramanujan 1980; Hiltebeitl 1988.
19. Kapferer 1983.
20. O'Flaherty 1984.
21. S. Daniel 1980.
22. Appadurai 1983; Singer 1972; Ramanujan 1980.
23. Schweder and Bourne 1984.
24. Gould 1965.
25. Beals 1962.
26. Lee Siegel (1987) provides many good examples of intentional ambiguity in Sanskrit poetry, especially poems involving puns.

27. Sanskrit and Tamil are so different grammatically that they necessarily cannot share all the same poetic conventions. Further, the context of composition of Tamil poetry has always been quite different from that of Sanskrit poetry. For instance, Tamil poetry, even "courtly" poetry, is and has always been closely connected with "folk" poetic traditions. Sanskrit, to the extent that it is noncognate with local vernaculars, is alienated from poetic traditions, especially oral poetic traditions, maintained within those vernaculars. While Tamil bards in ancient South India sang for kings in their palaces, grandmothers in the villages sang for the babies, goatherds sang for the goats, and field laborers sang for each other. The bards easily wove elements from these folk poetic traditions into their own songs, and the folk also learned from the bards. Therefore, classic Tamil poetry is not really "courtly" poetry. It has a strong rural flavor to it that Sanskrit courtly poetry seems to lack. Moreover, there is a high valuation of the "natural" (*iyaṯkai*) in Tamil poetry, which contrasts sharply with the high valuation of artifice in much Sanskrit poetry.

28. Dumont 1970.

29. Intentional ambiguity might be defined as something like the knowing and simultaneous attribution, by the "same person," of mutually exclusive "meanings" to a single "sign." If we follow this definition, we may see that an act of intentional ambiguity is, among other things, a metasemiotic act, an act that somehow makes reference to the sign system as such. The development of intentional ambiguity is dependent upon an understanding, on the part of the actor, that "signs" and their "meanings" are different things and may have different names. Thus in acts of intentional ambiguity there is often a focus upon the nonidentity of "sign" and "meaning," and a secondary focus upon the nonidentity of "signs" among themselves and the nonidentity of "meanings" among themselves. I put the words "sign," "meaning," and "person" in quotes, because the idea of the duality of the sign is not shared by all people, nor is the idea of the oneness of the person. Mauss, for instance, argued that the idea of the integral self that we now take as universal arose in particular historical circumstances. In his words,

> It is from the notion of the [Christian] "one" that the notion of the "person" was created—I believe it will long remain so—for the divine persons, but at the same time for the human person, substance and mode, body and soul, consciousness and act. (Mauss 1979, 86)

The idea of the sign as being a container ("sign vehicle") with a content ("sign substance") goes together with the idea of the person as being a soul inside a body. One is not only a metaphoric expression of the other. Latterly, Derrida (1976) has argued that it is just in order to save the notion of the "self" as an abiding being, the ultimate "substance," the "transcendent signified," that Western linguists have held to the principle of double articulation (language as an organization of sounds superimposed upon a different organization of meanings) in the first place. But it is not only within the domain of Christendom that the container–content model, both of person and of sign, has come into being. This model is present in India, too, and there has been in India too a recognition that selfhood and signhood are inseparable concepts. For instance in Tamil linguistic theory, which has been greatly influenced by Indo-European linguistic theory, the meaning (*poruḷ,* "substance") of a word is *in* the word, as the scent is in the flower, the heat is in the fire, the spirit is in the body. Meaning is the animating energy of a word, married, as it were, to its sound or form, and bearing the same relation to the sound as vowels (*uyir eṛuttu,* "spirit letters") bear to consonants (*mey eṛuttu,* "body letters"), essentially a relation of containment. This ancient model of meaning enters into Tamil poetics (see, for example, *Tolkāppiyam*), and thence into Tamil poetry itself, and is one source of the resonance between a Tamil poem and the rest of the world as many Tamil speakers perceive it.

As regards our own languages, Benveniste (1966) offers a discussion of the container–content model in Indo-European. Whorf (1956) attributes to "Standard Average European" languages a proclivity for fitting everything into the container–content mold.

What engenders this notion of an abiding, underlying self, coupled with a belief in the duality of the sign, a belief that meaning and appearance are different? It would not be saying anything new to suggest that circumstances of intense culture contact have something to do with it. We know that Christianity and Hinduism have both been forged and reforged in such a crucible. Thus in both Christianity and Hinduism there exists a high degree of reflexivity, self-consciousness, consciousness of the self, which goes along with a high degree of logocentrism, consciousness of thought processes, of linguistic processes, and it is all bound up with the thoroughgoing multilinguality and multiculturality of European and South Asian civilizations respectively.

With self-consciousness comes self-doubt. Thus in both South Asia and Europe a dialectic has grown up between logocentrism as belief in the Absolute and antilogocentrism as its denial. In their struggle with each other, each position becomes more extreme. Faith becomes orthodoxy, monism with a vengeance; doubt becomes anarchy and nihilism. In India in the sixth century A.D., Bhartrhari developed to perfection the idea that the single universal spirit (*brahman*) concealed within multiple bodies is identical to the single universal meaning concealed within multiple utterances:

> Brahman is the one object denoted by all words; and this one object has various differences imposed upon it according to each particular form; but the conventional variety of the differences produced by these illusory conditions is

> only the result of ignorance. Non-duality is the true state; but through the power of "concealment" (exercised by illusion) at the time of the conventional use of words a manifold expansion takes place. (Quoted in Coward 1976, 33)

On the opposing side of this struggle, the Buddhist philosopher Nagarjuna in his Madhyamika Sutra developed the principle that nothing exists in itself: what stands between a thing and its opposite is just emptiness, *śunyatā,* and this śunyatā is all that can be said to be, and even śunyatā itself is no less *śunya,* no less empty, than anything else.

But these two polar views of reality, śunyatā and brahman, in their pure forms are too frightening and too oppressive for any human being to live with for long. In between them, among people living in the world, there arises a hope or a faith or just a suspicion (something less than a conviction) that illusion does have an opposite, something abiding and real, lying behind or beneath what is perceived: a return to theism, sometimes a violent return, but never again with an innocent trust in the reality of one's own particular word, or world, or god. So in modern Indian villages, human blood is still shed in the names of different deities, but in the same villages, it is commonplace for the same deities to be mocked to their faces, and their existence denied, by their own worshippers; see Srinivas 1976, 326–329.

Perhaps the European peasantry of a few centuries ago, faced with the conflicting languages of the Bible and the manor, underwent a similar process. So Bakhtin suggests,

> As soon as a critical interanimation of languages began to occur in the consciousness of our peasant, as soon as it became clear that these were not only various different languages but even internally variegated languages, that the ideological systems and approaches to the world that were indissolubly connected with these languages contradicted each other and in no way could live in peace and quiet with each other—then the inviolability and predetermined quality of these languages came to an end and the necessity of actively choosing one's orientation among them began. (1981, 296)

In sum, intentional ambiguity requires a kind of relativism with respect to language and a kind of agnosticism with respect to the psyche. It depends initially upon belief in a distinction between sign and meaning, between the perceptually manifest and the unmanifest, between real and ideal. To say something knowing that it can be taken in more than one way is to recognize that words come from and can produce thoughts that are not identical to those words themselves. It is to admit a degree of uncertainty concerning the possibility of one person's knowing the mind of another. It is also to give room for longing. To those who think of the world as consisting of forms and contents, an ambiguous message can imply something "below the surface," different from what is "on the surface," and closer to the heart of the person purveying the message than what is "on the surface." An awareness of something hidden, a desire to get at that something, and an anxiety lest it not be gotten, are aroused by ambiguity. The meaning within a word, the soul within a body, the time before self and other were divided—such transcendent ideals are what ambiguity evokes, but does not supply. Ambiguity is the reminder that perfection, understanding, and wholeness are always to be desired, but rarely to be had. Since it does little to contribute to illusions of fulfillment (logical closure, social solidarity, personal integration) it is, in a certain sense, functionless. But just because it keeps monistic illusions from growing too powerful, perhaps it is necessary.

3: THE IDEOLOGY OF LOVE

1. Thoughts put into my head by Clifford's (1983) account of Griaule; Stocking's (1968) account of Boas; Allen's (1985) account of Mauss; Crapanzano's (1986) account of Geertz; Malinowski's (1967) account of himself; and work by Kristeva (1975) and Bakhtin (1981).

2. To them I was America, and they were India to me. They understood that I was watching them in order to learn about their way of life and write about it. It was important to them that they be represented well in the world, and so they offered a particular face to me. They would represent themselves in other ways to other people, the representation depending upon the audience, or, more precisely, upon what they thought the audience was. And their image of this audience would in turn devolve in part from what face the audience presented to them.

"A 'culture' can materialize only in counterdistinction to another culture," writes James Boon (1982). Just as a person can only emerge in counterdistinction to another person. Often enough, perhaps always, these two confrontations are one. Perhaps what we call cultures are always only persons representing themselves as cultures.

3. I write this in response to the idea, first articulated by Boas and still widely subscribed to by many anthropologists, that conscious explanations of cultural practices on the part of the practitioners are secondary elaborations that only obscure the true nature of the practices in question. The Marxist definition of ideology as an expression of class interest contributes to this view. Certainly descriptions of a culture coming from actors within the culture cannot be disinterested. The question is whether a disinterested description of human life is ever possible, and whether an ethnographer can in any case truthfully represent herself as being outside

the cultural system she describes. I find it most reasonable to assume that an indigenous analysis of a cultural system is no more likely to be erroneous and distorted than an outsider's analysis of that same system, and it will certainly have a larger store of information as its base.

4. A statement I heard only once, in the context of a very brief conversation. Some individuals regarded the expenditure of money as necessary to the enactment of love (*anpu*). Others saw the exchange of money as opposed to anpu. Because money exchanges often were a sign of market relationships devoid of personal commitments, some people that I interviewed refused offers of money in exchange for interview time; others accepted money as a gift in the expectation that more such gifts would follow.

5. One reader of an earlier version of this chapter has suggested that the apparent unkindnesses that took place in this family under the name of anpu were no more than outlets for suppressed tensions; in particular, mothers who mistreated their children were perhaps taking out on the children their resentment at being subordinated to men. I think that this would be an incorrect interpretation of events, for in this family, tensions even over such matters as money and sex were not suppressed but were freely ventilated. Nor were women as a class subordinated to men as a class: if a woman was angry with a man, she took it out on him directly. For reasons that I have discussed above, I think it would be misleading for us to imagine that Tamil people who enact anpu in ways that appear to us paradoxical are pasting an ideological veneer over their raw aggression. Culture is not just a set of labels for things, thoughts, or feelings. It shapes all three from the bottom up. For us to assume that we know how people of another culture feel, and that their accounts of their feelings are mere rationalizations for behavior whose underlying motivations we know better than they, would be counter to the spirit of anthropology.

6. *Kaṇ ḍrișṭi* would be most accurately glossed in English as "light from the eyes." The Tamil term itself, unlike the English term "evil eye," suggests not malice but dangerous power.

In Indian mythology and in everyday life, eyes are treated as receptacles of the most important life fluids and as emitters of powerful transformative emotional forces; see Maloney 1976; Eck 1981. These forces are as substantial and material as water, fire, or blood; see Babb 1981. The power in the eyes has a dangerous erotic component. A woman may lose her sakti by looking with desire at a man, or by being viewed with desire by one; see Trawick Egnor 1980, 1983. Emission of light from the eyes is, in Saiva and Buddhist mythology, parallel to emission of semen from the penis; see Obeyesekere 1984; O'Flaherty 1973.

For Indians, the emotional power of the mother in any form is dangerous: it is intense, and it can easily turn into rage. The child cannot protect himself against it, and there is no mediator between the child and his mother. The mother herself must keep it under control. Therefore she does not gaze too intently at the child she bore.

7. See Eck 1981.

8. The custom of a wife's avoiding her husband's name in India is interpreted by some observers as a sign of respect, even subordination. Yet in Tamil Nadu, name avoidance can occur even in the absence of any other signs of respect. Such signs include the use of respectful pronominal forms (*nīṅkaḷ, avar, avarkaḷ*), respectful bodily postures and facial expressions (crossed arms, smiling, standing or squatting rather than sitting or lying down), an attitude of assent and willingness to serve. Such external forms, which are quite complex and have many nuances, are in general supposed to indicate an internal feeling of respect for the person towards whom they are directed, though dissimulation is certainly part of the game. Expressions of respect occur in face-to-face encounters between people of clearly unequal caste, economic or political status, between people who are unequally educated, between people of widely separate ages, between the bride's and groom's kin at weddings. But these conventional expressions indicating acceptance of one's own subordination are noticeably absent in the behavior of many Tamil wives toward their husbands, and I have never heard of any Tamil woman explaining her avoidance of her husband's name in terms of his superiority to her or in terms of distance between them (distance and hierarchy being the two essential components of respect-relationships as social scientists are prone to see them). Moreover, name avoidance between spouses in Tamil Nadu is often reciprocal, and sometimes an individual will avoid the name of a kinsperson whose rank is lower than his own. For all of these reasons, I feel that a Tamil wife's avoidance of her husband's name cannot be adequately explained in terms of respect. Since Tamil women themselves explain this custom as a means of protection (*kāppu*) of the husband, I have chosen to discuss it under the topic of containment. It appears related to the observance of nōnpu, a fast to protect the husband's life, after which the wife ties a string around her wrist to show that she has fasted for this purpose.

Whether the husband is to be protected for the sake of anpu, or for some other reason (e.g., the guardianship of one's own status as a *cumaṅkali,* an auspicious married woman) is not such an easy question to answer. Certainly anpu is *supposed* to be what binds husband and wife to each other. One of the standard questions I asked interviewees in 1984 was, among what pair of persons in a family should there be the most anpu, and the stock answer was that anpu should be strongest between husband and wife.

9. Sometimes such practices were explained in terms of protecting the child from the evil eye, *kaṇ ḍriṣṭi*. The power of kaṇ ḍriṣṭi was not simply

a matter of malevolence or envy on the part of onlookers, as the danger of the mother's eye illustrates. Nor was it a matter of demonic forces, for demons are attracted to flaws and impurities and to people in isolation, not (in Tamil Nadu) to those who are well and surrounded by love. Rather, the hiding of a child's beauty and of one's love for it could be seen as a special case of the strong and pervasive sentiment in India that perfection in and of itself is deadly—see Daniel 1984; Narayan 1972, 52–55; and perfect love, perhaps, is most deadly of all.

10. Trawick Egnor 1986.

11. See also Kakar 1978.

12. One colleague suggests that pride turned humility into public acts meant to be interpreted as love, and dominance turned acts of servitude into acts meant to be interpreted as love. A compromise between this reader's formulation of events and my own might say that the availability of anpu as an interpretive device enabled actors to transform potentially humiliating situations into vehicles for the expression of pride, and so forth, and to do so in a way that was credible within the Tamil cultural context. Tamil Saiva mythology is replete with paradoxical expressions of love and antihierarchical messages. Ayya was simply bringing the spirit of this mythology home.

13. See Appadurai 1981*a* for a detailed discussion of ways in which acts of feeding and eating in Tamil Nadu become messages with negotiable interpretations about kinship, religion, and emotion.

4: DESIRE IN KINSHIP

1. An important exception to this and many other generalizations about kinship in India is the Nayar community in Kerala. Brahmans also tend to distinguish themselves from other communities in their locality by the use of certain kin terms, just as they distinguish themselves by the use of certain other marked patterns of speech. However, kinship terminology in general appears to vary more with regional dialect than it does from caste-to-caste within a region.

Information on kinship systems and terminologies in South India and Sri Lanka is patchy, therefore no overall statistical statements about South Indian kinship can be made with very great certainty. The statements made in this chapter are made on the basis of my own observations and on the basis of what is reported by other ethnographers and historians of South India. Major sources comparing kinship systems and terminologies between communities within a region and from region to region include Trautmann 1981; Yalman 1974; Karve 1965; McGilvray 1974; Gough 1956, 1959.

2. See Trautmann 1981, 218–219.

3. Trautmann 1981, 220–221.

4. Ideal types in the tradition of Weber, or categories and collective representations in the tradition of Durkheim and Mauss.

5. Dumont 1983.

6. Radcliffe-Brown 1953.

7. Levi-Strauss (1967) argues that overt and conscious structures of social organization may be, perhaps always are, only cover-ups of "real" social organization. People need these cover-ups for the sake of maintaining various necessary fictions—for example, in the case of the Bororo, for the sake of maintaining a fictional solidarity between social units that would otherwise be independent of each other. Here Levi-Strauss is following Boas 1911 who made a similar argument about native explications of traditions. Durkheim (1912/1965) argued that people in a community attribute sacred value to any object in which they invest their "collective effervescence." They do not realize the truth of their religion, which is that they are worshipping their own collective power. Levi-Strauss in his work on kinship as well as in his work on mythology suggests that a particular myth or kinship organization can only be fully understood as a piece of a larger puzzle—that is, in its relation to other myths or kinship organizations of which the particular teller of the myth or participant in the kinship system is unlikely to be aware.

8. See David 1983; Barnett 1976, 1982.

9. Schneider 1968; Marriott and Inden 1978; Inden and Nicholas 1977.

10. Trautmann 1981, 76–80 provides a lengthy discussion of theories of double unilineal exogamy which were earlier in this century held to account for systems of cross-cousin marriage in South India. Even where an overt named native system of double unilineal exogamy is found to exist, however (as for the Toda), Trautmann points out that it cannot explain the prohibition of marriage with parallel cousins, as there are parallel cousins who are not related to ego either through a line of males only or through a line of females only—as for instance father's mother's brother's daughter's daughter.

11. See Trautmann 1981, 302ff.

12. Alternate theories of conception in Tamil culture are offered by McGilvray 1982; Moffatt 1979; Trawick Egnor 1978; and Daniel 1984.

13. Fruzetti, Ostor, and Barnett 1982 seem to be accepting precisely this position, namely, that nontheoreticians are mere followers of the rules made by others, when, in defense of Dumont's Brahman-oriented vision of Indian society, they quote Lukacs (1971, 257):

> The organs of authority harmonize to such an extent with the [economic] laws governing men's lives, or seem so overwhelmingly superior that men experience them as natural forces, as the necessary environment for their existence. As a result, they submit to them freely, which is not to say they approve of them.

However, it is to be questioned whether the organs of Brahmanical authority do indeed harmonize with the laws governing men's lives in present-day India, especially in light of the fact that there are and have been for a long time other competing authorities at work on the subcontinent, undermining the strength of dharmaśāstra.

One might parry Lukacs with a quote from Gramsci:

> Every social group . . . creates together with itself, organically, one or more strata of intellectuals which give it homogeneity and an awareness of its own function not only in the economic but also in the social and political fields. . . . When one distinguishes between intellectuals and nonintellectuals, one is referring in reality only to the immediate social function of the professional category of intellectuals . . . The mode of being of the new intellectual can no longer consist of eloquence, which is an exterior and momentary mover of feelings and passions, but in active participation in political life . . . One of the most important characteristics of any group that is developing towards dominance is its struggle to assimilate and to conquer "ideologically" the traditional intellectuals, but this assimilation and conquest is made quicker and more efficacious the more the group in question succeeds in simultaneously elaborating its own organic intellectuals. (Gramsci 1971, 5–10)

In India, one might argue, there are many "organic intellectuals" of the kind envisioned by Gramsci.

14. Among recent works discussing the nonseparation of substance, spirit, and action in South Indian thought are Waghorne and Cutler 1985; Daniel 1984; Trawick Egnor 1978; Wadley 1980.

15. See, for example, chapter 3 this volume, on the relation between *paṛakkam* (habit) and *cupāvam, iyaṯkai,* and *kuṇam*—all terms for the "built-in" quality or nature of a person. Not even *uyir* ("soul") remains unchanged by *paṛakkam*. Further discussion of the fluidity and multiplicity of components of the Tamil person is found in Daniel 1984. Much of the literature on purity and pollution, as well as the literature on spirit possession in South Asian culture also bespeaks the inherent mutability and mutual interpenetrability of persons in South Asian thought.

16. Tamil *uyir* is said by scholars to be derived from *uy* (pronounced "whee"), "to rise up, to escape, to waft away." It is what goes when life goes, as when one says of a dead thing *Uyir pōccu,* "Its life is gone," or *Uyir illai,* "It has no life." In some dialects, *uyir* becomes *ucar,* and thus is reassimilated to *ucar* meaning "high." I heard an account of a woman who died because she was bending over and a buffalo gored her in the *ucar nāḍi* ("life channel" or "high channel"). I was unable to ascertain

whether this term referred to the vagina, as I suspected, or to some major artery.

In popular philosophy, the Ruler (*āṇḍavan*) is often said to be the Creator (*paḍaittavan*) of souls and the giver of life (*uyir koḍuttān*)—an idea that may be borrowed from Christianity. An unschooled Tamil Christian woman, on the other hand, when asked what happens to the uyir after a person dies, said, "If the person is evil, his soul comes back in the form of a worm or a bug." Her seminarian son standing by quickly corrected her, "The souls of the good go to heaven and the souls of the wicked go to hell." His mother then retorted, "After all, how do *we* know where the soul goes when the body dies."

In Saiva Siddhanta philosophy, a self-consciously South Indian philosophical system, there are said to be three mutually irreducible and independent elements in the world: *pati, pacu, pācam,* "the master, the beast, and the bond." The master is God, *iṟaivan*. The beast is the soul, *ānmā* or *uyir*. The bond is the material world, *ulakam*. In this philosophy, God did not create the souls or the world; all three have been around since the beginning.

The Tamil scholar Themozhiyar said that if you look ino the empty sky you can see the souls (*uyirkaḷ*) floating around there, like bubbles. At the time of intercourse, such a sky-floating soul will be attracted to the love of the man and the woman and will come down and enter the woman's womb. For Ayya, body and soul were to each other as man and woman. The body (*mey, uḍampu*) protects and contains the soul (uyir) as a husband protects and contains his wife. Themozhiyar never mentioned the notion that a mother contributes *uyir* to her child, and the father contributes the body (*uḍampu*).

In the theory of Ayurvedic medicine, which originated in North India but is widely practiced in the south as well, the mother's seed contributes the soft parts of the body of the fetus, the father's seed contributes the hard parts, the mother's blood nourishes the fetal body, and the soul of the fetus enters from without, in accordance with the dictates of its karma.

A common theory in Tamil Nadu says that life (uyir) enters the fetus in the fifth month of pregnancy, so that if one aborts the fetus before then, one is not guilty of killing.

There was an impoverished young Chettiar woman who had one child, a baby daughter, and could be seen to lavish much love upon this beautiful baby. She had had a baby son before, who had died. She said the death of her son had been the worst thing that ever happened to her. I asked her whether this new baby, being a girl, could be as valuable to her as the boy baby had been. *Atu oru uyir,* she said with a smile, "It's a living creature."

I hope that these examples will give the reader some idea of how complex is the notion of uyir in Tamil, and how various are the theories of conception in which this idea is implicated.

17. The continuity of theory with personality, and more generally with the particular socially and historically conditioned life-circumstances of the theoretician, is not true only of those people we call "natives." If I claim it is true of Indian intellectuals, this is because I think it is true of *all* intellectuals, including Western academicians and scientists, and including my own colleagues and myself. That all theories are actually "local knowledge" in this sense does not render them invalid. See for instance Keller 1985; Holton 1973; and Gramsci 1971 on this topic.

18. For discussion of the body–soul connection in South Indian culture see for instance Waghorne and Cutler 1985, especially introduction by Waghorne. See also other references in note 10 above.

19. Chomsky's approach to the study of language hinges largely on judgments of whether particular sentences are grammatically acceptable or unacceptable—that is, whether a given sentence follows the rules, or whether it doesn't. Rules are determined by the linguist on the basis of native speakers' judgments of the grammaticality of sentences—a speaker is presumed to know *when* a rule is broken, even if he doesn't know exactly *what* the rule is. Sociolinguists, especially those observing language education, can easily note the political implications of this attitude toward what is "correct" in language.

20. Needham 1962, 27 citing Levi-Strauss 1949, 96, 107, 108, 170–171, 175.

21. Levi-Strauss 1966.

22. Trautmann 1981, 201–204.

23. Leach 1951.

24. Dumont 1970.

25. Dumont 1970.

26. Fruzetti and Ostor 1982, 52.

27. Inden and Nicholas 1977.

28. This conclusion may be inferred from the notion that matrilateral marriage draws together into mutual dependency a larger number of lineages than does patrilateral marriage.

29. Moffatt 1979; Gough 1972; Berreman 1971; Mencher 1974; myself (1986, 1988), and others have asked just this question of Tamil untouchables and have gotten mixed answers, ranging from total acceptance of the legitimacy of social hierarchy (Moffatt), to total rejection of it (Mencher). My own finding is that many people on the bottom end of the social hierarchy ambiguously reinterpret the concept of encompassment to mean either love and protection (which they feel has been unjustly denied them) or imprisonment and exclusion (which they feel has been unjustly inflicted upon them).

30. See critique by Medick and Sabean 1984.

31. Schneider's (1961) anthropological definition of what Americans call "love."

32. See, for example, Gough 1955; Yalman 1963; Carstairs 1957;

Nicholas 1975; Kakar 1978; Ramanujan 1983; Obeyesekere 1984.

33. The notion of transsubstantiation of a wife's bodily substance to that of her husband is one such troublesome piece of ideology. So is the Bengali belief discussed by Fruzetti and Ostor (1982) that for a girl to marry into the line into which her mother's sister has married yields "bad blood" (i.e., bad feelings in the household). It turns out that such a marriage is disapproved because it would produce ritual inconveniences for the girl's male kin.

34. Levi-Strauss 1969, chapter 13. Also Levi-Strauss 1967*b*.

35. Dumont 1957, 19ff.

36. Homans and Schneider 1955, 51.

37. Radcliffe-Brown 1924.

38. Homans and Schneider 1955, 23. Quoted in Needham 1962, 30.

39. Mitchell and Rose 1982; Irigaray 1985; Clement 1983; Wilden 1968.

40. Clement 1983, 65. One North Indian psychoanalytic thinker commented on this idea (tongue-in-cheek) that female genitalia always did seem to him to be rather "cluttered."

41. This is where Lacan departs from Turner, in that for Turner carnival events were not private but eminently collective and shared. (Communitas is the felt, emotional side of social organization—beyond social order, yet ultimately affirming it.)

42. In Iśwara Krishna's Saṃkhyā-Kārikā (Guadapada 1887), in the beginning there are said to be two beings, Prakṛti ("she out of whom it is made") and Puruṣa ("the husband"). Prakṛti is the material substance of the universe, changeable and divisible. Puruṣa is spirit, indivisible and changeless. Prakṛti is Unmanifest (*avyakta*) until Puruṣa "impregnates her with his essence." Then Prakṛti enters a state of disequilibrium and proceeds to evolve out of herself the variegated phenomena of the universe as perceived by the embodied person; in this state she is manifest (*vyakta*). Puruṣa, imprisoned within Prakṛti, mistakes himself for her and thinks that he undergoes change and experiences pain. In fact, though he is the cause of the evolution of life, he is not really involved in it or altered by it. Ultimately, through yoga, the evolutionary process is reversed, Prakṛti becomes Unmanifest again, and Puruṣa is liberated from her.

43. Monier-Williams's Sanskrit dictionary includes these definitions for *brahman:*

> Lit. 'growth,' 'expansion,' 'evolution,' 'development,' 'swelling of the spirit or soul,' . . . the sacred word (as opp. to *vāc,* the word of man), the Veda, a sacred text . . . (exceptionally treated as m.) the Brahmā or one self-existent impersonal spirit, the one universal Soul (or one divine essence and source from which all created things emanate or with which they are identified and to

which they return), the Self-Existent, the Absolute, the Eternal . . . ; n. the class of men who are the repositories and communicators of sacred knowledge, the Brāhmanical caste as a body . . .

In this sense the Sanskrit concept of *brahman* is very close to the Greek concept of *logos,* as in John 1:1, "In the beginning was the Word (*logos*) and the Word was God . . . " See also note 1 to Preface, note 29 to chapter 1.

44. Yalman 1967.

45. Trautmann 1981.

46. Compare with the argument that Proto-Indo-European was not one language but many in Trubetzkoy 1939.

47. Trautmann 1981, 26.

48. Veena Das personal communication.

49. See Abu-Lughod's (1987) discussion of the trouble caused to her by her assumption that the "truest" sentiments expressed by her informants were those that defied social convention.

50. Compare this volume chapter 5, the section on "natural union" versus "artificial union," with A. K. Ramanujan's volume of poetry entitled *Relations.*

51. How central kin terms are to the grammar of Dravidian languages, and how closely implicated in Dravidian concepts of relations between self and other, are both evidenced by early Tamil literature, in which kin terms incorporated personal possessive pronouns: *ñāy,* "my mother"; *yāy,* "your mother"; *tāy,* "his/her/their mother"; *entai,* "my father"; *nuntai,* "your father"; *tantai,* "his/her/their father"; *nampi,* "our younger brother"; *tampi,* "his/her/their younger brother"; and so forth. Caldwell even argued that early Tamil kin terms were etymologically related to terms for body parts—for example, *taṅkai,* "younger sister," derived from *tan,* "his/her/their" + *kai* "hand"; *aṇṇan,* "older brother," derived from *kaṇṇan,* which is derived from *kaṇ,* "eye" + *-an,* masculine singular. Unfortunately, there is not enough systematic evidence to support Caldwell's attractive hypothesis.

52. I have observed in several families children who are marriageable cross-cousins growing up in the same household together. The children of course are taught that they are cross-cousins and not siblings, but they call each other by name (not by kin term) as born together (*uḍan pir̠anta*) siblings generally do, and the way they play together is indistinguishable from the way that siblings play together. An eight-year-old boy, for instance, may act as parttime caretaker for his two-year-old future wife.

53. In the villages where I did field research, most of the dead were buried. Cremation was a luxury that few could afford. See also Srinivas's (1976) account of burial of village men on ancestral lands in Karnataka.

54. For ethnographic references see Carstairs 1957; Daniel 1984; Mc-

Gilvray 1982; Davis 1976; Kakar 1982; Inden and Nicholas 1977. For textual references see Śuśruta and also Tirumūlar, O'Flaherty 1980.

55. If there is an analogous anxiety regarding women, it is in the matter of their not losing their sexual power (*kaṯpu,* often glossed as "chastity"). A woman may lose her kaṯpu if she has intercourse with someone not her husband, but in principle she may also lose it if a man not her husband merely looks at her with desire, or if she looks at him that way. Through chastity and mental steadfastness, a woman's kaṯpu is maintained. Unlike semen, kaṯpu is not a bodily substance but rather a moral condition. Women are said to possess semen like men. This female semen may be emitted as a vaginal discharge which has powerful, usually negative, effects upon what it touches; a woman for this reason must be very careful what or who she steps over. But the discharge of this female semen seems to have nothing to do with the loss of kaṯpu. There is an idea expressed by some that women are inherently leaky, they are losing their semen all the time. There is also an idea that a woman has an infinite supply of semen; no matter how much she loses, she will always have more.

56. In some Veḷḷāḷar families also in the same region, the head of the household consults the family deity in dreams. This custom is not confined to lower caste households.

Mauss (1938) speaks of archaic societies in which there are considered to be a finite number of spirits or souls, infinitely recycled. A man is only a person if he is in possession of (or possessed by) such an ancestral spirit; to the extent that he is a person, he is a reincarnation of his ancestor. This kind of society was probably more than anything else a product of Mauss's imagination, still in some respects it is present in Tamil Nadu. Patriliny there has much to do with possession—an eternal spirit, passing as a living substance through the bodies of many generations. Cf. also Dumont's statement on possession, quoted in note 3 for chapter 1.

57. A full description of this pilgrimage is given in Daniel 1984.

58. Ramanujan 1983.

59. Trawick Egnor 1986.

60. Shulman 1980, 256–257.

61. Miller 1981.

62. Note that the mother in this song is addressed as *attai,* which usually means "father's sister."

63. Kakar 1978.

64. See note 27 above.

65. Horney 1967.

66. See note 27 above.

67. See O'Flaherty 1980 and Shulman 1980 for scores of examples from mythology alone.

68. Beals 1962; Whiting and Whiting 1975.

69. Peterson 1986, 31; Shulman 1980, 243ff., 256–257; Trawick Egnor 1988; Hiltebeitl 1980.
70. Wadley 1975; Raheja 1988.
71. Bennett 1983.
72. Friedrich 1966, 1986.
73. Peterson 1986.
74. Wadley 1975.
75. Peterson 1986, 12.
76. Peterson 1986, 17.
77. Wadley 1980.
78. Trawick Egnor 1980.
79. Beck 1974.
80. Hudson 1978.
81. See Peterson 1986. Cf. Medick and Sabean 1984, 18–19: Anthropologists look at specific kin dyads, "searching for the central emotional moment around which structure is built"—for instance, trust and conflict between father and eldest son. Then they may ask, how are others affected by this central emotional moment? To what degree is it given ideological expressions? To what degree is this ideology accepted?
82. Reynolds 1980.
83. Peterson 1986, 21.
84. Peterson 1986, 23–24, following Shulman 1980, 256–257.
85. Beck 1982.
86. Peterson 1986, 40.
87. Shulman 1980, 257.
88. As far as I can tell, the only thing that this story has in common with the story of Ponnar and Caṇkar as recounted in Beck's *Aṇṇanmār Katai* is the theme of brother–sister love.
89. Peterson 1986b, 5.
90. Trawick Egnor 1986.

8: FINAL THOUGHTS

1. Similar thoughts are expressed in different ways by Bateson 1972 and Dimock 1966.
2. For elaboration on this theme see Trawick Egnor 1988*c*.
3. Cf. Tannen 1984 on the poetics of everyday conversation.
4. Boas 1927.
5. Bateson 1958.
6. Good exemplars of lovers of the quest in modern Euro-America are Frederick Jackson Turner and Karl Popper.
7. See for example Dumont 1983; Carter 1973; Vatuk 1982; Bean 1975; Trautmann 1981.
8. Trawick Egnor 1988*b*.

9. There is a type of bhakti, or devotional love, called *virodha bhakti*, devotion through enmity, in which a person (or in mythology more often a *rakshasa* or an antigod of some kind) devotes his full mind to hatred of the supreme being and in this way becomes bonded to the supreme being, and so is liberated from rebirth. In ordinary life in Tamil Nadu, people often give vent to feelings of intense anger at their god of choice, even challenge the god to a fight. Ayya once challenged Siva in this way. Trembling with emotion he said, "You'd better give me what I want, or I'll come there and make you give it." Consider also Naccan's angry shattering of the image of his family deity (see chapter 4, this volume).

10. Borges 1962.

11. McKim Marriott (1976*a*) has drawn attention to this contrast by his coinage of the term "dividual" to denote the Hindu notion of the person as an essentially nonbounded entity. O'Flaherty (1980) and Daniel (1984) elaborate on this concept and give further examples. Much of the data on pollution-avoidance (e.g., Harper 1964) may be reinterpreted, and partly explained, in terms of a Hindu view of living creatures as sharers of "coded substance," or as nondiscrete entities flowing into each other.

12. On the face of it, it is strange that studies of kinship in India rarely if ever consider the cultural elaboration of sexual affect as an important part of the kinship pattern.

13. See Foucault 1967 on the way that enlightened Western psychiatry established internal prisons of "conscience" to take the place of external, physical prisons in the confinement of madmen. See then Nandy 1983 on the way that similar mental prisons were established through education of the colonized, a process he refers to as "colonization of the mind." Richard Fox (personal communication) points out that Mohandas Gandhi is a good example of a man who did *not* feel determined by his own childhood—Gandhi's autobiography shows that he considered himself free to change his personality from point-to-point throughout his adulthood.

14. Cf. Daniel 1984, 64–67, on the problems associated with a simple question such as "Where are you going?"

15. Cf. Trawick Egnor 1978, 1988*a*.

References

Abu-Lughod, Lila. 1987. *Veiled Sentiments: Honor and Poetry in a Bedouin Society*. Berkeley, Los Angeles, London: University of California Press.

Adigal, Prince Ilango. 1965. *Shilappadikaram (The Ankle Bracelet)*. Trans. Alain Danielou. New York: New Directions.

Allen, N. J. 1985. "The Category of the Person: A Reading of Muass's Last Essay." In *The Category of the Person*. Ed. M. Carrithers, S. Collins, and S. Lukes, 26–45. Cambridge: Cambridge University Press.

Appadurai, Arjun. 1981*a*. "Gastropolitics in Hindu South Asia." *American Ethnologist* 3: 494–511.

———. 1981*b*. "The Past as a Scarce Resource." *Man,* n.s. 16 (2): 201–219.

———. 1986. "Is Homo Hierarchicus?" *American Ethnologist* 13: 745–761.

———. Forthcoming. "The Terminology of Measurement in Rural Maharashtra." In *Agricultural Discourse in South Asia*. Ed. Arjun Appadurai.

Babb, Lawrence. 1975. *The Divine Hierarchy*. New York: Columbia University Press.

———. 1981. "Glancing: Visual Interaction in Hinduism." *Journal of Anthropological Research* 37 (4): 387–401.

Bakhtin, Mikhail M. 1981. "Discourse in the Novel." In *The Dialogic Imagination*. Ed. and trans. M. Holquist and C. Emerson. Austin: University of Texas Press. First published in Russian, 1975.

Bateson, Gregory. 1958. *Naven*. Stanford: Stanford University Press.

———. 1972. "Style, Grace, and Information in Primitive Art." In *Steps to an Ecology of Mind*. San Francisco: Chandler.

Beals, Alan. 1962. *Gopalpur: A South Indian Village*. New York: Holt, Rinehart and Winston.

Bean, Susan. 1975. "Referential and Indexical Meanings of *Amma* in Kannada: Mother, Woman, Goddess, Pox, and Help!" *Journal of Anthropological Research* 31: 313–330.

Beck, Brenda. 1974. "The Kin Nucleus in Tamil Folklore." In *Kinship and History in South Asia*. Ed. Thomas Trautmann, 1–28. Michigan Papers on South and Southeast Asia, no. 7. Ann Arbor: Center for South and Southeast Asian Studies, The University of Michigan.

———. 1981. "The Goddess and the Demon: A Local South Indian Festival and its Wider Context." *Purusartha* (Paris) 5: 83–136.

———. 1982. *The Three Twins: The Telling of a South Indian Folk Epic*. Bloomington: Indiana University Press.

Bennett, Lynn. 1983. *Dangerous Wives and Sacred Sisters: Social and Symbolic Roles of High-Caste Women in Nepal*. New York: Columbia University Press.

Benveniste, Emile. 1966. *Problemes de linguistique generale*. Paris: Gallimard.

Berreman, Gerald. 1971. "The Brahmanical View of Caste." *Contributions to Indian Sociology,* n.s. 5: 16–23.

Blackburn, Stuart H. 1986. "Performance Markers in an Indian Story-Type." In *Another Harmony*. Ed. S. H. Blackburn and A. K. Ramanujan, Berkeley, Los Angeles, London: University of California Press.

Blackburn, Stuart H., and A. K. Ramanujan. 1986. "Introduction." In *Another Harmony: New Essays on the Folklore of India*. Ed. Stuart Blackburn and A. K. Ramanujan, 1–40. Berkeley, Los Angeles, London: University of California Press.

Boas, Franz. 1911. "Introduction." In *Handbook of American Indian Languages,* pt. 1 5–83. Smithsonian Institution, Bureau of American Ethnology. Bulletin 40. Government Printing Office. Washington, D.C.

———. 1927. *Primitive Art*. Cambridge, Mass.: Harvard University Press.

Boon, James. 1982. *Other Tribes, Other Scribes*. Cambridge: Cambridge University Press.

Borges, Jorge Luis. 1962. "The Approach to Al Mu'Tasim." *Ficciones*. Ed. Anthony Kerrigan. London: Weidenfeld and Nicolson.

Bourdieu, Pierre. 1977. *Outline of a Theory of Practice*. Cambridge: Cambridge University Press.

Carrithers, Michael, Steven Collins, and Steven Lukes, eds. 1985. *The Category of the Person*. Cambridge: Cambridge University Press.

Carstairs, G. Morris. 1957. *The Twice-Born: A Study of a Community of High-Caste Hindus*. London: Hogarth Press.

Carter, Anthony T. 1973. "A Comparative Analysis of Systems of Kinship and Marriage in South Asia." Proceedings of the Royal Anthropological Institute of Great Britain and Ireland, 29–54.

Claus, Peter. 1973. "Possession, Protection and Punishment as Attributes of Deities in a South Indian Village." *Man in India* 53 (3) 231–242.

———. 1975. "The Siri Myth and Ritual: A Mass Possession Cult of South India." *Ethnology* 14 (1): 47–58.

———. 1979. Spirit Possession and Spirit Mediumship from the Perspective of Tulu Oral Traditions. *Culture, Medicine and Psychiatry* 3 (1): 29–52.

Clement, Catherine. 1983. *The Lives and Legends of Jacques Lacan.* Trans. Arthur Goldhammer. New York: Columbia University Press.

Clifford, James, and George Marcus, eds. 1986. *Writing Culture: The Poetics and Politics of Ethnography.* Berkeley, Los Angeles, London: University of California Press.

Clifford, James. 1983. "Power and Dialogue in Ethnography: Marcel Griaule's Initiation." In *Observers Observed.* Ed. George Stocking, 121–156. Madison: University of Wisconsin Press.

Coward, Harold. 1976. *Bhartrhari.* Boston: Twayne Publishers.

Crapanzano, Vincent. 1986. "Hermes Dilemma: The Masking of Subversion in Ethnographic Description." In *Writing Culture: The Poetics and Politics of Ethnography.* Ed. James Clifford and George Marcus, 51–76. Berkeley, Los Angeles, London: University of California Press.

Daniel, E. Valentine. 1984. *Fluid Signs: Being a Person the Tamil Way.* Berkeley, Los Angeles, London: University of California Press.

Daniel, Sheryl. 1980. "Marriage in Tamil Culture: The Problem of Conflicting Models." In *The Powers of Tamil Women.* Ed. Susan Wadley, 611–692. Maxwell School of Foreign and Comparative Studies, South Asian Series, no. 6, Syracuse University.

Das, Veena. 1976. "Masks and Faces." *Contributions to Indian Sociology* 10 (1): 1–30.

David, Kenneth. 1973. "Until Marriage Do Us Part: A Cultural Account of Jaffna Tamil Categories for Kinsmen." *Man* n.s. 8: 521–535.

Davis, Marvin. 1976. "A Philosophy of Hindu Rank from Rural West Bengal." *Journal of Asian Studies* 36: 5–24.

Derrida, Jacques. 1976. *Of Grammatology.* Trans. G. C. Spivak. Baltimore: Johns Hopkins. First published in French 1967.

Dimock, Edward C. 1966. *The Place of the Hidden Moon.* Chicago: University of Chicago Press.

———. 1982. "A Theology of the Repulsive: The Myth of the Goddess Sitala." In *The Divine Consort.* Ed. John Stratton Hawley and Donna Marie Wulff, 184–203. Boston: Beacon Press.

Dirks, Nicholas. 1987. *An Ethnohistory of a Little Kingdom.* Cambridge:

Cambridge University Press.

Dumont, Louis. 1959. "Possession and Priesthood." *Contributions to Indian Sociology* 3: 55–74.

———. 1957*a*. *Une sous-caste de l'Inde du sud: organisation sociale et religion des Pramalai Kallar*. Paris and The Hague: Mouton.

———. 1957*b*. "Hierarchy and Marriage Alliance in South Indian Kinship." Occasional Papers of the Royal Anthropological Institute of Great Britain and Ireland, no. 12. London: Royal Anthropological Institute of Great Britain and Ireland.

———. 1970. *Homo Hierarchicus: The Caste System and Its Implications*. London: Weidenfeld and Nicholson.

———. 1983. *Affinity as Value: Marriage Alliance in South India, with Comparative Essays on Australia*. Chicago: University of Chicago Press.

Durkheim, Emile. 1965. *Elementary Forms of the Religious Life*. Trans. Joseph Ward Swain. New York: Free Press. First published in English 1912.

———. 1933. *The Division of Labor in Society*. Trans. George Simpson. New York: Macmillan. First published in French 1893.

Eck, Diana L. 1981. *Darsan, Seeing the Divine Image in India*. Chambersburg, Pa.: Anima Books.

Foucault, Michel. 1967. *Madness and Civilization*. New York: Random House.

Freud, Sigmund. 1930. *Civilization and Its Discontents*. Trans. Joan Rivers. London: Hogarth.

Friedrich, Paul. 1966. "Proto-Indo-European Kinship." *Ethnology* 5: 1–36.

———. 1986. "Kinship Alpha: Proto-Indo-European." In *The Language Parallax,* 112–114. Austin: University of Texas Press.

Fruzetti, Lina. 1982. *The Gift of a Virgin: Women, Marriage, and Ritual in Bengal*. New Brunswick, N.J.: Rutgers University Press.

Fruzetti, Lina, Akos Ostor, and Steve Barnett. 1982. "The Cultural Construction of the Person in Bengal and Tamil Nadu." In *Concepts of Person*. Ed. Akos Oster, Lina Fruzetti, and Steve Barnett, 8–30. Cambridge, Mass.: Harvard University Press.

Fruzetti, Lina, and Akos Ostor. 1982. "Bad Blood in Bengal: Category and Affect in the Study of Kinship, Caste, and Marriage." In *Concepts of Person. Ed. Akos Oster, Lina Fruzetti, and Steve Barnett, 31–56. Cambridge, Mass.: Harvard University Press.*

Gaudapada. 1887. *The Saṃkhya-Karika of Iśwara Krishna with the Commentary of Gaudapada*. Trans. Henry Thomas Colebrooke. Bombay: Tookaram Tatya.

Goffman, Erving. 1983. *Forms of Talk*. Philadelphia: University of Pennsylvania Press.

Geertz, Clifford. 1974. "From the Native's Point of View: On the Nature of Anthropological Understanding." Bulletin of the American Academy of Arts and Sciences 28, no. 1.

Goody, Jack, and Stanley J. Tambiah. 1973. "Bridewealth and Dowry." Cambridge Papers in Social Anthropology, no. 7. Cambridge: Cambridge University Press.

Gough, Kathleen. 1955. "Female Initiation Rites on the Malabar Coast." *J.R.A.I.* 82: 71–88.

———. 1956. "Brahmin Kinship in a Tanjore Village." *American Anthropologist* 58: 826–853.

———. 1959. "The Nayars and the Definition of Marriage." *J.R.A.I.* 89: 23–34.

———. 1972. "Harijans in Thanjavur." In *Imperialism and Revolution in South Asia*. Ed. K. Gough and H. P. Sharma. New York: Monthly Review Press.

Gould, Harold. 1965. "Modern Medicine and Folk Cognition in Rural India." *Human Organization* 84 (3): 201–208.

Gramsci, Antonio. 1971. "The Formation of the Intellectuals." In *Selections from the Prison Notebooks of Antonio Gramasci*. Ed. and trans. Quinton Hoare and Geoffrey Nowell Smith, 5–13. New York: International Publishers.

Harman, William. 1986. "Kinship Metaphors in the Hindu Pantheon: Siva as Brother-in-Law and Son-in-Law." *Journal of the American Academy of Religion* LIII/3: 411–430.

Harper, Edward B. 1957. "Shamanism in South India." *Southwestern Journal of Anthropology*. 13 (3): 267–287.

———. 1963. "Spirit Possession and Social Structure." In *Anthropology on the March*. Ed. Bala Ratman, 165–177. Madras.

———. 1964. "Ritual Pollution as an Integrator of Caste and Religion." *Journal of Asian Studies* 2: 151–197.

Hart, George. 1973. "Women and the Sacred in Ancient Tamilnad." *Journal of Asian Studies* 32: 233–250.

———. 1974. "Some Aspects of Kinship in Ancient Tamil Literature." In *Kinship and History in South Asia,* Ed. Thomas Trautmann, 29–60. Michigan Papers on South and Southeast Asia, no. 7. Ann Arbor: Center for South and Southeast Asian Studies, the University of Michigan.

Hiltebeitl, Alf. 1980. "Draupadi's Garments." *Indo-Iranian Journal* 22: 97–112.

———. 1981. "Draupadi's Hair." In *Autour de la Deesse Hindoue*. Ed. Madeleine Biardeau. *Purusarta* 5: 179–214.

———. 1988. *Mythologies: From Gingee to Kurukshetra*. Pt. I, *The Cult of Draupadi*. I. Chicago: University of Chicago Press.

Homans, George, and David Schneider. 1955. *Marriage, Authority and*

Final Causes: A Study of Unilateral Cross-Cousin Marriage. Glencoe: The Free Press.

Holton, Gerald. 1973. *Thematic Origins of Scientific Thought: Kepler to Einstein*. Cambridge, Mass.: Harvard University Press.

Horney, Karen. 1967. *Feminine Psychology*. Ed. Harold Kelman. New York: W. W. Norton.

Hudson, Dennis. 1978. "Siva, Minakshi, Visnu—Reflections on a Popular Myth in Madurai." In *Temples in South India: An Analytical Reconsideration*. Ed. Burton Stein, 107–118. Delhi: Manohar.

Hymes, Dell. 1974. "Studying the Interaction of Language and Social Life." In *Foundations of Sociolinguistics: An Ethnographic Approach*. Philadelphia: University of Pennsylvania Press.

Inden, Ronald B., and Ralph W. Nicholas. 1977. *Kinship in Bengali Culture*. Chicago: University of Chicago Press.

Inglis, Stephen. 1985. "Possession and Pottery: Serving the Divine in a South Indian Community." In *Gods of Flesh, Gods of Stone*. Ed. J. Waghorne and N. Cutler, 89–102. Chambersburg, Pa.: Anima Publications.

Irigaray, Luce. 1985. *Speculum of the Other Woman*. Trans. Gillian C. Gill. Ithaca, N.Y.: Cornell University Press.

Jakobson, Roman. 1960. "Why 'Mama' and 'Papa'?" In *Perspectives in Psychological Theory: Essays in Honor of Henry Werner*. Ed. Bernard Kaplan, 124–134. New York: International Universities Press.

Kakar, Sudhir. 1978. *The Inner World: A Psycho-analytic Study of Childhood and Society in India*. Delhi: Oxford University Press.

———. 1982. *Shamans, Mystics and Doctors: A Psychological Inquiry into India and its Healing Traditions*. New York: Alfred A. Knopf.

Kapferer, Bruce. 1983. *A Celebration of Demons: Exorcism and the Aesthetics of Healing in Sri Lanka*. Bloomington: Indiana University Press.

Karve, Irawati. 1965. *Kinship Organization in India,* 2d ed. Bombay: Asia Publishing House.

Keller, Evelyn Fox. 1985. *Reflections on Gender and Science*. New Haven: Yale University Press.

Kristeva, Julia. 1984. *Revolution in Poetic Language*. Trans. Margaret Waller. New York: Columbia University Press. First published in French 1974.

Lacan, Jacques. 1968. *Speech and Language in Psychoanalysis*. Ed. and Trans. Anthony Wilden. Baltimore: Johns Hopkins Press.

Lakoff, Robin. 1973. "The Logic of Politeness, or Minding Your P's and Q's." In Papers from the Ninth Regional Meeting of the Chicago Linguistics Society.

Leach, Edmund R. 1951. "The Structural Implications of Matrilateral Cross-Cousin Marriage." *J.R.A.I.* 81: 23–55.

Leis, Philip. 1970. "Accommodation in a Plural Kingdom (Cameroon)." *Man* 5: 671–685.

Levi-Strauss, Claude. 1966. *The Savage Mind* (*La pensee sauvage,* 1962). Chicago: University of Chicago Press.

———. 1967*a*. "Do Dual Organizations Exist?" In *Structural Anthropology*. Trans. Claire Jacobson and Brooke Grundfest Schoepf, 128–160. Garden City, N.Y.: Doubleday, Anchor Books.

———. 1967*b*. "Structural Analysis in Linguistics and Anthropology." In *Structural Anthropology*. Trans. Claire Jacobson and Brooke Grundfest Schoepf, Garden City, N.Y.: Doubleday, Anchor Books.

———. 1969. "Overture." In *The Raw and the Cooked*. Trans. John and Doreen Wightman. New York: Harper and Row.

———. 1969*a*. *The Raw and the Cooked* (*Le cru et le cuit,* 1964). Trans. John and Doreen Wightman. New York: Harper and Row.

———. 1969*b*. *The Elementary Structures of Kinship* (*Les structures elementaires de la parente,* 1949). Trans. James Harle Bell and John Richard von Sturmer. Ed. Rodney Needham. London: Eyre and Spottiswood.

Lewis, I. M. 1971. *Ecstatic Religion*. New York: Penguin.

Lukacs, G. 1971. *History and Class Consciousness: Studies in Marxist Dialectics*. London: Merlin Press.

Malinowski, Bronislaw. 1967. *A Diary in the Strict Sense of the Term*. New York: Harcourt, Brace and World.

Maloney, Clarence. 1976. "Don't say 'Pretty Baby' Lest you Zap it with the Evil Eye—the Evil Eye in South Asia." In *The Evil Eye*. Ed. Clarence Maloney, 102–148. New York: Columbia University Press.

Manu. 1886. *The Laws of Manu*. Trans. George Buhler. Vol. 25, *The Sacred Books of the East*. Ed. F. Max Muller. Oxford: Clarendon Press.

Marglin, Frederique. 1985. *Wives of the God-King: Rituals of the Devadasis of Puri*. London: Oxford University Press.

Marriott, McKim. 1955. "Little Communities in an Indigenous Civilization." In *Village India*. Ed. McKim Marriott, 171–222. Chicago: University of Chicago Press.

———. 1976*a*. "Hindu Transactions: Diversity without Dualism." In *Transaction and Meaning: Directions in the Anthropology of Exchange and Symbolic Behavior*. Ed. Bruce Kapferer. Philadelphia: Institute for the Study of Human Issues.

———. 1976*b*. "Interpreting Indian Society: A Monistic Alternative to Dumont's Dualism." *Journal of Asian Studies* 36, no. 3: 189–195.

Marriott, McKim, and Ronald B. Inden. 1974. "Caste Systems." *Encyclopedia Britannica,* 15th ed., vol. 3, 982–991.

———. 1977. "Toward an Ethnosociology of South Asian Caste Systems." In *The New Wind*. Ed. Kenneth David. The Hague: Mouton.

Marsella, Anthony, George DeVos, and Francis L. K. Hsu, eds. 1985. *Culture and Self: Asian and Western Perspectives*. New York: Tavistock.

Marx, Karl. 1932. *Capital* (*Das Kapital,* 1890). Trans. Max Eastman. New York: Modern Library.

Mauss, Marcel. 1938. "Un categorie de l'esprit humain: la notion de personne, celle de 'moi.' " *J.R.A.I.* 68. Reprinted in *Sociologie et anthropologie*. Paris: Presses Universitaires de France, 1950.

———. 1954. *The Gift: Forms and Functions of Exchange in Primitive Societies*. Trans. Ian Cunnison. London: Cohen and West.

McGilvray, Dennis. 1974. "Tamils and Moors: Caste and Matriclan Structure in Eastern Sri Lanka." Ph.D. diss. University of Chicago.

———. 1982. "Sexual Power and Fertility in Sri Lanka: Batticaloa Tamils and Moors." In *Ethnography of Fertility and Birth*. Ed. Carol P. MacCormack, 25–73. London: Academic Press.

Medick, Hans, and David Warren Sabean, eds. 1984. *Interest and Emotion: Essays in the Study of Family and Kinship*. Cambridge: Cambridge University Press.

Mencher, Joan. 1974. "The Caste System Upside-down, or the Not-So-Mysterious East." *Current Anthropology* 15: 469–493.

Miller, Barbara D. 1981. *The Endangered Sex: Neglect of Female Children in Rural North India*. Ithaca and London: Cornell University Press.

Mitchell, Juliet and Jacqueline Rose. 1982. *Feminine Sexuality: Jacques Lacan and the Ecole Freudienne*. New York: Norton.

Moffatt, Michael. 1979. *An Untouchable Community in South India: Structure and Consensus*. Princeton: Princeton University Press.

Moreno, Manuel. 1985. "God's Forceful Call: Possession as a Divine Strategy." In *Gods of Flesh, Gods of Stone*. Ed. Joanne Waghorne and Norman Cutler, 103–122. Chambersburg, Pa.: Anima.

Nandy, Ashis. 1983. *The Intimate Enemy: Loss and Recovery of Self Under Colonialism*. Delhi: Oxford University Press.

Narayan, R. K. 1972. *Malgudi Days*. New York: Viking Press.

Needham, Rodney. 1962. *Structure and Sentiment: A Test Case in Social Anthropology*. Chicago: University of Chicago Press.

Nicholas, Ralph. 1982. "The Village Mother in Bengal." In *Mother Worship: Theme and Variations*. Ed. James J. Preston, 192–209. Chapel Hill: University of North Carolina Press.

Obeyesekere, Gananath. 1981. *Medusa's Hair*. Chicago: University of Chicago Press.

———. 1984. *The Cult of the Goddess Pattini*. Chicago: University of Chicago Press.

Ochs, Eleanor, and Bambi Schieffelin. 1984."Language Acquisition and Socialization: Three Developmental Stories and their Implications." In

Culture Theory. Ed. R. Schweder and E. J. Bourne, 276–320. Cambridge: Cambridge University Press.

O'Flaherty, Wendy. 1973. *Asceticism and Eroticism in the Mythology of Siva*. London: Oxford University Press.

———. 1980. *Women, Androgynes and Other Mythical Beasts*. Chicago: University of Chicago Press.

———. 1984. *Dreams, Illusions and Other Realities*. Chicago: University of Chicago Press.

O'Flaherty, Wendy, ed. and trans. 1975. *Hindu Myths: A Sourcebook*. Harmondsworth: Penguin.

Ostor, Akos, Lina Fruzetti, and Steve Barnett. 1982. *Concepts of Person: Kinship, Caste, and Marriage in India*. Cambridge, Mass.: Harvard University Press.

Padmanabhan, Nila. 1968. *Talaimuraikal*. Nagarkoyil, India: Jayakumari Stores.

Parry, Jonathan. 1982. "Sacrificial Death and the Necrophagous Ascetic." In *Death and the Regeneration of Life*. Ed. Maurice Bloch and Jonathan Parry, 74–110. Cambridge: Cambridge University Press.

Peterson, Indira V. 1986. "The Tie that Binds: Brothers and Sisters in North and South India." Paper presented at the Conference on Religion in South India, Craigville, Massachusetts. Forthcoming in *South Asian Social Scientist*.

Preston, James J. 1982. "The Goddess Chandi as an Agent of Change." In *Mother Worship: Theme and Variations*. Ed. James J. Preston, 210–226. Chapel Hill: University of North Carolina Press.

Radcliffe-Brown, A. R. 1924. "The Mother's Brother in South Africa." *South African Journal of Science*. XXI: 542–555. Reprinted in *Structure and Function in Primitive Society*. New York: Free Press. 1965.

———. 1941. "The Study of Kinship Systems." *J.R.A.I.* 71: 1–18. Reprinted in *Structure and Function in Primitive Society*. New York: Free Press. 1965.

———. 1953. "Dravidian Kinship Terminology." *Man,* item 169, p. 112.

Raheja, Gloria. 1988. *The Poison in the Gift: Ritual, Prestation and the Dominant Caste in a North Indian Village*. Chicago: University of Chicago Press.

Ramanujan, A. K. 1971. *Relations: Poems*. London: Oxford University Press.

———. 1980. "The Relevance of South Asian Folklore." Paper presented at the Conference on Models and Metaphors in South Asian Folklore, Berkeley and Mysore.

———. 1983. "The Indian Oedipus." In *Oedipus: A Folklore Casebook*. Ed. Alan Dundes and Lowell Edmunds, 234–261. New York: Garland.

Redfield, Robert. 1957. *The Little Community: Viewpoints for the Study of the Human Whole*. Chicago: University of Chicago Press.

Reiter, Rayna. 1975. "The Traffic in Women." In *Toward an Anthropology of Women*. Ed. Rayna Reiter. New York: Monthly Review Press.

Reynolds, Holly Baker. 1980. "The Auspicious Married Woman." In *The Powers of Tamil Women*. Ed. Susan Wadley, 35–60. Maxwell School Foreign and Comparative Studies, South Asian Series, no. 6, Syracuse University.

Rudolph, Lloyd, and Suzanne Rudolph. 1967. *The Modernity of Tradition*. Chicago: University of Chicago Press.

Sapir, Edward. 1924. "Culture, Genuine and Spurious." *American Journal of Sociology* 29: 401–429.

Schegloff, Emanuel. 1968. "Sequencing in Conversational Openings." *American Anthropologist* 70: 1075–1095.

———. 1981. "The Relevance of Repair to Syntax-for-Conversation." In *Syntax and Semantics,* vol. 12: *Discourse and Syntax*. New York: Academic Press.

Schneider, David M. 1968. *American Kinship: A Cultural Account*. Englewood Cliffs, N.J.: Prentice-Hall.

Schneider, David M. and Kathleen Gough, eds. 1961. *Matrilineal Kinship*. Berkeley: University of California Press.

Schweder, Richard A. and E. J. Bourne. 1984. "Does the Concept of the Person Vary Cross-culturally?" In *Culture Theory*. Ed. Richard Schweder and Robert Levine. Cambridge: Cambridge University Press.

Shulman, David D. 1980. *Tamil Temple Myths: Sacrifice and Divine Marriage in the South Indian Saiva Tradition*. Princeton: Princeton University Press.

Siegel, Lee. 1987. *Laughing Matters: The Comic Tradition in India*. Chicago: University of Chicago Press.

Singer, Milton. 1959. "The Great Tradition in a Metropolitan Center: Madras." In *Traditional India: Structure and Change*. Ed. M. Singer. American Folklore Society Bibliographic and Special Series, no. 10, 141–82. Austin: University of Texas Press.

———. 1972. *When a Great Tradition Modernizes*. New York: Praeger.

Spiro, Melford. 1982. *Oedipus in the Trobriands*. Chicago: University of Chicago Press.

Srinivas, M. N. 1976. *The Remembered Village*. Berkeley, Los Angeles, London: University of California Press.

Stocking, George. 1968. *Race, Culture and Evolution*. New York: Free Press.

Susruta. 1907. *Susruta Samhita*. Ed. and trans. K. K. L. Bhishagratna. Calcutta.

Tannen, Deborah. 1984. *Conversational Style: Analyzing Talk Among*

Friends. Norwood, N.J.: Ablex.

Tedlock, Dennis. 1983. "The Analogical Tradition and the Emergence of a Dialogical Anthropology." In *The Spoken Word and the Work of Interpretation,* 321–338. Philadelphia: University of Pennsylvania Press.

Tirumular. 1975. *Tirumantiram Muvayiram*. Ed. Iramanatha Pillai. Tirunelveli, India: South India Saiva Siddhanta Works Publishing Company.

Trautmann, Thomas R. 1981. *Dravidian Kinship*. Cambridge: Cambridge University Press.

Trautmann, Thomas R., ed. 1974. "Kinship and History in South Asia." Michigan Papers on South and Southeast Asia, no. 7. Ann Arbor: Center for South and Southeast Asian Studies, The University of Michigan.

Trawick Egnor, Margaret. 1978. "The Sacred Spell and Other Conceptions of Life in Tamil Culture." Ph.D. diss. University of Chicago.

———. 1980. "On the Meaning of Sakti to Women in Tamil Nadu." In *The Powers of Tamil Women*. Ed. Susan Wadley, 1–34. Maxwell School Foreign and Comparative Studies, South Asian Series, no. 6, Syracuse University.

———. 1983. "The Changed Mother, or What the Smallpox Goddess Did When There Was No More Smallpox." *Contributions to Asian Studies* 18: 24–45.

———. 1986. "Internal Iconicity in Paraiyar (Crying Songs.)" In *Another Harmony: New Essays on the Folklore of India*. Ed. Stuart Blackburn and A. K. Ramanujan, 294–344. Berkeley, Los Angeles, London: University of California Press.

———. 1988*a*. "Spirits and Voices in Tamil Song." *American Ethonologist* 15 (2): 193–215.

———. 1988*b*. "A Song Out of Darkness: Code Defiance in the Art of a Tamil Untouchable." Ms.

———. 1988*c*. "The Guru in the Garden: Ambiguity in the Oral Exegesis of a Sacred Text." *Cultural Anthropology* 3 (3): 316–351.

Trubetzkoy, N. S. 1939. "Gedanken uber das Indogermanenproblem." *Acta Linguistica Hasniensia* I. 81–89. Copenhagen.

Turner, Victor. 1969. *The Ritual Process*. Chicago: Aldine.

———. 1985. "The Anthropology of Performance." In *On the Edge of the Bush: Anthropology as Experience,* 177–204. Tucson: University of Arizona Press.

Vatuk, Sylvia. 1982. "Forms of Address in the North Indian Family: An Exploration of the Cultural Meaning of Kin Terms." In *Concepts of the Person: Kinship, Caste and Marriage in India*. Ed. Akos Ostor, Lina Fruzetti, and Steve Barnett, 56–98. Cambridge: Harvard University Press.

Wadley, Susan Snow. 1975*a*. "Brother's Husbands, and Sometimes

Sons: Kinsmen in North Indian Ritual." *Eastern Anthropologist* 29 (2): 149–170.
———. 1975*b*. "Shakti: Power in the Conceptual Structure of Karimpur Religion." The University of Chicago Studies in Anthropology Series in Social, Cultural and Linguistic Anthropology, no. 2. Chicago: University of Chicago Department of Anthropology.
———. 1980. "The Paradoxical Powers of Tamil Women." In *The Powers of Tamil Women*. Ed. Susan Snow Wadley, 61–92. Maxwell School Foreign and Comparative Studies, South Asian Series, no. 6, Syracuse University.
Waghorne, Joanne P. 1985. "Introduction." In *Gods of Flesh, Gods of Stone: The Embodiment of Divinity in India*. Ed. Joanne Waghorne and Norman Cutler, 1–8. Chambersburg, Pa.: Anima Publications.
Wagner, Roy. 1975. *The Invention of Culture*. Chicago: University of Chicago Press.
Whiting, John W. M., and Beatrice B. Whiting. 1975. *Children of Six Cultures: A Psychocultural Analysis*. Cambridge, Mass.: Harvard University Press.
Whorf, Benjamin Lee. 1956. *Language, Thought and Reality*. Cambridge, Mass.: M.I.T. Press.
Yalman, Nur. 1967. *Under the Bo Tree: Studies of Caste, Kinship, and Marriage in the Interior of Ceylon*. Berkeley, Los Angeles: University of California Press.
———. 1963. "On the Purity and Sexuality of Women in the Castes of Ceylon and Malabar." *J.R.A.I.* 93: 25–58.
———. 1964. "The Structure of Sinhalese Healing Rituals." In *Aspects of Religion in South Asia*. Ed. Edward Harper. *Journal of Asian Studies* 23: 115–150.

Index

Compositor:	Interactive Composition Corporation
Text:	10/13 Times Roman
Display:	Times Roman
Printer:	Braun-Brumfield, Inc.
Binder:	Braun-Brumfield, Inc.